D0793370

REFORMATION AND REVOLT
IN THE LOW COUNTRIES

Shooting the Popinjay. Satire on the Inquisition (*c.* 1566)
(*Amsterdam, Rijksmuseum, Rijksprentenkabinet, FM 445-B*)

At Whitsun the companies of archers in the Low Countries would hold competitions to decide who should lead them in the coming year. The first archer to hit the popinjay on the pole became the *schutters'* 'king'. In the contest depicted here the mendicants and prelates are defeated by the Beggars: their crooked bolts are no match for their opponents' arrows, which fly straight and true.

REFORMATION
AND REVOLT IN
THE LOW COUNTRIES

ALASTAIR DUKE

THE HAMBLEDON PRESS

LONDON   AND   RONCEVERTE

Published by The Hambledon Press, 1990

102 Gloucester Avenue, London NW1 8HX (U.K.)
309 Greenbrier Avenue, Ronceverte WV 24970 (U.S.A.)

ISBN 185285 021 3

British Library Cataloguing in Publication Data

Duke, Alastair
 Reformation and Revolt in the Low Countries.
 1. Benelux countries. Christian church. Reformation.
 I. Title
 274.92

Library of Congress Cataloging-in-Publication Data

Duke, A.C.
 Reformation and revolt in the Netherlands / Alastair Duke.
 Includes bibliographical references.
 1. Reformation–Netherlands. 2. Reformation–Benelux countries.
 3. Netherlands–Church history–16th century.   4. Benelux countries–
 Church history–16th century.   I. Title.
 BR395.D85   1990
 274.92'06–dc20   90-4457
                                                                    CIP

Typeset by Ponting–Green Publishing Services, London
Printed on acid-free paper and bound in Great Britain by
The Camelot Press, Trowbridge, Wiltshire.

Contents

List of Illustrations

Frontispiece

Shooting the Popinjay. Satire on the Inquisition

Acknowledgements

The articles reprinted here first appeared in the following places and are reprinted by the kind permission of the original publishers.

1 This chapter appears here for the first time.
2 *Journal of Ecclesiastical History*, XXVI (1975), pp. 41–67.
3 *Bestuurders en geleerden: Opstellen over onderwerpen uit de Nederlandse geschiedenis van de 16e, 17e en 18e eeuw, aangeboden aan Prof. Dr. J.J. Woltjer bij zijn afscheid als hoogleraar van de Rijksuniversiteit te Leiden*, ed. S. Groenweld, M.E.H.N. Mout and I. Schöffer (De Bataafsche Leeuw, Amsterdam-Dieren, 1985), pp. 23–32.
4 *Britain and the Netherlands*, VII, *Church and State Since the Reformation*, ed. A.C. Duke and C.A. Tamse (Martinus Nijhoff, The Hague, 1981), pp. 45–74.
5 This chapter will also appear in a forthcoming publication of the Fryske Akademy, Leeuwarden, 1990.
6 *Tijdschrift voor Geschiedenis*, LXXXII (1969), pp. 316–37.
7 *Reformation Principle and Practice: Essays in Honour of Arthur Geoffrey Dickens*, ed. P.N. Brooks (The Scolar Press, London, 1980), pp. 137–56.
8 *Transactions of the Royal Historical Society*, 5th Series, XXXII (1982), pp. 113–35.
9 *Tijdschrift voor Geschiedenis*, LXXXIX (1976), pp. 373–93.
10 This chapter appears here for the first time.
11 *International Calvinism, 1541–1715*, ed. M. Prestwich (Clarendon Press, Oxford, 1985), pp. 109–34.

Opgedragen aan Juliaan en Ien
uit dank voor raad, daad, en vriendschap
gedurende vele jaren

Introduction

Open a standard English textbook on European history in the early modern period and you will probably look in vain for any mention of the Reformation in the Low Countries. Convention prescribes an Italian Renaissance, a German Reformation, French wars of religion and a Dutch Revolt. In the case of the Netherlands Reformation this neglect is not hard to explain. In the first place the evangelicals in the Low Countries conspicuously lacked inspirational leaders in the heroic mould of Knox or Zwingli, men who by the force of their personality impressed their identity on the messy complexity and so provided attractive subjects for their biographers. Professional historians may no longer care for the Carlylean creed that 'universal history ... is at bottom the history of great men', yet 'great men' undeniably popularise the times in which they lived. The one Dutchman from this period, Desiderius Erasmus, to command universal attention detached himself so completely from his native country, which he left behind fifteen years before his death, that scholars usually feel no reason to set him in the context of late medieval Holland or even of his 'beloved Brabant'.

In those countries where the Reformation is perceived as an event of national significance, the absence of 'great men' need not greatly matter. With the exception of Thomas Cranmer the English reformers were not religious leaders of genius, yet few doubt that the break with Rome and the Elizabethan Church Settlement decisively altered the course of English history. In the Low Countries however the Reformation lies in the shadow of the Revolt. In the southern provinces a resurgent Catholicism in the late sixteenth century wiped away the embarrassing memory of the earlier mass defections from the faith, an act of collective amnesia no doubt assisted by the exodus from the southern provinces of numerous Calvinist Walloons, Flemings and Brabanters. In the north the Reformed churches were indeed closely associated with the newly-independent United Provinces, but they neither gained the status of 'established' churches nor even probably the support of a majority of the people. After the dissolution of the 'Union of Church and State' in 1796, the Protestant Reformation became almost the private concern of the various denominations. They nurtured confessional traditions by

founding chairs of church history, safely located in faculties of theology
and in seminaries. The first half of the present century saw the publication
of solid monographs on Lutherans, Baptists (*wederdopers* and *doopsgezinden*), Reformed Protestants, Remonstrants, Socinians and, of course,
Catholics. Even if the church historians showed an awareness of the
Reformation's original complexity, their readers, brought up in a *verzuilde*
(compartmentalised) society, expected to discover their denominational
roots in the first half of the sixteenth century. This may partly explain
why to this day there is no survey of the sixteenth-century religious
changes in the Low Countries to match the breadth of A.G. Dicken's
classic account of *The English Reformation.*

When Dickens wrote his masterpiece in 1964 he enjoyed certain advantages denied his colleagues in Belgium and the Netherlands. In the first
place he worked within an established Protestant historiography, which
has only recently been challenged. Moreover he could weave his account
of the English Reformation into a well-defined political and constitutional
context. The centralised character of the Tudor state and the preponder-
ance of London within the kingdom encouraged historians to look at
events from the perspective of the King's government and the south-
eastern counties.

One cannot write an adequate account of the Reformation in the Low
Countries from the standpoint of Brussels. Both the fledgling condition
of the Habsburg Netherlands and the hostility of that state to the
Reformation call for a different approach. Charles V certainly strengthened the central institutions of government, clarified the constitutional
standing of the *Nidererblanden* within the Empire and determined the
boundaries of the 'seventeen Netherlands' whose cartographical image
mapmakers then fixed for the next hundred years.[1] Yet the special
relationship between each province and the centre and the important
differences between the provinces, which extended to systems of law,
forms of local government, social structures and cultures, make general-
isations about the history of the Netherlands in the early modern period
especially hazardous. It is not therefore surprising that those most recently
concerned with the development of early Protestantism in the Low
Countries have chosen to study the spread of heresy within a single town
or province. In this way they can observe the different character of the
towns and give weight to local political circumstances. Yet if the confessional historiography no longer offers a satisfactory framework, it remains
to be seen whether the Reformation can be made more intelligible for
the general reader through the practice of *Landesgeschichte.*

---

[1] For the cartographical tradition of the 'seventeen Netherlands' see H.A.M. van der
Heijden, 'De oudste kaarten van Nederland en de opkomst van het nationaliteitsbesef',
Spiegel Historiael, XXI (1986), pp. 547–55. Mr.P.J. Regan kindly drew this article to my
attention.

These essays provide no solution for they do not offer a connected history of the Reformation in the Low Countries. They reconnoitre various problems which are examined in relation to particular periods and provinces. Yet they may introduce English readers to those circumstances and early experiences which have left an enduring mark on Protestantism in the Low Countries. We should never forget that the Reformation in these parts only succeeded, and then only partially, in despite of the central government. From the outset the Habsburg government and, for that matter, the rulers of Liège, Utrecht and Gelre, showed little sympathy for the new religious ideas. Luther's books were burnt in the Low Countries even before the edict of Worms and between 1520 and 1550 the Habsburg authorities piled edict upon edict until the mere possession of a forbidden book became a capital offence.

The persecutions had two important consequences. Many of those charged with the enforcement of the edicts had no liking for the legislation. They took exception to those punitive sanctions which seemed to threaten property rights, secured with privileges of non-confiscation, and the commercial prosperity of the country. To a limited, yet significant, degree the religious policy of Charles V and his son strained the natural loyalty the governing classes felt for the dynasty. Secondly, the repression aggravated the sectarian character of dissent by forcing it underground. Many evangelicals hoped at first for the reform of the Roman church, which they had no wish to leave. Accordingly they went in good conscience to the Bible meetings, where they discussed the religious issues of the day, as well as to mass. As conservatives tightened their grip on the Catholic church and evangelism beyond the frontiers of the Netherlands slowly crystallised into separate churches, these Dutch evangelicals had to steer an increasingly difficult passage between the Scylla of Roman orthodoxy and the Charybdis of confessional Protestantism.

Some dissidents readily entered into separatist brotherhoods. In the 1530s Anabaptists began to withdraw from both the Roman church and from the world in expectation of the Second Coming; they developed an exclusivist theology of the church to match. Reformed Protestants too regarded the Church of Rome as the seat of Antichrist, although they took refuge in sectarianism to escape persecution rather than out of doctrinal necessity. Yet others held all forms of external religion in contempt. Such 'enthusiasts' (*geestdryvers*) feigned outward conformity with the Catholic church, partly to escape detection, while pursuing the path of inward spiritual regeneration in secret.

Apart from those Netherlanders who studied at Wittenberg in the second and third decades of the sixteenth century, most dissidents from the Low Countries gained their knowledge of the new doctrines unsystematically. They might attend Protestant services while in Germany, listen at home to sermons given by sympathetic priests, eavesdrop out of curiosity on religious discussions in taverns or buy whatever heretical literature the book pedlars had in stock. Evangelical theology in the Low Countries owed most to Luther, (although his later writings attracted less notice), yet the teachings of his opponents like Karlstadt and Hoffman also found favour, sometimes in the selfsame circles as welcomed Luther. Spiritual interpretations of the eucharist developed by the Swiss and south German reformers, themselves influenced by the Hollander, Cornelis Hoen, jostled with crude materialist rejections of the real presence whose arguments and language probably hark back to late medieval oral traditions of dissent. Erasmus's denunciation of monasticism and superstitious forms of piety also coloured the religious debate in the Netherlands. Since the economies and cultures of the various provinces overrode the newly-established boundaries of the country, they also stood open to a wide range of religious influences. Evangelicals in the Walloon towns followed in the train of their coreligionists in France, while Anabaptists in the northern Netherlands moved to and fro across the border with Westphalia.

Such doctrinal diversity was not itself unusual: the German Reformation passed through a far more extreme period of confusion and religious experimentation in the 1520s and 1530s until the evangelical princes eventually imposed a new orthodoxy. In the Netherlands the Reformation remained in the melting-pot for longer. In the north-eastern provinces, incorporated though scarcely integrated into the Habsburg Netherlands under Charles V, a relatively mild regime allowed evangelicals (apart from the Anabaptists) to continue on the margins of the Catholic church until 1566. In Holland, Flanders and Brabant repression hastened the pace of confessionalisation, but also seriously hampered the organisation of dissent. Only the self-conscious Anabaptist congregations achieved any sort of doctrinal uniformity but razzias frequently dislocated their rudimentary organisation and forced their leaders to flee. Menno Simons, Dirk Philips and David Joris spent much of their lives on that account outside the Low Countries. In the 1540s the authorities quickly scotched an attempt to set up Reformed congregations in Tournai and Valenciennes.

By the mid sixteenth century it seemed as though the Reformation had lost its momentum. Until 1535, when the Anabaptists threatened to seize power in Amsterdam as they had done in Münster, even radical evangelicals in Holland had enjoyed tacit support from within the governing elites. The events of 1534-35 caused the central government to replace the easy-going magistrates of Amsterdam with sound Catholics. Anabaptism continued to win recruits in the Dutch-speaking maritime provinces but rarely attracted followers from among the upper social echelons: their apocalypticism, which acquired an other-worldly quality under the leadership of Menno Simons, chiefly appealed to the *kleyne luyden* – to the craftsmen in the towns and seafaring folk. Consequently the Anabaptists ceased to pose a significant challenge to the political and religious establishment. Yet the urban elites, who had not entirely lost their appetite for new religious ideas, could find no vehicle for their piety apart from attendance at informal bible-reading conventicles. In the mid 1540s the Counter-Reformation began to take effect in the Netherlands. At the instance of Charles V the theologians at Leuven published a succinct statement of Catholic doctrine (1545) and drew up a list of forbidden books (1546). Having defeated the German Lutherans at Mühlberg (1547), the Emperor set about the reform of the Catholic church in both Germany and the Netherlands. Charles held the alleged shortcomings of the late medieval clergy responsible for the wholesale apostasy from the Catholic faith. Accordingly the *Formula reformationis* (1548) forbade the cumulation of benefices and required the bishops to hold visitations and synods to implement the reforms. Nevertheless at this moment, when the future of Protestant dissent in the Low Countries seemed far from assured, the situation suddenly changed again.

In the first place evangelicals began to respond to the challenge, which Calvin and other reformers had issued to evangelicals in the 1540s and 1550s to abandon the Roman church. Privy Calvinist churches came into being, the first at Antwerp in 1555. In these congregations accredited ministers preached the Word and administered the Lord's Supper to select bodies of professed Reformed Protestants. Secondly, Dutch and Walloon dissidents, who fled abroad to escape persecution, gravitated for economic as well as religious reasons towards either the local Reformed church, as happened at Emden in East Friesland, or towards the stranger churches, of which the Walloon congregation at Wesel (1545) and the Dutch church at London (1550) were the first. Here they could receive a thorough grounding in Reformed doctrine and practice: if they had not already been aware of themselves as Protestants before they left the Low Countries, many became so in exile. The churches at Emden and London also provided ministers and pastoral advice for the 'congregations under the cross' and, through them, access to the wider Calvinist world. In this period also Emden became the centre of Dutch Reformed printing: from the East Frisian town Bibles, metrical psalms and catechisms were smuggled in large quantities into the Low Countries. As a result of these changes religious dissent gradually took on a more systematic, and specifically Calvinist content, although non-Calvinist evangelicals continued to value the gospel of Christian freedom taught by the young Luther, the early native evangelical theologians, and above all Erasmus.

In the early 1560s the heretics in the southern Netherlands grew bolder. They started to hold public services outside the Walloon towns and in the Westkwartier of Flanders. The more extreme among them openly defied the authorities, organising psalm-singing demonstrations (*chanteries*), delivering fellow-believers from prison and threatening violence against their persecutors. This did not however signal, as has been suggested, 'the start of the armed resistance against Spain'.[2] These Calvinists wanted nothing so much as an end to the persecutions and freedom of worship, conditions enjoyed, at least nominally, by French Protestants since 1562. Nevertheless the slow and imperfect fusion between political and religious dissent began at this time: a small number of Calvinist gentry campaigned for the abolition of the 'inquisition' and for a new religious policy to be worked out in conjunction with the States General. This programme initially attracted widespread support, but during the summer of 1566, when the Calvinists came out into the open, many Catholic gentry, who had entered the Compromise of the Nobility, drew back. The hedge-preaching and above all the iconoclastic riots shattered the fragile alliance. By the winter of 1566–67 the Calvinists found themselves a relatively small and increasingly isolated minority. Although they staged a series of revolts, their lack of coordination enabled government forces to put these down one by one.

In exile both Calvinists and *gueux d'état* gradually came to accept William of Orange as their leader. Relations between the disparate groups were, however, often strained. Some Reformed ministers remained wary of Orange and he, in turn, felt frustrated by their narrowly religious concerns. In order to overcome such divisions abroad and to mobilise opinion in the Low Countries against Alva, the publicists around Orange attempted to develop an all-embracing patriotic rhetoric. Although the 'seventeen Netherlands' was too recent a creation for this appeal to carry much conviction, the patriotic myth proved conveniently versatile. In the pamphlets published after 1568 the appeal to the 'whole fatherland' was often associated with the cause of the gospel, yet the linkage was opportunistic. When the Orangists sought in 1576 to foster a 'patriot' party among the overwhelmingly Catholic governing classes of Brabant and elsewhere in the south, they employed the notion of the *universa patria* in a bid to transcend provincial loyalties but left the religious issue in abeyance.

While in exile Dutch Protestantism became more explicitly presbyterian. In the early 1560s the Reformed congregations in the French-speaking towns, Flanders and Brabant adopted the forms of church government in use among French Protestants. The synod convoked at Emden in October 1571 reasserted the presbyterian principle of parity between churches, further developed the hierarchy of consistories, *classes* and synods proposed at Wesel and proceeded to divide the 'churches under the cross' into *classes*. Persecution had obliged the small Reformed congregations to operate behind closed doors. Prudence required the consistories to restrict access to the Reformed services to those with satisfactory credentials in order to keep out troublemakers and informers. This was not only a matter of expedience. The Belgic Confession (1561) placed a high value on discipline: for this reason the so-called Convent

[2] A.A. van Schelven, 'Het begin van het gewapend verzet tegen Spanje in de 16e-eeuwsche Nederlanden', *Handelingen en levensberichten van de maatschappij der nederlandsche letterkunde te Leiden* (1914-15), pp. 126-56.

of Wesel decided that only professed members who accepted the authority of the consistory should be admitted to the Lord's Table. The fateful decisions to adopt a presbyterian church order and consistorial discipline were taken by a relatively small, and possibly unrepresentative, number of ministers and elders meeting in secret or outside the Netherlands. Since neither the town magistrates nor the States of Holland had played any part in the making of these decisions, they could scarcely be expected meekly to accede to the demands of the Reformed church in 1572.

In the half century between the start of the Revolt in Holland and the National Synod of Dordrecht (1618–19) the nature of the religious settlement was gradually worked out. At first the town magistrates had not wanted to recognise the small Calvinist groups; instead they sought guarantees for the maintenance of the Catholic church. With Beggar garrisons in the towns and Catholicism identified with the Spanish enemy, this proved unrealistic and in the spring of 1573 the States abandoned Orange's policy of religious freedom for both Catholics and Protestants. Despite the continued presence of many Catholics in the town corporations and among the gentry in Holland, the governing classes accepted that the Revolt had made a reformation of the church in a Protestant sense inevitable. For that reason the town governments and the States of Holland agreed to the suppression of the mass and provided financial support for the Reformed ministers. When they negotiated the terms of the Union of Utrecht (1579) they also rejected Orange's policy of *religievrede* for Holland. Yet many, probably most, of them saw no reason to endorse a specifically Calvinist church order. They preferred a comprehensive and mildly Protestant church under the control of the magistrates. From their perspective the arguments for consistories and *classes* looked less compelling, more especially since the persecution had ended and 'godly magistrates' had taken the place of the tyrant ruler.

If the Revolt prepared the way for the Reformation of the church, it did not guarantee that the Calvinist form of Protestantism would find favour with the civil powers. The Union of Utrecht gave the right to determine religious policy to the provincial States, an opportunity which some did not fail to take. In the case of Holland the States produced draft ecclesiastical ordinances in 1576 and 1583 which showed scant regard for Calvinist susceptibilities. In Utrecht, where the Calvinist party was far weaker, the States prevented the formation of *classes* until 1620. If the opposition to the Reformed church were so formidable, the question arises why the Calvinists carried the day at the national synod of Dordrecht. To an extent they owed their success to the backing they received after 1610 from the then *stadhouder* of Holland, Zeeland and Utrecht, Prince Maurice, and from the magistrates of Amsterdam. The influx of southern Calvinists, who began to arrive in large numbers in the north in the 1580s and 1590s, also bolstered the position of the Reformed churches in the towns of Holland. The Calvinist party knew too what sort of church they wanted and, no less importantly, found in the *classes* and synods the means to bring that vision closer to reality. The *classes*, in particular, proved invaluable in raising up a Calvinist ministry, while the synods could obtain redress of grievances by their sheer persistence.

If the synod of Dordrecht sealed the victory of Calvinist theology in the church and of the presbyterian church order, Calvinist penetration of the countryside had only recently begun. The task of creating Calvinist congregations in the villages of Holland was far from complete by the late 1580s. For many years to come country folk, faced by some calamity, turned instinctively to 'papist superstitions' for comfort. In the matter of religion the United Provinces presented two faces to the world. Convinced Calvinists considered the Reformed religion to be 'the foundation and the bond binding together the United Provinces'. The States General appeared to concur when they declared in 1651 that the true Religion (*i.e.* Reformed) should be maintained, if necessary, by force. Insofar the Dutch Republic might be fairly described as a Calvinist state: only ministers of the 'true Christian Reformed religion' might preach in the parish churches. Yet by no means all of those in authority themselves professed the doctrines of the *publicque Kercken*. They hesitated to surrender the sovereign right of provinces to determine religious policy and to abandon the principle of freedom of conscience. Besides, as any visitor to the rural churches of Holland and Utrecht could confirm, the Dutch were still – even in the mid-seventeenth century – far from being a nation of Calvinists.

Eight of the essays in this collection first appeared in print between 1969 and 1985 and they have not survived the passage of time unscathed. Several of the essays (4, 7, 8, 9, 11) were written for particular conferences or publications and they betray the circumstances of their genesis. In particular there is some degree of repetition, but the integrity and balance of the individual essays would have suffered from the excision of the overlapping passages. Republication has however afforded an opportunity to incorporate many of the suggestions made by attentive readers and to correct errors of fact. If the articles in their revised state improve on the earlier versions, then the credit belongs to colleagues on both sides of the North Sea. In the light of their comments and of recent research I have amplified and modified quite substantial passages in both the body of the text and in the critical apparatus. To make the collection more amenable to the English reader, translations replace most of the foreign quotations in the text, although where there is doubt about the precise sense, the Dutch original may be found in the appropriate footnote.

Everyone who writes on the Low Countries in the early modern period encounters the problem of nomenclature. Charles V added to the Burgundian Netherlands, the *pays de par deçà*, which he inherited, Friesland in 1515–23, Tournai-Tournaisis in 1521, Utrecht and Overijssel in 1528, Groningen and the Ommelanden in 1536 and Gelre (Gelderland) in

1543. In these essays the terms the Low Countries and the Netherlands are used as synonyms for the 'seventeen Netherlands' as the patrimonial lands of the Habsburgs began to be known about the middle of the sixteenth century. As a result of the Revolt two new states emerged: the United Provinces of the Netherlands (*Belgium foederatum*) and the Catholic or 'Royal' Netherlands (*Belgium regium*).[3] Because the Netherlands as a political entity with fairly precise boundaries only came into existence during the first half of the sixteenth century, there was no clear consensus about the name for this region. Contemporaries employed either a geographical description – *Niderlandt, Low(er) Germany, Pays Bas* – or some variant of Flanders as a *pars pro toto*, because the Flemish cities of Ghent and Bruges had achieved an international fame in the later middle ages as the centres of commerce.[4] In this book, however, Flanders and Holland only refer to the counties or provinces of that name. In the case of place-names I have selected the version which is likely to be most familiar to English readers rather than striving after some pedantic consistency. Hence Ghent rather than Gand or Gent; Leuven and 's-Hertogenbosch instead of Louvain and Bois-le-Duc. On the other hand Brill, by which Elizabethans knew Den Briel seems now almost as quaint as the Burse and Bridges, the names used by the seventeenth-century English diplomat Sir William Temple for 's-Hertogenbosch and Bruges, and I have therefore adopted the modern Dutch spelling for the town at the mouth of the Maas.

While carrying out the research for these essays I have contracted a large number of debts to libraries, record offices and other institutions of higher learning, whose staff have smoothed my passage. In particular I am grateful to the staff at the Hartley Library of the University of Southampton, the British Library, the Koninklijke Bibliotheek at The Hague, the Koninklijke Bibliotheek Albert I at Brussels, the Bibliotheek der Rijksuniversiteit te Leiden and the Bibliotheek van de Rijksuniversiteit Gent. I benefited also from the knowledge and expertise of archivists in many Belgium and Dutch record offices, including the Algemeen Rijksarchief at The Hague, the Algemeen Rijksarchief at Brussels, the Rijksarchieven in Noord-Holland and Utrecht, and the Gemeentelijke Archiefdiensten at Alkmaar, Gouda and Leiden. I remember with gratitude the kindly interest in my work shown by J. Fox as rijksarchivaris of the Derde Afdeling (Archieven van Holland), by the late Dr. J.P. van Dooren when he presided over the former Archief van de Nederlandse Hervormde Kerk in the Javastraat and by the late J.H. Rombach of the Gemeentearchief, Alkmaar. I also wish to place on record my thanks to Carl van Dycken whose responsibilities in

[3] H. de Schepper, *'Belgium nostrum' 1500-1650: Over integratie en desintegratie van het Nederland* (Antwerp, 1987), pp. 22–23.

[4] An Elizabethan official, writing in 1571 about the depredations of the Sea Beggars on Vlieland and Texel, described these islands as being situated 'upon the cost of Fflannders'. I owe this reference to the kindness of Mr. M.J. French, a student in history at the University of Southampton.

the 1970s included the Archiv der Evangelisch-reformierte Gemeinde at Emden. Both the Stichting Atlas van Stolk Rotterdam and the Rijksprenten-kabinet Amsterdam responded most promptly and courteously to urgent appeals for illustrative material from their rich collections.

Over the years I have received help and encouragement from many fellow historians. These include J.N. Bakhuizen van den Brink, John Bromley, C.C. de Bruin and A.F. Mellink who are alas no longer with us. I am grateful to Patrick Collinson who first pointed me in the direction of the Dutch Reformation, to Henk van der Linden for making me aware of the importance of Dutch legal history and to both he and his late wife Gien for marvellous hospitality, to Ernst Kossmann and Koen Swart who supervised my first steps in Dutch history, to Coen and Willy Tamse-Aldersma for years of friendship, to Geoffrey Parker, Dirk Kolff, Johan Decavele, Hans Trapman, Wiebe Bergsma, Henk van Nierop, Simon Groenveld and Andrew Pettegree for challenging discussions about Dutch heretics, rebels and Calvinists. Before publication this collection was submitted as a doctoral dissertation to the Rijksuniversiteit te Leiden. In accordance with Dutch academic practice a *promotiecommissie* read the text. They courteously drew attention to errors and made suggestions which I have been glad to incorporate in the final version. The co-authors of chapters six and nine generously allowed me to include these pieces in the collection. I have learnt much from my postgraduates past and present. Stuart Moore introduced me to the world of the cathedral canons of Utrecht, Andrew Johnston extended my knowledge of evangelical literature, Marcel Backhouse has confounded my scepticism about the Flemish Calvinists at Sandwich and Paul Regan has made me aware of the importance of maps. I thank my colleagues in the History Department at Southampton for their forebearance and help, especially Ernest Blake and George Bernard. Like other students I have found discovered for myself the old truth that 'other men laboured and ye are entered into their labours' (John IV:38).

The production of a book is a team effort. This one would never have been completed in time without the dedication and ingenuity of Andrew Spicer, who selflessly set aside precious time from his own researches on the French-speaking Reformed Church in Elizabethan Southampton in order to prepare these essays for the computer. I am also obliged to the computing expertise of the HiDES team at Southampton, especially to Jean Colson, Robert Cruickshank, Paul Norris and Jason Clow. In Martin Sheppard I had the good fortune to find a publisher who took as many pains with the style of the typescript as he did with the publication of the book. My wife and children supported me throughout, giving encourage-ment when it was needed while understanding that there were also occasions when it was better not to ask after the book's progress. I thank them all.

Southampton

Abbreviations

AC	Archief van de classis.
AGKKN	*Archief voor de geschiedenis van de Katholieke kerk in Nederland.*
AGN	*Algemene geschiedenis der Nederlanden*, ed. J.A. van Houtte *et al.*, 12 vols. (Utrecht, 1949–58)
(Nieuwe) *AGN*	*Algemene geschiedenis der Nederlanden*, ed. D. P. Blok *et al.*, 15 vols. (Haarlem, 1977–83).
ARAB	Algemeen Rijksarchief Brussel.
Archives ou Correspondance	*Archives ou correspondance inédite de la* Maison d'OrangeNassau,1ère sér., ed. G. Groen van Prinsterer, 8 Vols. & suppl. (Leiden, 1835–47)
ARG	*Archiv für Reformationsgeschichte.*
BBH	*Bijdragen tot de geschiedenis van het bisdom Haarlem.*
BCHR	*Bulletin de la commission royale d'histoire.*
BGN	*Bijdragen voor de geschiedenis der Nederlanden.*
BLGNP	*Biografisch lexikon voor de geschiedenis van het Nederlandse Protestantisme*, ed. D. Nauta *et al.*, 3 vols. (Kampen, 1978–88).
BMGN	*Bijdragen en mededelingen betreffende de geschiedenis der Nederlanden.*
BMHG	*Bijdragen en medede(e)lingen van het Historisch Genootschap.*
BN	*Britain and the Netherlands.*
Bor	Pieter Bor (Christiaensz.), *Oorsprongk, begin en vervoligh der Nederlandsche Oorlogen*, 4 vols. (Amsterdam, 1679–84). Cross references to 3rd. edition (Leiden – Amsterdam, 1621–34) by book and folio.
Brandt	Geeraert Brandt, *Historie der reformatie en andre kerkelyke geschiedenissen in en ontrent de Nederlanden*, 4 vols. (Amsterdam, 1671–1704)

BRN   *Bibliotheca reformatoria neerlandica*, ed. S.
                               Cramer and J. Pijper, 10 vols. (The Hague,
                               1903–14).
CAD   *Classicale acta 1573–1620: Particuliere synode
                               Zuid-Holland*, I, *Classis Dordrecht, 1573–1600*,
                               ed. J.P. van Dooren (The Hague, 1980), Rijks
                               Geschiedkundige Publicatiën, Kleine serie
                               49.
CD   *Corpus documentorum inquisitionis haereticae
                               pravitatis neerlandicae: Verzameling van stukken
                               betreffende de pauselijke en bisshoppelijke inquisitie
                               in de Nederlanden*, ed. P. Fredericq, 5 vols.
                               (Ghent – The Hague, 1889–1902).
Corresp. Guillaume   *Correspondance de Guillaume le Taciturne*, ed.
                               L.P. Gachard, 6 vols. (Brussels, 1847–66).
Corresp. Marguerite   *Correspondance de Marguerite d'Autriche,
d'Autriche* (Gachard).   duchesse de Parme, avec Philippe II*, ed. L.P.
                               Gachard, 3 vols. (Brussels, 1867–88).
Corresp. française   *Correspondance française de Marguerite
Marguerite d'Autriche*   *d'Autriche, duchesse de Parme, avec Philippe
                               II*, ed. J.S. Theissen *et al.*, 3 vols. (Utrecht,
                               1925–42).
Corresp. Philippe II   *Correspondance de Philippe II sur les affaires des
                               Pays-Bas*, ed. L.P. Gachard, 5 vols. (Brussels,
                               1848–79).
Dagboek   *Dagboek van Broeder Wouter Jacobsz.*, ed. I.H.
                               van Eeghen, 2 vols. (Groningen, 1959–60).
DAN   *Documenta anabaptistica neerlandica.*
Emden   Archiv der Evangelisch-Reformierte
                               Gemeinde Emden.
GA   Gemeente archief.
Hoop Scheffer   J.G. Hoop Scheffer, *Geschiedenis der
                               kerkhervorming in Nederland van haar ontstaan tot
                               1531* (Amsterdam, 1873).
JEH   *Journal of Ecclesiastical History.*
KA   Kerkeraadsarchief (Kerkelijk archief).
NAK   *Nederlands(ch) archief voor kerkgeschiedenis.*
NK   W. Nijhoff and M.E. Kronenberg, *Nederlandsche
                               bibliographie van 1500 tot 1540*, 3 vols. (The
                               Hague, 1923–71).
NNBW   *Nieuw nederlandsch biografisch woordenboek*, ed.
                               P.C. Molhuysen and Fr. K.H. Kossmann, 10
                               vols. (Leiden, 1911–37).
ORA   Oud rechterlijk archief.

OSA	Oud synodaal archief.
Oude kerkordeningen	*Oude kerkordeningen der nederlandsche hervormde gemeenten, 1563–1638*, ed. C. Hooijer, (Zaltbommel, 1865).
RA	Rijksarchief.
RANH	Rijksarchief Noord-Holland.
Relations politiques	*Relations politiques des Pays-Bas et de l'Angleterre sous le règne de Philippe II*, ed. J.M.B.C. Kervyn de Lettenhove, 11 vols. (Brussels, 1882–1900).
RGP	Rijks Geschiedkundige Publicatiën.
ROPB	*Recueil des ordonnances des Pays-Bas sous le règne de Charles-Quint*, ed. C. Laurent *et al.*, 6 vols. (Brussels, 1893–1922).
RV	*Acta der provinciale en particuliere synoden gehouden in de noordelijke Nederlanden gedurende de jaren, 1572–1620*, ed. J. Reitsma and S.D. van Veen, 8 vols. (Groningen, 1892–99).
RvB	Raad van Beroerten
TG	*Tijdschrift voor geschiedenis.*
WMV	*Werken der Marnix-Vereeniging*, Serie I-III (Utrecht, 1870–89).

1

The Origins of Evangelical Dissent in the Low Countries

When the Sorbonne proscribed the teachings of Martin Luther in April 1521 frequent reference was made to earlier condemnations by the church of similar errors.[1] Luther thus stood convicted of having revived the pernicious heresies of Wyclif, Hus and the Waldensians, to say nothing of those which had beset the early church.[2] In this way Luther's judges unintentionally opened the debate about the relationship between the Protestant reformers and these earlier dissidents. At first the German evangelicals were afraid of being tarred with the Hussite brush, but they soon realised that the opposition of the Bohemians and other medieval dissenters to the Roman church provided them with the evidence they required to rebut the damaging allegation of their opponents that Luther and his adherents taught novel opinions. Accordingly, they saluted these dissenters as professors and witnesses of the 'true church'.

In the Low Countries, as in Germany, the learned supporters of Luther rummaged in the lumber-room of medieval anticlerical literature for any tracts which anticipated their denunciations of clerical celibacy, monastic vows and papal authority. In the 1520s a clutch of such works duly appeared in print along with the writings of Wessel Gansfort.[3] The early evangelicals soon came to appreciate that they could more easily counteract the weight of historical evidence on the Romanists' side by making a distinction between the 'true' church and the church of Antichrist. In 1525 a cleric from Woerden, on trial for his opinions, told his inquisitors that the holy church was 'an invisible and spiritual congregation', quite unlike the *ecclesia malignantium*, where the pope sits enthroned in the *cathedra pestilentie*.[3] Melchior Hoffman employed similarly apocalyptic language when he described the false church as 'the con-

---

[1] I wish to record my thanks to Dr. J. Trapman and Dr. A. Johnson who generously shared their knowledge of the period with me. An earlier version of this paper was given to the European History Seminar at the Institute of Historical Research and, when I came to revise it, I benefited from their constructive criticisms.

[2] P. Polman, *L'élément historique dans la controverse religieuse du XVIe siècle* (Gembloux, 1932), pp. 494–95.

[3] M.E. Kronenberg, *Verboden boeken en opstandige drukkers in de hervormingstijd* (Amsterdam, 1948), pp. 48, 61–63, 68–70.

gregation of Satan'.[4] Later Protestant martyrologists combed the ecclesiastical records for the names and testimonies of those who in times past had opposed the Roman church in order to demonstrate the lineage of the 'true' but persecuted church since the days of the Apostles, or indeed since Abel. For this reason a miscellaneous band of dissidents, including Arnold of Brescia (d. 1155), Savonarola and sundry Waldensians, Spiritual Franciscans and English Lollards, eventually secured a niche in the Dutch Reformed martyrology of Adriaen van Haemstede.[5] Likewise, Thieleman Jansz. van Braght devoted the first part of his account of the Mennonites' tribulations to their precursors since the start of the Christian era to prove that though the 'true church' might sometimes be hidden from sight, it had never been extinguished.[6] Dutch Calvinists and Mennonites alike measured this church by the quality, not the number, of its professors. It might, as the Belgic Confession acknowledged in 1561, seem at times 'very small and, in the eyes of men, even to have perished', yet it had been since the foundation of the world and would endure to the end.[7]

In their quest for witnesses to the *successio doctrinae* in a Protestant sense, the Dutch martyrologists did not confine themselves to the Low Countries. Indeed this region contributed conspicuously few medieval martyrs to suit the polemical and edifying purposes of van Haemstede and van Braght. They were not concerned to assert the particular election of the United Provinces by God.[8] The perspective shifted after the Dutch Republic came into being. Once the Reformed churches had been recognised as 'the public church' in the United Provinces, the original character of the Dutch Reformation became an urgent political, as well

[3] *CD*, IV, p. 477.

[4] C.A. Pater, 'Melchior Hoffman's Explication of the Songs(!) of Songs, *ARG*, LXVIII (1977), p. 179. Luther described the Council of Constance as 'die sinagoge van Sathan', *CD*, IV, p. 67. Heinrich von Kettenbach, the reformer of Ulm, denounced 'die kirchen der synagogam sathanae' in 1523, see *Die Schriften Heinrichs von Kettenbachs: Flugschriften aus den Jahren der Reformation*, ed. O. Clemen (Halle a.d.S., 1907), II, p. 68.

[5] *De gheschiedenisse ende den doodt der vromer martelaren* (s.l., 1559). For a listing of the numerous subsequent editions, several of which included additional material, see *Bibliographie des martyrologes protestants néerlandais* (The Hague, 1890), II, pp. 271–378. The account of the English Lollards first appeared in 1612, having been translated from Foxe's *Acts and Monuments of the Church*, probably by Henry Hexham, an English Presbyterian soldier in the employ of the United Provinces, see N.E. Osselton, *The Dumb Linguists: A Study of the Earliest English and Dutch Dictionaries* (Leiden-Oxford, 1973), p. 40 fn. 23.

[6] *The Bloody Theater or Martyrs' Mirror of Defenceless Christians* (Scottdale, 1951). p. 25. For bibliographical details on the various editions, see *Bibliographie des martyrologes protestants*, II, pp. 21–77.

[7] *De nederlandse belijdenisgeschriften in authentieke teksten*, ed. J.N. Bakhuizen van den Brink (Amsterdam, 1976), pp. 121–23 (art. xxvii). See also the testimony of Mennonite martyrs, *Het Offer des Heeren, BRN*, II, pp. 248–49, 314, 360.

[8] On this theme see G. Groenhuis, 'Calvinism and National Consciousness: the Dutch Republic as the New Israel', *BN*, VII, *Church and State since the Reformation*, ed. A.C. Duke and C.A. Tamse (The Hague, 1981), pp. 118–33.

as an ecclesiastical, issue. The zealous Calvinists insisted that the fragile unity of the state required the maintenance of the Reformed religion,[9] for, as the Contra-Remonstrant deputies from Amsterdam told the States of Holland in 1618, the bonds uniting the Reformed churches (in the Netherlands) had been forged before the Union of Utrecht.[10] In short, the church antedated the formation of the state.

But the Remonstrants and their political allies, the States' party, refused to allow the Contra-Remonstrants to annex the Reformation and the Revolt. Oldenbarnevelt believed that the salvation of the new state depended on the strict adherence to the doctrine of provincial sovereignty, even in the sphere of religion, as it was enshrined in the Union of Utrecht.[11] Though such leaders regarded the 'true Christian reformed religion' as the public church of Holland, they wanted supreme authority in ecclesiastical affairs to be vested in the provincial States and the town corporations. They also looked for the creation of a comprehensive Protestant church where all 'good patriots' might attend the Lord's Table without first having to submit themselves to the yoke of consistorial discipline or suffer the examination of some upstart *predikant*.[12]

More pertinently these non-Calvinist evangelicals called attention to the pluriformity of Dutch Protestantism. In 1622 Grotius warned the Reformed ministers that 'many magistrates and countless members of the church' had been schooled in the less exacting theologies of Bullinger, Melanchthon, Anastasius Veluanus and Erasmus.[13] In these circles Erasmus was revered and the demand for his books, in both Dutch and Latin, quickened in the early 1590s and again during the years of bitter theological wrangling which preceded the convocation of the National Synod in 1618.[14] Henceforth the Rotterdammer was assured a prominent place

[9] See the opinions of Willem Lodewijk, the *stadhouder* of Friesland, cited by H. Gerlach, *Het proces tegen Oldenbarnevelt en de 'Maximen in den Staet'* (Haarlem, 1965), pp. 265–67 and of the *predikanten* Wilhelmus Baudartius (1565–1640) and Johannes Fontanus (1546–1615), cited by J.C.H. de Pater, 'De religie als factor bij de vorming van den nederlandschen staat', *Bijdragen voor vaderlandsche geschiedenis en oudheidkunde*, 7de reeks, VIII (1937), pp. 114–15. For the same reason the provincial States undertook at the *Grote Vergadering* (1651) to maintain 'the true Christian Reformed religion', as defined by the National Synod of Dordrecht.
[10] H. Smitskamp, *Calvinistische nationaalbesef in Nederland vóór het midden der 17e eeuw* (The Hague, 1947), p. 20.
[11] Gerlach, *Het proces tegen Oldenbarnevelt*, p. 485.
[12] Brandt, II, 345–83; see below, pp. 247–48; 291–92.
[13] Cited by G.J. Hoenderdaal, 'Erasmus en de nederlandse reformatie', *Vox Theologica*, XXXIX (1969), p. 129. Johannes Uytenbogaert also read in his youth works by Luther, Melanchthon, Bullinger, Anastasius Veluanus and certain lesser known local evangelicals, A.J. van 't Hooft, *De theologie van Heinrich Bullinger in betrekking tot de nederlandsche reformatie* (Amsterdam, 1888), p. 100.
[14] S.W. Bijl, *Erasmus in het nederlands tot 1617* (Nieuwkoop, 1978), pp. 406–7. Between 1593 and 1596 the wooden statue of Erasmus in the marketplace at Rotterdam made way for one in stone. This in turn was replaced in 1622 by Hendrik de Keyser's bronze, see *Erasmus en zijn tijd: Tentoonstelling ingericht ter herdenking van de geboorte ... van Erasmus*, 2 vols. (Rotterdam, 1969), I, nos. 567, 570.

in the pantheon of Dutch reformers, at least in the opinion of Remonstrants and like-minded moderates. Erasmus, as Grotius remarked to the Remonstrant minister Johannes Uytenbogaert in 1632, 'had pointed the way to a reasonable reformation'.[15]

After their expulsion from the Reformed church the Remonstrants were concerned to vindicate their claim to be the authentic heirs – and therefore the proper guardians – of the original Dutch Reformation. Since their title was naturally contested by the victors at Dordrecht, the interpretation of the local Reformation[16] became a matter of fierce controversy, as the rival confessional traditions sought to establish their own pedigree and to discredit that of their opponents.[17] Without question the Remonstrant minister and belletrist Geeraerdt Brandt (1626–85) made the most impressive contribution to those exchanges with his *Historie der reformatie en andre kerkelyke geschiedenissen in en ontrent de Nederlanden.*[18] According to Brandt, the cause of the Protestant Reformation, to which he was devoted, had been disfigured by the intolerant treatment of dissidents and by the usurpation of authority in the public church by the Calvinist *predikanten* and the consistories. Similar concerns also informed his brief treatment of the medieval church. As a good Protestant he judged the pre-Reformation church harshly, though the general gloom was relieved for Brandt by the piety of Thomas à Kempis and the forthright attacks on scholastic theology, papal authority and indulgences made by Wessel Gansfort and Johannes Pupper of Goch.[19] In the incessant war against 'scandalous error' and 'ecclesiastical pride', the Protestant Reformation indeed constituted the decisive battle, yet the preliminary skirmishes had begun 'some hundreds of years before Luther was raised up'.[20] Brandt acknowledged Luther's part in the campaign, but the credit for teaching 'the world how to reform' belonged

[15] Brandt, I, pp. 49–50.

[16] This account of the historiography of the Dutch Reformation is indebted to D. Nauta, 'De reformatie in Nederland in de historiografie', *Serta Historica*, II (1970), pp. 44–71, reprinted in *Geschiedschrijving in Nederland*, II, *Geschiedbeoefening*, ed. P.A.M. Geurts and A.E.M. Janssen (The Hague, 1981), pp. 206–27.

[17] The strict Calvinist, Jacobus Trigland, denied in his *Kerckelycke Geschiedenissen* (Leiden, 1650) that Melanchthon and Bullinger's doctrine of election was at odds with the teachings laid down at Dordrecht. He also attempted to appropriate for his party the 'forerunners' of the Reformation. He asserted that before 'the open Reformation' of Luther and Zwingli had begun, certain Netherlanders had already come to a knowledge of the 'Holy Truth', above all Wessel Gansfort, *ibid.*, pp. 118–21.

[18] On Brandt, see P. Burke, 'The Politics of Reformation History: Burnet and Brandt', *BN*, VIII, *Clio's Mirror: Historiography in Britain and the Netherlands*, ed. A.C. Duke and C.A. Tamse (Zutphen, 1985), pp. 73–85.

[19] Brandt, I, pp. 49, 53–56. Blesdijk, David Joris' son-in-law, writing in the late 1550s, traced the start of the Reformation to Wessel Gansfort, S. Zijlstra, *Nicolaas Meyndertsz. van Blesdijk* (Groningen, 1983), p. 147.

[20] *Ibid.*, I, p. 3.

to Erasmus.[21] It was a conceit as congenial to Brandt as a Remonstrant as it was flattering to his pride as a Hollander.

If the author of the *Historie der reformatie* cast the German reformer in a subsidiary role, the ecclesiastical historians Annaeus Ypey (1760–1837) and Isaak Dermout (1777–1867) allowed Erasmus to steal the show. When the first volume of their collaborative history of the Reformed church in the Netherlands was published in 1819, Dutch Calvinists were still adjusting to the changes consequent on the separation of church and state and to their unaccustomed position as a religious minority in the newly-created Kingdom of the Netherlands.[22] The outburst of patriotic fervour with which they celebrated the tercentenary of the Reformation reflected their anxieties.[23] Such emotions help to explain the extravagant claims made by Ypey and Dermout for the Dutch Reformation. They audaciously declared that the process of spiritual enlightenment had begun, not in Italy or Germany, but in their 'fatherland'. In support they adduced the geniuses of Geert Grote, Rudolf Agricola, Laurens Jansz. Coster, honoured in nineteenth-century Holland as the inventor of printing from movable type, and, above all, Erasmus.[24]

Though church historians after Ypey and Dermout hesitated to press these claims, they continued to insist on the distinctive character of the Dutch Reformation. According to scholars associated with the so-called Groningen school of theology, the Brethren of the Common Life, Wessel Gansfort and, of course, Erasmus had nurtured a 'truly Dutch national theology', averse from bigotry and creedal statements. In the course of the Reformation this indigenous tradition had been thrust aside by the alien and legalistic system of Calvin, but Petrus Hofstede de Groot (1802–86) and his circle, whose watchword 'niet de leer, maar de Heer' (not doctrine, but the Lord) neatly epitomised their religious priorities, sought to revive this venerable native theology.[25]

With the conspicuous exception of those scholars who held confessional chairs in ecclesiastical history,[26] Dutch Protestant church historians until as late as the Second World War regarded the Reformation in the

---

[21] *Ibid.*, I, verse under portrait of Erasmus facing p. 64.

[22] A. Ypey and I. Dermout, *Geschiedenis der nederlandche hervormde kerk*, 4 vols. (Breda, 1819–27).

[23] A. de Groot, 'Sociocultureel en godsdienstig leven in de noordelijke Nederlanden 1813-circa 1840' (Nieuwe) *AGN*, XI (Bussum, 1983), p. 94.

[24] Ypey and Dermout, *Geschiedenis*, I, pp. 4–5, 9, 23, 29–30.

[25] Nauta, 'Reformatie in Nederland', pp. 54–56. On the Groningen school of theology see E.H. Kossmann, *De Lage Landen, 1780–1940: Anderhalve eeuw Nederland en België* (Amsterdam-Brussels, 1976), pp. 209–10; J. Huizinga *et al.*, *Academia Groningana MDCXIV-MCMXIV: Gedenkboek ter gelegenheid van het derde eeuwfeest der Universiteit te Groningen* in J. Huizinga, *Verzamelde Werken*, VIII, *Universiteit, wetenschap en kunst* (Haarlem, 1951), pp. 148–51. Dr. C.A. Tamse kindly supplied this reference.

[26] *E.g.* the Calvinist F.L. Rutgers (1836–1917); the Lutheran J. Loosjes, (1874–1935) and the Mennonite J.G. de Hoop Scheffer (1819–93).

Netherlands as a substantially indigenous creation, at least in origin, though they argued among themselves about the relative importance of Luther and the sacramentarians. When Laurentius Knappert (1863–1943) wrote his history of the rise and establishment of Protestantism in the Low Countries,[27] he treated the Reformation, despite his unsurpassed knowledge of the different sources, in a manner not so very different from that devised by Brandt some two and a half centuries earlier. If Thomas à Kempis no longer qualified as a 'forerunner of the Reformation', Johannes Pupper appeared as an avant-garde Protestant,[28] and Wessel Gansfort as 'the first representative of that religious humanism, which sought to unite scholarship, intellectual culture and piety'.[29] The 'original autochthonous reformation', according to Knappert, derived from the fusion of two religious traditions: Zwinglian eucharistic theology, itself indebted to the Hollander Cornelis Hoen for its symbolic interpretation of the words of institution, and the undogmatic, biblically-oriented Christianity of Erasmus, which made him an opponent of religious persecution.[30] Though Knappert was well aware of Luther's enormous influence on evangelicals in the Low Countries, he chose nevertheless to describe the earliest decade of the Reformation as 'the sacramentarian period', on the grounds that Luther's own teaching on the real presence did not find favour with them.[31]

Johannes Lindeboom (1882–1958), however, regarded Lutheranism as one of the chief constituents in the Dutch Reformation alongside Anabaptism, Calvinism and the so-called 'national-reformed' party.[32] Where earlier scholars had divided the Reformation into distinct chronological phases, as if it were a three-stage rocket, Lindeboom treated the varieties of Protestantism side-by-side in order to accentuate the blurred and shifting lines of religious allegiance in the first half of the sixteenth century. Though he still maintained the distinctive character of the Dutch Reformation and accorded the 'national-reformed' element a major part in its complex development, he was reluctant to claim that the biblical and practical Christianity professed by such reformers was

---

[27] *Het ontstaan en de vestiging van het protestantisme in de Nederlanden* (Utrecht, 1924). Although in many particulars outdated, it remains unsurpassed as a survey of the Reformation in the Low Countries for Knappert gave a prominent place to the southern Netherlands, treated Anabaptism at length and made extensive use of both the contemporary religious literature and archival sources. Apart from Lindeboom's concise essay, published in 1946, and Halkin's admirable short history of the Reformation in the southern provinces under Charles V, which appeared in 1957, Knappert's account represents the last serious attempt at a general history of the Reformation in the Low Countries in any language.

[28] Knappert, *Ontstaan*, pp. 52, 77–79.

[29] *Ibid.*, p. 87.

[30] *Ibid.*, p. 112.

[31] *Ibid.*, pp. 175–79.

[32] *De confessioneele ontwikkeling der reformatie in de Nederlanden* (The Hague, 1946).

peculiar to the Low Countries.[33]

By the later 1940s even these modest claims in favour of a distinctive, indigenous Reformation were slowly losing their plausibility as the liberal Protestant and patriotic assumptions, which underpinned them, ceased to correspond with the prevailing values of the postwar generation. As the pace of dechristianisation accelerated, interest in the Reformation slackened. Since the destiny of the Dutch people no longer seemed to be bound up closely with the Protestant faith, the significance of the religious changes in the sixteenth century for the national history diminished.

The notion of 'forerunners' suffered a damaging blow when medievalists and Catholic historians from Belgium and the Netherlands exposed the flaws in the arguments of those who regarded the Modern Devotion as having prepared the ground for the sixteenth-century evangelicals.[34] It had always been hard to explain why, if the religious spirit cultivated by the Modern Devotion bore some likeness to the evangelical piety of early Protestantism, the Brethren of the Common Life and the Canons of Windesheim should have displayed so little enthusiasm for the Reformation.[35] This indifference has become more understandable in the light of modern scholarship. The Modern Devotion instilled in its members an introspective spirituality induced by systematic meditation on Christ's Passion. Furthermore, pressures both within and without the movement caused many houses in the fifteenth century to adopt a monastic rule of life; at the same time, the proportion of lay brothers in the 'free congregations' tended to decline. For these reasons the Modern Devotion was out of sympathy with evangelical theology.[36] Even the well-attested enthusiasm for the Scriptures among the Brethren does not presage the Protestant demand for the Bible *tout court*, let alone anticipate the principle of *sola scriptura*. Since the imitation of Christ's example remained the object of their piety, they attached most importance to the gospels, but ranked the epistles of Paul behind the *Vitae patrum* and the accounts of Christ's Passion. When Gerard Zerbolt of Zutphen advocated

[33] *Ibid.*, pp. 41–42.

[34] *E.g.* L.J. Rogier, *Geschiedenis van het katholicisme in noord-Nederland in de 16e en 17e eeuw*, 3 vols. (Amsterdam, 1947), I, pp. 103–13; R.R. Post, *Kerkelijke verhoudingen in Nederland vóór de reformatie van ± 1500 tot ± 1580* (Utrecht-Antwerp, 1954), pp. 515–16; S. Axters, *Geschiedenis van de vroomheid in de Nederlanden*, 4 vols. (Antwerp, 1950–60), III, pp. 414–15; R.R. Post, *The Modern Devotion: Confrontation with Reformation and Humanism* (Leiden, 1968), ch. XIV-XV; A.G. Weiler, 'Recent Historiography on the Modern Devotion: Some Debated Questions', *AGKKN*, XXVI (1984), pp. 161–79.

[35] The Reformation did find a following in a few houses, notably at Deventer, Doesburg, Utrecht and Amersfoort. For a superficial appreciation of the Modern Devotion by an evangelical see J. Trapman, *De summa der godliker scrifturen (1523)* (Leiden, 1978), p. 70. These casual links cannot compensate for the fundamental antipathy between the practical spirituality of the Modern Devotion and Luther's Christian freedom.

[36] Weiler, 'Recent Historiography', pp. 177–79.

the translation of the Bible into Dutch, he deliberately excluded the Old Testament prophets, the epistles and Revelation on the grounds that these were too difficult for the unlearned.[37] This is a very different kind of Bible from that championed by Christian humanists and Protestants of all persuasions.

Once the historians of the early Reformation in the Low Countries could free themselves from patriotic and confessional constraints, they could acquire a fresh understanding of the local Reformation by looking at the progress of evangelical theology outside the Netherlands. Consequently the claims once made by pious and patriotic historians, often writing long afterwards, for those Dutchmen, whose protests against Rome had supposedly antedated Luther, lost credibility.[38] Even if the traditions concerning this handful of obscure proto-evangelicals could be anchored more securely in the contemporary records, this would not shake the scholarly consensus that religious attitudes among both the learned and the laity underwent a profound transformation around 1520.

Until then objections to the traffic in indulgences were apparently confined to a small circle of theologians and mendicant preachers, worried lest the indiscriminate use of indulgences undermine the sacrament of penance,[39] though the complaint, often reiterated in fifteenth-century Germany, that their sale drained the country of gold and silver, was also voiced in the Low Countries.[40] In the diocese of Utrecht the income from the sale of indulgences had largely paid for the upkeep of the cathedral fabric – until 1522. But in that year the pardoners unexpectedly found themselves unable to meet their obligations, 'on account', we are told, 'of the great dearth, the teachings of Martin Luther and the fighting in the Oversticht'. To quench any doubts about the value of indulgences the cathedral chapter printed 500 pamphlets for distribution by the indulgence-sellers, which recounted 'certain

---

[37] See J. Roelink, 'Moderne devotie en reformatie', *Serta Historica*, II (1970), 19–21; C.C. de Bruin, *De statenbijbel en zijn voorgangers* (Leiden, 1937), p. 69. Johannes Pupper of Goch permitted men, but not women and children, to interpret the Scriptures, see R.R. Post, 'Johannes Pupper van Goch', *NAK* n.s., XLVII (1965–66), p. 95. The French translator of biblical excerpts in 1510 made a similar distinction between suitable and unsuitable parts of the Bible for the laity, see D.J. Nicholls, 'The Nature of Popular Heresy in France, 1520–1542', *Historical Journal*, XXVI (1983), pp. 266–67.

[38] For a convenient list of these see Lindeboom, *Confessioneele ontwikkeling*, pp. 36–37. For a recent discussion about a certain Hilmar von Borssum see M. Smid, *Ostfriesische Kirchengeschichte* (Pewsum, 1974), p. 116.

[39] See M. van Rhijn, *Wessel Gansfort* (The Hague, 1917), pp. 222–28; for Jean Vitrier's attack on indulgences in 1498 see *CD*, I, p. 491 and for Tileman Spengenberg see Lindeboom, *Confessioneele ontwikkeling*, p. 36.

[40] Hoop Scheffer, p. 51 where he cites an extract from the *Divisiekroniek*, printed at Leiden in August 1517, attacking indulgences.

miracles against Luther's teaching'. Despite this counterblast the demand for indulgences did not recover.[41]

Were this an isolated incident it would prove little:[42] the spasmodic rhythm of popular piety, expressed in sudden surges of religious enthusiasm and ephemeral cults, warns us against reading too much into a single fluctuation, no matter how suggestive.[43] Yet there are other pointers, which together indicate a marked shift in religious sentiments at this time. In Antwerp freewill offerings and legacies had provided almost one-third of the revenues for the upkeep of the chief parish church between 1510 and 1519. In the next decade receipts from these sources accounted for less than one-sixth of the total income, a decline which the churchwardens attributed to the baleful influence of Luther.[44] Moreover, according to an evangelical, writing in the mid-1520s, several local shrines in Holland had recently lost popularity because people had ceased to believe in the miraculous powers of their relics.[45]

During the same period many religious houses in the northern Netherlands went into decline. In 1524 Erasmus informed Willibald Pirckheimer, the Nuremberg humanist, that 'in my Holland' monks were everywhere forsaking their monasteries to take wives.[46] The incidence of apostasy among the religious so alarmed the government that they published a succession of edicts in the later 1520s, fixing severe penalties for renegade monastics and their abettors.[47] Those who deserted could

[41] W.H. Vroom, *De financiering van de kathedraalbouw in de middeleeuwen, in het bijzonder van de dom van Utrecht* (Maarssen, 1981), pp. 300, 316, 318–20. No copy of this pamphlet has apparently survived.

[42] When reviewing Vroom's book in *AGKKN*, XXIV (1982), pp. 144–45, W. Frijhoff attributed the sudden fall in receipts from the sale of indulgences to the collapse of a financial system which had been overstretched: Luther was made the scapegoat. The consequences too of the great dearth of 1520–22 should not be overlooked: the faithful had less money to spend on indulgences in a time of hardship. On this crisis in Antwerp, the first in the sixteenth century, see E. Scholliers, *De levensstandaard in de XVe en XVIe eeuw te Antwerpen* (Antwerp, 1960), pp. 126–27, where the discontent was linked with heresy. H. Heller, 'Famine, Revolt and Heresy at Meaux: 1521–1525', *ARG*, LXVIII (1977), pp. 142–44 also postulates a connection between the attack of the 'Meaux Group' on prayers for the dead and the contemporary dearth.

[43] C.I. Kruisheer, *De Onze Lieve Vrouwe-Broederschap te Doesburg, ca. 1397–1580* (Ellecom, 1976) notes a decline in the legacies for memorial masses a decade *before* the Reformation and sees in this a reaction against the exuberance of the late medieval piety.

[44] W.H. Vroom, *De Onze-Lieve-Vrouwekerk te Antwerpen: De financiering van de bouw tot de beeldenstorm* (Antwerp-Amsterdam, 1983), pp. 58–60, 144–45.

[45] (Willem Gnapheus), *Een troost ende spiegel der siecken*, *BRN*, I, p. 196. Though not apparently printed until 1531, this evangelical work seems to have been written in late 1525 or early 1526, according to Gnapheus' introduction to a revised edition of the *Troost*, entitled *Tobias ende Lazarus* (Emden, 1557). Dr. Andrew Johnston kindly supplied me with a copy of this introduction.

[46] *CD*, IV, p. 284; see also IV, pp. 162, 246; V, pp. 166–67, 248–49; Hoop Scheffer, p. 332.

[47] Edicts for Holland 12 April 1526; 3 December 1527; 18 January 1528; 7 December 1528.

not easily be replaced. The convent ceased to offer a secure haven for the unmarried daughter and the life of religion no longer afforded a more certain road to salvation. Consequently many monastic and quasi-monastic communities, which had for the most part been surviving comfortably before 1520, if not always thriving, found themselves seriously depleted twenty years later; some indeed were abandoned well before the onset of the Revolt.[48]

Evidence of a different, though no less eloquent, kind of the radical shift in religious attitude is revealed by the appetite for the vernacular Bible and for preaching grounded in the Scriptures. The Bible was not, of course, a closed book to the laity in the fifteenth century, and most of the books were available in translation by 1480. The devout reader with small Latin could turn to Geert Grote's popular book of hours, which included a substantial anthology of psalms, and to the lectionaries, which contained the pericopes appointed for reading at public worship. Indeed no fewer than thirty-two Dutch lectionaries were printed between 1478 and 1522.[49] Yet this was a far cry from the complete Bible: the first full translation of the New Testament appeared in print in 1522 and another four years elapsed before Jacob van Liesvelt gave the Dutch public its first vernacular Bible. In other respects, too, the Protestant notion of the Bible, and nothing but the Bible, was far removed from the medieval understanding of the *sacrae scripturae*. Before the Reformation no rigid distinction was made in art and literature between the Bible and other devotional works. In the popular *Bibel int corte* non-biblical material was woven into the text without explanation or warning, and Geert Grote reckoned the litanies in his devotional manual to be no less inspired than those passages taken from the Bible proper. Since the epistles and gospels in the lectionaries were apportioned for reading on particular days the lay reader could not approach the New Testament systematically through the pericopes.

In the 1520s the Bible came to be viewed in an entirely different way. Between 1522 and 1540 thirty-eight complete editions of the New Testament and nine editions of the more expensive complete Bible were printed in Dutch. In the same period only three lectionaries came off the press. Such was the demand for sermons based on the Scriptures that the Dominicans were exhorted at their chapter in 1522 to familiarise themselves with the Bible 'and above all the New Testament' in order to

[48] Post, *Kerkelijke verhoudingen*, pp. 180–85; *idem, Modern Devotion*, ch. XIV-XV; the climate of opinion became less sympathetic towards monastics after 1520, see J.H.P. Kemperink (ed.), 'Johan van Ingen: Geschiedenissen', *Archief voor de geschiedenis van het aartsbisdom Utrecht*, LXXIV (1957), p. 87.

[49] Based on de Bruin, *Statenbijbel*, pp. 60–72, 98–101, 185–86.

disarm their critics, who accused them of preaching extravagantly.[50]

The mould of late medieval Catholicism had cracked. But was Luther alone responsible? The diehard conservatives in the faculty of theology at Leuven had wanted to include Erasmus in their condemnation of the German reformer in November 1519. Nor were they alone in confounding the causes of the two men. Several of the earliest scholarly advocates of evangelical preaching saw connections between the ideal of the *pia studia*, initiated by Wessel Gansfort, and the *vera theologia* pioneered at Wittenberg. To understand why men of very dissimilar sympathies made these connections, we should pay close attention to the relatively late triumph of Christian humanism in the Low Countries, to the debates which agitated the scholarly world in the second decade of the sixteenth century and to the common enthusiasm of many humanists and evangelicals for the Pauline epistles and for 'Christian freedom'.

Humanist pedagogy had been seeping into the grammar schools since the mid-fifteenth century, but the campaign against the barbarous grammarians – Donatus, Priscian and Alexander de Villadei – only began to bear fruit after 1510.[51] Significantly that classic statement of the 'philosophy of Christ', Erasmus's *Enchiridion militis christiani*, which had passed almost unnoticed when it first appeared in 1503, only became a bestseller after Luther had made his mark.[52] If Luther owed his understanding of the notion of repentance to Erasmus, he repaid that debt by creating a popular demand for religious works of which Erasmus was one of the chief beneficiaries. Conservative churchmen had been much alarmed by the humanists' plans for the reform of theology. In particular, they objected to the humanists' insistence that the text of the Bible should be studied in the original languages, rather than through the medium of approved commentaries. When the Trilingual College was founded at Leuven in 1518, Jacobus Latomus, by no means a reactionary, argued that a thorough doctrinal preparation should precede a training in

---

[50] *Acta capitulorum provinciae germaniae inferioris ordinis praedictorum ab anno MDXV usque ad annum MDLIX*, ed. S.P. Wolfs (The Hague, 1969) p. 50; for contemporary criticism of the friars' sermons see below p. 52; also S.P. Wolfs,'Dominicanen en de Colloquia van Erasmus', *NAK*, LXI (1981), pp. 40–41.

[51] M.A. Nauwelaerts, 'Scholen en onderwijs' in (Nieuwe) *AGN*, IV, pp. 369–70. Between 1484 and 1511 Alexander's *Doctrinale* was printed in forty-three editions at Deventer. According to R.R. Post, *Scholen en onderwijs in Nederland gedurende de middeleeuwen* (Antwerp-Utrecht, 1954), p. 146 the *Doctrinale* gradually disappeared from the school curriculum in the northen Netherlands between c. 1520–36; at Bruges the schools adopted the humanist Latin grammars in the 1520s, see A. Dewitte, 'Het humanisme te Brugge: een overtrokken begrip?', *Handelingen van de koninklijke zuid-nederlandse maatschappij voor taal en letterkunde en geschiedenis*, XXVII (1973), p. 11.

[52] R. Stupperich, 'Das *Enchiridion militis christiani* des Erasmus von Rotterdam nach seiner Entstehung, seinen Sinn und Charakter', *ARG*, LXIX (1978), pp. 9–10.

grammar or the sacred languages. Erudition was no guarantee of piety or orthodoxy.[53] The publication in 1516 of Erasmus's fresh translation of the New Testament from the Greek, which departed significantly from the authoritative text of the Vulgate, strengthened these fears. At this time too the controversy provoked by Reuchlin's defence of Jewish books against the fanatical Pfefferkorn reached a crescendo with the publication of the irreverent *Epistolae obscurorum virorum* (1515: 1517), which discredited the scholastic theologians. Though Erasmus stood aloof, many humanists did take Reuchlin's part in the paper war against the Dominican Inquisitor, Jacob van Hoogstraten.

By the time the shockwaves from the 'Luther affair' reached the Low Countries, the scholarly world was already engaged in a variety of debates and the positions theologians, humanists, mendicant preachers and schoolmasters had taken up in these debates coloured their perception of the German reformer. To a reactionary like Nicholaas van Egmond, who had long distrusted Erasmus, Luther's writings only confirmed the doctrinally subversive character of Christian humanism. Though Erasmus escaped condemnation with Luther, his departure for Basel in 1521 did nothing to redeem his reputation in the eyes of his detractors. Conservatives considered his books to be thoroughly pernicious. At Leuven penitents who confessed to having read his *Colloquia familiaria* were allegedly refused absolution by some priests in 1524,[54] and Dominicans and Crutched Friars in the Low Countries were forbidden to read any of Erasmus's works.[55] Equally, humanists could be attracted to Luther because his enemies were their enemies. Gerardus Listrius, the rector of the grammar school at Zwolle from 1516 to 1522, Gerardus Geldenhauer (Noviomagus), the court humanist of Philippe de Bourgogne, and the Westphalian poet Hermannus Buschius looked sympathetically on the evangelical cause because they had earlier supported Reuchlin and had no liking for his persecutors.[56]

Christian humanists welcomed Luther as an ally in their fight to make the Scriptures accessible to all men. Erasmus had stated the humanists' position most eloquently in his *Paraclesis* and others endorsed it, including Johannes Murmellius (d. 1517), the school rector at Alkmaar, who

[53] R. Guelley, 'L'évolution des méthodes théologiques à Louvain d'Erasme à Jansenius', *Revue d'histoire ecclésiastique*, XXXVII (1941), pp. 52–68.

[54] H. de Jongh, *L'ancienne faculté de théologie de Louvain au premier siècle de son existence (1432–1540)* (Leuven, 1911), pp. 252–53, 49*. In July 1523 students at Ingolstadt were reprimanded for reading the *Colloquies*, P.A. Russell, *Lay Theology in the Reformation: Popular Pamphleteers in Southwest Germany, 1521–1525* (Cambridge, 1986), p. 192.

[55] See below p. 83.

[56] Kronenberg, *Verboden boeken*, pp. 62–63, 67–70; on these humanists see J. Lindeboom, *Het bijbelsch humanisme in Nederland* (Leiden, 1913), pp. 134–40, 149–52, 183; S.P. Wolfs, *Das Groninger Religionsgespräch (1523) und seine Hintergründe* (Utrecht-Nijmegan, 1959), pp. 34–43; D. Grosheide, 'Enige opmerkingen over de reformatie en het humanisme in de noordelijke Nederlanden', *Serta Historica*, II (1970), pp. 73–74.

insisted that 'schoolboys should read the Psalms, Proverbs, Ecclesiastes and the Gospels, despite the opposition of some shavelings, more concerned with their own bellies and pockets than Peter's barque and their neighbour's salvation'.[57] Apart from the language of instruction, there was little difference between the schoolmaster, who expounded the scriptures to his pupils, and the bible-reading conventicles, which mushroomed in the towns after 1523. The authorities realised this and duly placed curbs on the former sort of assembly, while forbidding the latter.[58] There was also a convergence of doctrine: the antithesis between the flesh and the spirit, the notion of evangelical freedom, the high value set on Paul's epistles and the belief that baptismal promises rendered monastic vows superfluous.[59]

In the early 1520s the humanists were cock-a-hoop: obscurantism seemed at last to be in retreat and the Christian renaissance at hand. Cornelius Grapheus, the town secretary of Antwerp, rejoiced in 1521 that 'everywhere polite letters are being restored, the gospel of Christ has been re-born and Paul lives again'. To Grapheus, as to other humanists, it seemed as if the day prophesied by Joel (II: 28) when the Lord would pour out his spirit 'upon all flesh', was about to be accomplished.[60] In 1523 an unknown scholar at Groningen fervently hoped that many would turn at Easter 'from Aristotle to Paul, from Moses to Christ, from the Law to Grace, from the flesh to the spirit, from servitude to freedom, and from fear to gladness'.[61] This exultant mood soon faded. Grapheus and two fellow humanists from Antwerp had to recant their opinions in

---

[57] De Bruin, *Statenbijbel*, p. 97.

[58] D.P. Oosterbaan, 'School en kerk in het middeleeuwse Delft', *Spiegel der historie*, I (1966), p. 113; in September 1525 and again in March 1527 schoolmasters were told to expound the gospel and epistle on Sundays and feast days *grammaticale et non mistice* to avoid trouble, *CD*, V, pp. 4, 190.

[59] On this see Trapman, *Summa*, ch. VIII and *idem.*, 'Le rôle des "sacramentaires" des origines de la réforme jusqu'en 1530 aux Pays-Bas', *NAK*, LXIII (1983), pp. 11–12.

[60] *BRN*, VI, p. 38. Dr. Trapman first pointed out how much importance the humanists attached to this prophetic text in the 1520s. I am indebted to him for the following references: Erasmus (January 1522) in his epistle to the reader which accompanied his *Paraphrase* of St. Matthew, (*Opera omnia*, VII (Leiden, 1706 repr. 1962), fo. **3–3v.; Hans Sachs, *Disputation zwischen einem chorrherren und schuchmacher. Spätmittelalter, Humanismus Reformation: Texte und Zeugnisse*, II *Blütezeit des Humanismus und Reformation*, ed. H. Heger (Munich, 1978), p. 383; Anémond de Coct, the French evangelical, concluded a dedication, written in 1523, with the exhortation 'Adieu, et prie avec nous pour la paix de l'Eglise renaissante', *Correspondance des réformateurs dans les pays de langue française*, ed. A.L. Herminjard (Geneva, 1866), I, p. 151.

[61] *BRN*, VI, p. 551; see also Wolfs, *Groninger Religionsgespräch*, p. 27. The passage recalls Luther's assertion, made in his *Operationes in Psalmos* of 1519–21, that man's salvation depends on his passing 'de lege ad gratiam, de peccato ad iusticiam, de Mose ad Christum', see J.K. Steppe, ' "De overgang van het mensdom van het oude verbond naar het nieuwe." Een brussels wandtapijt uit de 16e eeuw ontstaan onder invloed van de lutherse ikonografie en prentkunst', *De gulden passer*, LIII (1975), p. 335.

April 1522 and two Augustinian monks were burnt in Brussels in the summer of 1523. Nevertheless the interweaving of Christian humanism and evangelical theology left its mark in the religious literature of those years. When the Franciscan warden at Amsterdam, Johannes Pelt, translated Matthew's gospel in 1522, he consulted the *Novum Instrumentum* and appended 'a precious exhortation ... from the worthy Doctor, master Erasmus'. Yet in his afterword he dwelt at length on justification by faith alone, insisting that man could be saved 'only by the grace and merits of Jesus Christ'.[62] The unknown author of *De Summa der godliker scrifturen* (1523) also took much of his theology from Erasmus. In characteristic manner he made baptism the gateway to Christian living and spurned monastic vows. He also set great store by the epistles of Paul and strongly advocated that the laity should be taught to read the Scriptures for themselves. Indeed of the typically Erasmian themes he only neglected *bonae literae*. Yet the same author clumsily incorporated an abridged translation of the first part of Luther's treatise *Von weltlicher Obrigkeit* (1523), which seems at odds with the rest of the work.[63] Whatever Luther and Erasmus thought about one another, conservatives and evangelical-humanists alike seem to have been more struck at this time by what they had in common than by what kept them apart.[64]

For all the points of contact between humanists and Protestant reformers, we need to keep a sense of proportion. Only a handful of prominent humanists, probably fewer than ten, persevered in the evangelical faith after 1525, that is after the persecutions and the open rupture between Luther and Erasmus.[65] Those chiefly concerned to cultivate polite letters – the *Schulhumanisten* – stayed aloof or agreed with Alardus of Amsterdam, when he asserted as early as 1522 that the cause of letters had been harmed by its association with the new theology.[66] Having entered this important caveat, it is clear that the evangelical theology appealed, however superficially, above all to those whom Erasmus

[62] Bijl, *Erasmus*, pp. 12–32. It is significant that Erasmus' translators were often evangelicals, who also made Luther's works available in the vernacular. Louis le Berquin and William Tyndale translated the *Enchiridion* into respectively French and English. The Zürich reformer Leo Jud made a German translation.

[63] Trapman, *Summa*, ch. IV.

[64] This explains why Canirivus, a humanist-schoolmaster at Delft, berated Erasmus in 1522 for not speaking out in support of the Lutheran cause, Oosterbaan, 'School en kerk', p. 113; Grosheide, 'Enige opmerkingen', pp. 78–79.

[65] Of the scholars listed in the repertory of humanists in the *Bibliographie de l'humanisme des anciens Pays-Bas*, ed. A. Gerlo and H.D.L. Vervliet (Brussels, 1972) only sixteen displayed any sympathy for Luther in the 1520s, including Cornelius Aurelius, Martin Dorp, Erasmus and Gerardus Listrius. Convinced evangelicals among the humanists included Herman van den Busche, Nicolaus Buscoducensis, Adrianus Cordatus, Wouter Delenus, Gerardus Geldenhauer, Willem Gnapheus and Joannes Sartorius.

[66] A.J. Kölker, *Alardus Aemstelredamus en Cornelius Crocus: Twee amsterdamse priester-humanisten* (Nijmegen-Utrecht, 1963), p. 50.

once described as the *mediocriter litterati*, the men of modest learning. Catholic polemicists habitually sneered at the 'barbers and toothdrawers' or 'furriers and weavers', who meddled with the Scriptures.[67] If they believed these stereotypes, which may reflect the unlearned character of late medieval dissent in the German lands,[68] then they deceived themselves. The printed records for the period 1518 to 1528 name 414 persons suspected of holding heretical opinions or of breaking the antiheresy edicts in force in the territories which constituted the Habsburg Netherlands after 1543.[69] An analysis of the 255 persons (61.6 per cent) whose profession or craft is known reveals that eighty-two (32.1 per cent) were clerics, conventuals or beguines; a further forty-four (17.25 per cent) were lawyers, schoolmasters, officeholders or printers, but only thirty-nine (16 per cent) made their living in the textile industry or garment-making trades. After 1530 the social appeal of the new doctrines changed markedly. Support from the learned classes declined and those recruited in to the ranks of the Anabaptists in Holland in the mid-1530s came above all from the ranks of the craftsmen and apprentices.[70]

Despite the grave misgivings of the conservatives about Erasmus, they never doubted that the *radix malorum* lay in Wittenberg. They therefore classified all dissidents as *lutheriaenen*, whether or not Luther would have recognised them as his disciples. Nor were they mistaken. Martin Luther was no less the author of the Reformation in the Low Countries than in Germany and Wittenberg the cynosure of all manner of nonconformists. The impact of his theology was felt most directly within the Augustinian houses at Antwerp, Ghent and Dordrecht, all of which belonged to the Saxon Congregation. Between 1516 and 1520 fifteen monks went from

[67] For a discussion of these stereotypes see below p. 37 fn. 60. An alternative stereotype of the dissident, which accords more closely with the occupational structure of the evangelicals in the 1520s, is given by the anonymous Catholic author of *Een cleyn Verclaringhe des gheestelijcken staets tegen tfenijen door Martijn Luyter* (NK 4017). He asserts that those most infected with heresy are 'dim witted and melancholic or whose minds have been given over to intellectual pursuits, or who brood deeply or who practise the arts and crafts concerned with the senses such as painters and engravers' [menschen die cleyn van herssenen sijn ende melancoloes, ofte die haer sinnen seer gemoeyt hebben met gheestelijcken oefeninghen oft met veel studerens, oft die constighe ambachten doen, ende ambachten die die sinnen moeyen, als schilders, beeldesniders ...].' Aiiiiv. I owe this reference to Dr. A. Johnston.

[68] S. Hoyer, 'Nicolaus Rutze und die Verbreitung hussitischer Gedanken im Hanseraum', *Neue Hansische Studiën*, ed. F. Konrad (Berlin, 1970), p. 164.

[69] Based on *CD*, IV-V (though the sixty persons investigated at Brussels in 1527 have been excluded because of Fredericq's incomplete documentation of this trial). Additional information has been taken from recent local studies of the Reformation in Flanders, Tournai, Mons, Lille, Namur, 's-Hertogenbosch, Maastricht as well as from a few older source publications not used by Fredericq (Zeeland and Overijssel). Schoolmasters were to the fore in the early German Reformation, H.A. Oberman, *Masters of the Reformation* (Cambridge, 1981), p. 265, especially fn. 19.

[70] H. Pirenne, *Histoire de Belgique*, III (Brussels, 1923), p. 116. For literacy among these 'small men' see below pp. 111-14.

these houses to study at Wittenberg,[71] where they lodged in the Augustinian monastery, of which Luther was the director of studies. By the early summer of 1519 the sermons delivered by the prior of the Antwerp Augustinians had already attracted the favourable notice of Erasmus.[72] Two years later a correspondent of Thomas Müntzer, writing from Brunswick, could report that 'there [Antwerp] the common folk are a thousand times more attached to the teachings of Christ and Martin [Luther] than they are here'.[73] Despite persecution and the suppression of their house Augustinians continued to disseminate the new doctrines at Antwerp until 1525. Meanwhile Luther kept a close watch over the evangelicals in that city and warned them against 'erring' and 'presumptuous spirits'.[74]

Netherlanders gained a knowledge of the evangelical theology from the many works of Luther circulating in their midst. In February 1519 the Basel printer, Johannes Froben, reported the despatch to Brabant, among other destinations, of his edition of Luther's *Omnia opera*.[75] The shrewd printers of Antwerp quickly grasped Luther's commercial potential. In a little over four months during the winter of 1520/21 one press there published five works by Luther, probably translated into Dutch by the local Augustinians.[76] By 1524 a score or more of Luther's works had appeared in Dutch.[77] This corpus of Luther translations was supplemented by Dutch editions of works by colleagues at Wittenberg and by like-minded reformers elsewhere in Germany.[78] The Saxon reformer's theology was also transmitted more subtly by his translation of the Bible;

[71] *Album Academiae Vitenbergensis: Altäre Reihe ...*, *1502–1602*, ed. K.F. Förstermann, O. Hartung and K. Gerhard, 3 vols. (Leipzig, 1841; Halle a.d.S., 1894–1905), I, pp. 65–100.

[72] *CD*, IV, p. 11.

[73] *The Collected Works of Thomas Müntzer*, trans. and ed. P. Matheson (Edinburgh, 1988), p. 38.

[74] On the evangelical activities of Augustinians at Antwerp after 1523 see M. Mélard, 'Les débuts de la réforme à Anvers, 1518–1530', (*Licence*, University of Liège, 1971–72), pp. 130–37; at Antwerp the people identified the Augustinians with the evangelicals and the Dominicans with the conservatives, *CD*, IV, p. 382; V, p. 117. Martin Oudermerck, an Augustinian, delivered certain sermons 'opt velt buyten Antwerpen', which were apparently printed by 1534, see M.E. Kronenberg, 'Nederlandsche drukken in de Catalogus der Librye van het Hof van Holland, 1533/4', *Het boek*, XXXI (1952–54) p. 31 (NK 01346). Oudermerck, like his confrères Adriaan Borschot, Hendrik van Zutphen and Jacobus Praepositus, later served the Lutheran cause in Germany.

[75] C.Ch.G. Visser, *Luther's geschriften in de Nederlanden tot 1546* (Assen, 1969), p. 3.

[76] *Ibid.*, pp. 31–38, 152–56.

[77] *Ibid.*, nos. 3–7, 14–16, ?17, 26–27, 29–30, 34–40, 42–45. In addition there were Latin editions and a few French translations.

[78] For example, works by Bugenhagen (NK 508), Urbanus Rhegius (NK 1791), Heinrich von Kettenbach (NK 0739), Melanchthon (NK 675; 01341), Benedictus Gretzinger (NK 01306), Joerg Birckenmayer (NK 01292), Caspar Huberinus, Andreas Althamer (NK 3317), Franciscus Lambertus (NK 1310), Hans Sachs (NK 3827) and probably Justus Jonas, Antonius Corvinus and Matthias Bienwald.

many of the Dutch vernacular editions, which appeared at this time, depended to a greater or lesser degree on his German Bible. Within a year of Luther's New Testament, a Dutch edition appeared, though the printer prudently omitted the contentious prologues and annotations. The men behind the so-called Deventer New Testament of 1525, however, audaciously brought out an unbowdlerised translation of Luther's text.[79] In the case of the Old Testament the Dutch translators and printers followed hard on Luther's heels: the Liesvelt Bible of 1526 adopted his text as far as the Psalms and inserted woodcuts prepared for an earlier German edition. As Luther worked through the Old Testament, van Liesvelt substituted his version for the Vulgate until in 1535 he published a Dutch Bible, which was based throughout on Luther's text.[80]

Luther's ascendancy in Dutch evangelical circles cannot be gainsaid. Yet in order to understand the protean character of the early Reformation in the Low Countries, we should remember that even in Germany, where the religious changes were guided by princes and town magistracies, many years elapsed before the theological revolution wrought by Luther found expression in evangelical church orders. Disorder, excitement and experimentation were the hallmarks of the 1520s as evangelicals, swept along by the wave of support for Luther, found themselves in uncharted waters bound for unknown destinations. Those Netherlanders who travelled to Wittenberg, Strassburg, Zürich or Emden encountered inchoate evangelical movements in the German towns. As a result they became acquainted with the divergent theologies of Oecolampadius, Bucer and Zwingli as well as with the opinions of still more radical spirits.[81] In these heady times even Luther's closest colleagues were not clones of the master. For example, during Luther's absence from Wittenberg in the autumn of 1521, Melanchthon and the Dutch Augustinian Hendrik van Zutphen apparently took the side of the extremists who

---

[79] De Bruin, *Statenbijbel*, pp. 154–55.

[80] *Ibid.*, pp. 161–69.

[81] The influence German radicals, especially Anabaptists and Spiritualists, exercised in the Low Countries before 1530 requires more investigation. Dutch evangelicals could read works by Karlstadt (NK 0262) and Hubmaier (NK 1145). The authorities certainly knew a little about the radicals. In July 1528 the bishop of Liège warned the English ambassador about a politically subversive Anabaptism, which had spread along the Danube and the Rhine (See below p. 58). In November 1528 an anti-evangelical poem, printed at Deventer, mentioned Melchior Hoffman by name (NK 964). Outside the Netherlands Gerardus Geldenhauer consorted with radicals, including Hans Denk and Ludwig Hätzer, when in Worms in 1527 (C. Augustijn, 'Gerard Geldenhouwer und die religiöse Toleranz', *ARG*, LXI (1978), pp. 144–45). In East Friesland and Jülich extreme forms of spiritualism had led some evangelicals to dispense altogether with the sacraments in advance of Anabaptism (Smid, *Ostfriesische Kirchengeschichte*, pp. 131–35; J.F.G. Goeters, 'Die Rolle des Täufertums in der Reformationszeit des Niederrheins', *Rheinische Vierteljahrsblätter*, XXIV (1959), pp. 220–25): in both regions Dutch evangelicals were active.

demanded the immediate abolition of private masses.[82]

Many dissidents in the Low Countries professed opinions, which for all their enthusiasm for Luther, owed little or nothing to the Saxon reformer. In particular some went beyond Luther's rejection of transubstantiation to deny the real presence of Christ in the eucharistic elements. For that reason J.G. de Hoop Scheffer (1819–94) and Knappert called these early evangelicals *sacramentisten*,[83] thus reviving a pejorative term, originally coined by Luther to denote the followers of Karlstadt and Zwingli and later applied by the Catholic authorities in the Low Countries to those who disparaged the sacrament of the altar.[84] Before we concern ourselves with the possible sources, varieties and chronology of 'sacramentarianism' in the Netherlands, it may be useful to look again at the German Reformation so as to appreciate the distinctive character of Dutch dissent, which in the view of many historians derives from the presence there of *sacramentarii*.[85]

In the Low Countries, as in Germany, the Reformation began when local clerics decided to preach the Wittenberg theology as they perceived it. The pattern in Antwerp and Amsterdam was in this respect no different from that in Nuremberg and Strassburg. But once the government of Charles V in the Netherlands had excluded the suspect clerics from the churches, the evangelicals there had to meet secretly in conventicles, which were increasingly led by laymen. By contrast the German Reformation evolved with fewer restraints: the mass was abolished or drastically altered and all manner of religious opinions, including sacramentarian

---

[82] R.J. Sider, *Andreas Bodenstein von Karlstadt: The Development of his Thought 1517–1525* (Leiden, 1974), pp. 155–56; U. Bubenheimer, ' "Scandalum et ius divinum" Theologische und rechtstheologische Probleme der ersten reformatorischen Innovationen in Wittenberg, 1521/22', *Zeitschrift der Savigny-Stiftung für Rechtsgeschichte*, 90 Kanon. Abt., LIX (1973), pp. 277–83, 295–303.

[83] Hoop Scheffer, pp. 107–10; Knappert, *Ontstaan*, pp. 112, 137–48.

[84] For a discussion of the terminology see Trapman, 'Rôle des "sacramentaires"' pp. 1–5. The term *sacramentarii* was current in Holland by September 1534: *DAN*, V, *Amsterdam (1531–1536)* ed. A.F. Mellink (Leiden, 1985), p. 45.

[85] Recently Professor C. Augustijn has urged students of the Dutch Reformation to jettison the term 'sacramentarianism', see 'Anabaptisme in de Nederlanden', *Doopsgezinde bijdragen*, n.r., XII-XIII (1986–87), pp. 13–28 and 'Sacramentariërs en dopers', *Doopsgezinde bijdragen*, n.r., XV (1989), pp. 121–27. He considers the evangelicals of the 1520s as participants in 'a still undifferentiated movement of renewal in which both Erasmus and Luther play a role'. While I find myself in substantial agreement, I have retained the term 'sacramentarian' because I am here especially concerned with the crude rejection of the real presence, and because the authorities regarded the repudiation of the real presence, like believer's baptism, as a readily recognisable and infallible mark of heresy. This is not to say that the so-called sacramentarians and Anabaptists themselves attached the same significance to these doctrines.

beliefs, were openly canvassed.[86] In the aftermath of the Peasants' Revolt, however, this period of more or less uninhibited and spontaneous Reformation gradually drew to a close as territorial princes and town magistrates tried to reach a *modus vivendi* with the popular evangelical movements. By dint of visitations, catechisms and church orders the ruling classes gave the German Reformation a confessionally Lutheran identity. In particular, Luther's teaching on the real presence became the touchstone of a new religious orthodoxy. In the Low Countries persecution prevented close Lutheran supervision of dissent,[87] and consequently the Reformation there lacked an explicitly confessional character until the middle of the century, when the formation of stranger-churches abroad and privy congregations at home drew it in a Calvinist direction.

The denial of the real presence was neither peculiar to dissent in the Low Countries, nor was it the central plank of the evangelical theology there. The Dutch authorities, however, chose to emphasise this aspect of dissent: it represented the most flagrant deviation from the teaching of the church and it could be more readily detected than other evangelical doctrines. For that reason the Reformation in the Low Countries gained a reputation for being 'sacramentarian'.

The first unambiguous expressions of popular hostility to the real presence in the Low Countries were recorded in 1525. In May a group of dissidents at Mons abjured several heretical opinions, including disbelief in Christ's presence in the host.[88] Two months later a witness at the trial of a cooper in Utrecht deposed that the accused had been heard to say, 'What's the sacrament but bread?'.[89] Thereafter suspects were frequently charged with denying the real presence. Significantly, similar opinions came to the notice of the authorities in Nuremberg in the winter of 1524/25 [90] and in France a year or so later.[91] It is surely no coincidence that popular 'sacramentarianism' attracted attention at more or less the same time as the evangelical theologians were at loggerheads concerning the real presence in the eucharist, but the nature of the relationship is far from straightforward.

[86] H. Zschelletzschky, *Die 'drie gottlosen Maler' von Nürnberg: Sebald Beham, Barthel Beham und Georg Pencz: Historische Grundlagen und ikonologische Probleme ihrer Graphik zu Reformations und Bauernkriegszeit* (Leipzig, 1975), pp. 24–55. For the religious anarchy in East Friesland in 1530 see Smid, *Ostfriesische Kirchengeschichte*, p. 134.

[87] Attempts were however made: at least two of Luther's polemics against Zwingli were translated into Dutch, Visser, *Luther's geschriften*, nos. 51 and 53.

[88] Antoine de Lusy, *Le journal d'un bourgeois de Mons, 1505–1536*, ed. A. Louant (Brussels, 1969), pp. 375–78.

[89] *CD*, IV, p. 372.

[90] H. Barge, *Andreas Bodenstein von Karlstadt*, II, *Karlstadt als Vorkämpfer des laienchristlichen Puritanismus* (repr. Nieuwkoop, 1968), p. 192.

[91] Nicholls, 'Nature of Popular Heresy in France', p. 271; see also M. Royannez, 'L'Eucharistie chez les évangeliques et les premiers réformés français', *Bulletin de la Société de l'histoire du Protestantisme Français*, CXXV (1979), pp. 548–76.

Before 1525 the reformers had attacked several crucial aspects of the Roman mass, and in particular the doctrine of transubstantiation and the notion of the mass as a repetition of Christ's sacrifice. They had also urged the administration of communion in both kinds to the laity. In some places an evangelical Lord's Supper had been held, though the mass was not abolished in Zürich and Nuremberg until April 1525. Yet until the publication at Basel in late October and early November 1524 of Andreas Karlstadt's eucharistic tracts, the evangelical theologians had, with one exception, been conspicuously silent, at least in public, about the real presence. The exception was Luther who in the spring of 1523 had denounced as blasphemous those who would interpret the words of institution in the eucharist 'Hoc est corpus meum' to mean 'this signifies my body'. Though Luther did not name the author of this 'blasphemy', he had in mind an exegesis of the eucharist which he had received from the Netherlands shortly before he left for Worms in April 1521.[92]

It was Cornelis Hoen, a jurist and member of the provincial *Hof van Holland*, who first proposed this controversial interpretation. Apparently Hoen had reached his conclusions after having read certain works on the eucharist by Wessel Gansfort (*c*.1419–89). Gansfort himself never repudiated the doctrine of transubstantiation, but he hinted that the worth of the sacrament of the altar depended to a degree on the spiritual disposition of the recipient. Besides, Christ's presence was not confined to the elements: the body and blood of Christ could be partaken by the faithful in spirit outside the eucharist.[93] Of course neither Gansfort nor Thomas à Kempis, who also allowed spiritual communion to those who were hindered from sacramentally receiving the elements, intended to belittle the sacrament of the altar.[94] On the contrary, they – and indeed Hoen too – held the sacrament in the highest regard. Nevertheless the spiritual interpretation advanced by Gansfort may have provided the springboard Hoen required to reach his more radical exegesis.[95] According to Hoen the words of institution should be taken symbolically in the same way as the statements of Jesus that He is 'the way', 'the cornerstone' and 'the true vine'.[96] Though Luther dismissed

---

[92] W.A. Kooloos, 'Cornelis Hoen en zijn avondmaalsbrief', (*Doctoraalscriptie*, Stichting Theologische Faculteit, Tilburg, 1981), p. 29. Dr. Trapman kindly obtained a copy for me of this sober analysis of Hoen's letter.

[93] Van Rhijn, *Wessel Gansfort*, p. 258; Post, *Modern Devotion*, p. 541.

[94] For example, Thomas à Kempis, *The Imitation of Christ*, bk. IV, ch. X, para. 6.

[95] Hoen's exegesis was not unknown in the middle ages. A Franciscan, writing *c*.1240, alleged that the Cathars also interpreted the words of institution in the sense 'This *signifies* my body' and adduced in support 1 Cor. X: 4, which text Hoen also cited. *Heresies of the High Middle Ages*, ed. W.L. Wakefield and P.A. Evans (New York-London, 1969), p. 304. Unlike Hoen the Cathars adopted the purely figurative interpretation because of their rejection of bread and wine as part of an evil creation.

[96] H.A. Oberman, *Forerunners of the Reformation: The Shape of Late Medieval Thought* (London, 1967), p. 271.

this interpretation out of hand, Hoen's little treatise found favour with the Swiss reformers whom Hinne Rode consulted in 1523.[97] On Zwingli's initiative a modified version of Hoen's letter appeared in print anonymously in the late summer of 1525. A few months later a second Latin edition was published and two German translations followed within a year.[98]

Both Zwingli and Bucer acknowledged their debt to the *Epistola christiana*. It is harder to determine what influence Hoen's letter exercised in the Netherlands: if he discussed his eucharistic theology with fellow evangelicals in The Hague and Delft, no evidence has survived. When, however, the Emden minister Aportanus composed the *Hovet Artikelen des hylligen Sacramentes* in 1526, he drew on Hoen in order to refute the literalist interpretation of the words of institution.[99] Yet Hoen cannot be the source for the sacramentarianism detected in the Low Countries in the summer of 1525, for it preceded by several months the publication of the letter in Zürich. Nor indeed is it easy to reconcile the crude repudiation of the real presence by these dissidents with Hoen's dignified statement on the eucharist. Whereas the former disparaged the sacrament, Hoen held it in high regard as a pledge given by Christ to those who partake of the eucharist, trusting in His promise of the forgiveness of sins.[100]

As a source for popular sacramentarianism in the Low Countries Karlstadt might seem a more plausible candidate than Hoen. The publication of his German eucharistic treatises antedated by several months the first recorded prosecutions of those who denied the real presence, and his books were forbidden by the government in Brussels in September 1525.[101] His doctrines too infiltrated into East Friesland, where they left a mark in Aportanus' eclectic eucharistic articles.[102] On the other hand we have no certain evidence that the German reformer's idiosyncratic

---

[97] For the chronology of Hinne Rode's journeys to Wittenberg, Basel, Zürich and Strassburg see Kooloos, 'Cornelis Hoen', pp. 24–36.

[98] *Ibid.*, pp. 36–38.

[99] The text is reprinted in E. Meiners, *Oostvrieschlandts kerkelyke geschiedenis*, 2 vols. (Groningen, 1738–39), I, p. 120.

[100] Trapman, 'Rôle des "sacramentaires"', pp. 19–20. Hoen's letter was not translated into Dutch until 1650, when it appeared in Trigland's *Kerckelycke Geschiedenissen*, pp. 125–30; Hoffman also used the metaphor of the ring which the bridegroom gives to his bride when he debated his eucharistic theology with the Lutherans in 1529, K. Deppermann, *Melchior Hoffman: Social Unrest and Apocalyptic Visions in the Age of the Reformation* (Edinburgh, 1987), p. 125.

[101] *CD*, V, p. 4. In February 1525 a scabbard-maker was prosecuted in Antwerp for having sold pamphlets which disparaged the holy sacrament. Was Karlstadt, whose eucharistic works had been printed in the autumn of 1524, the author of these anonymous pamphlets? See *CD*, IV, p. 308.

[102] Smid, *Ostfriesische Kirchengeschichte*, pp. 126–27.

exegesis of the words of institution were known in Dutch evangelical circles before 1529.[103] Besides Hoen and Karlstadt there were other theologians whose spiritualised interpretations of the eucharist did not pass unnoticed in the Low Countries. In 1527 a monk blamed Oeco- lampadius, the reformer of Basel, for the belief then held by Flemish dissidents that Christ was not present in the consecrated elements of bread and wine.[104] Luther himself accused Bucer of propagating an erroneous interpretation of the eucharist in the Netherlands. The Witten- berg theologians discovered to their chagrin that Bucer had insinuated into his German translation of Bugenhagen's commentary on the Psalms, published at Basel in 1526, his own memorialist view of the Lord's Supper. Since the Dutch translation of this commentary derived from Bucer's German text, Luther and Bugenhagen hastened to warn evangelicals in Antwerp, where the offending translation had been printed in 1526, of the deception practised by the Strassburg reformer.[105]

The eucharistic quarrel among the evangelical theologians was grist to the Romanist mill: disunity seemed clear proof of false doctrine. At the same time the public controversy between Karlstadt and Luther in 1524, and between Luther and the Swiss reformers in 1525, changed the theological agenda. Since none of the reformers had opposed the doctrine of the real presence directly until 1524, the Romanists had had no reason to give any attention to the matter: good works, confession, indulgences, papal power, purgatory, scriptural authority, transubstantia- tion and the sacrificial character of the mass provided stuff enough for the most conscientious inquisitor and the most ardent polemicist. In the wake of the argument among evangelical theologians about the real presence, the ecclesiastical authorities in the Low Countries began to examine suspects about their opinions on the eucharist. When they uncovered widespread scepticism about the real presence, they were inclined to attribute this apparent 'rise' of popular sacramentarianism to the influence of reformers like Karlstadt, Zwingli, Bucer and Oeco- lampadius. It seemed like a straightforward case of *post hoc ergo propter hoc.*

[103] Hoop Scheffer, p. 514.

[104] *CD*, V, pp. 189–90. In 1525 Oecolampadius had published *De genuina verborum Domini: 'Hoc est corpus meum' juxta vetustissimos authores expositione liber.*

[105] G. Hammer, 'Der Streit um Bucer in Antwerpen', *Lutheriana: Zum 500. Geburtstag Martin Luther von den Mitärbeitern der Weimarer Ausgabe*, ed. G. Hammer and K.-Heinz zur Mühlen (Cologne-Vienna, 1984), pp. 393–454. A manuscript version of the Dutch transla- tion, apparently commissioned by Floris von Egmond (1469–1539), significantly makes no mention of Bucer on the title page and suppresses his preface, J.V. Pollet, *Martinus Bucer: Études sur les rélations de Bucer avec les Pays-Bas, l'Électorat de Cologne et l'Allemagne du Nord*, 2 vols. (Leiden, 1985), I, pp. 352–58 and *Het boek in Nederland in de 16de eeuw* (The Hague, 1986), p. 61.

But, as we have seen, it is difficult to demonstrate the connections between the learned theologies of scholars like Hoen, Karlstadt and the Swiss reformers on the one hand and the blunt, pithy and occasionally eccentric opinions professed by the humbler sort of dissidents on the other. Lay evangelicals could of course advance reputable theological arguments. They did so when they asserted that the sacrament had been instituted 'for a remembrance and memorial' of Christ's Passion, when they opposed the real presence on the grounds that Christ is seated at the righthand of the Father after His Ascension, and when they insisted that God 'dwelleth not in temples made with hands' (Acts XVII: 24). But when they claimed that the sacrament of the altar was not one whit better than the bread in their larder,[106] or sought to refute the doctrine of the real presence of Christ by quoting the address of the Lord's Prayer to 'Our Father in heaven',[107] they employed a barbarous idiom and a country divinity far removed from the erudite theology of the major reformers.

Did then these dissidents draw unwittingly on some more ancient tradition of disbelief and scepticism for their arguments? Though the fragmentary evidence stops well short of proof, the hypothesis deserves to be taken more seriously than has been customary among students of the early Reformation. In the fifteenth century religious nonconformity was confined to the Waldensian enclaves in the Alps and Provence, to the Hussites in Bohemia and the Lollards in parts of southern England. Recent work on the Waldensians and the Lollards has established connections with the earliest Protestants, albeit of a complex character.[108] In the German lands overt heresy was rare: dissatisfaction with the state of the clergy here found expression in a series of disturbing prophecies, which foretold the imminent and drastic reform of the church.[109] In the Burgundian Netherlands likewise religious dissent did not pose a serious problem in the fifteenth century: the Hussite opinions which gained a following in some Walloon towns in the years immediately after Hus's execution in 1415 ceased to attract attention after 1430.[110] Paul Fredericq,

---

[106] For example, *CD*, V, pp. 344–45; J. Decavele, *De dageraad van de reformatie in Vlaanderen, 1520–1565*, 2 vols. (Brussels, 1975), I, p. 598.

[107] For example, *DAN*, V, pp. 8, 142.

[108] E. Cameron, *The Reformation of the Heretics: The Waldenses of the Alps, 1480–1520* (Oxford, 1984); J.A.F. Thomson, *The Later Lollards, 1414–1520* (Oxford, 1965); M. Aston, 'Lollardy and the Reformation: Survival or Revival?', *History*, XLIX (1964), pp. 149–70; *idem.*, 'John Wycliffe's Reformation Reputation', *Past and Present*, XXX (1965), pp. 23–51. These two last essays have been reprinted in *idem.*, *Lollards and Reformers: Images and Literacy in Late Medieval Religion* (London, 1984).

[109] R.F. Lerner, 'Medieval Prophecy and Religious Dissent', *Past and Present*, LXXII (1976), pp. 3–24.

[110] For the sources see *CD*, I, pp. 299–303; II, pp. 247–54, 57–9, 109–11.

who made a particular study of medieval dissent in these parts, once remarked that in the fifteenth century 'the heretics were usually only misguided individuals without much support'.[111] The incidence of heresy prosecutions may be as much an index of the concerns and anxieties of those in positions of authority as an objective record of religious sentiment: heresy, like witchcraft and political conspiracy, is detected whenever the powers-that-be are so minded.

The argument in favour of the survival of late medieval dissent in the early years of the Reformation in the Low Countries rests on three kinds of circumstantial evidence. There is first the trickle of prosecutions for religious offences which persisted until the edict of Worms. Most of those convicted were accused of unspecified blasphemies, a few religious were charged with preaching donatist heresies and one cleric was burnt in 1512 on account of his obstinate disbelief in the Christian revelation. In addition a small number were prosecuted for disparaging the holy sacrament. Unfortunately the laconic entries usually prevent identification of the precise character of these dissident opinions, but in one case Hussite opinions were justifiably imputed by a contemporary to a dissident on trial in 1485.[112] It would be surprising if this ill-defined hostility to the sacrament of the altar, detected as late as 1519, did not colour to some extent the language used by those prosecuted for sacramentarian opinions after 1525.

When questioned about their beliefs many evangelical nonconformists resorted to a common stock of images and metaphors, which do not recur in the extant Dutch evangelical literature. When Wendelmoet Claesdr. of Monnikendam, who holds a special place in the affections of Dutch Protestants as the first woman to die for her faith, was examined during her trial in November 1527 about the holy oil used to anoint the sick, she brusquely replied that the 'oil was good for a salad or for greasing boots'.[113] Though Wendelmoet is the first evangelical known to have made this irreverent suggestion, it seems unlikely that she coined it. Heretics in different parts of the Low Countries mocked the holy oil in like fashion on many occasions, and they were echoed by evangelicals as far afield as Switzerland and England: all of these ridiculed the sacred oil

---

[111] P. Fredericq, 'Geschiedenis der inquisitie in de Nederlanden. III: De nederlandsche inquisitie tijdens de vijftiende en het begin der zestiende eeuw' (1916), ch. III (unpaginated). MS. 3740 Rijksuniversiteit Gent. This unpublished volume concludes his *Geschiedenis der inquisitie in de Nederlanden tot aan hare herinrichting onder keizer Karel V (1025–1520)*, 2 vols. (Ghent-The Hague, 1892–97).

[112] *CD*, II, pp. 141–43. The heretical opinions alleged here resemble those professed by a group of heretics detected at Eichstätt (S. Germany) in 1460, F. Machilek, 'Ein Eichstätter Inquisitionsverfahren aus dem Jahre 1460', *Jahrbuch für fränkische Landesforschung*, XXXIV/XXXV (1974–75), pp. 426–28.

[113] *CD*, V, p. 281.

as fit only for greasing their boots.[114] Our surmise that the insult is older than the Reformation finds some support in the conduct of Saxon troops in Friesland in 1500 who, according to the chronicler, trod the holy oil underfoot 'and greased their boots with it'.[115] The trial depositions preserve the blunt speech of the early evangelicals as they reviled the statues of the saints in the churches as blocks of wood and stone; the old priests as 'soul murderers'; purgatory as a clerical invention to swindle the laity; Our Lady as a milkmaid, as an empty sack of cinnamon or pepper, as a lantern without a candle; [116] the consecrated host as no better than the corruptible bread in a man's larder and priestly confession as inferior to confession to a tree.[117] Such vehement derision of orthodox beliefs and practices recalls the homespun idiom of English Lollardy and the Hussite Taborites rather than the theologies of Wittenberg, Zürich and Strassburg.[118]

In our concern to trace the influence of the leading reformers on the earliest Dutch evangelicals, it is tempting to disregard those opinions which do not fit preconceived notions about evangelical theology. In this respect the sundry beliefs attributed to a cooper, on trial for heresy in Utrecht in 1525, are instructive. His stance on papal authority, confession and the saints was unambiguously 'Lutheran', but the provenance of certain of his other opinions cannot be so confidently established. From where did he gain his notion that Our Lady was 'an empty bag of flour'; that a priest must have a wife and children before ordination; that a

---

[114] To the list given on p. 43 fn. 96 and 97 should be added: *DAN*, II; *Amsterdam (1536–1578)* ed. A.F. Mellink (Leiden, 1980), p. 232; O.J. de Jong, *De reformatie in Culemborg* (Assen, n.d.), p. 139; G. Marnef, 'Het protestantisme te Brussel, *ca.* 1567–1585', *Tijdschrift voor brusselse geschiedenis*, I (1984), p. 59.

[115] Peter Jacobsz. van Thabor, *Historie van Vrieslant*, ed. R. Steensma (Leeuwarden, 1973), p. 156. See also H.C. Lea, *History of the Inquisition of the Middle Ages*, 3 vols. (New York, 1887–88), II, p. 144.

[116] See below p. 42, especially fn. 88; *Een cleyn Verclaringhe* Biiv (NK 4017); in English Lollard circles similar opinions were expressed, J. Davis, 'Joan of Kent, Lollardy and the English Reformation', *JEH*, XXXIII (1982), 230–33. Such vulgar gnosticism may have influenced the incarnational theology of Melchior Hoffman and the Dutch Anabaptists.

[117] In 1296 a heretic in southern France derided the host 'as nothing but baked dough, such as he had in good supply in his cupboard', W.L. Wakefield, 'Some Unorthodox Popular Ideas of the Thirteenth Century', *Medievalia et Humanistica*, IV (1973), p. 27, for a sixteenth-century parallel see fn. 106. A Flemish dissident in the early 1530s declared that he 'would rather confess to a tree' than to his the parish priest, Decavele, *Dageraad van de reformatie*, I, p. 269, fn. 176. This recalls the sentiment of a heretic from north-eastern France who asserted in 1307 'that it was better to confess to a tree trunk than to a priest because the tree would not reveal a confession', cited by R.E. Lerner, *The Heresy of the Free Spirit in the Late Middle Ages* (Berkeley, 1972), p. 69.

[118] In addition to the books mentioned in fn. 108 J.B. Russell, *Dissent and Reform in the Early Middle Ages* (Berkeley, 1965); *Heresy Trials in the Diocese of Norwich, 1428–31*, ed. N.P. Tanner, Camden Society, 4th Series, XX (1977); J.F. Davis, *Heresy and Reformation in the South-East of England, 1520–1559* (London, 1983); P. de Vooght, 'L'hérésie des taborites sur l'euchariste (1418–1421)', *Irenikon*, XXXV (1962), pp. 344–45.

bishop should not be invested until he had completed a seven-year stint of matrimony and that the Apostles were common criminals, not martyrs of the faith?[119] The religious position of mr. Jelys Vientsz. of Hoorn is no less enigmatic. When he likened the people processing about an altar in his native town to the Children of Israel dancing before the Golden Calf and compared Our Lady to a chimney or pisspot, he sounded like an evangelical, though he had evidently quarrelled with those who 'luthered'. Yet there is no obvious source for his propositions that the Devil had composed the Apostles' Creed or that St. Laurence, a third-century martyr, had been justly put to death on a gridiron for embezzling the treasury of the local congregation. In their perplexity the inexperienced local judges treated him leniently, perhaps on account of his inebriated condition when he made those remarks.[120] Though mr. Jelys was no Dutch Menocchio, his trial in 1528/29 gives us a glimpse of the fragmentary 'theology' an autodidact might construct. Though plainly informed by the Reformation debate, it was also nourished by an old hatred of the clergy and underpinned by a crude materialism, not uncommon in late medieval dissent.

The host of fanatics and heavenly prophets who appeared in the midst of the evangelicals as if from nowhere appalled Luther, though they did not altogether surprise him – the Devil after all had many disguises. 'The world', he warned the evangelicals at Antwerp in the spring of 1525, 'was once full of disembodied poltergeists, who made out that they were men's souls. Now it is filled with live flibbertigibbets, who all claim to be living angels.'[121] Luther had in mind Eloy Pruystinck, a slater from Antwerp, who had visited Wittenberg early in 1525, and disputed with Melanchthon. To put the evangelicals at Antwerp on their guard, Luther summarised the prophet's principal doctrines: every man possesses the Holy Spirit; the Holy Spirit is identical with human reason and intelligence; every man has faith; only the flesh (not the spirit) suffers hell and judgment; all souls enjoy eternal life; faith is to desire for one's neighbour what one desires for one's self; no sin is committed when one has an evil inclination, provided one does not succumb; those who do not possess the Holy Spirit (presumably children beneath the age of discretion) cannot sin because they are without reason.[122]

Luther called the Loists, as the followers of Eloy came to be known, 'a new breed of prophets'.[123] Evidently they owed little or nothing to the

---

[119] *CD*, IV, pp. 368–73, 396–67.

[120] Oud-Archief Hoorn, 6, pp. 5–43.

[121] *CD*, IV, p. 327.

[122] *CD*, IV, p. 328. See also E.M. Braekman, 'Un cas de dissidence à Anvers: Eloy Pruystinck', *Bibliotheca dissidentium: Scripta et Studia*, I, *Les dissidents entre l'humanisme et le catholicisme*, ed. M. Lienhard (Baden-Baden, 1983), pp. 197–98.

[123] J. Frederichs, *De secte der loïsten of antwerpsche libertijnen, 1525–1545: Eligius Pruystinck ... en zijne aanhangers* (Ghent-The Hague, 1891), p. 4.

Wittenberg theology, but Luther was probably mistaken when he supposed their doctrines to be novel. The radical dualism of flesh and spirit and the sinless state of the spirit recall the beliefs attributed to the so-called 'free spirits', though it would be rash to suppose that the Loists were descended from the *Homines Intelligentiae,* a sect of the free spirit discovered in Brussels in the early fifteenth century.[124] Nevertheless the affinities between the 'free of spirit' and the Loists remind us that the appeal of medieval mystical theology did not cease at the Reformation. Indeed Luther's discovery and publication of the anonymous *Theologia Deutsch* in 1516 revived interest in the mystical movements of the mid-fourteenth century. The emphasis which the South German Anabaptists and Thomas Müntzer put on the immanence of the divine within man's soul, on the abnegation of self and on the Christian's obligation to imitate Christ's suffering may be traced to this source.[125] The debt which the early Dutch radicals owed to the medieval mystical tradition has not yet been thoroughly assessed, but both Hoffman and Bernhard Rothmann were thoroughly familiar with the mystical concept of *Gelassenheit,* which became in Menno's vocabulary *lydsaemheyt.*[126] Medieval sources certainly determined other aspects of Dutch Anabaptist theology. Hoffman, who we are told 'grew up in an environment of medieval piety, rife with speculations about the end of the world, and the voice of prophecy', derived his spiritual exegesis of the Song of Solomon from the twelfth-century *Glossa ordinaria* and his tripartite scheme of church history from the Joachimite prophetic tradition.[127] As we read the apocalyptic and mystical writings of men like Hendrik Rol and David Joris, it is hard to resist the conclusion that they too owed much to late medieval spiritual traditions.

Luther's theology penetrated the Netherlands in the wake of Christian humanism and contemporaries therefore felt the early 1520s to be a time of momentous change. It was as though an abyss had opened up, cutting them off from their theological roots. Nor were they mistaken.

---

[124] On the *Homines Intelligentiae* see Lerner, *Heresy of the Free Spirit,* pp. 157–163. For the persistence of the Free Spirit in the later fifteenth century see *CD,* I, pp. 429–31.

[125] See esp. W.O. Packull, *Mysticism and the Early South German-Austrian Anabaptist Movement, 1525–1531* (Scottdale, 1977); G.H. Williams, 'Popularized German Mysticism as a Factor in the Rise of Anabaptist Communism', *Glaube, Geist, Geschichte: Festschrift für Ernst Benz zum 60. Geburtstage am 17. November 1967,* ed. G. Muller and W. Zeller (Leiden, 1967), pp. 290–312; S.E. Ozment, *Mysticism and Dissent: Religious Ideology and Social Protest in the Sixteenth Century* (New Haven-London, 1973).

[126] J.P. Jacobszoon, 'Gelassenheit. Enkele historische notities', *De geest in het geding: Opstellen aangeboden aan J.A.Oosterbaan* (Alphen aan den Rijn, 1978), pp. 111–26. Luther's edition of the *Theologia Deutsch* was translated into Dutch in 1521, see Visser, *Luther's geschriften,* pp. 56–60 (NK 2228).

[127] C.A. Pater, *Karlstadt as the Father of the Baptist Movement: The Emergence of Lay Protestantism* (Toronto, 1984), pp. 211, 223–26, 232; M. Reeves, *The Influence of Prophecy in the Later Middle Ages: A Study in Joachimism* (Oxford, 1969), pp. 490–92.

But while it is right to stress the discontinuity, we should never forget that the first *evangelische luden* [evangelical people] had been baptised into the Roman church. They were therefore heirs to the rich and diverse legacy of late medieval Christianity. The fifteenth-century church did not imprison the faithful in a narrow uniformity: it accommodated, more or less comfortably, a variety of theological traditions and a wide range of spiritualities and devotional practices. In the absence of any sort of counter-church, the motley assortment of mystics, scoffers, anti-clericals and religious dissidents, stood on the margins of the Roman church. In the case of the Low Countries, later medieval dissent left few traces and no literary legacy to compare with the English Lollards.[128] Yet the idiom and the gestures of defiance employed by Dutch evangelicals are reminiscent of pre-Reformation nonconformity. These images and turns of phrase clung, as it were, to the coat-tails of the grander theologies advanced by the reformers of Wittenberg, Strassburg or Zürich. The influence of late medieval dissent on the Reformation in the Low Countries may not have been profound, but it should not be overlooked.

---

[128] A. Hudson, ' "No newe thyng": The Printing of Medieval Texts in the Early Reformation Period' in *idem.*, *Lollards and their Books* (London, 1985), pp. 227–48. Between 1530 and 1550 nine different Lollards texts were printed.

2

The Face of Popular Religious Dissent in the Low Countries, 1520–30[1]

Writing to Wolsey from Bergen-op-Zoom in 1527 the English ambassador described the Low Countries as being in grave peril from heresy, 'for yf ther be tre men that speckes, the tweyn keppis Lutter ys openyon':[2] it was a pardonable exaggeration. Of Luther's immediate popularity in the Netherlands there can be no doubt. In taverns, private houses and on board barges and wagons the religious issues of the day were hotly debated; from pulpits the new doctrines were championed or denounced, and in public places posters appeared pillorying the mendicants. The succession of placards forbidding the reading, sale or printing of Luther's writings and the increasingly severe penalties prescribed for attendance at conventicles, for harbouring apostate religious and, above all, for spreading heretical notions tell the same tale. Already by 1525 Luther had become a household name in the Netherlands and a new synonym for heretics *Luytrianen* had entered common speech, displacing the older *Valdoysen ende Wijclevisten*.

According to a well-substantiated tradition the new doctrines were first brought to the Low Countries by the Augustinian Eremites. This is hardly surprising: the concern of Giles of Viterbo to reform the Augustinians meant that the order as a whole was then particularly receptive to reforming ideas, whatever their provenance.[3] Besides, by 1517 six of the Augustinian houses in the Netherlands belonged to the newly formed Saxon congregation within which there was much coming and going, so

---

[1] Earlier versions of this paper were read to the Low Countries Seminar at the Institute of Historical Research, the Medieval Seminar of Southampton University and the Sixteenth Century Local Ecclesiastical History Colloquium held at Reading in March 1974. I am indebted to the members of these seminars for their many useful comments and criticisms. The late Professor C.C. de Bruin and Dr. J.Trapman kindly gave assistance on a variety of matters. I should also like to acknowledge a grant from the Sir Ernest Cassel Educational Trust towards research in the Netherlands in 1972. The terminal date has occasionally been overstepped to allow consideration of some non-Anabaptist heretics in the early 1530s.

[2] *The Letters of Sir John Hackett, 1526–1534*, ed. E.F. Rogers (Morgantown, 1971), p. 81.

[3] F.X. Martin OSA,'The Augustinian Order on the Eve of the Reformation', *Miscellanea Historiae Ecclesiasticae*, II (Leuven, 1965), pp. 71–104.

that Luther was already known to several Augustinians in the Netherlands. Though the priors at Dordrecht[4] and Ghent[5] were close friends of
the Saxon monk, his influence was most deeply felt in the house at
Antwerp. During its brief existence from 1513 to 1523, when the buildings
were razed in a bid to expunge the embarrassing memory of apostasy, no
fewer than two, and possibly three, priors demonstrated their attachment
to Luther: Praepositus and Hendrik van Zutphen were later to preach
the Reformation at Bremen,[6] while Lambert Thoren probably died as an
obstinate heretic in a Brussels gaol in September 1528.[7] The same
monastery also furnished the protomartyrs of the Reformation, Hendrik
Voes and Johannes van (den) Esschen, whose execution at Brussels on 1
July 1523 Luther commemorated in the hymn beginning 'Ein neues Lied
wir heben an'.[8] To prevent the Lutheran contagion spreading further
the Dutch Augustinians broke away from the Saxon Congregation in
August 1522 and elected their own vicar.[9]

Yet, despite the fervour with which the Augustinians at Antwerp had
preached the new doctrines, their direct influence on the Reformation
in the Low Countries was shortlived. In part this was because they were
quickly silenced, but it may also be that their teaching was too subtle to
catch on: an examination of the doctrines attributed to Praepositus and
the martyrs shows them to be disciples of Luther's theology in the fullest
sense, a far cry from the crude anticlericalism of most contemporary
dissidents. But their memory could not be entirely effaced. When another
Augustinian heretic was drowned in the Scheldt in 1525 his followers
were overheard asking those present at the execution, whether they
believed after the Dominican or Augustinian fashion,[10] from which we

---

[4] According to a tradition, recently shown to be erroneous, the Augustinians at
Dordrecht incited the townspeople against indulgences as early as March 1518; see A. de
Meijer, OSA, 'Augustijnen in conflict met Dordtse magistraat?' *AGKKN*, V (1963), pp. 343–
50 In fact certain Franciscans, not Augustinians, were responsible for stirring up religious
passions in the town, but it is by no means clear that these monks were advocating heresy;
the accusations of the magistrates are vague. It is not impossible that these Franciscans, like
their *confrères* elsewhere, had irked the magistrates by denouncing evangelical theology
intemperately. Some Franciscans did, however, sympathise with the new doctrines. Chief
among such was Johannes Pelt, the warden of the Grey Friars in Amsterdam until his flight
to Bremen in 1524. He has been credited with the translation of the New Testament which
appeared during 1523 in three parts.

[5] J. Scheerder, 'Het lutheranisme te Gent', *Annales de la Société d'Histoire du Protestantisme
Belge*, 4ème série, VI (1963), p. 305.

[6] *CD*, IV, pp. 35–6, 136–41, 173–77; also H.Q. Janssen, *Jacobus Praepositus, Luthers leerling
en vriend* (Amsterdam, 1862), *passim*.

[7] *CD*, V, pp. 360–2.

[8] *CD*, IV, pp. 191–214.

[9] *CD*, IV, 132–4.

[10] *CD*, IV, p. 382; V, p. 117. *Collectanea van Gerardus Geldenhauer Noviomagus*, ed. J.
Prinsen, (Amsterdam, 1901), p. 67. The rivalry between the mendicant orders already
existed in the fifteenth century, see J. Huizinga, *The Waning of the Middle Ages* (London,
1955), p. 180. [*Verzamelde werken*, III, p. 212].

gather that the Augustinians were still popularly associated with the new doctrines.[11]

On 8 October 1520 eighty odd of Luther's books were burnt at Leuven. Even though not all the books then burnt were by Luther, for some students redressed the theological balance by throwing into the flames such evergreen favourites of the parish clergy as *Dormi secure* and *Sermones Discipuli*,[12] the authorities rightly saw in his writings one of the principal sources of heresy in the Low Countries, and during the next decade book-burnings took place in many towns.[13] It was a futile exercise, for in the same period at least thirty works by Luther appeared in Dutch translations,[14] an achievement which can better be gauged when we consider that, apart from Tyndale's adaptation of Luther's prefaces for his New Testament of 1526, only three of Luther's writings were Englished before 1530.[15] Nor was Luther the only evangelical theologian to be read in the Low Countries. The edicts forbidding his books also mentioned those of Melanchthon, Bugenhagen, Karlstadt, Justus Jonas, Lambert of Avignon and Oecolampadius,[16] and to these should be added Balthasar Hubmaier and Hans Sachs and the little known evangelical preacher Matthias Bienwald from Dantzig, Dutch translations of whose books probably circulated at this time;[17] Zwingli's writings were first proscribed in 1529.[18] Many of these books came from presses in Antwerp, whose printers employed a variety of subterfuges to avoid detection, sometimes sheltering behind a false or fictitious imprint, or giving a pre-1520 publication date, thereby ostensibly guaranteeing the orthodoxy of the text.[19] The risks taken by such printers are perhaps less a guide to their own religious convictions than a pointer to the appetite for such literature. The case of the baker from Ghent, Lieven de Zomere, shows how highly Luther's works might be regarded, even in comparatively uneducated

[11] For other Augustinians suspected of heresy see *CD*, IV, pp. 335, 366; V, pp. 8–9, 133, 168; see also the career of the apostate Augustinian, Pieter Daensius from Ghent, who was examined in 1538, J.G. de Hoop Scheffer, 'Geestelijken, van ketterij verdacht, in verhoor voor het Hof van Holland 1530–1540', *Kerkhistorisch archief*, IV (1866), pp. 200–7. A limiter from the Augustinian house at Dordrecht preached heretical doctrines at Heenvliet before 1532. A. de Bussy, 'De eerste informatie naar Merula's ketterij (1533)', *NAK* n.s., XVI (1921), pp. 131–32.

[12] M.E. Kronenberg, *Verboden boeken en opstandige drukkers in hervormingstijd* (Amsterdam, 1948), pp. 30–1. Returns from a visitation of the clergy carried out in Jülich in 1533 show that Herolt's *Discipuli sermones* was, after the Bible, the book most likely to be found in the priest's house.

[13] C.Ch.G. Visser, *Luther's geschriften in de Nederlanden tot 1546* (Assen, 1946), pp. 13–15.

[14] Visser, *op. cit.*, ch. II; see also list on pp. 130–33.

[15] W.A. Clebsch, 'The Earliest Translations of Luther into English', *Harvard Theological Review*, LVI (1963), pp. 75–86. Two of these translations were printed at Antwerp.

[16] Kronenberg, *op. cit.*, p. 16.

[17] Hoop Scheffer, pp. 405–20; *CD*, V, p. 151.

[18] Visser, *op. cit.*, p. 9.

[19] Kronenberg, *op. cit.*, ch. VII.

circles.[20] Shortly before his arrest in April 1522 Lieven, having proudly boasted that he had nineteen books by Luther at home, declared that he 'would rather go to the stake than abandon Luther or be parted from his books'. On hearing about Luther's *De captivitate babylonica* during a sermon, he had immediately tried to read it with the help of a cleric, though he soon gave it up, 'because the matter was too deep for him', possibly because of the Latin.

Probably most people gained their first inkling of Luther's teaching from sermons given in their parish churches or in other religious foundations. Following the condemnation of Luther by the faculty of theology at Leuven in November 1519, the conservative clergy, especially the Dominicans and Franciscans, mounted a fierce counter-attack against the Saxon reformer. His *doctrine démoniaque* was denounced in a flurry of sermons preached during 1520–22 throughout the Netherlands.[21] But, as Erasmus observed, a campaign of vilification was likely to advance the very cause it sought to injure,[22] and it was probably for this reason that in September 1525 limiters were forbidden to mention Luther in their public sermons.[23] In the preamble to the third placard against the *Lutherianen* the continued spread of heresy was blamed in part on the 'many preachers...who from the pulpit dwell on the errors of the aforesaid Luther and his adherents, as well as the opinions of heretics and heresies already condemned, thereby bringing them again to the notice of people and putting the same ideas into heads which had neither thought about nor heard of these before'.[24] In a bid to keep a tighter rein on preaching the *Raad van Holland* decided in March 1527 to impose a temporary ban on the public going to sermons outside the parish churches or friaries,[25] and when the hospitals in The Hague asked leave for their lay benefactors to attend their services, as was customary, they were firmly rebuffed.[26]

[20] *CD*, IV, pp. 110–13; A.G. Johnston, 'Lutheranism in Disguise: the *Corte Instruccye* of Cornelis van der Heyden', *NAK*, LXVIII (1988), pp. 25–26.

[21] For Ieper see B.de Troeyer, OFM, *Bio-bibliographia franciscana neerlandica saeculi XVI* I *Pars biographica* (Nieuwkoop, 1969), p. 48; Ghent, *CD* IV, p. 112; Dordrecht, Hoop Scheffer, pp. 77–78; Bergen-op-Zoom, J. Kleyntjens SJ and C. Slootmans, *Hervorming te Bergen-op-Zoom: Hare ontwikkeling en vestiging in de 16e eeuw* (Bergen-op-Zoom, 1933), p. 1; Tournai, G. Moreau, *Histoire du protestantisme à Tournai jusqu'à la veille de la Révolution des Pays-Bas* (Paris, 1962), p. 59; Antwerp, *CD*, IV, p. 43.

[22] *CD*, IV pp. 296–7.

[23] *CD*, IV, p. 501.

[24] *CD*, V, p. 3; see also *CD*, V, p. 207. In 1527 a Dutch translation of Johann Eck's *Enchiridion locorum communium adversos Lutheranos* was ordered to be burnt at Amsterdam, probably because it indirectly helped to spread Luther's teaching; see Hoop Scheffer, pp. 438–39. The Franciscan preacher Jean Glapion delivered a series of Lenten sermons in 1520, but he carefully avoided direct references to Luther, P. Hugolin Lippens, OFM, 'Jean Glapion. Défenseur de la réforme de l'observance, conseiller de l'empereur Charles Quint', *Archivum franciscanum historicum*, XLIV (1951), pp. 57–58.

[25] *CD*, V, pp. 188–89.

[26] *CD*, V, p. 211.

At first heresy seems to have been the near monopoly of the intelligentsia: the earliest prosecutions were against monks, parish clergy, schoolmasters and printers.[27] But the appeal of the new doctrines soon broadened to embrace the craftsmen in the large towns of Flanders and Brabant. Perhaps the 'small men' in rapidly expanding cites like Antwerp were first attracted less by the doctrines than by a desire to assert their own identity: by entering these evangelical circles they could achieve a greater measure of self-respect, for instead of being submerged in the despised and anonymous mob, *Heer Omnes*, they gained notoriety in the eyes of the law, while enjoying the camaraderie of the clandestine meetings. Early in March 1524 a conventicle was surprised at Antwerp and those present were summoned by the magistrates.[28] Virtually all of them were artisans: a cooper, painters, shearmen, a woodcarver, a cutler-cum-silversmith, girdlers, dyers, a pointmaker, a satinworker, grocers, a joiner, a shoemaker, tinkers, tailors (but no soldiers or sailors!), a saddler, smiths, labourers, a silk dyer, a locksmith, a carter and a dealer in earthenware; at least a third of them had been born outside Antwerp. In the absence of research into literacy rates the intellectual milieu of such men cannot be determined, though the ability to read and write was probably more common in the towns of Flanders, Brabant and Holland than in most other parts of Europe: Guicciardini, writing in 1567, remarked that most of the ordinary people in the southern provinces, including the farmers, were literate.[29] Yet clerics in the Netherlands of the sixteenth century were as prone as their peers in fifteenth-century England to equate lay literacy with heresy:[30] Christiaan Munters, a chaplain at Kuringen near Hasselt, recorded the following moral story in his journal:[31] sometime in 1535 a simple woman met, while at market

[27] Petrus van Thabor attributed the appeal of Luther's teaching to 'many educated people' to his knack of clearly proving his case from scripture: *CD*, IV, p. 246.

[28] *CD*, IV, pp. 259–61; C.C. de Bruin, *De Statenbijel en zijn voorgangers* (Leiden, 1937), p. 195.

[29] J.G.C.A. Briels, 'Zuidnederlandse onderwijskrachten in Noord Nederland, 1570–1630', *AGKKN*, XIV (1972), p. 91.

[30] *E.g.*, R.M. Haines, ' "Wilde wittes and wilfulnes": John Swetstock's Attack on those "poyswunmongeres", the Lollards', *Studies in Church History*, VIII, ed. G.J. Cumings and D. Baker (Cambridge, 1972), pp. 148–49.

[31] *Dagboek van gebeurtenissen opgetekend door Christiaan Munters, 1529–1545*, ed. J. Grauwels (Assen, 1972), p. 26. For a medieval cautionary tale associating knowledge with the devil see C.G.N.de Vooys, *Middelnederlandse legenden en exempelen: Bijdrage tot de kennis van de prozalitteratuur en het volksgeloof der middeleeuwen* (Groningen, 1926 repr. 1974), p. 177. Independent study of the Bible by the laity came to be seen in Catholic circles after the Reformation as highly dangerous, see A.Th. van Deursen, *Het kopergeld van de Gouden Eeuw*, IV, *Hel en hemel* (Assen, 1980), p. 96. By contrast Anabaptists strongly emphasised the importance of being able to read and write, see Menno Simons's advice to parents, K. Vos, *Menno Simons, 1496–1561: Zijn leven en werken en zijne reformatorische denkbeelden* (Leiden, 1914), p. 203 and the testimony of some Anabaptist martyrs in T.J. van Braght, *The Bloody Theater or Martyrs Mirror* (Scottdale, 1951), pp. 587, 760; for the reaction of hostile contemporaries to their ability to read, *op. cit.*, pp. 681, 775.

in Maastricht, a man who offered to teach her to read. She went to his house and by the time she left, she could read fluently. On her departure he gave her some books by Luther and she returned home, boasting of her newly acquired skill; but her troubled husband called in the priest to instruct his wife, so that she would abandon her heresy and confess. After receiving instruction she agreed to confess 'and having made her confession and received absolution, she was no longer able to read a word'. Ignorance remained the mother of devotion. By the early 1530s every town must have had its crop of reputed heretics, but heresy only penetrated the countryside where rural industries, commerce or fishing were important in the local economy; the villages in the landward provinces remained immune, except, of course, where a parish priest used his pulpit to expound the new doctrines.[32]

In the towns the Reformation had a disruptive effect. As early as 1520 a Dominican, preaching at Dordrecht against the local Augustinians, was stoned for his pains.[33] In January 1522 a crowd in Antwerp, anxious to thwart Praepositus's abduction to Brussels, was only restrained by the prior's plea that God's will be accomplished,[34] and later that year a mob of women delivered Hendrik van Zutphen from his captors.[35] Religious passions were so inflamed in Amsterdam that there was a serious risk of street brawling,[36] while in 's-Hertogenbosch the arrest of a suspected heretic triggered off a riot in 1526.[37] Since popular feeling was usually well-disposed towards the 'Lutherans', the authorities were obliged to change their tactics. In September 1521 the nuncio Aleander had thought that the burning of half a dozen heretics would do the trick,[38] but by May 1527 the *Raad van Holland* was reluctant to sanction any more dramatic public executions: the case of an heretical priest, burnt at The Hague in 1525, suggested that such events only confirmed the dissidents in their convictions. Experience had taught that the humiliating abjuration was more likely to be gained after a prolonged spell in prison, preferably on a diet of bread and water.[39] Counter-protests by Catholics

[32] For a survey of the situation in one diocese see P. Harsin, 'Les premières manifestations de la réforme luthérienne dans le diocèse de Liège, 1520–1530', *Académie royale de Belgique: Bulletin de la classe des lettres et des sciences morales et politiques*, 5ème série, XLVIII (1962), pp. 273–94.

[33] *The Correspondance of Erasmus*, VIII, trans. R.A.B. Mynors and annotated P.G. Bietenholz (Toronto, 1988), no. 1165.

[34] *CD*, IV, p. 86.

[35] *CD*, IV, pp. 136–39, 158.

[36] *CD*, IV, p. 246.

[37] *CD*, V, p. 133; the *schout*'s house at Hoorn was attacked in 1527 by the relatives of a heretic in custody there: *CD*, V, p. 196.

[38] *CD*, V, pp. 410–11.

[39] *CD*, V, pp. 225, 232, 323. Later the authorities advocated secret executions to avoid disorder. At Utrecht some Anabaptist women were, we are told by a chronicler, 'drowned during the night in wine barrels' in 1539, J.M. van Vliet, 'Ketterij en ketterbestrijding in de stad Utrecht (*ca.* 1520–1580)', (unpub. *scriptie*, Utrecht, 1977/78), p. 35.

seem to have been fewer, although there are instances of provocative heretics being ejected from taverns,[40] while a certain Willem die Cuper was expelled from his guild at Utrecht for advocating compulsory marriage for all priests and bishops.[41] In December 1529 Weyn Brouwers and her daughter had the unpleasant experience of being chased through the streets of Gouda by a crowd of women and children, shouting, 'Lutheran whore, Lutheran whore, burn, burn', but then Gouda seems to have been religiously more conservative than the other towns in the county of Holland.[42]

Often one cannot tell whether the violence was religiously inspired. What interpretation should one place on the raid on a Cistercian monastery outside Monnikendam in 1526,[43] or the three assaults made in 1529 on religious houses not far from Hoorn?[44] Possibly the intruders were impelled by nothing loftier than a knowledge that bread and beer would be plentifully available in these vulnerable communities. But when two weavers menaced a priest in Delft with a knife in November 1526 and smashed his monstrance, their conduct was almost certainly inspired by the sacramentarian abhorrence of the real presence.[45] Simon Gerbrantsz. de Glaesmaker from Hoorn was typical of these unruly supporters of the new ideas.[46] Having insulted the dean of West Friesland, accusing him of selling God for a doit, he then assaulted a chaplain in the parish church. Subsequently he flouted the ecclesiastical censure imposed on him and the dean had to invoke the secular arm to administer correction.

From the start of the Reformation the mendicants and in particular the Grey Friars, were the targets of popular abuse. As early as 1522 Erasmus remarked on their widespread unpopularity;[47] two years later, the Frisian chronicler, Petrus van Thabor, noted how bitterly they were hated in Amsterdam, where some people were refusing them alms.[48] In 1525 both Dominicans and Franciscans were hounded out of 's-Hertogenbosch by a crowd incensed at their fiscal privileges,[49] and scurrilous lampoons denouncing the friars appeared on the doors of Leiden's Pieterskerk.[50]

---

[40] *E.g.*, Geryt die Cuper, who was expelled from a tavern in Gouda after speaking offensively of our Lord's passion: GA Gouda, ORA, 146, fo. 138v-9.

[41] *CD*, IV, p. 373.

[42] GA Gouda, ORA, 146, fo. 149v. On the early Reformation at Gouda see below ch. III.

[43] *CD*, V, p. 172.

[44] RANH, ORA, 4515, fo. 13–13c.

[45] *CD*, V, p.170.

[46] RANH, ORA, 4515, fo. 6v-7.

[47] *CD*, IV, p. 161.

[48] *CD*, IV, p. 246.

[49] *CD*, IV, p. 392; Harsin, *op. cit.*, pp. 281–84. The guilds at Den Bosch threatened the religious that they might suffer as the German monasteries had at the hands of the peasants, L. van Meerendonck, OP, *Tussen reformatie en contra-reformatie: Geest en levenswijze van de clerus in stad en meierij van 's-Hertogenbosch en zijn verhouding tot de samenleving tussen ± 1520 en ± 1570* (Tilburg, 1967), p. 95 fn. 103.

[50] *CD*, V, pp. 106, 142.

While the threat to public order in the towns, posed by heresy should not be exaggerated – proceedings for heresy were rare, far outnumbered by those for the routine crimes of vagabondage, robbery and violence – the presence of a rival religious ideology was a potentially serious threat to the unity of the citizen body on which the prosperity and independence of the town largely depended. In an endeavour to prevent dissension and forestall bloodshed the magistrates of Hoorn ordered the townspeople in 1532 to desist from offensive name calling.[51] As yet the divisive influence of the Reformation was slight, but later in the century the towns of the Low Countries, like those in the Empire and France, would discover just how difficult it was to maintain the peace while permitting the public exercise of two faiths in the same *corpus*.

During the 1520s religious dissent was contained within the existing ecclesiastical framework: dissent had yet to develop into open schism. To many at the time the quarrels between those of the old and new light must have seemed just another expression of the traditional rivalries between the mendicant orders and between the regular and secular clergy.[52] Often the new ideas were put across during the ordinary services by *evangelijsche* priests. Mr. Dirck van Abcoude and Mr. Herman Gerrits, who attracted so much attention in Utrecht in 1521–22 until they were silenced, preached from the pulpits of their respective churches.[53] Again Jan Cornelisz. Winter, a vicar at Hoorn, and Regnier Dufour, an Augustinian at Tournai, both used their lenten sermons in 1532 to publicise their evangelical views.[54] At Bergen-op-Zoom the confessor to the béguines urged the sisters in his sermons to read the new *evangelye* books, if they wanted to understand the gospel.[55] Sometimes priests acted as mentors to evangelical discussion groups: brother Wouter, an ex-Dominican from Utrecht, worked at Delft and Mr. Nicholaas Jansz. van der Elst, an erstwhile parish priest in Antwerp, used to lead a circle in Brussels in 1527, composed largely of artists and tapestry weavers, meeting in private houses.[56] At Den Briel the priest attached to the Zuideinde Gasthuis preached covertly to a small group of laymen in 1528.[57]

Where there were no sympathetic clergy to give a lead lay preachers stepped into the breach. Much of the early poetry of Anna Bijns, who

[51] RANH, ORA, 4515, fo. 20v-21.

[52] *E.g.*, *CD*, IV, p. 382; V, pp. 51, 55, 254–55.

[53] *CD*, IV, pp. 85–86. The career of Mr. Dirck is outlined by L. Knappert, *De opkomst van het protestantisme in eene noord-nederlandsche stad* (Leiden, 1908), pp. 74–75, fn. 4. Though Visser, *op. cit.*, pp. 156–58 identifies the Utrecht priest with the 'Heer Dieric' who translated works by Luther, a verdict of 'non-proven' seems prudent given the unsatisfactory nature of the evidence. See J.D. Bangs, 'Reconsidering the Lutheran Booktrade: the so-called "Winkelkasboek" of Pieter Claesz. van Balen', *Quaerendo*, IX (1979), pp. 227–60.

[54] Hoop Scheffer, p. 575; G. Moreau, *op. cit.*, pp. 76–77.

[55] *CD*, V, p. 46.

[56] *CD*, V, pp. 237–42.

[57] *CD*, V, pp. 325–27.

defended the Catholic cause in Antwerp, expresses her complete contempt for these *duytsce clercken,* meaning the self-appointed preachers without any Latin, the cobblers who now think themselves superior to the doctors of the church, and, especially, the spinsters and béguines, those *doctorin-nen* (doctresses) who suppose they can interpret scripture:[58]

> It's no wonder that we see so many going astray.
> People nowadays have no respect for the universities;
> Instead they go to school in the woods and hedgerows.
>
> . . . They bring the gospel into the tavern,
> Interpreting it after their fashion
> Or else in some haunt outside the town moat.
>
> . . . You foolish people, what have you brought about?
> I now fear the birth of the Antichrist.
> You wreak more damage than an hundred devils,
> You begetters of discord;
> By your errors many souls have now been lost.
> Carpenters, masons have become our theologians,
> While tinsmiths, pipers, painters,
> And slaters, chandlers, dyers and cloth-dressers,
> Barbers and toothdrawers busy themselves
> With the scriptures, in fact scoffers and mockers,
> Scandalmongers, who thrive on gossip,
> These are the doctors with talents abounding.[59]

Nor was she alone in despising these hot-gospellers: during the examination of Heer Jan van Woerden in 1525 one inquisitor angrily asked whether scriptural interpretation should be left to 'furriers and weavers', to which he replied it could safely be entrusted to the whole congregation.[60] Before his abjuration in April 1522 the Antwerp humanist Cornelius

[58] *Refereinen van Anna Bijns naar de nalatenschap van Mr. A. Bogaers,* ed. W.L. van Helten (Rotterdam, 1875), pp. 45–54, Bk. I, refr. xiv. This 'refereyn' bears the date 21 November 1523. The poetry of Anna Bijns should be used circumspectly, for many of her allusions to the evil consequences of the Reformation refer to events in Germany, especially the Peasants' War, rather than to the situation in the Netherlands.

[59] *Ibid.,* p. 30, (Bk I. refr. ix, b. 11., 1–3; 12–14; c. 11. 1–13). Though this 'refereyn' is not dated, it appears in a collection of poems published in 1528. L. Roose has detected an allusion to the sect of the Loists, who came to notice in Antwerp in 1525, *Anna Bijns een rederijkster uit de hervormingstijd* (Ghent, 1963), p. 234.

[60] *CD,* IV, p. 467. 'Pelsers ende wevers' were singled out by Catholics as the least suitable interpreters of the scripture on account of their lack of education. The parish priest in the evangelical rhetoricians' play *Een schoon Tafelspel van drie personagien* (*c.* 1538–40) declares that 'where weavers and furriers will interpret the scriptures, there must the holy church sleep miserably', L.M. van Dis, *Reformatorische rederijkersspelen uit de eerste helft van de zestiende eeuw* (Haarlem, 1937), p. 193 (11. 1563–64). A Catholic pamphlet of 1580 also accused 'the uneducated weavers and furriers' of propounding 'democratic' notions acquired from their preachers, G. Griffiths, 'Democratic Ideas in the Revolt of the Netherlands', *ARG,* L (1959), p. 60.

Grapheus had maintained that interpretation of the Bible should be open to all, save women,[61] and Regnier Dufour looked forward to the time when the gospel would be preached by all and sundry.[62]

We know little of what went on at these meetings. At the time their clandestine character gave rise to improbable tales of immorality: according to one report of a conventicle at Amsterdam in 1525, the men and women used to go upstairs after the Bible study to play at 'crescrite [sic] et multiplicamini'.[63] The essential feature of these conventicles was the reading from the Bible. In 1530 the magistrates of Leiden learnt of gatherings outside the town at which 'one of those present would preach from a large book on his lap, interpreting the holy scripture after their [evangelical] fashion'.[64] Such gatherings would be arranged locally by word of mouth and any links with similar coteries elsewhere would depend on personal contacts. Sometimes a particular preacher found favour with evangelicals, who would make a point of attending his sermons: by 1535 Jannichgen, a sacramentarian from Gouda, had not heard mass for at least five years, though she went to sermons given by a certain 'broeder Wouter'.[65] There is no evidence to suggest that these informal groups ever held evangelical communion services. From the returns of a visitation conducted in parts of the neighbouring duchy of Jülich in 1533, we can glimpse the way in which such meetings could develop where evangelicals enjoyed more freedom. In some parishes there was pressure for communion in two kinds to which a priest from Susteren acceded.[66] At Waldfeucht evangelicals, disappointed at what they considered their priests' failure to preach the pure Word, used to meet separately to read and discuss the gospel and epistles,[67] and likewise at Havert, where children read the Bible aloud to their presumably illiterate elders, and where a rudimentary congregational discipline was exercised to settle quarrels within the circle.[68] But the prime purpose of these meetings of *bijbellezers* was to spread a knowledge of scripture at a time when illiteracy was widespread and Bibles were still beyond the

[61] *CD*, IV, p. 106. On several occasions Anna Bijns speaks of women preachers, especially *Refereinen*, Bk. I. xiv, xv, xxii, but there is no evidence of their activity, at least for the 1520s.

[62] Moreau, *op. cit.*, p. 76.

[63] *CD*, IV, p. 387. Similar aspersions were also cast by Anna Bijns, Roose *Anna Bijns*, p. 230. This accusation was, of course, commonplace: charges of sexual license had been levelled at the so-called 'Free Spirits', Waldensians and Fraticelli and in the sixteenth century they would be made against Anabaptists and Jorists.

[64] Knappert, *op. cit.*, p. 119.

[65] GA Gouda, ORA, 147, fo. 80v. It is tempting to identify this 'broeder Wouter' with the Dominican apostate of that name who preached to evangelicals in Delft, but he fled in 1528 to Strassburg and this deposition apparently relates to events after *c.* 1530.

[66] O.R. Redlich, *Jülich-Bergische Kirchenpolitik am Ausgang des Mittelalters und der Reformationszeit*, II, *Visitationsprotokolle und Berichte*, II, *Jülich, 1533–1589* (Bonn, 1911), pp. 90–95.

[67] Redlich, *op. cit.*, p. 520.

[68] Redlich, *op. cit.*, p. 502.

pocket of ordinary men and women.[69]

Although the resort to conventicles in the Netherlands about 1524 marked a stage in the growth of a separate ecclesiastical organisation, for some time to come they supplemented, rather than replaced, the mass.[70] Round about 1526 suspects started being asked whether they had discharged their paschal obligations: refusal to confess and neglect of communion came to be seen as the hallmarks of the incipient schismatic.[71] With sacramentarian opinions cropping up in heresy trials after 1525, it would seem that the denial of the real presence led to avoidance of the mass: for the sacramentarian continued attendance at mass would become harder to stomach or justify. It is perhaps no accident that in June 1527 the regent ordered the arrest of all those inhabitants of Monnikendam, who had failed to make their Easter communion that year or in previous years,[72] for that town was notorious as a hotbed of sacramentarianism.[73] In Jülich also neglect of the Easter communion was most commonly encountered in those parishes where sacramentarianism was flourishing by 1533. On the other hand by no means all sacramentarians shunned the mass: Jan Romersz. and his father Romert Zijvertsz. emphatically denied the real presence, yet some witnesses testified that they had still fulfilled their religious obligations like other Catholics.[74] So long as Protestants were liable to persecution, withdrawal from the mass was bound to be a slow process, accompanied by much heartsearching.

[69] De Bruin, *op. cit.*, pp. 87–89.

[70] The evangelical author of the *Summa der godliker scrifturen* advised parents to send their children to church to 'hear mass and in particular the sermon', J. Trapman, *De Summa der godliker scrifturen (1523)* (Leiden, 1978), p. 33. In the villages around Ghent evangelicals in the early 1530s used to withdraw to the tavern to discuss the gospel of the day after having attended mass, J. Decavele, *De dageraad van de reformatie in Vlaanderen, 1520–1565*, I (Brussels, 1975), pp. 268–70.

[71] It would however be quite wrong to suppose that all those who neglected these obligations were heretics, or even suspected of heresy. There were non-religious grounds for failing to comply with these regulations. For example, many of the sturdy beggars sentenced by the *schepenbank* at Gouda confessed to not having been to confession or communion for several years. Presumably these vagrants had slipped through the ecclesiastical net before the spread of Protestantism caused the courts to investigate such negligence more closely. Anabaptists offered the following 'explanations' for absenting themselves from mass: failure to resolve quarrels with neighbours, *DAN*, I, *Friesland en Groningen, 1530–1550*, ed. A.F. Mellink (Leiden, 1975), pp. 75, 78 fear of receiving unworthily *ibid.*, p. 80; no decent clothes *DAN*, II, *Amsterdam, 1536–1578*, ed. A.F. Mellink, (Leiden, 1980), p. 257. Such excuses only make sense if they were also current outside heretical circles.

[72] ARAB, Papiers d'État et de l'Audience, 1475 (i), 27 June 1527.

[73] Hoop Scheffer, pp. 577–87.

[74] W. Bezemer, 'Geloofsvervolging te Rotterdam, 1534–1539', *Archief voor Nederlandsch Kerkgeschiedenis*, VI (1897), pp. 50–51.

The theology of these early dissenters is elusive. Though some of the writings of the popular Reformation survive, the still largely unsolved problems of authorship and chronology rule out even the most tentative conclusions as to their influence.[75] By comparison the heresy trials have the substantial advantage of recording the opinions of named individuals at a given moment. But the drawbacks of the judicial sources are too serious to be lightly passed over. In the first place, the intention behind these proceedings should be kept in mind. The inquisitors were not concerned to provide posterity with an accurate impression of the accused's religious outlook, but to determine whether he had erred from the teaching of the church and, if so, whether he could be persuaded to abjure. The secular courts were likewise only concerned to discover whether the edicts against heresy had been contravened.[76] In these records anti-Catholic statements and acts, therefore, attract disproportionate attention, while the same sources are uninformative on other facets of evangelical piety. Paradoxically, although these records cannot provide a rounded picture of early dissent, they can sometimes exaggerate the coherence and conviction of some anti-Catholic gestures. A brash remark made over a pot of ale might well sound much more portentous in court. Occasionally dissenters struck defiant postures without necessarily subscribing to, or even appreciating, the doctrinal implications. An evangelical might, for example, advertise his contempt for the ordinances of the church by eating meat in Lent, but the same act could be done simply out of bravado, or even to satisfy the craving of a pregnant woman.[77] Moreover since the interrogators were inclined to follow well-worn avenues in their examinations, a considerable interval might elapse before an emerging heresy made its presence felt in the courts. But, used cautiously, these records, many of which were edited at the turn of this

---

[75] The most important of the early evangelical writings have been reprinted in *BRN* I *Polemische geschriften der hervormingsgezinden*, ed. F. Pijper (The Hague, 1903). For recent discussions of these and other evangelical works consult Trapman, *Summa der godliker scrifturen*, and A.G. Johnston, 'The Eclectic Reformation: Vernacular Evangelical Pamphlet Literature in the Dutch-speaking Low Countries, 1520–1565' (unpub. Ph. D. thesis Southampton, 1987).

[76] For the relationship between the inquisition and the secular courts in the Habsburg Netherlands see *CD*, V, pp. 207, 255–59; also E. Poullet, 'Histoire du droit pénal dans le duché de Brabant depuis l'avénement de Charles-Quint jusqu'à la réunion de la Belgique à la France, à la fin de XVIIIe siècle', *Mémoires couronnés et mémoires des savants étrangers publiés par l'académie royale des sciences, des lettres et des beaux-arts de Belgique*, XXXV (1870), pp. 53–80, and L.T. Maes, *Vijf eeuwen stedelijk strafrecht: Bijdrage tot de rechts- en cultuurgeschiedenis der Nederlanden* (Antwerp-The Hague, 1947), pp. 177–87.

[77] Hoop Scheffer, pp. 538–39; it was widely supposed that refusal to indulge women in their pregnancy might have harmful consequences for both mothers and their offspring, D.Th. Enklaar, *Varende luyden: Studiën over de middeleeuwse groepen van onmaatschappelijken in de Nederlanden* (1956, repr. Arnhem, 1975), pp. 27–28.

century by Paul Fredericq and his indefatigable assistants,[78] can still tell us much about the nature of popular heresy. As it will not be possible to review all the dissident opinions being aired in the 1520s, the emphasis has been placed on those which did most to mould the evangelical consciousness.[79]

On the eve of the Reformation many had misgivings about indulgences, or at least the razzamatazz associated with their promotion. In 1498 that ardent Franciscan reformer, Jean Vitrier, was condemned for denouncing pardons as a device of the devil and a similar undercurrent of disapproval found an outlet in some popular works of piety.[80] At first Luther was seen in the Low Countries as an opponent of indulgences,[81] and in his wake the attacks became more strident: Praepositus preached against indulgences in Antwerp and Mr. Herman Gerrits was compelled in January 1522 to abjure the opinion that pardons were blasphemous.[82] Yet this concern seems only occasionally to have been echoed in popular evangelical circles: when Dirck den Roeyen Cuper was asked in 1525 for his opinion of indulgences, he told his judges that he had once spent a golden guilder (*i.e.* a Rhenish guilder) on them, but he wished now he had kept his money.[83] Though the opposition to indulgences rumbled on,[84] this particular controversy was lost to sight as the onslaught on Catholic doctrine broadened and deepened. As the concern with indulgences faded, the focus shifted to purgatory, with which it was closely bound up. After 1525 heretics in the Netherlands were increasingly inclined to deny the existence of purgatory, dismissing it as nothing but a device to line the pockets of the clergy.[85]

With the exception of the mass, no aspect of Catholicism aroused such strong aversion among evangelicals as the mediatorial role of Our Lady and the saints. Whereas some merely wanted to correct what they believed

[78] Paul Fredericq edited the records as far as 31 December 1528. The promised sixth volume, which would have carried the work to 1531, unfortunately never appeared. In *CD* are to be found excerpts from chronicles, letters, papal bulls, edicts, trial proceedings and extracts from the various exchequers relating to the pursuit of heretics. This scholarly edition can be supplemented by, for example, material from the record offices of Rotterdam and Gouda in Holland.

[79] The most serious omission concerns the Loists whose activities in Antwerp alarmed Luther; see J. Frederichs, *De secte der Loisten of Antwerpsche libertijnen, 1525–1545: Eligius Pruystinck (Loy de Schaliedecker) en zijne aanhangers* (Ghent-The Hague, 1891).

[80] *CD*, I, p. 491; Hoop Scheffer, pp. 50–52.

[81] *E.g.*, R.R. Post, *The Modern Devotion: Confrontation with Reformation and Humanism* (Leiden, 1968), pp. 585–88; *CD*, IV, p. 246.

[82] *CD*, IV, pp. 35–36, 87.

[83] *CD*, IV, p. 397.

[84] See Hoop Scheffer, p. 566; Moreau, *op. cit.*, p. 76.

[85] *E.g.*, Hoop Scheffer, pp. 514, 575; *CD*, V, pp. 222, 225, 334; Bezemer, *op. cit.*, 50; RA Utrecht, Bisschoppelijk archief, no. 537, unfoliated. Dr. C. Dekker generously drew my attention to this last reference: it concerns a certain Heer Andries Anna, who was accused of heresy by his colleagues in 1532.

was the exaggerated veneration paid to the Virgin, the more radical spirits saw the devotion to Mary as blasphemous, and demanded its abolition. Many who would not have regarded themselves as favouring the new doctrines would nevertheless have agreed with Regnier Dufour when he taught in 1532 that, though it was not wrong to invoke the saints, it was better to pray to God alone.[86] Nicolaus Christi took the same line when he told the béguines at Bergen-op-Zoom that Our Lady was entitled to honour and respect, but she was not a 'goddess', adding that he would 'make her no greater than she is in fact'. When urging the sisters to pray directly to God, he drew a distinction between petitioning the emperor, where an intermediary was necessary, and God where none was required.[87] Pieter Florisz., a crippled tailor in Gouda, strenuously denied the mediatorship of Our Lady and quaintly compared her to 'a sack that had once held cinnamon, but now only retains the sweet savour',[88] an image also used by Willem die Cuper when he unflatteringly likened her to a flourbag from which the flour had been emptied.[89] More extreme were those evangelicals who insisted that Mary was 'a simple woman', no different from any other.[90] Jan Goessen put it bluntly when he asked rhetorically, 'If our blessed Lady is so holy, how much more sacred must then the ass be which carried the whole caboodle'.[91] Anger at the misplaced devotion to the statues of saints 'made of stone and wood' led one heretic to declare that 'if the images were burnt, wood would be cheaper',[92] and others to break the statues and crucifixes. The first iconoclastic incidents were signalled at Antwerp and Delft in the summer of 1525.[93] Sporadic as these outbreaks were, they are a reminder that the iconoclasts of 1566 drew on a tradition going back to the start of the Reformation in the Low Countries.

[86] Moreau, *op. cit.*, p. 76; see also the *Refutacie vant Salve regina* in BRN, I, pp. 17–19.

[87] *CD*, V, pp. 45, 52. The same contrast between petitioning the emperor and God is made in *Vanden Propheet Baruch*, BRN, I, pp. 265–66.

[88] GA Gouda, ORA 147, fo. 45v. This imagery was employed also by English Protestants. Robert Barnes was accused at his trial in 1540 of likening Our Lady to a saffron bag, *Remains of Myles Coverdale*, Parker Society, (Cambridge, 1846), pp. 347, 350; and Hugh Latimer in his 'Sermon of the Plough' referred to Mary similarly, *Sermons of Hugh Latimer*, Parker Society (Cambridge, 1844), p. 60. For further discussion and references see above p. 25.

[89] *CD*, IV, p. 372.

[90] *E.g.*, *CD*, IV, p. 403; V, pp. 227–28; Bezemer, *op. cit.*, p. 47.

[91] *CD*, IV, p. 385: 'Is Onse Lieve Vrouwe soo heylich, hoe heylich mach dan wesen de esel, die den hutschpot all te same gedragen heeft?'

[92] *CD*, IV, p. 399.

[93] *CD*, IV, pp. 356–57, 376, 393. In May the States of Holland had complained about baseless rumours then current in Mechelen to the effect that at Delft all the images of the saints had been banished from the churches and that a statue of St. Nicholas had been towed behind a ship, *ibid.*, p. 338.

Jacques Toussaert has shown that in late medieval Flanders the laity set great store by the last rites of the church.[94] By roundly abusing the consecrated oil used to anoint those in danger of dying the evangelicals were reacting against a widely cherished ceremony. Again and again one finds them expressing their aversion, using the same coarse humour. When Wendelmoet Claesdr. was asked at her trial in November 1527 for her views on the chrism, she replied that 'oil was good for a salad or for greasing boots',[95] an application also considered appropriate by evangelicals at Veere in 1529 and at Düren in Jülich in 1533.[96] Was it by chance that Protestants as far afield as Switzerland and England should hit on the same expression?[97] Did they borrow it from some anti-Catholic pamphlet, or were they tapping an immemorial and instinctive tradition of blasphemy?

Just as the evangelicals retaliated against the cult of the Virgin by repudiating the claims made on her behalf, so they turned against the reverence due to the consecrated elements by nicknaming and profaning the host.[98] Although there were many objectionable aspects of the mass to evangelicals, including the practice of placing a sanctuary lamp before the altar,[99] the sacrifice of the mass,[100] and the denial of the cup to the laity,[101] it was on the miracle of transubstantiation and the real presence that they concentrated their fire. Yet in the first years of the Reformation the issue of the real presence seems to have been neglected. Cornelis Hoen, who served as a counsellor-at-law in the *Hof van Holland*, had concluded some time before the end of 1520 that the words of consecra-

[94] J. Toussaert, *Le sentiment religieux en Flandre à la fin du Moyen-Age* (Paris, 1963), pp. 205–11.

[95] *CD*, V, p. 281.

[96] Hoop Scheffer, p. 514; Redlich, *op. cit.* p. 203; for later instances of the expression, see G.Grosheide, *Bijdrage tot de geschiedenis der Anabaptisten in Amsterdam* (Hilversum, 1938), p. 166; ARAB, RvB, 110, fo. 119; *Kroniek eener kloosterzuster van het voormalig Bossche Klooster 'Marienburg'*, ed. H. van Alfen ('s-Hertogenbosch, 1931), p. 72; *Handvesten rakende de wederdoopers en de calvinisten der XVIde eeuw in de voormalige kastelnij van Kortrijk*, ed. Th. Sevens (Kortrijk, n.d.), pp. 58–59. For additional references see above p. 25.

[97] For examples outside the Low Countries see C.E. Herford, *Studies in the Literary Relations of England and Germany* (repr. London, 1966), p. 42 and F.D. Price, 'Gloucester Diocese under Bishop Hooper, 1551–3', *Transactions of the Bristol and Gloucestershire Archaeological Society*, LX (1938), p. 140. For these references I am indebted to Professor W.A. Coupe and Miss I. Luxton.

[98] Amongst the abusive descriptions current in the 1520s were 'den witten God', 'papen Godt', 'bacte goeen'; for some later nicknames see J.G.R. Acquoy, *Jan van Venray en de wording en vestiging der hervormde gemeente te Zalt-Bommel* ('s-Hertogenbosch, 1873), p. 43.

[99] *E.g.*, Hoop Scheffer, p. 564; GA Gouda, ORA, 147, fo. 45.

[100] *E.g.*, *CD*, IV, p. 198; V, p. 243; GA Gouda, ORA, 147, fo. 45v; P. Fredericq, 'Sentence prononcée contre Guillaume van Zwolle par l'inquisiteur général des Pays-Bas, 1529, *Bulletin de l'académie royale des sciences, des lettres et des beaux-arts de Belgique*, 3ème série, XXX (1895), p. 263

[101] Apparently there was little demand for communion in both kinds in the Low Countries, but see *CD*, IV, p. 198; P. Fredericq, *op. cit.*, p. 263

tion 'Hoc est corpus meum' should be interpreted as 'this signifies my body', but his essay on the eucharist was only published by Zwingli in the summer of 1525.[102] Though his views may have won acceptance among evangelicals in The Hague and Delft,[103] there is no evidence of concern about the real presence until about 1525–26, by which time sacramentarian opinions were also gaining ground in East Friesland and the lower Rhineland.[104] Nor is Hoen necessarily the only source of the sacramentarian interpretation, even in the Netherlands. Livinus Ammonius, a Carthusian from Ghent, attributed it in 1527 to Oecolampadius,[105] while, by rare good fortune, we know that Karlstadt's idiosyncratic interpretation was current in evangelical circles at Veere by 1529:[106] as Gordon Rupp has said, 'at this time the notion of a symbolic, spiritual real presence was in the air'.[107]

Menno Simons's doubts about the real presence date from his ordination in 1524,[108] but the first unambiguous indication of sacramentarianism comes in the northern Netherlands in September 1525, when a witness testified that Willem die Cuper of Utrecht had insisted that the sacrament of the altar was only bread.[109] Thereafter sacramentarian opinions turn up with growing regularity.[110] In June 1526 a slater from Leiden was charged with maintaining a 'hideous opinion' on the sacrament of the altar.[111] After pleading drunkenness in extenuation – drink was accepted by the courts as a mitigating circumstance – he explained that, while working with his master at a nearby monastery, the guestmaster had told them of the impious conduct of the heretics in Germany, who

[102] H.A. Oberman, *Forerunners of the Reformation: The Shape of Late Medieval Thought* (London, 1967), pp. 252–53.

[103] See the justified scepticism about 'sacramentarianism' in Delft of D.P. Oosterbaan, *De Oude Kerk te Delft gedurende de middeleeuwen* (The Hague, 1973), pp. 234–35.

[104] E. Kochs, 'Die Anfange der ostfriesischen Reformation', *Jahrbuch der Gesellschaft für bildende Kunst und vaterländische Altertümer zu Emden*, XIX (1916–18), pp. 281–20, 253–60; H. Forsthoff, *Rheinische Kirchengeschichte*, I, *Die Reformation am Niederrhein* (Essen, 1929), esp. ch.VII.

[105] *CD*, V, pp. 189–90. Possibly he had in mind Oecolampadius's *De genuina verborum Domini: 'Hoc est corpus meum' juxta vetustissimos authores expositione liber*, also printed in the summer of 1525. The inclusion of Oecolampadius's *Dat Testament Jesu Christi* in the *Summa der godliker scrifturen* (NK 1968), which appeared c. 1528, strengthened the association with the reformer of Basel. See Trapman, *Summa der godliker scrifturen*, pp. 16, 18, 51–52 and the revised bibliographical data in his 'Le rôle des "sacramentaires" des origines de la réforme jusqu' en 1530 aux Pays-Bas', *NAK*, LXIII (1983), fn. 54, 62 and 90.

[106] Hoop Scheffer, p. 514.

[107] E.G. Rupp, *Patterns of Reformation* (London, 1969), p. 142.

[108] K. Vos, *op. cit.*, pp. 13–15. Menno's account of his doubts about the real presence was not, however, set down in print until 1554, see Menno Simons, *The Complete Writings*, ed. J.C. Wenger (Scottdale, 1956), p. 668.

[109] *CD*, IV, p. 372.

[110] For the period 1526–28 Fredericq records at least fourteen prosecutions, some of which involved more than one person.

[111] *CD*, V, pp. 139–41.

desecrated the holy sacrament by trampling it underfoot, whereupon the apprentice interrupted to say that since it was only bread, he could not see that much harm had been done. In support of this opinion he quoted scripture, including Acts XVII: 22–4, where Paul tells the Athenians that God is lord of heaven and earth and 'dwelleth not in temples made with hands', a passage later cited by others wishing to make the same point.[112] Jacob Keymuelen was banished from Ghent in 1528 for insisting that the host was no more miraculous than the bread in his larder,[113] while a locksmith from Amsterdam had his tongue pierced for declaring that it was 'a daft God who would put himself in the hands of you priests'.[114] The womenfolk were every bit as forthright. Wendelmoet Claesdr. told her inquisitors that she regarded the sacrament 'as bread and flour and, though you hold it as a God, I tell you it's your devil',[115] and, at Gouda, Jannichgen boasted that she could bake bread every whit as good as that used for the host.[116] Usually these sacramentarians defended their rejection of the real presence on the grounds that since Christ was substantially in heaven his body could not simultaneously be present in the host.[117]

Yet by no means all the dissenters after 1525 denied the real presence. When Cornelis Wouters was examined in 1527 he still apparently accepted the teaching of the church on the holy sacrament,[118] while Pieter Florisz. spoke up strongly in support of the real presence in 1533; indeed, he derided the custom of placing a light before the tabernacle on the grounds that the sacrament was God, who as the true and eternal light, had no need of other illumination.[119]

By comparison with the eucharist the other sacraments passed more or less unnoticed and infant baptism, which aroused so much controversy in south Germany after 1525, did not become an issue in the Netherlands until the coming of Anabaptism in 1531. But even before the controversy about the real presence the church's teaching on confession had been challenged. In 1522 Praepositus attacked the canonical obligations to confess once a year to the parish priest.[120] Heer Andries Anna, the incumbent of Midsland, on the island of Terschelling, so annoyed his colleagues by his teaching on confession that they drew up a formal protest in May 1532: not only had Heer Andries attacked the canon

---

[112] Bezemer, *op. cit.*, p. 49.

[113] *CD*, V, pp. 344–45.

[114] *CD*, V, p. 364.

[115] *CD*, V, p. 280.

[116] GA Gouda, ORA, 147, fo. 79v.

[117] *E.g.*, Bezemer, *op. cit.*, p. 47; GA Gouda, ORA, 147, fo. 80v; Redlich, *op. cit.*, p. 310.

[118] *CD*, V, p. 224.

[119] GA Gouda, ORA, 147, fo. 45v. On the other hand, Nicolaus Christi would only tolerate lights before the reserved sacrament on the grounds that God alone should be worshipped: *CD*, V, p. 61.

[120] *CD*, IV, p. 91.

Omnis utriusque sexus and the ecclesiastical sanctions used to enforce it, but he had also taught that auricular confession was unnecessary, unless guidance were being sought, in which case he had advised his parishioners to choose a priest who 'absque ullo timore profert ewangelium Christi'.[121] Before their execution Heer Jan van Woerden and Wendelmoet Claesdr. both refused to make a full confession, contenting themselves with a general confession to Christ,[122] and Cornelis Wouters told the inquisitor that since his conversion he had confessed to God alone.[123] At Rotterdam a lay preacher taught that one should first confess to God and seek reconciliation with one's fellowmen, before showing oneself to the priest.[124]

During the 1520s the question of authority in the Church does not seem to have aroused controversy. Possibly the notion of papal supremacy was too remote from ordinary Christians to excite much interest, or the inchoate condition of dissent, still lacking any organisation, made this a rather academic issue.[126] Be that as it may, the rejection of papal supremacy lacked the passion associated with, say, the denial of the real presence or the mediatorial role of Our Lady. Even denunciations of the pope as the Antichrist were comparatively rare.[127] True, the Augustinian disciples of Luther denied that the pope was *de jure divino* head of the church and asserted that Peter's primacy among the apostles, and hence that of his successors, was based *solo jure humano*: consequently, the pope had no authority to compel Christians to obey man-made ordinances on pain of mortal sin.[128] The martyrs of 1523 even went so far as to insist that the validity of any ecclesiastical decree, be it conciliar or papal, was dependent on its scriptural basis.[129] But one has to wait until 1525 before finding an outright rejection of the power of the keys,[130] and only with Heer Jan van Woerden does one encounter an explicit defence of the principle of *sola scriptura*. At his trial he refused to define or uphold anything 'which is not clearly expressed in the holy scriptures, these being understood as their author the Holy Spirit intended'.[131] Asked whether he would then believe nothing unless it were found in the Bible, he bluntly replied 'not a letter'. When his inquisitors tried to convince

[121] RA Utrecht, Bisschoppelijk archief, no. 537.
[122] *CD*, IV, pp. 488–91; V, p. 280.
[123] *CD*, V, p. 224.
[124] Bezemer, *op. cit.*, pp. 48–9.
[126] Moderate conciliar opinions surfaced in the disputation held at Groningen in 1523, S.P.Wolfs, OP, *Das Groninger "Religionsgesprach" (1523) und seine Hintergrunde* (Nijmegen, 1959), pp. 138–43; 164–65; 173–74.
[127] See *CD*, V, p. 224.
[128] *CD*, IV, p. 91; *cf.* IV, p. 106.
[129] *CD*, IV, pp. 196; see also P. Fredericq, *op. cit.*, p. 263.
[130] *CD*, IV, p. 370.
[131] *CD*, IV, p. 459; *cf.* Latin version IV, p. 419.

him of the superiority and priority of the church by arguing that it was the church which had originally determined the canon of scripture, he riposted by declaring that, to believers, the scriptures were self-authenticating[132] and that 'the meaning of holy scripture is not hidden beneath the glosses of the doctors or the definitions of councils: we are given the sense [*conclusie*] by the clear and true Word of God.'[133] Again he claimed that 'there is but one true holy doctor in the holy church, that is the Holy Spirit who teaches us all the truth'.[134] It is perhaps no accident that Heer Jan, almost alone among the dissenters at this time, attempted a definition of the true church which excluded the Roman church: 'I have told you (i.e. his inquisitors) that the holy church is an invisible and spiritual gathering of all those who will be saved through Christ, defending herself with nothing but the Word of God. Your church, to which you bow the knee, that is the *ecclesia malignantium* and the pope sits there in the highest throne, which is known as *cathedra pestilentie*; I will have nothing to do with this your church and will be pleased to be banished from her.'[135]

The late Professor R. Post once observed that 'for the contemporary the most spectacular and for many the most attractive aspects of Luther's preaching ... [may have been] comprised in the concept "evangelical freedom"'.[136] If this is so, it is because here Luther's denunciation of works righteousness coincided with, and reinforced, Erasmus's attack on a religion of outward observance: though Erasmus and Luther had different objectives, the practical effects of their teaching at this point were so similar as to make it sometimes very difficult to determine under whose influence an individual acted. Monasticism was the butt of their fiercest criticism and the religious houses in the Low Countries soon felt the disturbing impact of their teaching.[137] In the summer of 1524 Erasmus himself told Pirckheimer that 'in Hollandia mea' monks were everywhere deserting and taking wives.[138] The scale of the flight from the monasteries is uncertain, but vagrant religious were sufficiently numerous for the problem to call for special legislation.[139] We shall never know how many religious shared the opinion of the two Augustinian martyrs who, having discovered *christlichen freyheyt*, no longer felt themselves bound by their monastic vows. Certainly no aspect of evangelical liberty, with the possible

[133] *CD*, IV, p. 473.

[134] *CD*, IV, p. 457.

[135] *CD*, IV, p. 477. Jan van Woerden's definition of the church recalls the opinion of Wessel Gansfort. See M.H. Ogilvie, 'Wessel Gansfort's Theology of Church Government', *NAK*, LV (1975), pp. 132–33.

[136] Post, *op. cit.*, p. 587; the Leiden printer and bookseller Jan Zevertsz., who supplied books to Willem Vorsterman, apparently sold seven copies of Luther's *De libertate christiana* in the early 1520s, Bangs, 'Reconsidering the Lutheran Booktrade', pp. 227–48.

[137] *E.g.*, *CD*, IV, pp. 162, 246, 247; Post, *op. cit.*, pp. 586–88.

[138] *CD*, IV, p. 284.

[139] *E.g.*, *CD*, V, pp. 124–25, 286–88. 368–70.

exception of priestly celibacy, exercised so strong an appeal to the religious in the early 1520s. Already by January 1522 Mr. Herman Gerrits had been obliged to retract the opinion that Christians should remain free and not bind themselves to a way of life which God had not laid down,[140] a point of view echoed by Lodewijk Roelants, an Augustinian canon, in 1527.[141] Nicolaus Christi was accused of scoffing at the rule followed by his béguines and he would urge them to seek the best advice before making their profession,[142] and Regnier Dufour, preaching in a monastery at Tournai in 1532, asked the religious in his audience, 'What are you doing here? Do you suppose that your veils, be they black, white, blue or green can save you?'[143] It was this climate of opinion which persuaded Cornelius Grapheus to publish Johannes Pupper of Goch's late medieval treatise *De libertate religionis christianae*, with its insistence that monastic vows were in conflict with the evangelical law.[144]

In the Netherlands clerical celibacy does not seem to have been a controversial issue until 1525, when Willem Gnapheus penned his spirited defence of Heer Jan van Woerden's marriage.[145] He argued that clerical celibacy had no scriptural foundation and that purity of heart was more important than formal abstinence. [146] During his examination Heer Jan was more outspoken, maintaining that God had created man with a natural inclination to the opposite sex and insisting, with Paul, that it was better to marry than burn. His own father put it more crudely when he turned on his son's inquisitors, asking whether it was 'better to go to the beasts or to a wife? Where else should you seek a remedy?', which drew the tart rejoinder, 'qualis pater, talis filius'.[147] Heer Andries on Terschelling made no secret of his marriage, saying that he felt under no obligation to keep vows made at ordination, and pointing to the example of Paul, whom he alleged had taken Germana for his wife.[148] The laity had a less personal interest in this debate, but Willem die Cuper was in

[140] *CD*, IV, p. 87.

[141] *CD*, V, p. 243.

[142] *CD*, V, p. 44.

[143] Moreau, *op. cit.*, p. 76.

[144] R.R. Post, 'Johann Pupper von Goch', *NAK*, n.s., XLVII (1965–6), pp. 83–97.

[145] Though clerics married before 1525, Luther's own marriage on 13 June 1525 may have encouraged evangelicals to defend their action openly; an apostate religious on Texel defended his departure from the monastery and his subsequent marriage by citing Luther's example: *CD*, V, p. 357.

[146] Hoop Scheffer, pp. 372–75.

[147] *CD*, IV, pp. 453–95 *passim*. Heer Jan only entered the priesthood at his father's bidding and he had striven unsuccessfully to dampen his sexual desires by fasting, watches, hard work and living celibately for two years.

[148] RA Utrecht, Bisschoppelijk archief 537. Heer Andries had Philippians IV: 3 in mind. Erasmus had paraphrased 'germana compar' as 'vera germana coniunx': F.F. Beare, *Commentary on the Epistle to Philippians* (London, 1944), p. 144. I am indebted to Dr.E.O. Blake for discovering the probable source of Heer Andries's improbable exegesis.

favour of compelling all priests to marry for three years before taking the cloth, while bishops should first have to complete a marital stint of seven years before their election.[149]

The regulations governing fasting were regarded by evangelicals as man-made [*de insettinge van de menschen*].[150] According to Jan Romersz, fasts simply brought on headaches, while Our Lady was indifferent whether men fasted or not, for she was deaf.[151] Others, notably the clergy, attacked the notion of fasting as a good work: its only purpose, according to Mr. Herman Gerrits, was as a brake on our sensual proclivities.[152] Ironically the superficially permissive character of evangelical freedom allowed conservatives like Anna Bijns to misrepresent Luther's teaching as 'a soft, easy law', devised to suit the sensual appetites of the evangelicals.[153]

When Luther abolished the distinction between cleric and layman, declaring that 'baptism, gospel and faith alone make men religious', he furnished those jealous of the privileged station of the clergy with a formidable weapon. True to form, Praepositus and his Augustinian *confrères* espoused Luther's teaching,[154] but they were not alone. Heer Jan van Woerden dismissed episcopal ordination as worthless, not least because it was sold: priests are not made by bishops, but should be chosen following the practice of the apostolic church. Asked whether he believed that all men were priests, he carefully distinguished between 'the priesthood of Christ', to which all Christians belong, and those called by God to preach and minister to his congregations.[155] Though Heer Jan was accused of teaching that 'any layman filled with the Holy Spirit could consecrate the sacrament of the altar', he was clearly not in favour of allowing any Tom, Dick or Harry to preach.[156] The notion of the priesthood of all believers also found acceptance among the laity, some of whom interpreted this doctrine more radically than Luther: in 1528 Dyeuwer Reyersdr. boasted that she could celebrate mass as well as any priest,[157] and a tailor from Middelburg claimed, while in his cups,

---

[149] *CD*, IV, pp. 371–73. Karlstadt considered that bishops should be married in conformity with I Timothy III: 2, see H. Barge, *Andreas Bodenstein von Karlstadt*, I (Leipzig, 1905), p. 265.

[150] It should, however, be noted that conservative humanists too distinguished between universally valid and immutable doctrinal statements, and disciplinary and administrative regulations, subject to time and place. According to one participant in the disputation organised by the Dominicans at Groningen in 1523, the latter should be regarded as purely human ordinances and therefore liable to alteration, Wolfs, *Groninger "Religionsgesprach"*, pp. 165–66.

[151] Bezemer, *op. cit.*, p. 47; *cf. Refereinen van Anna Bijns*, p. 74, Bk. I refr. xix, e l. 7: 'Vasten maect hooftsweer'.

[152] *CD*, IV, p. 87; see also *CD*, IV, pp. 197, 480–81; V, p. 55.

[153] *Refereinen van Anna Bijns*, p. 74, Bk. I refr. xix, e ll. 5–12.

[154] *CD*, IV, pp. 92, 196.

[155] *CD*, IV, p. 458; Latin version IV, p. 418.

[156] *CD*, IV, pp. 494; *cf.* Doesburg Chronicle cited by Post, *op. cit.*, p. 586.

[157] *CD*, V, p. 347.

that 'he was also a priest and had the power to consecrate the holy sacrament as well as any ordained priest'.[158]

Among the earliest writings of Luther to be printed in the Netherlands were several dealing directly with justification. Yet it is difficult to determine the extent to which his theological revolution was understood. Apart from the Antwerp Augustinians, who were exceptionally conversant with Luther's theology and probably had a hand in translating his books,[159] the principle of *sola fide* was certainly accepted by several of the clergy. In January 1522 a secular at Utrecht was obliged to retract the opinion that 'homo sola fide sine operibus salvari potest',[160] while the catalogue of Heer Andries's offences included his teaching that 'our faith alone can save us all'.[161] At Leuven an Augustinian canon admitted in 1527 having said 'quod fides tantum salvat et non opera'.[162] Unfortunately these statements, abstracted for judicial purposes, are tantalisingly laconic. For this reason the case of Nicolaus Christi, the confessor to the béguines at Bergen-op-Zoom, is especially interesting.[163] When Nicolaus was examined in May 1525 his orthodoxy had already been in doubt for several years: at the time of Praepositus's arrest (in December 1521 or May 1522) Nicolaus had taken refuge in Antwerp and Holland and subsequently he attracted the unwelcome attention of the then inquisitor, Mr. Frans van der Hulst. Despite these brushes with the law, Nicolaus continued to associate with suspected heretics, both in Antwerp and Bergen-op-Zoom.[164] Though his accusers had grounds for their allegations, these were probably coloured by jealousy, for we learn that whereas few went to hear the preachers in the parish church of Bergen, the sermons of Nicolaus at the béguinage were thronged. To judge from the excerpts taken down by discontented sisters, his delivery was as colourful as his theology was daring. The nature of true faith seems to have been a favourite topic. One alert witness counted no fewer than fifty-three references to *fidem* in a sermon preached in May 1525. On another occasion Nicolaus was at pains to distinguish between the various

[158] K.R. Pekelharing, *Bijdragen voor de geschiedenis der hervorming in Zeeland, 1524–72* (Middelburg, 1866), p. 10.

[159] Visser, *op. cit.*, pp. 153–56.

[160] *CD*, IV, p. 86.

[161] RA Utrecht, Bisschoppelijk archief, no. 537.

[162] *CD*, V, p. 243.

[163] *CD*, V, pp. 41–62.

[164] Nicolaus Christi confessed that he had conversed with a certain Nicolaus Antwerpienis, but had broken off his links after the latter had been reprimanded by Mr. Frans van der Hulst, *CD*, V, p. 43. Nicolaus Antwerpiensis' identity is uncertain: Nicolaus Buscoducensis was in trouble with the authorities before Van der Hulst's term as inquisitor (23 April 1522 – September 1523). Other candidates are Nicolaus van der Elst, a parish priest in Antwerp, who had to abjure suspect opinions in April 1524 and Nicolaus Antwerpiensis, an ex-Augustinian from Ieper, executed at Antwerp on 31 July 1525 for having preached heresy.

sorts of faith: using the traditional nominalist terminology, he spoke in turn about *credere deum*, belief that God exists, *credere deo*, acceptance of the holy scripture as true, and *credere in deum*, that is saving faith.[165] He did not spare his audience: 'Until now you have not had a faith, but you have been in despair. You couldn't be saved with the sort of faith you've had up to now. Shall I speak plainly? You are all unbelievers. O holy faith, how long have you been slumbering? Your *'credo in Deum'* [creed] is that your faith? It's a sham, it's an historical faith'.[166] Outside the pulpit Nicolaus harped on the same theme. One of the béguines recalled the confessor finding her in tears on account of her sister's recent death. When she told him of her hopes for the salvation of her parents and sister, he replied that if they had the same sort of faith as she had, then he 'wouldn't even bother to read one Ave Maria for them'. When she enquired whether he then doubted that her parents had been saved, he replied by asking what sort of faith she had. When she had demonstrated her faith by reciting the creed in Dutch, he asked whether she had any other sort of faith. Perplexed, she asked what was wrong with it, since she intended to live and die in this faith as her parents had done, to which the priest retorted, 'then stay in it and die in it'.[167] On at least two occasions Johanna Adriaens had heard Nicolaus preach justification by faith alone. It comes then as no surprise that he had once owned a copy of Luther's *De captivitate babylonica* though he had since burnt it; more remarkable was his ability in June 1526 to find ten priests ready to vouch for his faith and morals less than a year after his abjuration at Leuven.[168]

Yet, given the cardinal importance of justification by faith alone in Reformation theology, there are disconcertingly few explicit references to the doctrine. Those who espoused it might like Sartorius in Amsterdam, be attacked by local conservatives,[169] but they were less likely to attract general condemnation than if they denounced the real presence or the cult of saints. True, Anna Bijns sneers at those who teach 'faith is enough since Christ has paid',[170] and the denunciations of works righteousness might be interpreted as implicit acceptance of the doctrine of *sola fide*. But the relatively small number of references suggests that justification by faith was either less obviously contentious or less well understood outside a small knot of evangelically-minded priests.

---

[165] H.A. Oberman, *The Harvest of Medieval Theology* (Harvard, 1962), pp. 464–65.

[166] *CD*, V, pp. 48–49.

[167] *CD*, V, p. 53.

[168] *CD*, V, p. 137.

[169] A.J. Kölker, *Alardus Aemstelredamus en Cornelis Crocus: Twee Amsterdamse priester-humanisten* (Nijmegen-Utrecht, 1963), pp. 196–98. Jan Pelt, who translated Matthew's gospel, added a postscript which revealed his conviction that 'all our works are vain, defective, impure, corrupt and sinful', S.W. Bijl, *Erasmus in het nederlands* (Nieuwkoop, 1978), p. 14.

[170] *Refereinen van Anna Bijns*, p. 58, Bk. I refr. xv, g. l. 3; *cf.* Bezemer, *op. cit.*, p. 47: 'God has done enough for us all'.

The new religious mood was marked, above all else, by a consuming passion for the vernacular scriptures. By 1480 all the books of the Bible had appeared in Dutch, but the first complete translation did not come until 1526. Yet in the period 1522–30 no fewer than twenty-five complete Dutch editions of the New Testament were printed, most of which were fairly cheap to buy and small enough to be easily hidden.[171] The translators used a variety of texts: for example, the Liesvelt Bible of 1526 followed in Luther's footsteps as far as this was possible for the Old Testament, incorporating the illustrations from his Pentateuch of 1523, while for the rest making do with the Cologne Bible of 1478 and the Vulgate; for the New Testament Luther's text was again preferred.[172] When Grapheus, the humanist town secretary of Antwerp, wrote 'the gospel has been reborn and Paul revived, thanks to the writings of Luther and others',[173] he was conveying the contemporary sense of excitement about the renewed interest in the Bible. Some evangelicals explained that they had come to a new understanding through scripture and for this reason they resented the eponymous tags conferred on them by their opponents; for the same reason they counselled others to exchange their traditional devotional aids for reading the Bible.[174]

Bound up with this concern for the Bible was a demand for preaching based on the scriptures, which extended far beyond the coteries of dissenters on the fringes of the church. Before the Edict of Worms the *stadhouder* of Holland was alleged to have advised the Dominicans in The Hague to take a leaf out of Luther's book and preach Christ's gospel sincerely and honestly.[175] According to Petrus van Thabor, writing about 1524, the sermons given by Franciscans in Amsterdam were being interrupted by people, demanding to know chapter and verse when they preached extravagantly, 'since Luther taught that the holy gospel, the epistles of Paul and indeed the essence of holy scripture should be preached with [only] a short commentary'.[176] When a Dominican took the pulpit in a small village in north Holland on the feast of the Conception in 1528, he undertook to preach the *heylige evangelie* and to

---

[171] De Bruin, *op. cit.*, pp. 185–86.

[172] Between 1523–28 fifteen complete or partial translations of the Bible based on Luther's text appeared in Dutch. To these should be added the eight translations which, though they bear no publication date, probably appeared in the same period. See M.E. Kronenberg, 'Uitgaven van Luther in de Nederlanden verschenen tot 1541', *NAK*, n.s., XI (1953), pp. 20–21.

[173] *CD*, IV, p. 106.

[174] *CD*, V, p. 55; GA Gouda, ORA, 147, fo. 46.

[175] *CD*, IV, p. 36. At a chapter meeting of the Dominicans at Haarlem in 1522 the friars were urged to familiarise themselves with Bible 'et maxime in Novo Testamento': *Acta capitulorum provinciae germaniae inferioris praedicatorum ab anno MDXV usque ad annum MDLIX*, ed. S.P. Wolfs, OP (The Hague, 1969), p. 50.

[176] *CD*, IV, p. 246. Erasmus recalled with indignation the extravagant praise heaped on Catherine of Sienna by a Dominican in a sermon he had attended in 1523, see S.P. Wolfs, OP, 'Dominicanen en de *Colloquia* van Erasmus', *NAK*, LXI (1981), pp. 40–41.

edify the congregation, instead of which he spoke about indulgences and told improving tales to the annoyance of the evangelical priest.[177] For fervent evangelicals preaching the Word acquired an almost sacramental significance: in their eyes a non-preaching clergy deprived their flock of the ordinary means of grace. This explains why priests were frequently abused by evangelicals as 'soul-murderers'.[178] At Veere the evangelical preaching made a deep impression on its audience, moving some to tears and causing one man to declare that he would rather risk his property, even his life, than stay away.[179]

In response to demands for biblical preaching and also in a bid to calm religious passions, the German diet decided in March 1523 that henceforth the clergy should preach 'only the holy gospel in accordance with the writings approved and accepted by the holy Christian church', by which was meant the works of Jerome, Ambrose, Augustine and Gregory the Great.[180] By placing these restraints on biblical exegesis, it was hoped to safeguard the Catholic interpretation, though in practice this decision gave the evangelicals in the empire a free hand to preach as they saw fit. In the Habsburg Netherlands the authorities took measures to restrain the preachers. These were apparently bidden to avoid obscure or controversial subjects and 'to preach on the gospel and epistle of the day, in accordance with the exposition of the ancient and approved doctors'.[181] The government also tried to curb the unsupervised reading of the Bible by laymen. By the placard of 24 September 1525, which attributed the spread of heresy in part to the unfettered interpretation of scripture, it was forbidden to attend gatherings where the Bible was read or discussed, and, in the following year, Charles V ordered the burning not only of heretical but also suspect vernacular editions of the

---

[177] Hoop Scheffer, pp. 566–67.

[178] For *zielmoerder* see GA Gouda, ORA, 146, fo. 112v; Roose, *Anna Bijns*, p. 257; Andries Anna, the evangelical cleric on Terschelling, denounced his fellow preachers as 'ziele morders, verleiders der menschen', RA Utrecht, Bisschoppelijk archief, no. 537; in the 1570s the priests in Gouda were vilified by some as 'eerloosde scelmen ende verleyers oft zielverliesers', *Dagboek*, p. 746.

[179] Hoop Scheffer, p. 513.

[180] C. Augustijn, ' "Allein das heilig Evangelium": het mandaat van het Reichsregiment, 6 maart 1523', *NAK*, n.s., XLVIII (1968), pp. 150–65.

[181] In 1616 Grotius recalled an order, sent by the *Hof van Holland* in 1536, to this effect, Brandt II, pp. 363–64. *Cf.* I, pp. 140–41, which is cited in the text here. This order apparently repeats one made earlier, for in August 1534, during the Anabaptist troubles, the Gouda *vroedschap* agreed with the States of Holland that the best antidote against heresy was the preaching of the "'t eeuwangelium', GA Gouda 43 fo. 153v. There exists an ordinance for Groningen to the effect that the clergy were obliged to preach 'the true and manifest gospel' in conformity with the interpretation of the 'four doctors', (Stadsarchief Groningen, Handschrift in folio 12). This was originally drawn up before the incorporation of the province into the Habsburg Netherlands, but it only survives in a text dated 26 March 1538. It was republished in 1558. The late Professor A.F. Mellink kindly drew my attention to this document and supplied me with a copy.

scriptures.[182]

Gradually 'evangelical' shed its original connotation of one who opposed speculative theology and preferred plain scriptural preaching to the elaborate allegorical exegesis favoured by the religiously conservative; instead it came to be applied in the Low Countries, as in Germany and France,[183] almost wholly to denote an adherent of the new doctrines. Already by 1525 'evangelical' had begun to acquire a contentious ring, though Nicolaus Christi could still claim that when he had advised his béguines to buy 'the new evangelical books' he had not meant works by Luther.[184] 'Evangelical' became the antithesis of 'monastic': the posters found on the Pieterskerk in Leiden in July 1526 took for granted the hostility of the monks towards the *Evangelie*.[185] When Jan Romersz. claimed in 1529 that many priests in his home town of Delft were *evangelijsche mannen*, he made his meaning clear when he explained that a preacher 'could not be a true evangelical so long as he said mass'.[186] Perhaps this is what Menno Simons meant when, looking back on his conversion almost twenty years after he had quit the priesthood, he deprecated those who had considered him to be 'an evangelical preacher' while he was still a priest simply because he 'preached the Word of God and was an upright man'.[187] This was insufficient. Gradually 'evangelical' was annexed by the adherents of the Protestant Reformation, though some Catholics registered a protest.[188] The original association of 'evangelical' with the open Bible, coupled with the edicts forbidding the reading of tendentious vernacular translations and the unsupervised discussion of scripture, gave rise to the notion that the Catholic church was itself hostile to the vernacular Bible. When David Joris put it about that the authorities had forbidden ordinary men and women to read or speak about the scriptures, he was probably expressing a widely held opinion, even though, as the judges at his trial in 1528 were at pains to point out, it was not strictly true.[189]

Hitherto little has been said of Erasmus and 'biblical humanism',

[182] De Bruin, *op. cit.*, pp. 191–92. In 1535 the bishop of Liège ordered the surrender to the authorities of all Bibles printed during the previous twenty years, see *Dagboek van ... Christiaan Munters*, p. 31.

[183] W. Richard, *Untersuchungen der Genesis der reformierten Kirchenterminologie der Westschweiz und Frankreichs mit besonderer Berücksichtigung der Namengebung* (Zürich, 1959), pp. 8–13.

[184] *CD*, V, p. 46.

[185] *CD*, V, p. 142; Willem van Zwolle believed that 'monasticism was contrary and repugnant to the gospel': P. Fredericq, *op. cit.*, p. 263.

[186] Bezemer, *op. cit.*, pp. 47, 49. Heer Andries was accused of omitting the canon of the mass, RA Utrecht, Bisschoppelijk archief, no. 537.

[187] H.W. Meihuizen, *Menno Simons: IJveraar voor het herstel van de nieuwtestamentische gemeente, 1496–1561* (Haarlem, 1961), p. 165.

[188] For example, Alardus Aemstelredamus, *Descriptio ecclesiasticae sive Concionatoris Evangelia*, (1539); Martinus Duncanus, *Vant rechte evangelissche avontmael Christi Iesu* (1558); *Die evangelische lanterne* (1525, 1565); *Die grote evangelische peerle* (1551, 1564).

[189] *CD*, V, p. 350.

chiefly because the relatively late appearance of translations of his works limited his direct influence on the formation of popular religious dissent.[190] Nevertheless, many evangelicals were clearly more indebted to the *Enchiridion*, a Dutch translation of which did appear in 1523, than to Luther's *De captivitate babylonica*. Cornelius Grapheus is a striking example of the humanist evangelical:[191] not only did he come out strongly in favour of scriptural preaching and denounce scholastic theology, he also bitterly attacked what he considered as the papal usurpation of imperial authority, while ridiculing superstitious and empty religious observances. Yet even he developed ideas, notably on the priesthood of all believers (from whom he excluded women and children) and the worthlessness of human works, which are reminiscent of Luther: the cleavage between Christian Humanism and Protestant Dissent still lay in the future. Ten years after Grapheus's abjuration in 1522, Regnier Dufour was constrained to recant opinions not so very different.[192] He was accused of teaching that 'the Word of God should be received as reverently as the body of Our Lord in the holy sacrament of the altar'[193] and that 'hypocrisy was a greater sin than heresy'. With a moderation worthy of Erasmus, he claimed that while it was not wrong to invoke the saints, he preferred to pray to God alone. Like Grapheus he displayed a naive enthusiasm for the gospel, looking forward to the time when it would be preached by one and all. At Gouda Pieter Florisz. espoused moderate views, restricting his criticism of the mass to the practice of the officiating priest mumbling the words of consecration and the notion of the mass as a sacrifice.[194] Characteristically he denied the virtues of consecrated water and the recitation of the rosary, advocating the reading of our Lord's passion as the only worthwhile act of devotion. Especially repugnant was the placing of lighted candles before the saints and the sanctuary, and he was fond of saying that the money squandered on such trifles would be better given to the poor and the lighted candles used to louse their infested clothing. On the matter of mediation Pieter Florisz. was more outspoken, for he flatly denied Our Lady any part whatsoever in the scheme of salvation. Yet he was silent about the central doctrines of Protestantism: though he consorted with known sacramentarians in Gouda, he remained critical of their radical interpretation of the doctrine of the priesthood

---

[190] G.J. Hoenderdaal, 'Erasmus en de nederlandse reformatie', *Vox Theologica*, XXXIX (1969), p. 127.

[191] J. Lindeboom, *Het bijbelsch humanisme* (Leiden, 1923), pp. 200–10; *CD*, IV, pp. 105–10.

[192] Moreau, *op. cit.*, p. 76.

[193] *Cf.* the opinion of Geiler von Kayserberg that the Bible ranked equally with the sacrament of the altar as a means of grace, E. Delaruelle, E.R. Labande et P. Ourliac, *L'Eglise au temps du Grand Schisme et de la crise conciliaire, 1378–1449*, XIV (II) *Histoire de l'Eglise depuis les origines jusqu'à nos jours*, (Tournai, 1964) p. 712.

[194] GA Gouda, ORA, 147, fo. 45–46.

of all believers.[195] Jan Romersz. is typical of the more extreme brand of evangelical: his loathing for Catholicism went beyond opposition to masses for the dead and the ecclesiastical regulations governing fasting, and included an outright rejection of purgatory, the mediatorial role of Mary, priestly confession and the real presence.[196] Together these four dissenters personify the spectrum of evangelical opinion.[197]

The term 'evangelical' provides, then, a broad umbrella beneath which many shades of dissenting opinion could shelter. Humanists and intellectuals like Cornelis Hoen, Frederik Hondebeke, Joannes Sartorius and Grapheus had little in common with the coarse-tongued popular sacramentarians. This is borne out when we consider their respective religious positions. In two dozen cases, rather less than half of whom were clerics, there is enough information to obtain a rough impression of the individual's religious position. Dissenting clergy and laity of all shades were agreed that the church had no authority to bind consciences to keep ordinances lacking a clear scriptural basis. Under this head they lumped lenten fasting, monastic vows, clerical celibacy as well as the obligations of annual confession and Easter communion. There was also a common antipathy to indulgences, purgatory and priestly confession. But the ordinary laity were understandably less bothered than the clergy by the claims of the papacy and the issue of authority in the church. Again, it was perhaps only to be expected that explicit support for the principle of justification by faith alone should come from the clergy, with their superior theological schooling. The laity, for their part, reacted more vigorously against what one might call the superstitious aspects of late medieval popular piety, associated with the use of holy oil, consecrated water, relics and images. It is difficult to determine whether their rejection of these badges of popular Catholicism amounted to a conscious repudiation of the entire sacramental system. Their vehement denial of the mediatorial powers of the Virgin and the saints, coupled with their emphatic rejection of transubstantiation and the real presence – a subject on which the dissenting clergy were strangely silent – suggests that their

---

[195] The anonymous crippled tailor's apprentice, seen attending conventicles at Jannichgen's house in Gouda, is probably one and the same as the tailor Pieter Florisz. 'de Crepel', see GA Gouda ORA, 147, fo. 79v, 81r.

[196] Bezemer, *op. cit.*, pp. 47–52.

[197] With the exception of their opposition to tithes, all the opinions held by the three Dutchmen prosecuted for heresy before the church court at York in the period 1528–34 were shared by contemporary Dutch sacramentarians. This is perhaps yet another reason for placing a question mark against their Lollard origins; see A.G. Dickens, *Lollards and Protestants in the Diocese of York, 1509–1558* (Oxford, 1959), pp. 17–23 and J.A.F. Thomson, *The Later Lollards, 1414–1520* (Oxford, 1965), p. 200.

theology was more than a reaction to excesses in late medieval religion. Whereas the clergy and the better educated laity could appreciate the profundity of Luther's challenge to scholastic theology, the rank-and-file among the dissenters were most affronted by those aspects of Catholicism of which they would have personal experience. In the light of the observations and interpretations of Keith Thomas one might venture to suggest that these ordinary laymen were attacking the magical elements in religion.[198] Reading accounts of their conduct one cannot but be struck by their coarse language and the violent, even obscene, nature of their anti-Catholic acts. These, of course, conveyed their deep loathing, but at the same time they provided a sort of Dutch courage, emboldening them to challenge hallowed traditions and powerful myths, from whose sway they were still not fully emancipated.

During the first decade of the Reformation in the Low Countries religious dissent drew on a variety of sources. Luther was far and away the most important. Erasmus also had helped, with his satires on conventional expressions of piety and his emphasis on the need to cultivate a religion of the spirit, where intentions mattered more than routine gestures. Late medieval theologians like Wessel Gansfort and Johannes Pupper of Goch could be reinterpreted in the light of the new doctrines, while on the eucharist, and possibly also on images, the dissenters borrowed from Oecolampadius and Karlstadt, ignorant of the friction between these theologians and Luther. Although the Marburg articles were soon translated into Dutch,[199] it took many years before evangelicals in the Low Countries could distinguish between the theologies of Luther and Zwingli.[200] The same eclecticism is apparent when one looks at where religious dissidents from the Netherlands took refuge. While the Antwerp Augustinians looked naturally to Wittenberg, brother Wouter the apostate Dominican from Utrecht, the humanist Geldenhauer and the future Anabaptist leader Hendrik Rol and many others chose Strassburg; yet others went to Bremen, Wesel and Emden.

The flight of so many prominent evangelicals by 1530 is an index of the vigour with which the central government prosecuted heresy. Although the tally of convictions for heresy and related offences during the decade is unknown, probably twenty and possibly as many as thirty persons were executed in this period for their religious opinions: fourteen of these were put to death in the Habsburg Netherlands and another five were

---

[198] K.V. Thomas, *Religion and the Decline of Magic: Studies in Popular Beliefs in Sixteenth- and Seventeenth-Century England* (London, 1971), chs. II, III.

[199] Visser, *op. cit.*, pp. 81–82.

[200] Hoop Scheffer, p. 109.

probably condemned by the Duke of Gelre.[201] Such severity contrasts sharply with the fitful persecution of dissenters at this stage in France and it was to leave an abiding mark on the character of the Reformation in the Low Countries.[202] The disappearance of monks, parish clergy, schoolmasters and printers from the forefront of the evangelicals, as a result of execution, flight or abjuration, combined with the imposition of still harsher edicts, to assist the growth of religious radicalism.

Long before 1530 heresy had penetrated to the grassroots of society and shown, on occasion, a disposition to violence, but as the decade went on dissent took on a more popular and aggressive note, as if in preparation for Anabaptism. Doctrinally, also, the ground for Anabaptism had been prepared. True, believer's baptism was unknown in the Netherlands before 1531, while the millennial excitement generated by Melchior Hoffman and his disciples was singularly absent, but here and there Anabaptist positions had been anticipated. For example, at least two heretics had opposed the taking of oaths before 1530,[203] but developments in the territories bordering the Netherlands were more important. In East Friesland the clergy were divided by 1530 on baptism, some wanting it postponed until the age of thirty-three and others urging its omission,[204] while in the lower Rhineland some evangelicals were also disposed to belittle the importance of this sacrament.[205] Even before 1530 the authorities in the Low Countries knew something about Anabaptism: in July 1528 the bishop of Liège warned Wolsey through the English ambassador about 'a nywe concept of baptisme that the comunalities abowt the rewers of Danowe and the Ryn ussys by nyght ... the ton baptissing the todyr with othe and promes newyr to obbey lord nether pryst'.[206] The passage from radical sacramentarianism to Anabaptism was not difficult. As the sacra-

---

[201] As no convenient list of persons executed for heresy or affiliated crimes in the 1520s has been compiled, the following may serve as a rough guide: Joannes van Esschen (Brussels, 1523); Hendrik Voes (Brussels, 1523); Clara 't Roen (Aalst, 1523/4); Nicolaas (Antwerp, 1525); Heer Jan van Woerden (The Hague, 1525); 'juffer van Wely' (Arnhem, 1526); two 'jofferen van Nymegen' (Arnhem, 1526); Hector van Dommele (Bruges, 1527); Wendelmoet Claesdr. (The Hague, 1527); Henri de Westphalie (Tournai, 1528); Lambrecht Thoren (Brussels, 1528); Willem van Zwolle (Mechelen, 1529); Anthonis Fredericks (The Hague, 1529); Cornelis Wouters (The Hague, 1529); Catalijne Bouwens (The Hague, 1529); unnamed man from Turnhout (Brussels, 1529); Arnoldus Kuyck from Doesburg, (Arnhem, 1529); unnamed Carthusian (Arnhem, 1529). There is more doubt about the execution of the following: Willem Dircksz. die Cuper (Utrecht, 1525); Bernard the Carmelite (Mechelen, 1525); a French priest (Liège, 1528); a chaplain (? drowned at Arnhem, 1529); four men and two women (Bergen-op-Zoom, 1529).

[202] R.J. Knecht, 'The Early Reformation in England and France', *History*, LVII (1972), pp. 1–16.

[203] *CD*, IV, p. 396; V, p. 112.

[204] E. Kochs, 'Die Anfange der ostfriesischen Reformation', *Jahrbuch der Gesellschaft für bildende Kunst und Vaterländische Altertümer*, XX (1920), pp. 26–7.

[205] H. Forsthoff, *op. cit.*, chs. IV, V.

[206] *The Letters of Sir John Hackett*, p. 158.

mentarians had made the validity of the communion dependent on the faith of the communicant, it followed that, when applied to baptism, that sacrament would be understood as the visible sign of an individual's conversion. For this reason the Dutch Anabaptists have recently been described as 'consistent sacramentarians'.[207] No wonder, then, so many evangelicals of the first hour embraced Anabaptism after 1530.[208] Allowing for poetic licence, Anna Bijns had said as much when she wrote;

Sire, it is all cloth of the same stripe,
From the Lutherans have Anabaptists sprung.[209]

[207] C. Krahn, *Dutch Anabaptism: Origin, Spread, Life and Thought, 1450–1600* (The Hague, 1968), p. 81; see also J.F.G. Goeters, 'Die Rolle des Taufertums in der Reformations-geschichte des Niederrheins', *Rheinische Vierteljahrsblatter*, XXIV (1959), p. 224.

[208] For the names of sacramentarians who later became Anabaptists, see Hoop Scheffer, pp. 618–19 and A.F. Mellink, *De wederdopers in de noordelijke Nederlanden, 1531–1544*, (Groningen-Djakarta, 1953), pp. 334–44.

[209] *Refereinen van Anna Bijns*, p. 143, Bk. II, refr. xii, e, ll. 1–2. The original contains a possible pun which does not lend itself to translation: 'het is al laken van eenen loye' may allude to the notorious Antwerp spiritualist, Eligius Pruystinck or Loy de Schaliedecker.

3

Dissident Voices in a Conformist Town: the Early Reformation at Gouda

The influence of the Christian humanists had barely begun to make itself felt in the schools and universities of northern Europe, when the writings of Martin Luther set all Christendom by the ears. As a result the third decade of the sixteenth century saw the intellectual and spiritual mood in the Low Countries change almost beyond recognition. For centuries schoolboys had conned their Latin grammar from Alexander's *Doctrinale*, of which no fewer then forty-three editions had been printed at Deventer before 1511.[1] Yet by 1536 the *Doctrinale* had been ousted from the syllabus.[2] The fashionable interest in the study of Greek and Hebrew even induced the magistrates of Haarlem to appoint a certain Mr. Wouter Henricz. in 1523 to provide instruction in these languages.[3] Outside the classroom of the *litterati*, the burghers began to demand new sorts of religious literature. Once satisfied with lectionaries, books of hours, bibles *int corte* and *passieboexcken* [passionals], they began to develop a taste for unadulterated and unabridged translations of the scriptures. The first complete Dutch translation of the New Testament only appeared in 1522, yet within the next eight years some twenty-five editions issued from the presses. By contrast the market for *plenaria* collapsed and only three appeared between 1522 and 1540.[4] There is also evidence that conventional expressions of piety no longer commanded the respect of the populace. It is otherwise difficult to account for the exodus of religious from the monasteries,[5] the sharp decline in the generosity of Antwerpenaars towards their senior parish church throughout the 1520s,[6]

---

[1] R.R. Post, *Scholen en onderwijs in Nederland gedurende de Middeleeuwen* (Utrecht-Antwerp, 1954) p. 146. The *Doctrinale* disappeared from the syllabus of the grammar school at Gouda *c.* 1521.

[2] *Ibid.*, p. 143. During the same period the *Doctrinale* went through thirty-three editions at Cologne and ten editions at Antwerp.

[3] H.J. de Jonge, ' "Caro in spiritum": Delenus en zijn uitlegging van Joh. VI:51', *De geest in het geding: Opstellen aangeboden aan J.A. Oosterbaan* (Alphen aan den Rijn, 1978), pp. 147–48.

[4] C.C. de Bruin, *De statenbijbel en zijn voorgangers* (Leiden, 1937), p. 196.

[5] *CD*, IV, p. 284; see also IV, pp. 162, 246; V, pp. 166–67, 248–49; R.R. Post, *Kerkelijke verhoudingen in Nederland vóór de reformatie van ± 1500 tot ± 1580* (Utrecht, 1954), pp. 180–85.

[6] W.H. Vroom, *De Onze-Lieve-Vrouwekerk te Antwerpen: De financiering van de bouw tot de beeldenstorm* (Antwerp–Amsterdam, 1983), pp. 58–60, 144.

and the slump in the sales of indulgences in the diocese of Utrecht at the same time.[7]

This loss of confidence in the church's spiritual ministrations was accompanied by a recrudescence of virulent anticlericalism. Broadsheets denouncing the papacy and the mendicants appeared on churches in several towns in Holland,[8] and in Den Bosch townspeople, irked by the refusal of the religious houses there to relinquish their fiscal privileges, stormed the monasteries in 1525, thereby causing those in authority to fear a repetition of the violence characteristic of the German Peasants' war.[9] Occasionally priests were set on in the streets,[10] and the dean of West Friesland alleged in December 1524 that he hardly dared to venture out of doors in Hoorn.[11] In nearby Monnikendam, a hotbed of dissent even before the advent of the Anabaptists, a parish priest died in 1530 from injuries inflicted, as we are told by Alardus Aemstelredamus, by a 'sicario Lutherano'.[12]

Contemporaries were naturally sharply divided in the manner they responded to these changes. Staunch Catholics, dismayed by the over-turning of the religious order, saw heresy lurking in every proposal for reform, be it as innocent as the schemes for the rationalisation of poor relief in the towns of Flanders. To the *rederijkster* Anna Bijns, writing in 1523, the world appeared 'everywhere to abound with tumults, false doctrines, dissension, and quarrels'.[13] Her forebodings were shared by Peter Jacobsz. van Thabor, a lay brother in Friesland. The conjunction of the planets led him to expect 'a great transformation and alteration' in 1524 and this he attributed in large part to the writings of Martin Luther.[14] The Doesburg chronicler was more judicious in his statements, but he too acknowledged that Luther's writings had been responsible for the overthrow of authority in the monastery.[15] On the other hand the Christian humanists saw in the quickening interest in the classical authors and the scriptures the promise of a new, and better, age. In 1523 an

---

[7] *Idem., De financiering van de kathedraalbouw in de middeleeuwen, in het bijzonder van de dom van Utrecht* (Maarssen, 1981), pp. 300, 316, 318–320.

[8] *CD*, V, pp. 106, 142, 349.

[9] L.J.A. van de Laar, 'De opkomst van de reformatie in 's-Hertogenbosch *c.* 1525–1565', *AGKKN*, XX (1978), pp. 115–16.

[10] *CD*, IV, p. 356; V, pp. 170, 328–29.

[11] *Bronnen voor de geschiedenis der kerkelijke rechtspraak in het bisdom Utrecht*, VII, ed. J.G.C. Joosting and S. Muller (The Hague, 1924), pp. 385–87.

[12] A.J. Kölker, *Alardus Aemstelredamus en Cornelius Crocus* (Nijmegen, 1963), pp. 134–35; the attack is confirmed in *Register op de parochiën, altaren, vicarieën en de bedienaars*, II, *Amstellandia*. ed. H.N.P.J. Berkhout (Haarlem, 1928), p. 51.

[13] *Refereinen van Anna Bijns naar de nalatenschap van Mr. A. Bogaers*, ed. W.L. van Helten (Rotterdam, 1875), p. 1 Bk.I refr. 1, e, ll. 5–6.

[14] *CD*, IV, pp. 245–46.

[15] R.R. Post, *The Modern Devotion: Confrontation with Reformation and Humanism* (Leiden, 1968), pp. 585–88.

unknown scholar in Groningen, using language strongly reminiscent of Luther,[16] fervently hoped that at Easter many would turn 'ab Aristotle ad Paulum, a Moyse ad Christum, a lege ad gratiam, a carne ad spiritum, a servitudine ad libertatem, a metu ad hilalaritatem'.[17] To the town secretary of Antwerp, Cornelius Grapheus, it seemed by 1522 that the *bonae literae* were everywhere reviving, that the gospel had been rediscovered and that Paul lived once more.[18] However deeply contemporaries differed in their assessment of these changes, none doubted that their generation was living at a time of crisis.

In many parts of Germany after the Peasants' War evangelical church orders, which supplanted the institutions and liturgy of the medieval church, provided a new measure of stability. In the Habsburg Netherlands, however, Charles V resolutely supported the conservative theologians and bolstered the faltering authority of the church. Those who advocated a Reformation in an evangelical sense were ruthlessly harried. Though the central government did not succeed in closing the Pandora's box Luther had opened, the evangelicals did lose the support they had enjoyed in the 1520s from the intelligentsia. Indeed it looked after the savage repression of the Anabaptists in the 1530s as though the Reformation had lost its momentum in the Netherlands. More than a generation separated the original reception of Luther's theology here and the formation of the first 'privy' Reformed church at Antwerp in 1555, and another seventeen years were to elapse before a determined minority of Calvinists drove the mass from the parish churches in Holland. Until then and, in the case of Friesland and Groningen until still deeper in the sixteenth century as Juliaan Woltjer has demonstrated,[19] the religious dissidents lived at odds with the Roman church without feeling the need to leave it in order to embrace confessional Protestantism.

The first Dutch dissidents derived most of their heterodox opinions from the writings of Luther and lesser-known German reformers. In the absence of any sort of Lutheran church order, they could not become systematic disciples of Luther. Without uniform liturgies, confessions of faith and catechisms, without visitations and the means to enforce discipline dissent in the Netherlands therefore long remained in a state of flux.

[16] M. Luther, *Operationes in psalmos 1519–21, Kritische Gesamtausgabe* V (Weimar, 1892), p. 61. Cited by J.-K. Steppe, ' "De overgang van het mensdom van het oude verbond naar het nieuwe." Een brussels wandtapijt uit de 16e eeuw ontstaan onder invloed van de lutherse ikonografie en prentkunst', *De gulden passer*, LIII (1975), p. 335.

[17] *Disputatio habite Gruningae...anno redempti orbis*, BRN VI, p. 551. See also discussion of text in S.P. Wolfs, *Das Groninger 'Religionsgesprach' (1523) und seine Hintergrunde* (Nijmegen, 1959), p. 27.

[18] *CD*, IV, p. 106.

[19] J.J. Woltjer, *Friesland in hervormingstijd* (Leiden, 1962); *idem*, 'Van katholiek tot protestant', *Historie van Groningen: Stad en Land*, ed. W.J. Formsma *et.al.* (Groningen, 1976), pp. 207–32.

Considering the nature of evangelical dissent at Gouda before 1535, we need to keep in mind how inchoate, derivative and protean the early Dutch Reformation was. Few of the native evangelicals were theologians of the first water and their knowledge of the teaching of the major reformers was acquired haphazardly. At Gouda, moreover, the dissidents lacked any sort of clerical leadership. Our evidence about their beliefs comes from depositions made by witnesses during the course of judicial investigations.[20] These cannot supply an accurate and complete picture of the system of beliefs professed by those under suspicion. The testimony was partial, often based on hearsay and given by uncomprehending, even hostile witnesses. Nor can we rule out the possibility that the evidence was warped by contemporary stereotypes and perceptions of heresy. On the other hand these depositions contain snatches of conversations, which enable us to come a little closer to the language and imagery employed by Gouwenaars as they argued about the religious issues of the day over a pot of ale or discussed these while working at home. Used cautiously such evidence can supplement, and sometimes correct, our knowledge of the early Reformation which derives in the main from the study of learned theology.

By the early sixteenth century Gouda's economy was in decay, chiefly because the brewing industry, which in 1514 still yielded around forty per cent of the excise revenue, was losing its outlets in Flanders.[21] Yet if this link with the southern Netherlands was weakening, the traffic on the *binnenvaart* (inland waterways) kept Gouwenaars in touch with the world outside. Along the waterway came all and sundry, including the Hanseatics or *oosterlingen*, who ate meat on Fridays and other fast days at the house of a certain Jannichgen in the Turfmarkt.[22] It was while travelling by barge from Amsterdam to Gouda in the autumn of 1533 that one Willem Vroesz. fell into conversation with Jutte, the wife of Jan Wouterssen. Her husband had been confined to Amsterdam 'on account of *die lutherie*', but this did not deter Jutte from avowing her admiration for those who had died at the stake for their faith and from decrying the priests, who trafficked in the sacraments.[23]

The first reference to the dissemination of evangelical ideas at Gouda concerns another outsider. Sometime before 10 September 1526 a Walloon printer or bookbinder, Martin Mathysz. from Mons, was arrested at Gouda for colporting a Dutch translation of Hans Sachs'

---

[20] ORA Gouda, 146–47.

[21] V.C.C.J. Pinkse, 'Het goudse kuitbier', *Gouda zeven eeuwen stad: Hoofdstukken uit de geschiedenis van Gouda* (Gouda, 1972), p. 96.

[22] ORA Gouda, 147, fo. 79v.

[23] ORA Gouda, 147, fo. 77. Jutte's husband may be identified with Jan Woutersz. who was ordered to make an expiatory pilgrimage to Rome on 31 December 1533 for his part in an anticlerical play performed in Amsterdam, *DAN*, V, *Amsterdam (1531–1536)*, ed A.F. Mellink (Leiden, 1985).

Disputation zwischen einen chorherren und schuchmacher, a copy of which he had sold to a barber in the town.[24] Banished from Holland in October 1526, Martin made his way to Friesland, where his irreverent tongue led to his conviction for blasphemy.[25]

Everywhere the new religious ideas aroused dissension in the community. But whereas the records for Amsterdam and Hoorn suggest that evangelical and anticlerical sentiments struck a chord, the depositions for Gouda give a very different impression. Here outraged conservatives were inclined to take the law into their own hands when they encountered dissent. Martin, the Walloon printer, may have been delated to the parish priest by one such and another 'luteriaen' narrowly escaped being struck by a pair of tongs.[26] In 1529 Weyn Brouwers and her daughter were reputed to have handed over some handbill or '*briefgen*' in a chapel and they were chased through the streets by a crowd, including many children, who shouted 'Lutheran whore, Lutheran whore, burn, burn'.[27] The readiness of the courts at Gouda to continue to enforce the edicts against blasphemy into the 1560s is yet another indication of the conservative religious climate prevailing in the town.

The defective state of the records make it impossible to give any precise estimate of the number of dissidents. For the period before 1535 the surviving depositions refer directly or obliquely to a dozen individuals, several of whom came from outside the town. Certainly the dissidents were not numerous. One of them, Pieter Florisz. a lame tailor, implies as much when he declared that not twenty people in the whole town had made their Easter communion in 1533 'honestly as they should'.[28] Nor do we hear about conventicles at Gouda such as took place elsewhere at this time. Usually the investigations arose following some incident in a tavern or discussion at home. Pieter Florisz. took part in conversations in private houses, where he had been sewing.[29] Only once is there any hint that the dissidents knew one another or came together. When Jannichgen's husband was away from home, her maidservant noted that 'Bartolomeeus the tailor, a bookbinder [living] in the Tiendeweg along with another cripple tailor' came and went frequently, though she knew nothing of their business.[30] If, as we suppose, the 'crippled tailor' was none other than Pieter Florisz., these few evan-

---

[24] ORA Gouda, 146, fo. 112v; CD, V, pp. 151–52. Possibly Martin was one of the ten unnamed 'lutherans' sentenced at Mons on 26 May 1525, see *Antoine de Lusy: le journal d'un bourgeois de Mons, 1505–1536,* ed. A. Louant (Brussels, 1969), pp. 357–59. For the Dutch translation of Sachs' pamphlet see NK 3827.

[25] *CD*, V, p. 252.

[26] ORA Gouda, 146, fo. 112v; 147, fo. 79v.

[27] ORA Gouda, 146, fo. 149v.

[28] ORA Gouda, 146, fo. 45; 45v.

[29] ORA Gouda, 146, fo. 45, 45v; 46.

[30] ORA Gouda, 147, fo. 81.

gelicals did not even share the same religious outlook. Jannichgen inclined to a radical sacramentarianism, whereas the crippled tailor still believed that the sacrament 'is god'.[31]

Religious dissent did not present a serious challenge to the church at Gouda. Only five persons are known to have been put to death for offences against the antiheresy edicts before the Revolt and even the troubled period of 1566–67 passed off with little incident.[32] In 1542 several prominent Gouwenaars found themselves under suspicion as a result of the perjured testimony of Maritgen Symonsdr., but they were acquitted.[33] True the trial of Faes Dirksz. who was executed in 1570, brought to light the presence in the town of a small band of Anabaptists who were in touch with their coreligionists in Rotterdam,[34] but when Gouda admitted the Sea Beggars in June 1572, the inhabitants had still to display any great enthusiasm for the Reformation.

Before the spread of Anabaptist doctrines changed society's perception of heresy, dissidents were indiscriminately labelled as 'Lutherans', whether or not their opinions owed anything to the theology of the reformer. This appears from the case of Geryt die Cuper. This cooper provoked a quarrel with a soldier, who was reading 'die passie ons heeren' (Our Lord's Passion) in a tavern in the town shortly after Easter 1529, by denying the resurrection. Whereupon the soldier retorted: 'What do you mean? Will you speak ill of the Passion, ... will you *luyteren?*'[35] Geryt belongs to a tradition of radical disbelief which found isolated champions in the sixteenth century, as it had done in earlier periods.[36] Pieter Florisz. however has a far better claim to be considered a 'Lutheran', even though his homespun 'theology' probably contains elements from several sources. Pieter certainly denied that he was a 'Lutheran', when accused by one of his companions of despising the saints.[37] Five witnesses attested at the end of May 1533 to remarkable conversations they had had with Pieter in the last ten days of April. Shortly after Low Sunday Pieter had sat sewing at the house of Oede die Bacster and her daughter,

---

[31] ORA Gouda, 146, fo. 45v.

[32] Two Anabaptists were executed before 30 June 1535, ARAG, Grafelijkheidsrekenkamer, Rekening 4460; Aert Aertssen was executed in 1547 (ORA Gouda, 176, 208–9); Lambrecht Vrenckesz. was burnt in the same year (ORA Gouda, 176, 211); for the fifth victim Faes Dirksz. see fn.34. For 1566 see C.C. Hibben, *Gouda in Revolt: Particularism and Pacifism in the Revolt of the Netherlands, 1572–1588* (Utrecht, 1983), p. 32.

[33] ARAG, Grafelijkheidsrekenkamer, Rekening 4462, fo. 107–7v; Hof van Holland, 5654, fo. 100–101v.

[34] ORA Gouda, 177, fo 51–52v.

[35] ORA Gouda, 146, fo. 138v-39.

[36] For late medieval examples see *CD*, I, pp. 490, 493; for sixteenth century see *DAN*, I, *Friesland en Groningen (1530–1550)*, ed. A.F. Mellink (Leiden, 1975), pp. 4–5; W. Bax, *Het protestantisme in het bisdom Luik en vooral te Maastricht, 1505–1557* (The Hague, 1937), p. 382. See also A. Murray, 'Piety and Impiety in thirteenth-century Italy', *Studies in Church History* VIII, ed. G.J. Cuming and D. Baker (Cambridge, 1972), pp. 83–106.

[37] ORA Gouda, 146, fo. 45v.

Katryn Martynsdr. Both women evidently set much store by the usual
devotional aids – books of hours, vigils and the rosary – and they were
therefore upset when Pieter asserted that with these 'you did yourself a
disservice rather than a service and that merit only came from reading
the passion of Our dear Lord'.[38] Pieter insisted that neither Mary nor
the saints had any powers of intercession. When Katryn would hear no
more of such impious language, Pieter had replied: 'You won't listen to me.
If you listened to me I would bring from death to life'.[39] On another
occasion the crippled tailor spent the day working at the house of mr.
Barentssen. It was 29 April, the eve of St. Quirinus, and mr. Barents'
wife, Jannetgen, wanted to make ready a candle to be offered in church
next day. She believed that the saint had interceded on her behalf with
God and that as a result she had been healed of her infirmity, and she
wished to be spared any further affliction. Pieter took her to task: 'Are
you then so simple as not to know that the saints that stand in the
church are made of stone and wood? How have you fallen into error?'[40]
Jannetgen replied that she knew this very well, but the saints in heaven
interceded. Pieter denied this: the saints in heaven were deaf and she
should therefore pray directly to God. In the afternoon a priest called to
speak with mr. Barent and the tailor took the opportunity to ask him for
his views on Jannetgen's intention to light a candle to St. Quirinus.
When Heer Cornelis Gherytssen took Jannetgen's part, Pieter
vehemently declared that it was an idolatrous and blasphemous practice.
The conversation turned to the custom of placing a sanctuary lamp
before the holy sacrament. Pieter argued that since the sacrament 'is
God and God is the true light', He had no need of our candles. The
money so spent should be given to the poor and the candles used to
louse their vermin-ridden clothing.[41] When Pieter asked why the priest
recited the canon under his breath, Heer Cornelis retorted that it was
none of his business. If Pieter cared so much about such matters, he
should present himself at Utrecht for ordination. To this Pieter pertly
remarked that his mouth was too small to swallow the host, an allusion
probably to the larger hosts used by celebrants.[42] Despite these arguments
the tailor seems to have remained at mr. Barent's house during the
evening, when a votive candle was carried through the rooms. During
these proceedings Pieter continued his sarcastic sallies, which attest the
strength of his convictions and his assurance. The fact of these investigations suggests that his confidence may have been misplaced, though it
seems unlikely that he was condemned to death.

[38] ORA Gouda, 146, fo. 45v.
[39] ORA Gouda, 146, fo. 46.
[40] ORA Gouda, 146, fo. 45.
[41] ORA Gouda, 146, fo. 45.
[42] ORA Gouda, 146, fo. 45.

In Jannichgen the evangelical doctrines found a still more truculent proponent. According to the depositions made between 27 February and 2 March 1535 Jannichgen had not gone to mass for a period of five years, though she had attended the sermons of a certain friar, 'broeder Wouter'.[43] The religious controversy provoked by the Reformation here set husband against wife. Not only did Jannichgen's husband, who appears in the records anonymously as 'my lord', not share her convictions, he even, or so it was alleged, beat her for refusing to come to church at Easter and on feast days.[44] She seems to have lived in some fear of 'the devil' as she called her husband, for she warned her three-year-old child to be sure to genuflect before the sacrament if he were present.[45] When he was not at home, she would disregard the obligations to fast and, as we have already noticed, keep suspect company.

Jannichgen did not conceal her contempt for the priests and mendicants. On seeing the clergy in a funeral procession, she was heard to remark: 'See how they [the priests] go peck, peck in the hope of getting something like ravens on a carcass'.[46] In her opinion the friars were rogues and vagrants, who squandered their money on whores.[47] Such anticlerical sentiments seem to have been provoked by 'the ancient hatred... of the laity towards the clergy', by the envy of the laity for the privileged first estate. That was what the official from the diocese of Cologne had in mind when he complained in 1500 about the disposition of the laity 'ab ineunte aetate' to place the worst possible construction on the motives of the clergy.[48] In the case of sacramentarians like Jannichgen this hatred of the clergy was reinforced by a repudiation of the miracle of transubstantiation. The priests were not only immoral, they were redundant. In this respect Jannichgen took a more radical stance than Pieter Florisz. Indeed, if we may identify the unnamed apprentice tailor who was observed working in her house with the crippled tailor, Pieter once chided Jannichgen. When she boasted that she could bake bread as good as that used for the sacrament, he reminded her that she had not been anointed.[49] Characteristically, she replied by insisting that she could recite the words of consecration as well as any priest. Once she told one of her maid-servants, who respected the obligations to fast: 'You go as well together with pilgrimages and sacra-

---

[43] ORA Gouda, 147, fo. 80v.

[44] ORA Gouda, 147, fo. 79v.

[45] ORA Gouda, 147, fo. 80v.

[46] ORA Gouda, 147, fo. 81.

[47] ORA Gouda, 147, fo. 81.

[48] Cited by F.W. Oediger, 'Niederrheinische Pfarrkirchen um 1500. Bemerkungen zu einen Erkundungsbuch des Archidiakonates Xanten', *Annalen des historischen Vereins für den Niederrhein*, CXXXV (1937), p. 40, fn. 171.

[49] ORA Gouda, 147, fo. 79v.

ments as a sack in tatters does. God's in heaven and He stays there. He's is not to be found in any sacraments; these [hosts] are baked gods. It's all done for money'.[50] When the blessed sacrament was borne past her door Jannichgen refused to pay her respects; instead she deliberately continued with her housework as if she had not seen it. Such irreverence enraged some of her neighbours, including Dirckgen die Clerckswyf, who had ordered her from across the water to fall on her knees 'as the Lord your God passes'.[51] But Jannichgen, whose God was in heaven, simply ignored the rebukes and returned the insults.

The provenance of these early dissidents' opinions and robust idiom remains a matter of conjuncture. One thinks naturally of Luther in the first place, yet on the slender evidence available it is difficult to *demonstrate* that these heterodox Gouwenaars were conversant with his theology, or indeed that of any of the leading reformers. Even Pieter Florisz.'s convic-tion that 'merit' only comes from reading the account of the passion, not from books of hours or praying the rosary, is ambiguous. It may evince a Lutheran understanding of justification, but it could also be plausibly read as an Erasmian assertion that the gospel should be the source of true piety. Nor would all the dissident opinions have found favour with Luther. Jannichgen's crude sacramentarianism would have been especially offensive, while Pieter's invective against images would have seemed too drastic.

Apart from the availability of Hans Sachs' dialogue, we know nothing about the nature of the evangelical literature then presumably circulating at Gouda. Some of the dissident opinions recall passages in Gnapheus' *Een troost ende spiegel der siecken*, which was printed in 1531, and in the anonymous *Vanden Propheet Baruch*, which appeared c. 1525. For example, Jannichgen's comparison between the priests at a burial with ravens around a carcass puts one in mind of Gnapheus' parish priest hovering 'like a vulture around the carcass' at the sickbed of the burgomaster's widow.[52] Pieter's scornful dismissal of the practice of burning candles before the statues of saints in church to obtain their intercessory support finds its parallel in the ridicule of Timotheus, the evangelical spokesman in Gnapheus' *Troost*, on those who set lights before blind images.[53] Again, the notion that it is better to give money to the poor, 'the living temples', than waste it on votive candles and on costly vestments and elaborate images recurs in both evangelical works as well as in the

---

[50] ORA Gouda, 147, fo. 80v. The Dutch text reads: 'Ghy hangt mit beverden ende sacramenten samen gelick en sack mit lappen doet. God die es inden hemel ende daer en compt hy niet vuyt, hy en compt in gheen sacramenten, tsyn bacte goeen, tes al om ghelt te doen'.

[51] ORA Gouda, 147, fo. 80.

[52] (W.Gnapheus), *Een troost ende spiegel der siecken*, BRN, I, p. 155, (NK 1010).

[53] *Ibid*, p. 192.

depositions.[54] It would, of course, be foolish to make too much of such similarities, which no doubt reflect a common dependence on biblical imagery[55] and on earlier denunciations of extravagance in the church.[56]

The vulgar theology of Pieter Florisz. and Jannichgen most closely resembles the expressions of dissent current in Lollard circles in England in the late fifteenth and early sixteenth century.[57] Here one discovers the same insistence that images were merely 'dead stocks and stones', that it was better to distribute money to the poor than to make offerings to saints, that the layman had as much authority as the priest to administer the sacraments and that the eucharist was 'the baken god'. There is, of course, no reason to suppose that English Lollard beliefs exercised any formative influence on early evangelical dissent in the Low Countries. But students of the Reformation in the Low Countries may find it helpful to bear in mind the possibility that the sort of popular dissent, which is recorded in the trial evidence, may contain elements derived from pre-Reformation heterodox traditions, as well as the familiar motifs taken from Christian humanist and Lutheran sources. Certainly this might account for some of the more bizarre religious beliefs, which cannot be found in any of the standard expositions of Protestant theology.[58] The pithy and memorable remarks of Pieter Florisz. and Jannichgen evidently did not originate with them. Nor can Wendelmoet Claesdr. take the credit for the suggestion that the chrism 'oil is fine on a salad or to grease your boots with'.[59] These beliefs are conveyed in such a robust and terse terminology that one suspects the previous existence of a tradition of oral dissent, transmitted in the form of aphoristic sayings, which were polished and honed by repetition.[60] Such opinions were only

[54] *Vanden Propeet Baruch, BRN,* I, p. 263 (NK 246); *Troost,* pp. 163, 192.

[55] For example the comparison between the clergy and ravens and vultures may have been inspired by Matthew XXIV: 28. I am grateful to my former student Andrew Johnston for drawing my attention to this passage.

[56] See for example the opinions of the priest Jaspar Fournier (1557), *CD,* II, p. 285; the author of the *Oeconomica,* cited by J. Trapman, *De Summa der godliker scrifturen (1523)* (Leiden, 1978), p. 27; Peter of Dieburg cited by R.R. Post, *The Modern Devotion,* p. 464; Geert Groote, cited by Post, *ibid,* p. 127.

[57] On the Lollards see J.A.F. Thomson, *The Later Lollards, 1414–1520* (Oxford, 1965); J.F. Davis, 'Lollardy and the English Reformation', *ARG,* LXXIII (1982), pp. 217–236; *idem,* 'Joan of Kent, Lollardy and the English Reformation', *JEH,* XXXIII (1982), pp. 225–233.

[58] For example, Willem de Cuper believed the apostles had been put to death for their crimes *CD,* IV, p. 373; mr. Jelijs Vientsz. of Hoorn believed St. Laurence, deacon and martyr of the third century, had been put to death 'om sijn misdaet en boeverye', Oud-Archief Hoorn, 6, 9.

[59] See above p. 43. In 1500 the troops of Albrecht of Saxony were accused of having abused the holy oil 'ende smeerden hoer schoenen daer mede', P.van Thabor, *Historie van Vrieslant,* ed. R. Steensma (Leeuwarden, 1973), p. 156.

[60] For a discussion of the 'proverbial' nature of late medieval dissent see E.Cameron, *The Reformation of the Heretics: The Waldenses of the Alps, 1480–1580* (Oxford, 1984) pp. 69, 73, 79, 123, 216–17, 255.

detected when the authorities had cause, as they had of course in late medieval England and in France and the Low Countries after 1520,[61] to take the menace of heresy seriously.

The relative absence of heresy prosecutions in the Burgundian Netherlands after the 1430s gravely handicaps the student of dissent in this region. Yet a careful study of the language used by dissidents in the early stages of the Reformation may yet provide some telling clues. When Pieter Florisz. was asked by Oede die Bacster whether he despised Mary, he denied the charge, saying, 'Our Lady was no more than a sack which had contained cinnamon and keeps its sweet fragrance'.[62] This vivid image was neither coined by the tailor nor, so far as I know, borrowed from any of the major reformers. Yet it was certainly current. In a Catholic polemic, *Een cleyn verclaringhe des gheestelijcken staets tegen tfenijn door Martijn Luther*, printed *c.* 1530, the anonymous author reports that some contemporaries doubted the propriety of invoking Our Lady 'seeing that Mary is no more respected than a milkmaid and a sack of pepper without any pepper and as a lantern without a candle as the Lutherans say'.[63] A dissident under investigation at Utrecht in 1525 was alleged to have replied, when asked why he did not respect Our Lady, 'Our Dear Lady, in what way did she differ from your wife or mine? She was like a bag from which the flour had been emptied',[64] while mr. Jelijs Vientsz. of Hoorn was accused of likening Mary to 'a pisspot or chimney'.[65] Across the North Sea precisely the same imagery was employed in Lollard and evangelical circles. At least as early as 1520, when an inhabitant of Rochester (Kent) admitted to holding the opinion that 'as for ouer blessid lady She is but a sakk'; one of the dissident beliefs proscribed in 1536 was that Our Lady was like 'a bag of saffron or pepper when the spice was out'[66]. It is therefore possible – though by no means certain – that the dissident voices overheard at Gouda in the early 1530s used an idiom that owed something to a tradition of dissent older than the Reformation proper and one which would eventually be drowned as that same Reformation systematically inculcated its theology by means of confessions of faith, catechisms and uniform liturgies.

---

[61] For a recent study of pre-Calvinist dissent in France see D.J. Nicholls, 'The Nature of Popular Heresy in France, 1520–1542', *Historical Journal*, XXVI (1983), pp. 261–75.

[62] ORA Gouda, 146, fo. 45v.

[63] NK, 4017. Biiv. I am indebted to Dr. Andrew Johnston for this reference.

[64] *CD*, IV, p. 372.

[65] Oud-Archief Hoorn, 5.

[66] J.F. Davis, 'Joan of Kent', p. 231.

4

Building Heaven in Hell's Despite: The Early History of the Reformation in the Towns of the Low Countries

Between 1 July 1523, when the protomartyrs of Protestantism were burnt in the market-place at Brussels, and the summer of 1566 more than 1,300 people are known to have been sentenced to death in the Low Countries for offences against the antiheresy edicts.* Indeed, if the repression in Flanders and the cities of Antwerp and Tournai was typical, the number of those prosecuted may have been five to ten times as high.[1] The judicial slaughter of Anabaptists in south Germany and Austria between 1527 and 1533 and the Marian persecutions in England may be more notorious, but in both cases the fury soon abated.[2] Valois France

---

* I wish to thank the late John Bromley for his generous assistance with the revision of this paper.

[1] Of the several attempts to compute the number of heretics who were executed, mention should be made of N. van der Zijpp, *Geschiedenis der doopsgezinden in Nederland* (Arnhem, 1952), p. 77; A.L.E. Verheyden, 'De martyrologia in de optiek van de hedendaagse martelaarslijsten', *Bronnen voor de religieuze geschiedenis van België: Middeleeuwen en moderne tijden* (Leuven, 1968) pp. 355–61 and J. Decavele, 'Historiografie van het zestiende-eeuws protestantisme in België', *NAK*, LXII (1982), pp. 7–10. My own estimate of the numbers executed before 1566 differs insofar as it is based on local studies of the Reformation, which use official sources in preference to the martyrologies. For Holland I have relied on court proceedings and exchequer records. Heretics executed without trial, *e.g.* the Anabaptists put to death at Oldeklooster in 1535, have been left out of account. Although lacunas in our sources remain, notably for Artois, Lille-Douai-Orchies and Mechelen, the present state of research gives us a fairly accurate notion of the *minimum* number who were executed for either the canonical offence of heresy or for crimes against the antiheresy legislation in each of the seventeen provinces before the iconoclastic riots in 1566: Artois *c.* 9; Brabant 228; Flanders 265; Friesland 102; the duchy of Gelre 16; Groningen 1; Hainaut 44; Holland 403; Lille-Douai-Orchies *c.* 60; the duchy of Limburg 6; Luxemburg 0; Mechelen 11; Namur 12; Overijssel 35; Tournai-Tournaisis 53; Utrecht 31; Zeeland 23; the condominium of Maastricht 21. The figures for the independent prince-bishoprics are: Liège 26 and Cambrai 6. For the repression in Flanders see J. Decavele, *De dageraad van de reformatie in Vlaanderen (1520–1565)*, 2 vols. (Brussels, 1975), II, pp. 52–57; for Antwerp see *The Mennonite Encyclopedia*, 4 vols. (Scottdale 1955–57), I, p. 134 and for Tournai see G. Moreau, *Histoire du protestantisme à Tournai jusqu'à la veille de la révolution des Pays-Bas* (Paris, 1962), pp. 251–381.

[2] For the number of Anabaptists executed in south Germany and Austria see C.-P. Clasen, *Anabaptism: A Social History, 1525–1618* (Ithaca-London, 1972), pp. 370–1; according to A.G. Dickens, *The English Reformation* (London, 1964), p. 266 the authorities executed 282 persons between February 1555 and 1558.

might seem to offer a closer parallel, for here, as in the Habsburg Netherlands, the ruler remained hostile to heresy. Yet the religious policy of the French king was swayed by considerations that counted for little with either Charles V or his son Philip. As a Renaissance prince Francis I protected the evangelicals at court when the *sorbonistes* accused them of heterodoxy, and even after the Affair of the Placards the King's need of support from the Lutheran princes of the Empire obliged him to mitigate the persecution from time to time.[3] By contrast the Protestant Reformation in the Low Countries proceeded in prolonged defiance of the state: a circumstance which goes far to explain why the Reformed churches never enjoyed the same constitutional standing within the United Provinces as the church established in England by the Crown-in-Parliament.

The urban Reformation in the Low Countries followed a very different course from that taken by the evangelical movement in the free cities of the Empire. This is hardly surprising. Although the towns in the Low Countries impressed contemporaries by reason of their size and number, even the most overmighty were subject to the will of the prince. For this reason they could not foster a civic patriotism to compare with that bred by the Hanseatic League or the cities of south Germany;[4] the presence of the brilliant Burgundian Court also diminished the importance of the towns as centres of patronage and learning. Above all, fear of persecution forced religious dissent in the Low Countries to go underground. For forty years the heretics lived 'under the cross' until the Reformed Protestants were granted a measure of recognition in 1566; then almost at once they were forced to flee abroad or return into hiding when the central government recovered the initiative. Almost fifty years elapsed between the onset of the Reformation and the 'planting' of 'the new religion' in Holland and Zeeland in the wake of the Beggars' successes. For most of this period Anabaptist and Reformed alike led a sectarian existence and even when the 'tyranny had been banished' the Reformed could not easily slough off the traits of that experience. By contrast, the evangelical movement in the German towns developed in comparative security: Luther's books were openly printed and sold in contempt of the Edict of Worms; his cause was championed in municipal councils as well as in public debates staged to ascertain the doctrinal leanings of the

[3] R.J. Knecht, 'Francis I, "Defender of the Fa*ith*"?', *Wealth and Power in Tudor England: Essays Presented to S.T. Bindoff*, ed. E.W. Ives *et al.* (London, 1978), pp.106–27.

[4] Many German town chronicles go back to the late middle ages, whereas the Dutch towns had to wait until the seventeenth century for their historians. Before then the monastery, dynasty or province, rather than the town, provided the framework for the historian, R. van Uytven, J.A. Kossmann-Putto *et al.*, 'De geschiedschrijving in de Nederlanden', *AGN*, XII, pp. 445, 457. For medieval chronicles of German towns see H. Schmidt, *Die deutschen Städtechroniken als Spiegel des bürgerlichen Selbstverständnisses im Spätmittelalter* (Göttingen, 1958).

burghers. This fundamental difference is reflected in the sources available for the study of the Reformation in the Low Countries. Apart from the martyrologies and a small number of theological and devotional writings, the student has to rely on the deficient and commonly hostile testimony furnished by inquisitions, court proceedings, government correspondence and exchequer records.

Charles V's determination to preserve the Catholic church in his hereditary lands was only to be expected. When he stated that the prince bore 'le soing principal de garder et de faire observer ladicte religion catholique',[5] he was simply echoing the sentiments of his Burgundian predecessors. The dukes had fostered the observance movement among the mendicant orders for the spiritual well-being of their subjects; blasphemy and heresy had been prosecuted to avert divine retribution.[6] At the close of the fifteenth century the town magistrates apparently still shared these concerns. They valued the moral and spiritual blessings that men and women, dedicated to the pursuit of holiness, bestowed on the wider community and they called on the religious to pray faithfully for the towns where they resided.[7] The urban authorities also sustained the late medieval church in other ways. Municipal ordinances forbade the sale of meat on fast-days, regulated behaviour during church services and protected the sanctity of the churchyard. Magistrates punished severely those who maligned Christ and the saints, because they believed, with the late fifteenth-century jurist and town magistrate, Willem van der Tanerijen, that deliberate acts of blasphemy provoked plague, dearth, tempests and earthquakes.[8] By appearing in the solemn processions held on Corpus Christi and the patronal festivals the magistrates affirmed their continued support for the church and her teachings. Charles V might be excused, then, for supposing that the town corporations would share his abhorrence of 'l'impieté luthérienne'. Many certainly did, but by no means all.

In fact the government in Brussels never ceased to deplore the shortcomings of those responsible for the enforcement of the edicts. Zealous Catholics came to the conclusion that heresy would only be halted when all the venal and laodicean *schouten* and *schepenen* had been purged. In so doing they overlooked the conflict of loyalties brought about by the Reformation and the antiheresy legislation.

---

[5] *ROPB*, V, p. 576.

[6] For the policy of the Burgundian dukes towards the religious houses and the matter of heresy see A.G. Jongkees, *Staat en kerk in Holland en Zeeland onder de Bourgondische hertogen, 1425-1477* (Groningen, 1942), pp. 44–47, 110–13, 249–50.

[7] R. van Uytven, 'Wereldlijke overheid en reguliere geestelijkheid in Brabant tijdens de late middeleeuwen', *Bronnen voor de religieuze geschiedenis van België*, p. 53; L. van Meerendonck O. Praem., *Tussen reformatie en contra-reformatie: Geest en levenswijze van de clerus in stad en meierij van 's-Hertogenbosch en zijn verhouding tot de samenleving tussen ± 1520 en ± 1570* (Tilburg, 1967), p. 185.

[8] *CD*, II, p. 288; for the edicts against blasphemy see *ibid.*, IV, pp. 5–6, 10–11, 41–42.

Since religious dissent was scarcely a force in the late fifteenth century, the problems of keeping order in a community with divided religious loyalties were unfamiliar. Such heresy trials as there were, moreover, had been conducted in the ecclesiastical courts: consequently the lay magistrates, of whom only a handful had more than a smattering of Roman and canon law,[9] were not familiar with the legal principles governing the prosecution and punishment of heretics. Their innocence came to an abrupt end with the Caroline edicts against 'heresy': not only were these to be enforced through the lay courts, but they were based on the medieval canon law of heresy. The canonists had treated heresy as though it were a species of lese-majesty against God and this doctrine was embodied in the penal code of Charles V. Since a crime against these edicts might therefore be treated as tantamount to high treason, customs and privileges, which would otherwise have secured the property of burghers against total confiscation and governed the conduct of the trial, could be set aside or even abrogated. The concern excited by these edicts and the so-called inquisition became so universal that the Compromise of the Nobility subsequently decided to make their abolition the chief point in a programme that was intended to have a broad appeal.[10]

By appearing to curtail the chartered liberties of towns and provinces, the central government compromised the ruling urban oligarchies, who in turn dominated the States of Brabant, Flanders and Holland. Although by the sixteenth century the burghers in most towns no longer had any voice in municipal government, the burgomasters and *vroedschap*, who as representatives of the *burgerij* were looked on as the guardians of the privileges, could ill afford to forfeit their trust. Failure to uphold the privileges in the face of Brussels could damage the standing of the corporation with the *corpus*. Precisely this explains why the civic militias in Leiden and Amsterdam were prepared in 1566–67 to take the defence of their town into their own hands: they suspected, not without some cause, that the corporation was prepared to open the gates to garrisons hostile to the interests of the community.[11]

If the prince had a clear duty to uphold the church, the town magistrates had the no less certain obligation to maintain harmony within the walls – the *stadsvrede*. As the internal peace of a town was always endangered

---

[9] R.C. van Caenegem, 'Boekenrecht en gewoonterecht: het Romeinse recht in de Zuidelijke Nederlanden op het einde der middeleeuwen,' *BMHG*, LXXX (1965), pp. 12–35.

[10] For a fuller discussion, with documentation, see below ch. VII.

[11] See J.C. Grayson, 'The Civic Militia in the County of Holland, 1560–81: Politics and Public Order in the Dutch Revolt', *BMGN*, XCV (1980), pp. 42–43; for the dramatic events in Amsterdam in February 1567 see H.K.F. van Nierop, *Beeldenstorm en burgerlijk verzet in Amsterdam, 1566–1567* (Nijmegen, 1978), pp. 53–58. A discussion of the dilemma posed by the antiheresy edicts for the town corporations may be found in *Resolutiën van de Staten van Holland*, 295 vols. (The Hague, 1772–98), 12 July 1565, pp. 20–21.

by the formation of parties and factions, the burghers had long been forbidden to engage in judicial duels or to hurl political insults at one another.[12] Though the sense of communal solidarity had suffered by the exclusion from government of the *schutterijen* and *métiers*, the notion of the *stadsvrede* lingered on into the sixteenth century.

The Reformation destroyed the religious unity of the town. As early as 1524 it was feared that verbal abuse would end in street brawls in Amsterdam, where the crowd heckled Franciscan preachers.[13] The situation in some towns already seemed so ominous to the president of the *Raad van Holland*, that he recalled the civil commotions which had periodically disrupted urban life in the fifteenth century when the factions of *Hoeken* and *Kabeljauwen* had struggled for control; he even feared that the bloodshed and violence of the German Peasants' War would engulf the county.[14] In an endeavour to keep the peace the magistrates of Hoorn forbade their townspeople to trade such insults as 'You're a Lutheran of the new light', or 'You're of the old light and belong to the devil'.[15] To the town magistrates, struggling to keep order, the inflammatory sermons preached by the friars against Luther, and sometimes Erasmus, after the theologians of Leuven had condemned the Wittenberger in 1519, were most unwelcome:[16] at Amsterdam some of the more obstreperous mendicants were driven from the town.[17] Even at this early stage, the magistrates came to appreciate that the conservative religious policy of Charles V could not easily be reconciled with the imperative of peace within the local community. The qualities most esteemed by town corporations in their clergy were succinctly listed by the magistrates of Delft, when they petitioned the Privy Council in 1557 for 'a good learned and peaceable priest to maintain the aforesaid town in the true

---

[12] K. de Vries, 'Het middeleeuwse burgerschap: condities en consequenties', *TG*, LXXIV (1961), pp. 220–25.

[13] *CD*, IV, p. 246.

[14] *ibid*, V, p. 189; the Anabaptist disorders of the 1530s revived memories of the disturbances in Kennemerland in 1491–92 known as the *Kaas- an Broodspel*, J.D. Tracy, 'Heresy, Law and Centralization under Mary of Hungary: Conflict between the Council of Holland and the Central Government over the Enforcement of Charles V's Placards', *ARG*, LXXIII (1982), p. 296.

[15] In Dutch 'ghy zyt luters van tnyeuwe licht' and 'ghy zyt vant ouwe licht ende vande duvel', RANH, ORA, 4515, fo. 20v-21; a similar ordinance was published for IJsselstein on 29 May 1532, see H.R. de Breuk, 'Twee stukken betreffende de geschiedenis der kerkhervorming te IJsselstein', *Kerkhistorisch archief*, II (1859), pp. 109–10; concern to avoid disorder induced the magistrates of Kortrijk to forbid people to jeer at those who reputedly went to conventicles, Decavele, *Dageraad*, I, pp. 287–88.

[16] See above p. 32; also *CD*, IV, pp. 42–43. For the association of Erasmus with Luther by the friars see Decavele, Dageraad, I, pp. 109–10.

[17] C.A. Cornelius, *Geschichte des münsterischen Aufruhrs*, 2 vols. (Leipzig, 1855–60), II, p. 406.

1. Anabaptists on the Gallows at Amsterdam
(Stichting Atlas van Stolk, Rotterdam, 241-23)

After the Anabaptists tried to seize control of Amsterdam in May 1535, the ringleaders were put to death. After execution the corpses were taken across the IJ, where they were strung up by the feet 'like dogs' on the gallows in De Volewijk.

2. The Battle between True Faith and the False Clergy. Woodcut *c.* 1530-35
(Amsterdam, Rijksmuseum, Rijksprentenkabinet, Nijhoff, plates 253-54)

The two deer symbolise the Christians who have placed their trust in God's Word. They are assailed from all sides. The apocalyptic Beast, seated on a canopied litter and escorted by wolves, proclaims a worldly wisdom, which the Philosophers on the bridge endorse. Behind them Schismatic and Hypocrisy lead a donkey, inscribed 'Loathing of Scripture', to a cistern of their own making (Jeremiah 2: 13). Two hounds, who recall the Dominicans, snarl at the deer, while Self Interest opposes the Christian with decretals and Ignorance attacks with a cudgel. High up in the barren tree of Conceit, a representative of the False Clergy dangles a rosary and a pardon. Naked Truth, armed with the helmet of Hope and the shield of Faith, wields the Sword of the Spirit. On the left a deer slakes his thirst for God's Word at the fountain of True Wisdom, fed by the Old and New Testaments.

Catholic faith as well as in peace and concord'.[18] Unhappily this blend of virtue, talent and tact proved as rare then as in the seventeenth century, when the civil authorities frankly preferred ministers of sound doctrine, edifying demeanour, and 'mild and peaceable' disposition.[19]

The execution of unrepentant heretics often threatened public order. As early as 1525 an apostate monk had been unceremoniously drowned in the Scheldt after the authorities in Antwerp deliberately misled the public about the place of execution.[20] When a couple of sacramentarian heretics were burnt in front of the townhall at Amsterdam in 1546, a wooden palisade had to be put up lest the throng of angry burghers and Hanseatics interrupted the grisly proceedings.[21] Precisely these fears were realised in 1558, when a riot broke out during the execution of some Anabaptists in Rotterdam and the crowd freed several prisoners. Only a few years later two Reformed Protestants were snatched from the stake at Valenciennes in a famous episode, aptly known as *la journée des maubruslez*.[22] According to the church it is not the suffering, but the cause, that makes a martyr. Experience taught otherwise. In a bid to deny the heretics the martyr's crown that the crowd conferred at their public execution, the *Hof van Holland* recommended in 1527 that those who stubbornly persisted in error should be kept in prolonged confinement until they had faded from the fickle memory of the people, and then put to death secretly.[23] This advice was heeded. Anabaptists were dispatched covertly in The Hague in 1534. A few years afterwards some of their coreligionists were drowned in wine-casks in the *Raadhuis* of

[18] Cited by D.P. Oosterbaan, *De Oude Kerk te Delft gedurende de middeleeuwen* (The Hague, 1973), p. 149. In 1540 the magistrates of Harderwijk asked for clergy 'die ons ind onsze gemeinde mit de woerde Goetz klar ind onvermenght trouwelicke leren ind vermanen, in die gelove, lyefde ende vreze Goitz ind tot frede, eyndracht int fruntschap onder eynanderen', C.H. Ris Lambers, *De kerkhervorming op de Veluwe, 1523–1578* (Barneveld, 1890), p. ciii; see also the terms of the agreement reached with a vicar at Kampen in 1567, S. Elte, 'Rumor in casa. Kampen 1567', *Kamper almanak* (1940), p. 201.

[19] See G. Groenhuis, *De predikanten: De sociale positie van de gereformeerde predikanten in de Republiek der Verenigde Nederlanden ± 1700* (Groningen, 1977), pp. 33, 95.

[20] M. Mélard, 'Les débuts de la Réforme d'Anvers, 1518–1530' (University of Liège, licence, 1971–72), pp. 135–37.

[21] G. Grosheide, *Bijdrage tot de geschiedenis der anabaptisten in Amsterdam* (Hilversum, 1938), p. 299.

[22] I.M.J. Hoog, *De martelaars der hervorming in Nederland tot 1566* (Schiedam, 1885), pp. 31–33, 237–41; C. Paillard, *Histoire des troubles religieux de Valenciennes*, 4 vols. (Brussels - The Hague, 1874–76), I, pp. 69–73. When Gillis Tielemans was executed in Brussels on 27 January 1544 the civic militia was on hand to quell any disturbances, A.L.E. Verheyden, *Le martyrologe courtraisien et le martyrologe bruxellois* (Vilvoorde, 1950), pp. 63–64. For details of other disturbances at the execution of heretics see [A. van Haemstede], *Geschiedenis der martelaren* (Arnhem, 1868), p. 554 (The Hague); p. 679 (Brussels); pp. 680–81, 685, 831 (Antwerp).

[23] *CD*, V, p. 225.

Utrecht under cover of darkness.[24] Later, other heretics were executed 'sans bruyt' in Middelburg and Antwerp to avoid disturbances.[25] In principle, however, public executions were staged as dramatic events, intended to point a sharp lesson; for that reason the hangman and the condemned wore special dress and symbolic devices were displayed to explain the nature of the crime to onlookers, who might expect to be summoned to the scene by the town-bell. Exemplary justice required public executions. By resorting to the clandestine execution of heretics the local authorities tacitly recognised that religious dissent was a crime *sui generis*, although Philip II only reluctantly countenanced the secret execution of heretics in 1565.[26]

The Reformation made its influence felt early in the chief towns of Holland. In December 1524 the disconsolate dean of West Friesland tendered his resignation to the cathedral chapter at Utrecht. He gave an odd assortment of reasons for this decision, but among these the insolence of the 'Lutherans' at Hoorn bulked large, for the dean ended his letter with the remarkable assertion that he was afraid to walk through the streets on their account.[27] In Amsterdam the *sincere ende goede*, as the traditionalists described themselves, were dismayed to see how quickly people abandoned the customary religious practices. Priests were jeered in the streets, church services interrupted, and scandalous songs circulated among the commonalty, who also watched irreverent plays. As the Holy Sacrament was taken through the streets to the sick, people ostentatiously advertised their contempt for the 'breadgod' by closing their doors and shutters. An incident during a procession in the town in 1534 shows vividly how low respect for the sacrament had already sunk. It was a wet, blustery day in September and the parish priest was having difficulty in keeping the sacrament aloft. As the cortege made its way across a bridge, the people in the neighbourhood were heard to shout, 'Rain harder, rain harder, drench the priest and his god'. Small wonder that priest had little enthusiasm for such processions in the future.[28]

At Antwerp the evangelical cause also commanded popular support from the outset, thanks, chiefly, to the Augustinian Eremites, several of whom knew Luther personally. In 1523 their monastery was levelled in a

[24] Hoog, *De martelaars*, p. 17; J.M. van Vliet, 'Ketterijen en ketterbestrijding in de stad Utrecht, *ca.* 1520–1580' (*Doctoraalscriptie*, University of Utrecht, 1977–78), p. 35.

[25] J.J. Mulder, *De uitvoering der geloofsplakkaten en het stedelijk verzet tegen de inquisitie te Antwerpen, 1550–1566* (Ghent-The Hague, 1897), pp. 23–24, 31; K.R. Pekelharing, *Bijdragen voor de geschiedenis der hervorming in Zeeland, 1524–1572*, (Middelbury, 1866), pp. 267–72; also Decavele, *Dageraad*, I, p. 36 fn. 127.

[26] *Corresp. française de Marguerite d'Autriche*, I, p. 102.

[27] *Bronnen voor de geschiedenis der kerkelijke rechtspraak in het bisdom Utrecht in de middeleeuwen*, ed. J.G.C. Joosting and S. Muller, 7 vols. (The Hague, 1906–24), VII, pp. 385–87.

[28] Cornelius, *Geschichte des münsterischen Aufruhrs*, II, pp. 378, 392.

bid to blot out the shameful memory of their wholesale apostasy.[29] Inside
the teeming metropolis English Bibles were printed with near impunity;
'certeyn Englishemen beyng Lutherans' could evade arrest and extradi-
tion by recourse to legal subterfuges that drove Henry VIII's ambassador,
Sir John Hackett, to distraction.[30] His complaint about the magistrates'
'denegacion of justice' in the pursuit of heretics was endorsed by certain
lay Catholics who, discouraged by the shilly-shallying of the local authorities, felt bound to call the Council of Brabant's attention to the
flagrant heterodoxy of some prominent clerics and printers. In their
opinion Antwerp would only be rid of heresy and 'false books', if a
Spanish-style inquisition were introduced to examine the inhabitants
street-by-street and guild-by-guild about those under suspicion of
holding erroneous opinions.[31]

It would be foolhardy to conclude, from the testimony of Amsterdam
and Antwerp alone, that the new doctrines had taken the townspeople
everywhere by storm. On the basis of quite flimsy evidence, it would
appear that religious dissent enjoyed a popular following in at most a
dozen towns by 1530.[32] On the other hand, the prevailing mood of
others seems to have been decidedly conservative. At Gouda, for example,
a woman and her daughter, reputedly heretics, had to flee through the
streets in 1529 chased by an angry crowd of women and children. When
news of the defeat of the German peasants, 'ennemys de Dieu et sa
sainte foy catholique' reached Douai in 1525, it was celebrated amid
great rejoicing by the common people.[33]

The attractiveness of the early Reformation may be gauged by an
analysis of the occupations of those prosecuted by the inquisition and
the lay courts for heresy and affiliated offences. Of the 380 dissidents
mentioned in Paul Fredericq's *Corpus documentorum inquisitionis* for the
period 1518–28, we know the occupations of 209 (*i.e.* sixty per cent).[34] A
breakdown into broad occupational groupings shows that roughly two in
every five might be classed as craftsmen. Among the crafts printing was
comparatively strongly represented, but the textile industry was apparently
not yet as closely identified with heresy as it was to become a generation

[29] The fullest account of the fate of the Augustinian monks is to be found in Mélard,
'Débuts', pt. I.

[30] *The Letters of Sir John Hackett, 1526–1534*, ed. E.F. Rogers (Morgantown, 1977). Among
the English Protestants signalled in Antwerp at this time were Richard Herman, Richard
Akerstone and George Constantine.

[31] R. van Roosbroeck, 'Een nieuw dokument over de beginperiode van het lutheranisme
te Antwerpen', *De gulden passer*, V (1927), pp. 267–84.

[32] Namely Amsterdam, Delft, Hoorn, Leiden and Monnikendam in Holland; Antwerp
and 's-Hertogenbosch in Brabant, Bruges and Ghent in Flanders; Tournai and Maastricht.

[33] See above p. 64; P. Beuzart, *Les hérésies pendant le moyen âge et la réforme jusqu'à la mort
de Philippe II, 1598, dans la région de Douai, d'Arras et au Pays de l'Alleu* (Le Puy, 1912), pp.
106–7.

[34] *CD*, IV-V. See above p. 15, fn. 69.

later: weavers, shearmen, dyers, woolcombers and spinners accounted for only one-tenth of those whose occupation can be established. The theology of the Reformation called the monastic way of life into question and profoundly changed both the standing of the priest in the community and his religious function, as the focus of attention shifted from the altar to the pulpit. No social group was more directly affected, not to say threatened, by the new doctrines than the clergy, yet they failed to meet the challenge as a united body: if Luther's sternest opponents were found among their ranks, so also were many of his warmest supporters. Indeed clerics and religious account for two-fifths of those whose occupation has been recorded. They came from all walks of life within the church: beneficed priests, stipendiary chaplains, monks, nuns, béguines, canons regular and mendicants, especially Augustinians of the Saxon Congregation;[35] this number does not include those brethren of the cloister who took advantage of the turmoil to return to a secular way of life that they had never willingly forsaken. It was only through this *trahison des clercs* that the religious conservatism of the countryside was ruffled. In the remoter corners of the land, including the Wadden Islands, the occasional priest denounced prayers for the dead and the cult of the Virgin, no doubt to the bewilderment if not consternation of their parishioners, few of whom seem to have followed their pastors into apostasy.[36] Even after a decade of evangelisation the Reformation remained confined to the towns.

It is not at all easy to explain why the religious mood in certain towns changed so drastically in the 1520s. Here we encounter what the late Jan Romein once called the 'problem of "transformation"'.[37] Quite abruptly, or so it would seem, the miracle of the mass and the mediatorial role of our Lady lost their spiritual meaning for many townspeople, at the same time as the new theology challenged the value of penance, prayers for the dead and a celibate clergy. In the early 1520s the old religious practices were disparaged as recklessly in Amsterdam or Antwerp as in Nuremberg, Strassburg or Regensburg, but whereas in these German cities medieval Catholicism dissolved so quickly that, in the vivid phrase

[35] In Tournai the exodus from the clergy ceased about 1530, but in Flanders a second generation of apostate clergy matured after 1557. In Holland the pattern was different again: a small, though significant, number of parish clergy joined the evangelicals and the Reformed (but only rarely the Anabaptists) during the first half of the century. Larger contingents of priests apostasised in 1566 and again immediately after 1572.

[36] The villages along the Limburg-Jülich border appear to have been more affected by radical Protestant doctrines already by 1533.

[37] J. Romein, 'Change and Continuity in History: The Problem of "Transformation"', *BN*, II, ed. J.S. Bromley and E.H. Kossmann (Groningen, 1964), pp. 205–20.

[38] For Regensburg, see B. Moeller, 'Probleme des kirchlichen Lebens in Deutschland vor der Reformation', *Probleme der Kirchenspaltung*, ed. H. Jedin *et al.* (Regensburg, 1969), pp. 12–30.

of the medievalist Heimpel, 'the images were broken by the very men who had donated them',[38] Charles V's stand against heresy in the Low Countries gave the existing religious order there an important breathing-space.

Certainly the intense devotion characteristic of the late fifteenth century ill prepares us for the apostasy after 1520. The last medieval century stands out as one of the greatest ages of church-building in the Low Countries.[39] Much of the building was spurred on by the need to accommodate the numerous side-chapels, where ceaselessly multiplying services for the dead could be read. If it is true that the physical features of the city reflect 'the view that man [has] of its function and purpose', then the medieval Dutch townscape, dominated by the bristling array of spires, bears eloquent witness to the deep religious sensibilities of the age.[40] Within the parish churches the liturgy was enriched by the daily singing of the divine office – the *zevengetijden* – as the townspeople sought to honour God more splendidly and, incidentally, to emulate the collegiate foundations.[41] To all appearances the Catholic religion was as firmly rooted in the affections of the commonalty in 1500 as it had been a century earlier. An Italian ecclesiastic, who toured the Low Countries in the summer of 1517, admired the fine town churches with their lofty spires and richly furnished interiors – the candelabra, finely wrought lecterns and pews – and he praised the conscientious piety of the townspeople, who thronged the churches, even on weekdays.[42] Yet barely ten years later the English ambassador considered the Low Countries to be in grave peril from heresy, 'for if there be three men that speak, the twain keep Luther's opinion'.[43]

If late medieval society had no quarrel with the teaching of the church, its attitude towards the clergy was ambivalent: the office of priest was extolled and ordination keenly sought, yet the first estate often had to endure the envy of the laity, to say nothing of the obloquy of ascetic reformers. The episcopal official from Cologne who complained in 1500 that the laity had always been ready to abuse the clergy was not alone in his opinion.[44] A vein of anticlericalism ran through late medieval

---

[39] R.R. Post, *Kerkelijke verhoudingen in Nederland vóór de Reformatie van ± 1500 tot ± 1580* (Utrecht-Antwerp, 1954), pp. 508–14, supplemented by *idem.*, *Kerkgeschiedenis van Nederland in de middeleeuwen*, 2 vols. (Utrecht – Antwerp, 1957), II, pp. 266–67.

[40] *The Historian and the City*, ed. O. Handlin and J. Burchard (Harvard, 1963), p. vi.

[41] P. Declerck, 'Commuun en zevengetijden in de Brugse parochiekerken', *Handelingen van het genootschap 'Société d'Émulation' te Brugge*, CVIII (1971), pp. 117–43; A. Viane, 'Lichten op rood', *Biekorf*, LXIV (1963), pp. 275–76.

[42] *The Travel Journal of Antonio de Beatis: Germany, Switzerland, the Low Countries, France and Italy, 1517–1518* (Hakluyt Society, 2nd series, no. 150), ed. J.R. Hale (London, 1979) pp. 85–103.

[43] *The Letters of Sir John Hackett*, p. 81.

[44] Cited by F.W. Oediger, 'Niederrheinische Pfarrkirchen um 1500', *Annalen des historischen Vereins für den Niederrhein*, CXXXV (1939), p. 40 fn. 171.

culture, finding expression in the plays performed by the *rederijkers*, in the paintings of Hieronymus Bosch and even in the so-called Cologne Bible, printed about 1478, in which a woodcut of the Last Judgment shows a pope, a cardinal and a bishop among those condemned to eternal perdition.[45] During the fifteenth century the ranks of the clergy had been swollen by an influx of chantry priests and unbeneficed chaplains, employed to meet the demand of the laity for obits. When the clergy from the Oude Kerk in Delft processed on Corpus Christi 1523, no fewer than 140 priests took part.[46] In addition to the secular clergy, a host of monastic and quasi-monastic communities had sprouted in the towns in the early fifteenth century. 's-Hertogenbosch, where one inhabitant in twenty belonged to a religious order in 1526, was probably exceptional,[47] but even Amsterdam counted around 1,000 religious among its 30,000 inhabitants.[48] To the magistrates the burgeoning of these religious foundations represented both a benediction and a fiscal burden. When the urban prosperity that had helped make possible these new foundations faltered about 1460,[49] the town corporations looked more critically at the terms on which the men of prayer lived in their midst. A fresh wave of municipal ordinances curbing mortmain and limiting the number of looms kept by the religious houses testifies to their concern.[50] Yet far from spurning the monastic ideal, the magistrates looked for a *modus vivendi* that, whilst encouraging the religious to pursue their vocation, would take into account the frail state of the urban economy.

[45] The intention behind such representations was not invariably hostile; the depiction of prelates among the damned underlined the moral that the sins of pride and lust were universal and no one escaped punishment. On this theme see C. Harbison, *The Last Judgement in the Sixteenth Century Europe: A Study of the Relations between Art and the Reformation* (New York, 1976), pp. 36–41. By the mid sixteenth century such statements were suppressed because they offered a hostage to Protestantism. I am indebted to David Freedberg of the Courtauld Institute of Art for alerting me to the following particularly neat illustration of this shift of official opinion. In 1524–25 Jan Provost was paid by the civic authorities of Bruges for a 'Last Judgment' to hang in the *schepenzaal*. This showed a cart carrying clergy and a monk with a naked lady on his shoulders among the damned, but in 1549–50 this detail, now considered to be offensive, was removed at the behest of the magistrates; it was also conspicuously absent from the copy painted by Jacob van den Coornhuise in 1578 for the church of Sint-Donaas. M.J. Friedländer, *Early Netherlandish Painting*, 14 vols. (Leiden-Brussels, 1967–76), IXb, pp. 85–86, 114 and plates 169 and 170; in 1534 the authorities 'having', as they said, 'regard for the present time' prosecuted a painter in Amsterdam for depicting devils with cowls fishing for money, *DAN*, V, *Amsterdam (1531–1536)*, ed. A.F. Mellink (Leiden, 1985), p. 43. See below p. 105 fn.16.

[46] Oosterbaan, *De Oude Kerk*, p. 169.

[47] Van Meerendonck, *Tussen reformatie en contra-reformatie*, p. 132.

[48] Van Nierop, *Beeldenstorm en burgerlijk verzet*, p. 17.

[49] R. van Uytven, 'Politiek en economie: de crisis der late XVe eeuw in de Nederlanden', *Revue belge de philologie et d'histoire*, LIII (1975), pp. 1097–149.

[50] D. de Man, 'Maatregelen door de middeleeuwsche overheden genomen ten opzichte van het oeconomische leven der kloosterlingen en leden van congregaties', *Bijdragen voor vaderlandsche geschiedenis en oudheidkunde*, Ve reeks, VIII (1921), pp. 277–93.

This circumstance helps to explain the enthusiasm of the town magistrates for the observant movement among the friars: not only would their stricter life confer greater spiritual benefits than the unreformed conventuals, but they undertook to renounce all ownership of property.[51] Yet the spread of the observance does not seem to have brought about a lasting improvement in relations between the friars and the towns. The high expectations aroused by the reformers were not always realised, partly because many houses were dragooned into the observance. Moreover, the very success of the observant movement increased the number of foundations dependent on the alms of the townspeople. The paucity of endowments did not matter so long as the friars enjoyed the favour of the lower orders, but this could not be taken for granted, as the mendicants in 's-Hertogenbosch found to their cost in 1525. In the late middle ages relations between the town corporations and the friars had usually been cordial: magistrates acted as *procuratores* for the mendicant orders and eminent townspeople sought burial in the friary churches. When a gap opened up between the religious values of the better educated burghers and the more conservative Franciscans – in Bruges, Ghent and Amsterdam – the friars had good reason to feel threatened.

The formation of 'humanist Christianity',[52] which stressed an interior, sober piety, sustained by Bible-reading and systematic expository preaching in preference to the exempla, was bound up with the reform of the grammar schools. Besides improving a student's command of classical Latin, the authors of the new textbooks aimed to bring him to a fuller understanding of *sacrae litterae*. Erasmus, through his *Enchiridion militis christiani* and *Novum Testamentum*, which were significantly the first of his works to be translated into Dutch, did much to shape this 'humanist Christianity'; his *Colloquia* made his adversaries, especially the obscurantists among the mendicants, appear ridiculous to the youth reading them at school.[53] By the second and third decades of the sixteenth

[51] Post, *Kerkgeschiedenis van Nederland*, II, pp. 154–59.

[52] J. IJsewijn, 'The Coming of Humanism to the Low Countries', *Itinerarium Italicum: The Profile of the Italian Renaissance in the Mirror of its European Transformation*, ed. H.A. Oberman and T.A. Brady, Jr. (Leiden, 1975), p. 224.

[53] Erasmus's *Colloquies* were blamed by one prelate for the contempt in which young men of law held the clergy: Moreau, *Histoire du protestantisme à Tournai*, p. 134, fn. 1; Erasmus's ridicule of pilgrimages was held responsible for the decline in the numbers of pilgrims to the Holy Land, S.P. Wolfs, 'Dominican en de *Colloquia* van Erasmus', *NAK*, LXI (1981), p. 67, fn. 157.

[54] R.R. Post, *Scholen en onderwijs in Nederland gedurende de middeleeuwen* (Utrecht-Antwerp, 1954), p. 146.

[55] For Greek and Hebrew in Haarlem and Amsterdam see H.J. de Jonge, '*Caro in spiritum*: Delenus en zijn uitleggingen van Joh. VI:51', *De geest in het geding: Opstellen aangeboden aan J.A. Oosterbaan*, ed. I.B. Horst *et al.* (Alphen aan den Rijn, 1978), pp. 147–48; for Bruges, A. Dewitte, 'Het humanisme te Brugge: Een overtrokken begrip?', *Handelingen van de Koninklijke Zuidnederlandse maatschappij voor taal- en letterkunde en geschiedenis*, XXVII (1973), pp. 7–8; for the Westkwartier, Decavele, *Dageraad*, I, pp. 106–7.

century the rising generation of jurists, schoolmasters, clergy and urban patricians was being educated along Erasmian lines. School syllabuses were purged of the grammarians scorned by Murmellius and Erasmus.[54] Greek, and occasionally Hebrew, was on offer not only in the Trilingual College at Leuven, but in Amsterdam, Haarlem and Bruges, and even in many of the smaller towns in the Flemish Westkwartier.[55] Before long humanist scholars began to enter the service of the most important towns.[56]

In 1517 Erasmus still looked forward to the time when the *philosophia Christi* would dispel religious superstition. These bright hopes faded when he found himself entangled in the Lutheran controversy. Though 'magister Erasmus' escaped censure in 1519, when the theologians of Leuven condemned Luther, the conservatives continued to insist that he, and those who shared his religious outlook, were Lutherans at heart. On that account the Dominicans in the province of *Germania Inferior* were forbidden to read Erasmus in 1531 and the Crutched Friars followed suit in 1534.[57] Nothing Erasmus said or wrote could allay the suspicions of the conservatives. When Leo X published *Exsurge domine* in 1520 and Charles V obediently enforced the bull in his hereditary territories with a series of bookburnings and edicts, those humanists who believed that on certain cardinal matters Erasmus and Luther spoke with one voice,[58] had somehow to demonstrate their orthodoxy without relinquishing their principles. Had not both men prized the vernacular Scriptures, above all the epistles of Paul, and condemned a religion of outward observance? Grapheus, the humanist secretary to the magistrates of Antwerp, could write in 1521: 'The gospel has been reborn and Paul brought to life again, thanks to the writings of Luther and others.'[59] It was naturally difficult for these to sympathise with the restrictions placed on Bible study. In 1525 the authorities forbade meetings where the Scriptures

---

[56] *E.g.*, Frans van Craneveld, pensionary of Bruges, Pieter Gillis and Cornelius Grapheus, clerks to the Antwerp council, and Jacob Battus, secretary of Bergen-op-Zoom. In 1533 Ieper sponsored the Dutch translation of Vives's *De subventione pauperum* to win support for its controversial ordinance on poor relief. In Holland humanists like Quirinus Talesius, Dirck Volckertsz. Coornhert and Jan van Hout acted as town secretaries.

[57] *Acta capitulorum provinciae germaniae inferioris ordinis fratrum praedicatorum ab anno MDXV usque MDLIX*, ed. S.P. Wolfs, OP (The Hague, 1964), p. 112; P. van den Bosch, 'De bibliotheken van de kruisherenkloosters in de Nederlanden vóór 1550', *Archief- en bibliotheekwezen in België*, Extranummer XI, *Studies over boekenbezit en boekengebruik in de Nederlanden vóór 1600* (Brussels, 1974), p. 579.

[58] J. Trapman, *De Summa der godliker scrifturen* (1523) (Leiden, 1978), p. 117.

[59] *CD*, IV, p. 106. In 1522 an evangelical schoolmaster at Delft, writing to Caspar Hedio, accused Erasmus of being a nicodemite, see D.P. Oosterbaan, 'School en kerk in het middeleeuwse Delft', *Spiegel der historie*, I (1966), p. 113, yet Dürer, on hearing a rumour of Luther's death in 1521, believed Erasmus might take up the Wittenberger's struggle, see A. Dürer, *Diary of his Journey to the Netherlands, 1520–1521*, ed. J.-A. Goris and G. Marlier (London, 1971), pp. 90–93.

were discussed; a year later vernacular Bibles with tendentious prologues and glosses were ordered to be burnt. Rumour had it that the laity were forbidden to read the Scriptures altogether. The allegation was ground-less, but given the hostility of conservative churchmen it must have seemed plausible.[60] Monasticism also came under sharp attack, from humanists and evangelicals alike, and many deserted the religious houses on the pretext of 'christian liberty'.[61]

As already observed, the friars had special cause for alarm. Not only was their religious calling disparaged; their way of life was called into question by the new ordinances then being introduced in certain Flemish towns for the relief of the poor. Even though the mendicant orders were exempted from the regulations against indiscriminate alms-giving, the friars felt threatened by a society which no longer associated poverty with holiness. Nor could they be blind to the evangelical teaching which represented them less as apostles to the urban poor than as parasites. In reaction the friars struck out wildly at both Luther and Erasmus, roundly condemning as heretical any change contrary to the interests of the clergy, even where no matter of doctrine was at issue.[62]

The religious ferment that characterised the 1520s proceeded from the concurrence of several, initially unrelated, tendencies. Among the educated urban classes, respect for the piety of the late middle ages weakened as christian humanism penetrated the schools. Anticlericalism itself had been sharpened by the frequent refusal of the secular clergy and the monasteries to contribute to the excises levied on the laity, at a time when many towns were in decline. In the early sixteenth century the process known to German historians as the *Verbürgerlichung des Kirchen-wesens* was hastened by schemes to place poor relief under the supervision of the magistrates. There was no necessary connection between Protest-antism and christian humanism, anticlericalism or laicisation but there were, as the conservatives instinctively appreciated, points of contact. In practice it was almost impossible to tell whether those who ransacked the religious houses in the 1520s were impelled by hatred of the clergy, the lure of food and drink, heresy or some combination of these. Even if the intentions of the assailants were uncomplicated by ideology, those in

---

[60] *CD*, V, p. 350.

[61] In 1521 two anti-monastic works were published, the anonymus *Lamentationes Petri* at Zwolle and the late medieval treatise *De libertate christiana* by Johannes Pupper von Goch, which Grapheus had published for the first time. On this theme see J. Trapman, *De Summa*, pp. 24–26, 107–9.

[62] Decavele, *Dageraad*, I, pp. 107–36. In 1526 the Spanish humanist Johannes Vives remarked that 'nowadays some people label anything unfamiliar as heretical', *Literae virorum eruditorum ad Franciscanum Craneveldium, 1522–1528*, ed. H. de Vocht (Leuven, 1928), p. 478. For other examples of the indiscriminate use of 'heresy' and 'heretical' by conservatives see L.J.A. van de Laar, 'De opkomst van de reformatie in 's-Hertogenbosch, *c.* 1525–1565', *AGKKN*, XX (1978), p. 136.

authority, prompted by fear and suspicion, were likely to interpret such acts as the work of heretics. It is no less difficult to determine whether those who criticised the monastic vocation had been influenced by Erasmus or by Luther. Burghers who demanded sermons based on the Bible might easily be converted to the principle of *sola scriptura*, while those who resented the privileged position enjoyed by the clergy in the towns could discover in Luther's assertion that 'baptism, gospel and faith alone make men religious' a theological solution to their problems.

Such confusion helps to explain the erratic policy pursued by the magistrates of Amsterdam towards the religious dissidents in their town. Although the central government had been irritated by the nonchalant treatment of heretics in Amsterdam ever since 1525, it could do little but issue reprimands, for the corporation formed a self-perpetuating clique. Moreover, the post of *schout*, which ordinarily would have been in the gift of Brussels, had been leased to the town. The officer at this critical time made no secret of his interest in the new religious ideas: Mr. Jan Hubrechtsz. had read books by Melanchthon and discussed points of Scripture with a priest who had sat at the feet of Luther. Not surprisingly, the edicts were enforced with little enthusiasm during his time in office; it was indeed alleged that the *schout* tipped off notorious heretics so that they might evade arrest.[63] The *schout* moreover had the support of at least some magistrates. These were responsible, so it was later claimed, for advancing clergy of dubious orthodoxy to benefices under their control. To make way for one such chaplain, a loyal Catholic priest had been ousted and the corporation had agreed that his successor need celebrate mass only as often as he wished. Nor was their choice of schoolmasters any more satisfactory in the eyes of conservatives, for they appointed two humanists with strong evangelical leanings. The magistrates made no secret of their aversion from the execution of heretics. After certain Anabaptists from Amsterdam had been executed at The Hague in 1531 on the orders of the provincial council, one burgomaster told government officers that no more heretics would be delivered to 'the butcher's block'. Disgruntled conservatives complained that unless one took the side of the Lutherans one would find no favour with the magistrates of Amsterdam.[64]

At first the religious dissidents did not leave the Catholic church. They sought out the sermons of well-disposed clerics and made their confessions to sympathetic or undemanding priests. As early as 1523, it is true, clandestine meetings took place in private houses in the town, and at these the Scriptures would be read and discussed; but such exercises

---

[63] A.F. Mellink, *Amsterdam en de wederdopers in de zestiende eeuw* (Nijmegen, 1978), pp. 10–11. Additional information about Jan Hubrechtsz.'s evangelical sympathies is given in the sentence of 1540, when he was banished, ARAG, Hof van Holland, 5654 fo. 42v-45v.

[64] Cornelius, *Geschichte des münsterischen Aufruhrs*, II, pp. 403–13.

supplemented, rather than replaced, the mass.[65] As opposition to the
mass intensified, some evangelicals began after 1525 to stay away from
confession and communion, and to form rudimentary congregations.
The transition from dissent to schism was not completed overnight:
many hesitated to break with the church into which they had been
incorporated by baptism, partly out of fear for the legal consequences,
but also because they, like Calvin himself, first had to be convinced that
the evangelicals were not wilful schismatics.

Nevertheless, around 1530, religious dissent in Amsterdam began to
attract popular support. Among the many sympathisers of radical reform
there developed a separated brotherhood, with an inchoate church
order. Preachers were commissioned, alms distributed to the needy by
deacons, baptism on confession administered to those who abjured the
Roman faith and the Lord's Supper commemorated: a counter-church
was born. Melchior Hoffman's proclamation of the Second Coming and
the expectation that only the regenerate would be saved in the Day of
the Lord induced a state of eschatological excitement in Amsterdam. By
late 1533 the city was in the grip of a religious hysteria which might be
compared with the mood in towns like Bruges and Tournai at the height
of the flagellant movements in the wake of the Black Death.

The reasons for the remarkable metamorphosis that dissent underwent
in Holland in these years are still debated by historians. The strongholds
of the Anabaptists in the northern part of the county, Leiden, Amsterdam and Waterland and the Zaanstreek, were acutely sensitive to any
adverse change in the pattern of trade. It so happened that both the
cloth industry of Leiden and the grain trade of Amsterdam were
disrupted at this time, creating widespread unemployment and a sense of
insecurity.[66] According to the government, it was the 'gens non letterez,
povres, mécanicques' who were most susceptible to the apocalyptic
tidings.[67] Such an impression is reinforced by an examination of the
occupations of those who came to the notice of the courts during 1534–
35 for their part in the Anabaptist movement in Amsterdam. In these two
years 178 individuals were tried: twenty by the *Hof van Holland* and the
remainder by the magistrates of Amsterdam. At least seven of these
appeared on two separate occasions. The occupation of seventy-nine of
the 171 different dissidents, of whom the great majority were Anabaptists,
can be discovered with some confidence. Nineteen made a living in

[65] Mellink, *Amsterdam en de wederdopers*, p. 12; *CD*, IV, pp. 259–61; V, 237–42.

[66] A.F. Mellink, *De wederdopers in de noordelijke Nederlanden, 1531–1544* (Groningen-
Djakarta, 1953), pp. 1–19.

[67] Cited by H. Pirenne, *Histoire de Belgique*, 6 vols. (Brussels, 1900–29), III, p. 116. In
Amsterdam a distinction was drawn in the 1530s between the *sacramentisten*, who found
some support among the propertied classes, and the penniless Anabaptists. *E.g.* ARAG,
Stukken afkomstig van ambtenaren van het centraal bestuur, 93, letters dated 15 and 24
March 1535.

metalworking (cutlers, glassblowers, armourers, smiths, potters, pin-makers and pewterers); sixteen in the clothing sector (tailors, cobblers, shoemakers, furriers, pursemakers, secondhand clothes' dealers) twelve in the textile industry (fullers, dyers, weavers, shearmen, sailmakers, card and combmakers), ten in the building trades (slaters, sawyers, carpenters). We also find five bakers and five pedlars as well as the odd basketmaker, bookbinder, carrier, and lighterman. But the liberal professions, and especially the clergy, so prominent among the dissidents a few years earlier, were conspicuously under-represented among the Anabaptists of Amsterdam, though several still entertained evangelical notions. The convicted dissidents included sixty-two women some of whom evidently worked as maidservants, seamstresses and spinners, but as the sparse references in the sources do not indicate on what basis they were employed, we have only counted the handful who apparently gained their livelihood by the practice of some trade or craft.[68] Anabaptism in Wurttem-berg has been called 'a movement of the non-intellectual classes', and the same could be said of its counterpart in Amsterdam.[69] The Anabaptists inhabited the twilight world of back alleys, cheap lodgings and inns and they often held their meetings on the edge of the town. Unlike the Reformed Protestants of 1566 they made few converts among the wealthy merchants living in the fashionable Warmoesstraat. More than half of those prosecuted had apparently been born outside Amsterdam. Some, of course, had only recently arrived in readiness for a rising planned for May 1535; others may have been victims of the courts' notorious bias against strangers. It is quite possible that the large immigrant population was predisposed to religious radicalism. Drawn to the city in the hope of employment, they missed the stability furnished by family ties and local tradition. Such people might find the prospect of the Second Coming more inviting than those with a greater social and material stake in the existing order: most of them had, as the government discovered to its chagrin when it confiscated their property, little to lose.[70]

[68] The list of convicted dissidents is taken from G. Grosheide, *Bijdrage tot de geschiedenis der Anabaptisten in Amsterdam* (Hilversum, 1933), but the information about their occupations is taken from *DAN*, V, *Amsterdam (1531–1536)*, ed. A.F. Mellink (Leiden, 1985), occasionally supplemented by the list of heretics then executed in ARAG, Rekeningen 4460. For another analysis which employs slightly different data see G.K. Waite, 'The Anabaptist Movement in Amsterdam and the Netherlands, 1531–1535: An Initial Investigation into its Genesis and Social Dynamics', *Sixteenth Century Journal*, XVII (1987), pp. 249–65. Some of those convicted earned their living by engaging in two occupations.

[69] C.P. Clasen, 'The Sociology of Swabian Anabaptism', *Church History*, XXXII (1963), p. 154.

[70] The disposal of the assets of convicted religious dissidents proved of little financial benefit to the state. The net profit to the fisc from the confiscated estates of heretics between 1525 and 1535 amounted to less than 990 Holland £. *i.e.* 4.7 per cent of the total sum fetched by the sales of property, Grosheide, *Bijdrage tot de geschiedenis der anabaptisten*, p. 85.

The social composition of religious radicalism at Amsterdam, when analysed, confirms Pirenne's famous description of Anabaptism as 'the Protestantism of the poor'.[71] Yet the upper reaches of urban society, at least in Deventer and Amsterdam, were more in touch with the radicals and less hostile to their theology than one might suppose from the harsh punishment meted out to the Anabaptists by the magistrates in 1535.[72] Jan Beukelsz., better known as John of Leyden, was received at table by one burgomaster; another member of the corporation died a martyr to the Anabaptist cause; still others had relations among the heretics.[73] Even the seizure of Münster and an Anabaptist plot to take Amsterdam in 1534 failed to persuade the magistrates to abandon their humanist and evangelically-coloured Catholicism. As late as February 1535 certain Anabaptists could still address the burgomasters as 'our brethren'. While such confidence was surely misplaced, the claim did not seem at all fanciful to the critics of the corporation. But that rash assertion, uttered in the hearing of the *procureur-generaal*, may have been the Anabaptists' undoing.[74] To scotch so damaging a rumour the magistrates were compelled to make a volte-face. Any lingering sympathy for the Anabaptists evaporated in May 1535, when the hotheads tried to seize control of Amsterdam. For the past decade the central government had been convinced that the latitudinarianism of certain magistrates would lead to disorder and events had proved it right. The political logic was inescapable. Between February and July 1535 sixty-two heretics were executed at Amsterdam, and many more banished, as the chastened corporation strove to impress Brussels with a belated display of exemplary severity.[75] In vain, for those most compromised by their earlier irresolution were driven from office in 1538, and for the next forty years a staunchly orthodox oligarchy governed the city. Throughout the county of Holland Anabaptists were hunted down: between 1534 and 1536 more than 200 are known to have been put to death in a wave of repression whose severity surpassed even that endured by the Protestants of Flanders from

---

[71] Pirenne, *Histoire de Belgique*, III, p. 117.

[72] The Deventer patrician family Van Wynssem included several convinced Anabaptists, J. de Hullu, *Bescheiden betreffende de geschiedenis der hervorming in Overijssel: Deventer 1522–1546* (Deventer, 1899), pp. 144–50, 235.

[73] Mellink, *Amsterdam en de wederdopers*, pp. 27–28, 42. At Münster the wealthier burghers were over-represented among the local Anabaptists, K.-H. Kirchhoff, *Die Täufer in Münster, 1534–35* (Münster, 1973), p. 42.

[74] Mellink, *Amsterdam en de wederdopers*, pp. 48–49.

[75] Grosheide, *Bijdrage tot de geschiedenis der anabaptisten*, pp. 60–61, 304–7. Among the fugitives was a certain Mr. Wouter Henricz. *hebreeuwsmeester*, who later entered the service of Henry VIII as *biblioscopus*. For the career of this evangelical humanist better known as Gualterus Delenus see De Jonge, '*Caro in spiritum*', pp. 146–51.

1559 to 1564, when 120 were executed.[76] The town magistrates were by now thoroughly alarmed and they prosecuted Jorists and Batenburgers ruthlessly in 1539 and again in 1544. For at least a decade heresy in Holland was equated with Anabaptism, and Anabaptism in turn with disorder, even rebellion. For almost all this period the provincial States, so loud in the 1520s in the defence of privileges allegedly infringed by the antiheresy legislation, kept an eloquent silence.[77]

Nevertheless, by the middle of the century the governing classes in Holland had lost their dread of heresy. The pace of magisterial repression slackened palpably after 1553, despite the insistence of Charles V, and later Philip II, that the government's draconian edicts should be enforced to the letter. Once more, militant Catholics among the magistrates found themselves on the defensive. The conservatives nourished dark suspicions about the orthodoxy of prominent burghers in the towns of Holland. In the most sensational case the *schout* of Amsterdam was eventually acquitted of heresy and of failing to prosecute Anabaptists, while the authors of these charges were themselves found guilty of suborning witnesses, perjury and slander.[78]

Not surprisingly this verdict, which shows how the obsession with heresy had faded amongst the judges, cast the conservatives into despair. In the States of Holland, too, the deputies from the town corporations again ventilated grievances over the methods used to suppress heresy. The more dispassionate treatment of heresy owed much to the changed nature of urban dissent. Among the Anabaptists the pacific teachings of Menno Simons gradually prevailed and the fanaticism of earlier years ebbed away. The refusal of Anabaptists to bear arms in the town militias and to take the oath required of burghers, coupled with their rejection of the office of magistrate as unchristian, limited their appeal to the *kleine luyden* in the towns, whereas by contrast Reformed Protestantism respected the ethos of the burghers. In the late 1550s this form of religious dissent began to make some headway among the merchants and artisans in Amsterdam and the smaller towns of the Noorderkwartier. In the broader perspective of the Netherlands Reformation the towns of

[76] According to a list, inserted loose in ARAG, Rekeningen van de rekenkamer, 4460, 126 persons were condemned to death 'vuyt saicke van lutherie ende anabaptisterie' by the *schepenbanken* between 1534 and *c.* 1537. As this list was intended for the *rekenkamer*, it includes several natives of Holland, who were executed outside the county. Inexplicably it omits five Anabaptists executed at Hoorn in 1535. For the repression in Flanders see Decavele, *Dageraad*, II, p. 57. For the relative severity of the persecutions in Holland, Flanders and the Walloon towns see below p. 99.

[77] For a lone defence by Amsterdam *in casu* its privilege of limited confiscation see, *Resolutiën van de Staten van Holland*, 18 April 1537, p. 281.

[78] J.J. Woltjer, 'Het conflict tussen Willem Bardes en Hendrick Dirckszoon', *BMGN*, LXXXVI (1971), pp. 178–99. Around 1558 one Edelinck Vrericxz. called Hoorn 'jongen Eembden' and later accused prominent inhabitants of that town of attending conventicles, see RANH, ORA, 4153, fo. 334, 408, 409v, 410, 415, 416; *ibid.*, 4515, fo. 108–11v.

Holland had by then, or perhaps even earlier, ceased to play a central part. The decisive confrontation was taking place in the southern provinces.

The towns of Brabant and Flanders had been little affected by the religious agitation that had convulsed the northern provinces during 1534–35. Most Anabaptists in the south at this time came from Holland or, in the case of Antwerp, from Maastricht and they were flushed out before they could build up a following.[79] Because the settled political order was not at this stage menaced by the heretics, the magistrates had less reason to agree with those zealots who pressed for the extirpation of religious dissent, heedless of the risk to their trade or privileges. Perhaps, too, because of their great civic awareness, symbolised by their campaniles and ornate gothic townhalls, they were determined that no ecclesiastical courts should encroach on their liberties. In Bruges and Ghent, moreover, the cultivated political and intellectual elites had been attracted by the biblical and eirenic Catholicism of Erasmus and Cassander – so much so, indeed as to bring them into conflict with the friars, who obstinately defended scholastic theology and late medieval piety.[80] For these reasons the triumph of the conservatives that occurred in Amsterdam in the wake of the Anabaptist challenge was postponed.

As already observed clergy, lawyers, schoolmasters and printers were to the fore in the reforming circles of the 1520s. They continued to dominate the evangelical movement at Ghent until at least 1545.[81] Indeed the Reformation at Leuven was confined almost entirely to such groups. Between 1530 and 1550 some eighty persons were prosecuted for heresy and related offences: to a man, they were skilled craftsmen, leading burghers and graduates of the university.[82] Protestantism failed to develop a popular base here – a striking fact because Leuven suffered a severe economic decline in the sixteenth century and its streets swarmed with paupers and unemployed.

The religious issues of the day were brought to the notice of the townspeople in Flanders and Brabant through the morality plays performed by the influential Chambers of Rhetoric – the *rederijkerskamers*. From conventional satires of clerical avarice some chambers proceeded to question the veneration shown to images and relics. If explicit statements in favour of Protestant theology are rare, many of the plays betray evangelical sympathies by their appeal to Scripture and their Christo-

---

[79] Decavele, *Dageraad*, I, 299–32 1; A.F. Mellink, 'Antwerpen als anabaptistencentrum tot ± 1550', *NAK*, n.s., XLVI (1964), pp. 155–68.

[80] Decavele, *Dageraad*, I, pp. 53–192.

[81] *ibid*, I, pp. 524–26.

[82] R. van Uytven, 'Bijdrage tot de sociale geschiedenis van de protestanten te Leuven in de eerste helft der XVIe eeuw', *Mededelingen van de geschied- en oudheidkundige kring voor Leuven en omgeving*, III (1963), pp. 3–38.

centric bias. This appears transparently in the plays presented at a celebrated national contest in Ghent during 1539. On that occasion the Chambers were asked to take as their theme 'the best consolation for a dying man'. Remarkably, not one of the nineteen companies so much as mentioned the sacrament of extreme unction: instead, the dying were urged to put their trust in Christ.[83] The Erasmian flavour of this advice alarmed conservative churchmen, who were quick to discern in such neglect of the sacraments a dangerous dilution of the Catholic faith. Some plays also incurred ecclesiastical disapproval because they encouraged people to read the Scriptures on their own. When in 1585 the bishop of Tournai's censor banned a play, based on the Book of Samuel, he did so 'chiefly because the actors as well as the spectators buy Bibles in the French language and thumb through them'.[84] Yet long before then the chambers had gone into decline, partly because of the growing preference among the educated for *le théâtre scolaire*, but also because they had been subjected to a stifling supervision by the central government and the church, both fearful of their contamination by heterodox ideas.[85]

Somewhere between 1545 and 1550 the urban Reformation in Flanders acquired a more popular and organised character. Following a savage bout of persecution during 1544–45 it seemed as though interest in the Reformation would be confined in Ghent, as in Leuven, to the intelligentsia and the great merchants, who retreated into a 'sort of salon Protestantism'.[86] If some were prompted to cloak their religious beliefs in a discreet silence before the world, others were compelled to seek safety abroad in the churches of refuge. From 1556 onwards a few returned as ministers to preach doctrines that may be described quite properly as 'Reformed Protestant'. Meanwhile in Bruges, where dissent attracted more support among the artisans than in Ghent, humble French-speaking workers began to propagate Calvinism among their fellows.[87] By 1560 the chief towns of Flanders possessed organised congregations. What is more, they were in correspondence with their coreligionists in Antwerp and the Walloon towns, as well as with London

[83] Decavele, *Dageraad*, I, pp. 199–200.
[84] R. Lebègue, 'L'évolution du théâtre dans les provinces du Nord' *La Renaissance dans les provinces du Nord (Picardie-Artois-Flandre-Brabant-Hainaut)*, ed. F. Lesure (Paris, 1956), p. 126. The custom of electing abbots of misrule and boy bishops also fell victim to the new censoriousness. In the context of the Protestant repudiation of transubstantiation and the sacrifice of the mass, the element of parody in these mock rituals shocked conservatives.
[85] Nor did the *rederijkerskamers* survive any better in the northern Netherlands, where the Reformed synods disliked their meddling in sacred matters. The contribution the rhetoricians had made to undermining the religious values of the old faith was soon forgotten. J.G.C.A. Briels, '"Reyn genuecht": Zuidnederlandse kamers van Rhetorica in Noordnederland, 1585–1630', *Bijdragen tot de geschiedenis*, LVII (1974), pp. 4–15, 38–49.
[86] Decavele, *Dageraad*, I, p. 322.
[87] *ibid*, I, p. 339.

and Emden. The growth of confessional Protestantism in Flanders after 1550 was further assisted by the arrival of Mennonite 'elders' from the northern Netherlands. And yet, though the Protestant communities in the larger Flemish towns were becoming bolder and more self-aware, they could not match the daring of their coreligionists in the industrialised countryside of the Westkwartier. In the centres of the new draperies – Hondschoote, Belle, Armentières – heresy commanded such massive support that it seemed as though Catholicism in these towns would be entirely effaced.

Having acquired a confessional identity, the Protestant communities in the southern towns had to consider on what terms they should live, as Calvin put it, 'among the papists'. In the Reformer's opinion the choice before the faithful Christian was disconcertingly stark: he might remain at home, provided he shunned all contact with idolatry, or he could withdraw to some place where the gospel was professed publicly. Such uncompromising counsel dismayed the Reformed Protestants of Tournai and Valenciennes in 1543–44, for those who failed to attend mass or refused to have their infants baptised by the priests courted banishment and even death.[88] For so long as Reformed congregations lived 'under the cross', these issues would preoccupy their synods.

Probably only a quite small proportion of those well-disposed to the new doctrines were prepared to abjure their Roman faith and place themselves under the discipline of the consistory. Around the small core of committed Reformed Protestants, a much larger number of *prudents* coalesced.[89] These preferred to profess their faith in their hearts, but they would not as a rule join the congregation for worship. Relations between the *fidèles* and the *prudents* were sometimes strained, not least because the *prudents* included many *gens de qualité*, who hesitated to risk their lives and property, though the intelligentsia may also have felt some uneasiness about the growing dogmatism of the Reformed leadership.

At Antwerp social differences between the members of the Reformed congregation and fellow-travellers, who remained on the fringes, gave rise to a serious dispute during 1557–58. The newly-formed congregation plainly expected their minister, Adriaen van Haemstede, to serve only

---

[88] Moreau, *Histoire du protestantisme à Tournai*, pp. 90–91.

[89] When the Reformed achieved a quasi-official status in 1566 some *prudents* entered the consistories. Until then these bodies had been dominated by *gens de petite qualité*. E.g. the consistory at Valenciennes was reinforced in 1566 by several prominent *marchands et bourgeois*, P. Beuzart, *La répression à Valenciennes après les troubles religieux de 1566* (Paris, 1930), p. 119. At Middelburg the original consistory had been composed of those 'who had nothing to lose', whereas the new consistory, responsible significantly for policy, had a leavening of more respectable burghers, J. van Vloten, *Onderzoek van 's konings wege ingesteld omtrent de Middelburgsche beroerten van 1566 en 1567* (Utrecht, 1873), pp. 70, 128, 160. Cf. A.J.M. Beenakker, *Breda in de eerste storm van de opstand: Van ketterij tot beeldenstorm* (Tilburg, 1971), pp. 61–62.

those who had broken with the Roman church. The elders in the consistory were therefore indignant when Van Haemstede insisted that he had an obligation to preach the gospel outside the closed circle of the congregation. What irked the elders was Van Haemstede's willingness to preach discreetly to the rich, who had refused to join the congregation for fear, so it was alleged, of being delated to the authorities by spies among the poorer brethren.[90] In this way the repression aggravated the social differences among the Protestants in the southern towns. If the dissidents in Holland were exempt from such pressures until the coming of Alva and the creation of the Council of Troubles,[91] this may be attributed to the lax enforcement of the edicts after 1553 and the slower growth of confessional consciousness among the heretics in that county.

The course of Protestantism in the Walloon towns differs so markedly from that observed in Flanders and Brabant as to constitute yet another pattern of urban reformation. In the first place Anabaptism made little or no headway in the French-speaking towns. Although a small Anabaptist congregation existed at Tournai, its members were either Dutch-speaking immigrants to the town or else Tournaisiens with close family or professional ties with Ghent, Kortrijk and Antwerp.[92] The failure of Anabaptists to surmount the language barrier, in marked contrast to the Reformed, who evidently found this no obstacle, may be attributed to the relatively humbler background of its preachers, few of whom had an adequate command of French.[93]

Even in 1566, that *annus mirabilis* in the calendar of the Reformation in the Low Countries, the hegemony of the Catholic church was over-thrown, and then but for a season, in only two substantial towns, Tournai and Valenciennes. Here the stampede into Protestantism, followed by the near elimination of heresy once these towns had been brought to heel in 1567, recalls the violent fluctuations of religious allegiance observed in certain French towns in the same period. On the eve of the

[90] A.J. Jelsma, *Adriaan van Haemstede en zijn martelaarsboek* (The Hague, 1970), pp. 28–30, 36–42, 49–60. At Ghent a schoolmaster also insisted on the need to evangelise outside the congregation, Decavele, *Dageraad*, I, p. 323. As Professor Roelink once remarked, 'The class conflict was found within, as much as outside, Calvinism', 'Het Calvinisme' *AGN*, IV, p. 287.

[91] *E.g.* H.J. Jaanus, *Hervormd Delft ten tijde van Arent Cornelisz., 1573–1608* (Amsterdam, 1950), p. 26. A similar problem seems to have arisen among the evangelicals at Groningen in 1560–61. Some of these had declined to attend the meetings, alleging that 'one could obtain salvation outside the same', J. Lindeboom, 'De kerkhervorming in de provincie Groningen', *Groningsche volksalmanak* (1943), p. 17.

[92] Moreau, *Histoire du protestantisme à Tournai*, pp. 118–20, 199–205. The thirteen Anabaptists, executed at Lille in 1563, were natives of Halewijn (Halluin), a Dutch-speaking village in the province of Lille-Douai-Orchies, M.P. Willems-Closset,'Le protest-antisme à Lille jusqu'à la veille de la révolution des Pays-Bas, 1521–1565', *Revue du nord*, LII (1970), p. 215.

[93] One leading Flemish Anabaptist admitted he could not help some French-speaking coreligionists 'on account of the language', Decavele, *Dageraad*, I, p. 448.

civil wars in France, around one-fifth of the inhabitants of Rouen and one-third in the case of Lyon embraced Protestantism, but many of these defected after the massacres had demoralised the Calvinist congregations.[94] In more important respects also the Reformation in these Walloon towns seems to have followed in the train of French Protestantism. Until 1534 the *luthériens* of Tournai kept personal links with evangelical circles in Paris. When in need of counsel or succour the Protestants from the southern Netherlands turned, like their French coreligionists, to Strassburg and, after the Lutherans gained the ascendancy in that city, to Geneva, though some refugees from the Walloon towns also forged links with the Protestant churches in the Lower Rhineland.[95]

Towards the close of the Habsburg-Valois wars the heretics grew more audacious. On Christmas Day 1554 Bertrand Le Blas sealed his fate by snatching the host from the priest and denouncing it as idolatrous. In 1561 psalm-singing crowds filed through the streets of Tournai and Valenciennes in closely concerted *chanteries*, similar to the demonstrations staged in Lyon ten years earlier. When two noted Calvinists were on the point of execution in April 1562 at Valenciennes, the crowd rioted and released the prisoners, and in the following year many townspeople, some of them armed, flocked to the public *prêches* in imitation of their coreligionists across the border. Taunts and threats against the Catholic clergy also recall the 'triumphalism' displayed by Parisian Protestants before the outbreak of hostilities, though the Catholic townspeople, unlike their counterparts in the towns of northern France, were as yet too cowed to meet insult with injury.[96] The contrast between the strongly protestantised towns and a countryside still preponderantly Catholic is more typical of France north of the Loire than of the Low Countries. The Reformation made headway among the rural population in the Low Countries, where proximity to a large market-town or the presence of the fisheries and textile industry challenged the supremacy of agriculture, as in the Flemish Westkwartier and its Walloon adjunct, the Pays de

[94] Based on P. Benedict, 'Catholics and Huguenots in Sixteenth Century Rouen: The Demographic Effects of the Religious Wars', *French Historical Studies*, IX (1975), pp. 223–26; N.Z. Davis, 'Strikes and Salvation at Lyon', *Society and Culture in Early Modern France* (London, 1975), p. 1; J. Estèbe, *Tocsin pour un massacre: La saison de Saint-Bathélemy* (Paris, 1968), ch. IX.

[95] Moreau, *Histoire du protestantisme à Tournai*, pp. 142–43; between 1557 and 1559 nine residents of Valenciennes enrolled as *habitants* of Geneva, yet only two Protestants from Flanders had registered before 1566, P.F. Geisendorf, *Le livre des habitants de Genève*, 2 vols. (Geneva, 1957–63) and Decavele, *Dageraad*, I, p. 330.

[96] See D. Richet, 'Aspects socio-culturels des conflicts religieux à Paris dans la seconde moitié du XVIe siècle', *Annales: Economies, Sociétés, Civilisations*, XXXII (1977), pp. 764–89. A Tournaisien observed that no one molested the crowds coming away from the hedge services around the town, whereas Huguenots in France had sometimes been set upon by Catholics as they returned from the *presches*. *Mémoires de Pasquier de le Barre et de Nicholas Soldoyer pour servir à l'histoire de Tournai, 1565–1570*, ed. A. Pinchart, 2 vols. (Brussels, 1859–65), I, pp. 75–6.

l'Alleu, as well as in Voorne and Waterland in Holland. Yet only in Artois and Hainaut were the rural smallholders prepared to stand up for their Catholic convictions. On more than one occasion these delated heretical assemblies to the authorities and they bloodily repulsed bands of icono-clasts in 1566, who elsewhere met little or no resistance.[97]

In both Tournai and Valenciennes the new religion exercised a strong attraction for the whole spectrum of urban society, though few clergy joined the Protestant ranks after 1531.[98] Between 1559 and 1573 some 630 persons were prosecuted as heretics or rebels in Valenciennes. The occupations of 346 are known.[99] Given the central importance of the cloth industry – there were said to be between 1,600 and 1,700 small master weavers in a population of around 12,000 – it is hardly surprising

Analysis by Occupation of those Prosecuted for Heresy and Sedition at Valenciennes, 1559–73[100]

	Number Employed	% of 346
Cloth Industry	131	37.8%
	(including 14 merchants)	
Clothing	38	10.9%
Victualling	37	10.6%
Building Trades	31	8.9%
Metalworking	23	6.6%
Other Trades/Crafts	28	8.4%
Services/Transport	24	6.9%
Merchants (unspecified)	21	6.0%
Professions	18	5.2%
Magistrates, Officials	18	5.2%

[97] *E.g. Le journal d'un bourgeois de Tournai: Le second livre des chroniques de Pasquier de le Barre: 1500–1565*, ed. G. Moreau (Brussels, 1975), pp. 414, 420–21; E. Mahieu, 'Le protestantisme à Mons des origines à 1575', *Annales du cercle archéologique de Mons*, LXVI (1966–67), pp. 180–81; J. Scheerder, *De beeldenstorm* (Bussum, 1974), pp. 20, 35, 49, 51.

[98] G. Moreau, 'La corrélation entre le milieu social et professionel et le choix de religion à Tournai', *Bronnen voor de religieuze geschiedenis van België*, pp. 289, 293.

[99] Based on P.J. Leboucq, *Histoire des troubles advenues à Valenciennes à cause des hérésies*, ed. A.P.L. de Robaulx de Soumoy (Brussels-The Hague, 1864); C. Paillard, *Histoire des troubles religieux de Valenciennes* and C. Muller, 'La réforme à Valenciennes pendant le révolution des Pays-Bas, 1565–1573' (Liège, *licence*, 1973–74). Professor Moreau kindly arranged for me to consult this thesis. No account has been taken of those prosecuted for their part in the rebellion in 1572, unless there is evidence that they had been involved in the events of 1566–67. For the rhythm of the persecutions in the Walloon towns see below p. 99 .

[100] In all 369 occupations are recorded, several having two employments or an office with a craft.

to discover that fully one-third of those prosecuted worked in this sector, the majority earning a livelihood as serge and linen weavers and wool-combers.[101] Slightly less than half were employed in the other main sectors: in the building trades, metalworking, chandlering, clothing, and victualling. The professional classes, on the other hand, were poorly represented, with only one schoolmaster and no physicians or lawyers, a fact which may reflect simply the relative absence of a vigorous intel-lectual life in Valenciennes. At Tournai the occupational profile of the dissidents was broadly similar to that found in Valenciennes, though here the *prudents* included some leading officials and lawyers.[102]

The economic and social structure of these towns provides no obvious explanation for the success enjoyed by the Reformation there. Lille, though larger, also depended on numerous small master weavers.[103] In all three towns the new draperies had been introduced and organised under guilds, which, however, enjoyed no political power.[104] Why then should Protestantism go from strength to strength in Valenciennes and Tournai, when the heretics in Lille had been forced on to the defensive by 1555? Lille, it has been suggested, was distinguished by the stability of its governing elite in which both the great merchants and the *rentiers* were represented. At Valenciennes, by contrast, the town government failed to mirror the economic hierarchy. Power remained with the *magistrat,* many of whose members were *rentiers,* despite the complaints of merchants aggrieved at their exclusion. This tension favoured Protest-antism. The ruling faction was faced with a dilemma by the antiheresy edicts. These apparently infringed the chartered privileges of Valen-ciennes: failure to uphold the privileges would leave the *magistrat* exposed to criticism from the merchants, whereas refusal to enforce the edicts would cause them to forfeit the trust of Brussels. Until December 1566 merchants and *magistrat* sank their political differences in order to forward the town's interests, but once Valenciennes was declared to be in a state of rebellion, most of the *magistrat* went, leaving the great merchants in control of the Calvinist-dominated town.[105] In other words, the Reformation at Valenciennes profited from a split between the political and mercantile elites. The history of the Reformation at Amster-dam offers a close parallel. Power was concentrated here in the hands of zealous Catholics after 1538. In 1564 this clique faced a formidable

[101] G.W. Clark, 'An Urban Study during the Revolt of the Netherlands: Valenciennes, 1540–1570' (Unpublished Ph.D. Columbia, 1972), pp. 15, 39–40.

[102] Moreau, 'La corrélation' pp. 286–99.

[103] R. Saint-Cyr Duplessis, 'Urban Stability in the Netherlands Revolution: A Comparative Study of Lille and Douai' (Unpublished Ph.D. Columbia, 1974), pp. 88–110.

[104] *ibid.*, pp. 318–30; Clark, 'An Urban Study', pp. 27, 30.

[105] Clark, 'An Urban Study', pp. 59–75, 120–30, 218–65, 364–80, 417–22.

and entrepreneurs, irritated because they could not exercise political influence commensurate with their wealth. During 1566 the Protestants and the *doleanten*, as the political dissidents in Amsterdam were known, moved closer to one another. When the ruling oligarchy was overthrown in 1578, the way was clear for the triumph of Reformed Protestantism.[106]

In both Valenciennes and Tournai the well-being of the community came to be briefly but closely identified with the cause of Reformed Protestantism. This remarkable state of affairs may be ascribed to the irritation aroused in the towns, oversensitive to outside interference, by the maladroit enforcement of the central government's policy. As early as 1544 Brussels had been concerned about the complacency of those responsible for the prosecution of the heretics.[107] Special inquisitorial commissions were sent then, and again in 1561, to sit alongside the local magistrates to ensure that the edicts were enforced punctually.[108] The crowning insult came in 1563. Angered by the insolence of the Protestants, who had organised outdoor services, Brussels concluded that the local magistrates were neither willing nor able to keep order in these strategically important frontier towns and garrisons were inflicted on both. Although calm was restored, the leading *bourgeois*, already incensed at the violation of their privileges, regarded the soldiers, and the authority they represented, with repugnance. From this perspective the inhabitants regarded the religious policy of the King as a greater threat to their privileges and property than the Protestantism of their fellow townsmen.[109]

During the winter of 1565–66 the political and religious dissidents tried to devise a common programme, based on mutual horror of that conveniently protean nightmare – the 'inquisition'. The growing political maturity of this opposition was reflected in the contemporary vocabulary, for the disaffected gentry as well as the committed Protestants came to be known collectively as the *gueux*. Only a few years earlier French Protestantism had undergone a similar metamorphosis, from which its adherents emerged as *huguenots*. We should not deceive ourselves, however, about the tensions that remained between the *gueux d'état* and the *gueux de religion*. In any case, the degree of politicisation was far from uniform: weakest in the non-patrimonial provinces, it was most advanced in Tournai and Valenciennes.

The politicisation of the Reformation that occurred in these towns can be paralleled by the case of La Rochelle. This stronghold of French Protestantism only entered into an alliance with Condé in 1568, after

---

[106] For the convergence of political and religious dissidents at Amsterdam in the 1560s see Van Nierop, *Beeldenstorm en burgerlijk verzet*, esp. ch. III.

[107] Moreau, *Histoire du protestantisme à Tournai*, p. 106.

[108] Clark, 'An Urban Study', pp. 202–24, 224–29.

[109] *ibid*, pp. 247–65.

having suffered a Catholic garrison. Traditionally the Rochelais secured their municipal autonomy by negotiation with the Crown, but in the exceptional circumstances caused by the breakdown of royal authority they were reluctantly driven to the conclusion that their privileges would be better protected by the Huguenot leader.[110] The tragedy of Valenciennes and Tournai was that at this stage William of Orange was unwilling, and Hendrik van Brederode unable, to play the role of Condé.[111] Ironically the Protestants of Valenciennes refused offers of aid from Condé in the expectation that the great nobility of the Low Countries would give them political and military support. When this failed to materialise, the Calvinist rebellion became a lost cause.

It would be foolish to suppose that the history of the urban Reformation in the Low Countries can be told in terms of the three patterns outlined here. The diversity of constitutions, and of economic and social structures, to be found among the forty or so chief towns rules that out. Besides the thriving commercial cities, there were towns that lived from the manufacture of specialised cloths. Others derived their prosperity from salt, brewing or the herring fisheries, or served as markets for the sale of dairy produce or grain. There were Hanseatic towns in the north-east, seats of government like Brussels, Mechelen and The Hague, bloated villages like Hondschoote that had grown in disorderly haste, *villes aux églises* like Utrecht, where the local gentry were entrenched in the powerful chapters. There were towns, especially in the north-east, where the guilds or burghers still retained a measure of political influence, and many more where a quite small number of closely-related families controlled the corporation. Each had its traditions and privileges, each stood in a different relationship to the central government.

By no means all these towns proved receptive to the Reformation: Douai, Arras, St. Omer, Mons, Gouda, Utrecht, Amersfoort and Groningen were, for example, only lightly affected. The urban magistrates in the Habsburg Netherlands could not permit the Protestants to worship openly even had they so wished, except when the central government was paralysed, as happened briefly in the summer of 1566. Yet neither did they respond uniformly or consistently to the religious policy of Charles V. At Mons, Lille and Douai the magistrates seem to have done the bidding of the central government, possibly because they believed that their economic interests would thus be better served. In other towns the

---

[110] J.C. Pugh Meyer, 'Reformation in La Rochelle: Religious Change, Social Stability and Political Crisis, 1500–1568' (Unpublished Ph.D.Iowa, 1977), esp. ch. IV–V.

[111] Early in 1567 Brederode was recognised by the Reformed churches of the Low Countries as their *chef*, a position reminiscent of the protector generalship to which Condé was appointed by the Reformed churches of France. See R.C. Bakhuizen van den Brink, 'Hendrik van Brederode en Willem van Oranje in 1566 en 1567', *Cartons voor de geschiedenis van den Nederlandschen vrijheidsoorlog*, 2 vols. (The Hague, 1891–8), II, pp. 184–85.

Executions for Heresy, 1524–66

	Flanders	Holland	Walloon Towns[1]
1524	1		
1525		1	
1526			
1527	1	1	
1528			1
1529		3	
1530	2	1	
1531	3	11	4
1532	2	2	
1533	3	1	6
1534	1	57	2
1535	3	125	
1536	4	24	
1537		3	
1538	10	3	
1539	2	51	
1540	3	15	1
1541	2	5	1
1542	4	4	4
1543	2		
1544	3	23	
1545	10	3	13
1546	1	4	2
1547	4	2	5
1548			1
1549	4	10	6
1550		6	1
1551	15		
1552	2	17	4
1553	12	6	1
1554	4	1	4
1555	3	2	12
1556	6		2
1557	13	3	1
1558	12	11	1
1559	20	2	1
1560	17	1	2
1561	23		16
1562	40	1	11
1563	16	1	32
1564	9	1	6
1565	3		3
1566	5		
TOTAL	265	403*	141

[1] Mons, Tournai, Valenciennes, Lille.
* This figure includes two executions which cannot be precisely dated.
Sources: J. Decavele, *De dageraad van de reformatie in Vlanderen (1520–1565)* (Brussels, 1975) II, p. 57; M.P. Willems-Closset, 'Le protestantisme à Lille jusqu'à la veille de la Révolution des Pays-Bas (1521–1565)' *Revue du Nord*, LII (1970), pp. 199–216; E. Mahieu, 'Le protestantisme à Mons des origines à 1575', *Annales du cercle archéologique de Mons*, LXVI (1965–66), pp. 129–247; G. Moreau, *Histoire du protestantisme à Tournai jusqu'à la veille de la Révolution des Pays-Bas* (Paris, 1962); M. Hodeigne, 'Le protestantisme à Valenciennes jusqu' à la vielle de la Révolution des Pays-Bas' (University of Liège *licence*, 1966–67).

magistrates effectively frustrated the antiheresy legislation out of dislike for the edicts themselves, out of fear of disorder, or occasionally out of sympathy for the religious outlook of the evangelicals. All urban magistrates alike were bound to work for the maintenance of order, to uphold the privileges, and to seek the material and spiritual well-being of their community. They judged both the Reformation and the religious policy of the government from this perspective. Opportunities for the Reformation were most favourable where and when the Protestants gained the backing of the civil authorities or, failing that, of some powerful lobby in the town. For that reason Reformed Protestantism carried the day briefly at Tournai and Valenciennes. Equally the suppression of the Reformation in these towns in 1567 revealed that Protestantism, unless it became politicised on an altogether grander scale, could not hope to succeed in the prince's despite.

5

Nonconformity among the Kleyne Luyden in the Low Countries before the Revolt

1525

Mr. Johannes Harmanni, surgeon in the town of Utrecht, aged fifty-three or thereabouts replied on oath, being examined [by the inquisition] in the vulgar tongue that: sometime ago, being afflicted by plague (*Godsgave*), he took a vow to visit Our Blessed Lady at Amersfoort. When he was about to set out to make the pilgrimage, the cooper [on trial for heresy] asked him where he was going. The witness replied that he wanted to make a pilgrimage to Amersfoort. Then the cooper said, 'What will you do there? Do you place your faith in wood and stone?' Thereupon the witness replied, 'I do not, but I believe that although the Mother of God is in heaven and exercises great power everywhere, it is her wish that she be more visited in one town than another'. Then the cooper said, 'The notions these ignorant folk have about pilgrimages and other inventions [*luyren*] are sheer nonsense'.

CD, IV, p. 373.

1534

Adriaen Pietersz. was sentenced to death by the court at Amsterdam for, among other offences, having said of the Holy Sacrament that ' "if God is there present, it would bleed when the priests break that sacrament in three pieces during the mass', adding thereby, 'fetch me fifty hosts, I will cut them in pieces with a sword; if they bleed, I will take your [*ie.* Catholic] faith" '.

DAN, V, Amsterdam (1531–1536), ed. A.F. Mellink (Leiden, 1985), p. 40.

1567

A tailor giving sworn testimony about the disturbances at 's-Hertogenbosch in 1566 stated that a certain Moyses, 'brought a large crucifix into the kitchen [of the Franciscan monastery] and threw it on the fire, saying, that he wanted to conjure the Devil out of it and [see] him fly out the chimney'.

Documents pour servir à l'histoire des troubles religieux du XVIe siècle dans le Brabant septentrional: Bois-le-Duc (1566–1570), ed. P. Cuypers-Van Velthoven (Brussels, 1858), p. 469.

It is no simple matter to discover the role of religion in the lives of Netherlanders who found themselves at odds with the Catholic church before the Revolt.[1] Since the rulers in the Low Countries strongly resisted the Reformation and persecuted the nonconformists in their dominions, those who sympathised with the evangelical theology could only give vent to their religious feelings in secret. Usually details about the practices and beliefs of the nonconformists only came to light when the authorities interrogated suspects. The earliest dissidents did not subscribe to a particular confession of faith, nor did they belong to some well-defined ecclesiastical body with a specific liturgy. They had been baptised in the Catholic church and, for the most part, they long continued to attend its services, although they also took part in conventicles, attacked the clergy and criticised aspects of the mass. With the important exception of the Anabaptists, dissent in the Low Countries lacked a corporate identity until small Reformed congregations evolved in the early part of Philip II's reign. The amorphous, doctrinally eclectic and individualistic nature of dissent before the Revolt should make us cautious about the conclusions we draw from the fragmentary evidence.

Even if we choose to interpret 'religion in everyday life' as 'popular religion', the problem of sources remains acute. Our task would have been easier if German Protestantism had been the focus of attention. Students of the German urban Reformation, 'the people's Reformation' and the 'Reformation of the common man' can call on an enviably abundant and varied range of sources: printed sermons, polemical pamphlets, illustrated broadsheets, simple catechisms and devotional manuals.[2] Although the records of popular dissent in the Low Countries are more problematic and generally less abundant, they can still, when used with care, give insights into popular religious nonconformity before the advent of Protestant churches in the Low Countries with their church orders, confessions of faith and professional ministries.

The campaigns against heresy mounted and sustained by Charles V and Philip II as well as by the prince-bishops of Utrecht and the dukes of Gelre largely explain the comparatively meagre literary and visual legacy left by the religious dissidents in the Low Countries. Between 1520 and 1540 some 170 separate vernacular pamphlets are known to have been published in the Dutch language. This total includes the writings of Anabaptists and Spiritualists as well as books, which are mentioned on

---

[1] An earlier version of this paper was read at the Colloquium on *Religion in Everyday Life* organised by the Fryske Akademy in October 1988. In its revised form it owes much to the comments of Professor L. Laeyendecker who presided over the Colloquium and to Dr. L.G. Jansma and C.H.A. Verhaar of the Fryske Akademy.

[2] R.W. Scribner, *For the Sake of Simple Folk: Popular Propaganda for the German Reformation* (Cambridge, 1981); L.J. Abray, *The People's Reformation: Magistrates, Clergy and Commons in Strasbourg, 1500–1598* (Oxford, 1985); P. Blickle, *The Revolution of 1525: the German Peasants' War from a New Perspective* (Baltimore, 1981).

the lists of forbidden works, inventories and trial proceedings, but of which no copies have survived.[3] No doubt others have disappeared without trace, the victims of wholesale destruction by the authorities or, in the case of the cheapest publications, the ravages of time. The recent chance discovery of six evangelical books concealed since the mid sixteenth century under the floor-boards of a house in Delft suggests as much. This cache included no fewer than four previously unknown titles or editions, one of which came from the press of a previously unknown printer.[4] Yet even when we keep such losses in mind, count the sixty-one vernacular editions of the Bible and New Testament printed between 1520 and 1540,[5] and throw in for good measure Protestant works published in the Low Countries in Latin and the few French evangelical titles printed at Antwerp, we have to admit that the stock of Protestant publications intended for readers in, or from, the Low Countries is quite modest. Protestant pamphlets published in Germany during the first half of the sixteenth century are reckoned not in hundreds, but in thousands.[6]

Despite the ingenious subterfuges employed by the printers of evangelical books in the Low Countries, the censorship of the booktrade and the exemplary punishment of those guilty of publishing heretical books undoubtedly stifled the trade in Dutch Protestant literature, even though these measures did not eliminate illicit printing.[7] At first printers in the Low Countries published evangelical literature because there was a market and therefore a profit to be made. Subsequently the risks increased. Of the seven printers responsible for more than half of the Dutch evangelical pamphlets and Bibles produced between 1520 and 1565, two, and possibly three, were put to death; one other was imprisoned and yet another decided to move his business from Antwerp to London and thence to

[3] A.G. Johnston, 'The Eclectic Reformation: Vernacular Pamphlet Literature in the Dutch-speaking Low Countries, 1520–1565' (Unpub. Ph.D. thesis, Southampton 1987), p. 1. This figure does not allow for different editions of the same title. A copy of this thesis has been deposited in the Koninklijke Bibliotheek.

[4] H. van Nierop, 'Verboden zestiende-eeuwse boeken: ketterij uit Utopia', *Supplement: NRC Handelsblad*, 24 February 1989; B.J. Spruyt, 'De zes, in het grachtenpand te Delft gevonden boeken, met name de *Summa der godliker scrifturen*', *Té-èf. Blad van de faculteit der godgeleerdheid van de Rijksuniversiteit te Leiden*, XVIII (1989), pp. 25–32.

[5] C.C. de Bruin, *De statenbijbel en zijn voorgangers* (Leiden, 1937), p. 185. The breakdown of the sixty-one publications is as follows: thirty-eight complete editions of the New Testament; five partial editions; nine complete Bibles; nine incomplete editions of the Old Testament.

[6] Johnston, 'Eclectic Reformation', p. 4; apparently the number of Dutch editions of the Scriptures matched more closely the production of German Bibles. See Johnston, 'Eclectic Reformation', p. 29, who cites W.C. Poortman, *Bijbel en prent*, I (The Hague, 1983), pp. 201–10.

[7] H. van Nierop, 'Censorship, Illicit Printing and the Revolt of the Netherlands', *BN*, IX, *Too Mighty to be Free: Censorship and the Press in Britain and the Netherlands*, ed. A.C. Duke and C.A. Tamse, (Zutphen, 1988), pp. 30–44.

Emden.[8] To the extent that the repression restrained the demand for evangelical books, it presumably reduced the profitability of the trade and therefore deterred printers from venturing into this market. Even though the supply of Dutch Protestant literature improved after 1554, when the centre of evangelical printing shifted from Antwerp to Emden, the distribution and ownership of forbidden books remained as risky as before.[9]

In general Dutch evangelical writers did not make a major contribution to the corpus of Protestant literature in the first half of the sixteenth century. There are a few exceptions: Gnapheus, the unknown author of the *Summa der godliker scrifturen*, Hendrik Rol, Menno Simons, David Joris, the mysterious Niclaes Peeters and Anastasius Veluanus have claims to be regarded as theologians and reformers of some distinction and originality. Around two-fifths of the 170 evangelical titles were in fact written by Luther and other less well-known German reformers.[10] The works chosen for translation do not, however, represent the full range of German evangelical writings. In the case of Luther, far more of whose works appeared during his lifetime in Dutch than in any other foreign language, Netherlanders showed most interest in his work as a translator of the Bible and in his more popular religious writings. The other German evangelical works selected for translation into Dutch show a strong preference for catechisms and works of edification. Some German polemics did appear in Dutch, but Luther's attacks against the Roman church and the boisterous and often ribald propaganda deployed by German pamphleteers against the papacy did not find a public or, more accurately, translators in the Low Countries.[11] This omission cannot be attributed to a greater delicacy and sense of decorum on the part of the Dutch *burgerij*: the satirical broadsides subsequently fired against Granvelle, Alva and the Spanish Inquisition were no less scurrilous than the rabid anti-Catholic publications which had circulated in German Protestant circles. Presumably the non-confessional character of the works reflects the backward condition of the Reformation in the Low Countries and the desire of the Dutch evangelical public for works of an edifying sort.

In the battle with the old religion German Protestants often employed visual propaganda in order to vilify the Roman church and to convey the

---

[8] Johnston, 'Eclectic Reformation', pp. 12–20.

[9] A. Pettegree, 'The Exile Churches and the Churches ' "Under the Cross": Antwerp and Emden during the Dutch Revolt', *JEH*, XXXVIII (1987), pp. 194–200.

[10] For translations of Luther see C.Ch.G. Visser, *Luther's geschriften in de Nederlanden tot 1546* (Assen, 1969) and for translations of works by other German reformers see Johnston, 'Eclectic Reformation', Part II, sections A and D.

[11] Visser, *Luther's geschriften*, pp. 130–37; B. Moeller, 'Luther in Europe: his Works and Translations, 1517–46', *Politics and Society in Reformation Europe*, ed. E.I. Kouri and T. Scott (Basingstoke, 1987), pp. 236–38; Johnston, 'Eclectic Reformation', pp. 251–52.

classic Lutheran teaching on the Law and Grace to those on the margins of the print culture. In the Low Countries illustrations of an evangelical sort were usually found only in vernacular Bibles whose woodcuts were sometimes copied from the German originals.[12] There are two outstanding exceptions: the spiritualists David Joris and Hendrik Niclaes both included elaborate prints in their books in order to explain their esoteric doctrines. At a secret Jorist assembly in Alkmaar the leader displayed 'the figure of a man and all his members' presumably to put across his master's teaching on the New Man.[13] The marked decline in the number of woodcuts in books in the third quarter of the sixteenth century has been linked with the triumph of the humanist notion that classical and theological texts had no need of illustrations.[14] In the case of evangelical books commercial considerations probably also played a part; the demand was for cheap, black-letter pamphlets in octavo, small enough to be concealed up a sleeve.[15]

Yet these reasons do not sufficiently explain the virtual absence of the single-sheet woodcuts and illustrated broadsheets such as brought the message of the Reformation to the attention of the public in Germany. Only a handful of Dutch evangelical woodcuts and engravings from the first half of the sixteenth century have survived, though others certainly circulated.[16] In the early 1520s a painter of stained glass let the town secretary of Brussels see prints depicting the pope in chains and cloven-hoofed cardinals. It may, however, be significant that he had received

---

[12] Johnston, 'Eclectic Reformation', pp. 31–33, 275.

[13] ARAG, Hof van Holland, 5654, fo. 128–29.

[14] P. van Boheemen, 'De vorm van het gedrukte boek in de noordelijke Nederlanden in de 16de eeuw', *Het boek in Nederland in de 16de eeuw* (The Hague, 1986), pp. 39, 50–51.

[15] Johnston, 'Eclectic Reformation', pp. 22–24.

[16] On these see K.G. Boon, 'Divers aspects de l'iconographie de la réforme aux Pays-Bas', *Gazette des beaux-arts*, CXXVI (1984), pp. 207–16; CXXVII (1984), pp. 1–14. An evangelical at Leuven had in his possession a suspect painting with the caption in Dutch, 'We have become a gazing-stock of the world', *Mededelingen van de geschied- en oudheidkundige kring voor Leuven en omgeving*, III (1963), p. 15. An anonymous satirical woodcut which depicts the pope as a fisherman vainly trying to lure evangelicals with indulgences is probably of German origin despite the contemporary Dutch title which has been added by hand, Stichting Atlas van Stolk, no. 334. Unflattering representations of the clergy which had been tolerated in the late middle ages caused embarrassment after the Reformation. Such delicacy may have persuaded Bernard van Orley or his patron not to proceed with a commission on the theme *De contemptu mundi et eorum quae in eo sunt*. All that remains is a preliminary though detailed drawing, now in the Rijksprentenkabinet. The message of the allegory is plain: the church which has been corrupted by its pursuit of secular power and fleshpots should flee the world and place its trust in Christ's words. Orley's drawing was subsequently reworked as an engraving. See N. Beets, 'Een godsdienstige allegorie door Barent van Orley', *Oud-Holland*, XLIX (1932), pp. 129–37: K.G. Boon, 'Divers aspects', *Gazette des beaux-arts*, CXXVII (1985), pp. 1–7, who invests the drawing with a more heterodox character than seems warranted.

these from an acquaintance in Basle.[17] None of the extant Dutch evangelical woodcuts can be described as popular works of art: their artistic sophistication and religious ambivalence reflect the preference of the sympathetic intelligentsia for an undifferentiated evangelical Christianity. The Protestants in Germany exploited popular visual images which pulled no punches because they needed to enlist the support of the 'common man' in the fight against the Antichrist. In the Low Countries, however, the repressive legislation and, in the case of the Anabaptists, an exclusive doctrine of the church, combined to push dissent out of the public arena. After the debacle of Münster and the bloody suppression of religious radicalism in Holland in the mid 1530s, dissent retreated behind closed doors. The opportunity for mass proselytism was temporarily past – and therefore the need for popular propaganda.

The chambers of rhetoric provided one quasi-legitimate public forum where a broadly evangelical message could occasionally be heard by the townspeople in the Netherlands. Though conservative churchmen regarded the chambers as nests of heresy, their fears were exaggerated. If they had a fair sprinkling of evangelicals and anticlericals, they also performed works by sincere Catholics like Cornelis Everaert.[18] The rhetoricians naturally took a close interest in the social and religious preoccupations of the day, for their success depended on the topicality of their plays. Since the religious issues raised by the Reformation aroused the curiosity of the urban elites, these provided subject matter for the chambers. At the height of the Anabaptist agitation in Holland the rhetoricians of Haarlem staged a play in which the Catholic clergy refuted Hoffman's incarnational theology and brought the errant laity back to the fold.[19] Thirty years later the same chamber took up another matter of immediate concern when they pilloried the sharp practices of the speculators and hoarders of grain during the dearth.[20]

The chambers in Holland responded quickly to the sudden interest in the new religious ideas. Already in 1526 the *Hof van Holland* had to investigate a *luyterspel* performed at Monnikendam as well as plays at Amsterdam, which treated the sacraments with irreverence.[21] This intervention did not deter rhetoricians staging another controversial play in

[17] J. Duverger, 'Lutherse predicatie te Brussel en het proces tegen een aantal kunstenaars (april-juni 1527)', *Wetenschappelijke tijdingen*, XXXVI (1971), col. 225. The authorities burnt certain 'prentes de la doctrine' of Luther at Bruges in 1521–22, *CD*, IV, p. 134.

[18] J. Decavele, *De dageraad van de reformatie in Vlaanderen (1520–1565)*, I (Brussels, 1975), pp. 196–220; Johnston 'Eclectic Reformation', pp. 204–6; K.P. Moxey, 'Image Criticism in the Netherlands before the Iconoclasm of 1566', *NAK*, LXXXVII (1977), pp. 151–56.

[19] S. Voolstra, ed., 'Een spel van sinnen vande menswerdinge Christo', *Doopsgezinde bijdragen*, n.r., IX (1983), pp. 53–61.

[20] E. Kuttner, *Het hongerjaar 1566* (Amsterdam, 1964), pp. 202–4.

[21] *CD*, V, pp. 171, 172.

Amsterdam a few years later. In this case they criticised the veneration of images in the church under the guise of a play about Daniel's triumphant overthrow of the cult of Bel and his destruction of the dragon (Daniel XIV).[22] It was, however, the plays written for the rhetorician's festival at Ghent in 1539, which alerted Brussels to the dangers of heterodox ideas being presented in dramatic form to an unsuspecting public. As was customary in such competitions, the chambers had been asked to perform a morality play on a particular theme. At Ghent the rhetoricians had to answer the question: 'What is the greatest consolation for the dying man?' Six of the contestants gave a place to good works in the process of justification, in keeping with the teaching of the Catholic church. Yet five others advanced the Lutheran doctrine of salvation by faith in Christ's promises, which had not then been condemned as erroneous. Some plays satirised pilgrimages and the veneration of images; more ominously not one thought to recommend the sacrament of extreme unction to the man on his deathbed. The participating chambers all advocated renewal within the Catholic church with a typically evangelical emphasis on the scriptures and on the doctrine of grace.[23]

The debates among literary scholars and historians about the precise theological stance of these and other plays only continue the controversies which broke out when they were first performed. The dramatic form lends itself to the treatment of sensitive subjects which when presented less subtly provide a more obvious target for opponents. It was possible to make anticlerical remarks, to criticise aspects of popular piety, for example, pilgrimages and the veneration of saints, and to explore evangelical teaching on grace and salvation without either playwrights or chambers having to nail their colours to the mast. This ambivalence infuriated the inquisitors; they insisted texts should be scrutinised in advance of performances so that offensive and tendentious passages might be excised.

These pamphlets, woodcuts and plays can only tell us what Dutch religious dissidents might have read, seen or heard; we should look elsewhere to discover how they appropriated the new theologies. For obvious reasons persecuted lay evangelicals with little formal education leave little behind in the way of *ego-documenten* – journals, spiritual autobiographies and letters. Ironically the repressive machinery, which largely silenced dissent, has compensated, though only very partially, for the paucity of personal records. The decision of the governments in the Low Countries to prosecute heresy and related offences generated exten-

---

[22] *DAN*, V, pp. 10–11, 21. Maarten van Heemskerk produced in the 1560s a series of engravings which took as their theme Old Testament idols and their destruction. D. Freedburg, 'Art and Iconoclasm, 1525–1580: the Case of the Northern Netherlands' *Kunst vóór de beeldenstorm* (The Hague, 1986), p. 79 and figs. 12–17.

[23] This analysis is based on the much fuller discussion in Decavele *Dageraad*, I, pp. 197–201 and Johnston, 'Eclectic Reformation', ch. VIII.

sive judicial and administrative archives and gave impetus to the publication of martyrologies. Such records are of special importance for the social history of the early Dutch Reformation.

German Protestants were of course no strangers to persecution, and government archives have been used by historians there to investigate the structure and nature of Anabaptism.[24] But apart from the grim years of 1527–31, when some 600 Anabaptists perished in Central and Southern Germany, and the executions in the aftermath of Münster, both the death toll and the intensity of the repression were lower there than in the Habsburg Netherlands.[25] The total number of heretics (chiefly Anabaptists and Calvinists) put to death in the Netherlands before 1566 exceeded 1300, with a peak of repression in Holland and Friesland between 1534 and 1536 and a further period of sustained persecution in the southern provinces between 1557 and 1564.[26] Thanks to the endeavours of Paul Fredericq and, more recently, Albert Mellink a substantial proportion of the official records relating to the suppression of dissent in the northern Netherlands have been published.[27] To these may be added the numerous documents from the *Raad van Beroerten* which local historians have edited.[28] The martyrologies have long been plundered by church historians, but in the absence of scholarly editions which establish the accuracy and reliability of these literary texts, it is difficult to make systematic use of them.[29]

Both kinds of sources present problems. Insofar as the martyrologies include trial interrogations and court sentences they duplicate the official records. The letters of spiritual comfort and edification, the religious songs and testimonies of faith, addressed to the persecuted brethren and subsequently treasured by their descendants, raise problems of veracity, narrative structure and literary convention about which I am unqualified

[24] C.-P. Clasen, *Anabaptism: A Social History, 1525–1618* (Ithaca, 1972).

[25] C.-P. Clasen, 'Executions of Anabaptists, 1525–1618: A Research Report', *Mennonite Quarterly Review*, XLVII (1973), p. 119.

[26] See above p. 99.

[27] *CD*, IV, V; For Friesland and Groningen,*DAN*, I, *Friesland en Groningen (1530–1550)*, ed. A.F. Mellink (Leiden, 1975); Deventer,*Bescheiden betreffende de hervorming in Overijssel*, ed. J.J. Hullu (Deventer, 1889); Utrecht, 'Bescheiden betreffende het eerste tijdvak van de geschiedenis der hervorming in de stad en provincie Utrecht 1524–1566', ed. A.H.C. van Asch van Wijck, *Berigten van het historisch genootschap te Utrecht*, IV (1851), pp. 109–74; for Amsterdam, *DAN*, II, *Amsterdam (1536–1578)*, ed. A.F. Mellink (Leiden, 1980); *DAN*, V, *Amsterdam (1531–1636*, ed. A.F. Mellink (Leiden, 1985).

[28] For a convenient listing of the most important source publications see bibliography in J. Scheerder, *De beeldenstorm* (Bussum, 1974), pp. 121–30.

[29] The most important martyrologies are Jean Crespin, *Le Livre des Martyrs* (1554); Adriaen van Haemstede, *De Gheschiedenisse ende den Doodt der vromer Martelaren* (1559); *Het Offer des Heeren* (1562); Thieleman Jansz. van Braght, *Het Bloedigh Toneel der Doopsgesinden en weereloose Christenen* (1660).

to comment.[30] The martyrologists certainly took pains to document their accounts, but this was by no means their only or even chief concern. What they above all offered was a 'theology of martyrdom' which was intended to confirm those facing persecution in their faith, to prepare them for the ordeal of interrogation and to provide exemplary patterns of conduct.[31]

Government records with a direct bearing on religious dissent fall into two categories: administrative and legal or judicial. The former is more heterogeneous: it includes correspondence between Brussels and the provinces about heresy and documents from the exchequer, where may be found payments to all those involved in the enforcement of the edicts and the apprehension of suspects as well as matters relating to the confiscation of heretics' property. For present purposes the court proceedings are more obviously rewarding. We should not of course expect to find impartial and full accounts of the beliefs of those on trial. When the proceedings opened there was a strong presumption that the accused was guilty: it was the responsibility of the court to determine whether offences under the antiheresy legislation had been committed and, if so, to induce the accused to confess openly to the same. The magistrates were expressly bidden to proceed to judgment 'without flourishes of legal rhetoric and as briefly as was consonant with reason and equity'.[32] Little is known about the social background and training of those who sat in the provincial courts and the *schepenbanken*. Apparently the university-educated jurists in the provincial courts, the *gens lettrez*, who might have been expected loyally to cooperate with the central government, did not endorse the religious policy of Charles V and Philip II unreservedly. Lawyers in the provincial courts of Holland and Flanders, who had made no secret of their admiration for Erasmus in the 1520s and 1530s, were unlikely to be zealous reactionaries; some indeed complained that the edicts were unreasonably harsh.[33] For several years after 1529 enforcement of the edicts against the 'Lutherans' was entrusted to special commissioners attached to the provincial courts, but as the volume of such business expanded, cognizance was restored to the local criminal courts. This arrangement proved no more satisfactory. The government complained that the local magistrates sabotaged the drive against heresy

---

[30] When Professor Becker delivered his paper at the Colloquium on *Religion in Everyday Life* he remarked that believers from different religious movements give distinctive accounts of their conversion and asked whether such accounts were in fact structured in accordance with pre-existing 'scripts'. The same question might fruitfully be asked about the narratives in the martyrologies.

[31] E. Stauffer, 'The Anabaptist Theology of Martyrdom', *Mennonite Quarterly Review*, XIX (1945), pp. 179–214; O. Swartzentruber, 'The Piety and Theology of the late Anabaptist Martyrs in Van Braght's *Martyrs' Mirror*', *Mennonite Quarterly Review*, XXVIII (1954), pp. 5–26, 128–42.

[32] *ROPB*, II, p.582; cf. *CD*, IV, p. 125.

[33] See below p. 155–56.

by their reluctance to prosecute dissidents rigorously while the lower courts, wishing to rid themselves of this bothersome and politically embarrassing duty, alleged that they lacked the requisite legal expertise.[34]

The deposition of witnesses and the interrogation of suspects allow us to eavesdrop in the taverns where stubborn nonconformists brawled with good Catholics and to walk the streets of Amsterdam where clergy found themselves the targets of irreverent abuse. These records also inform us about the clandestine world of nonconformity with its Bible-reading artisans, conventicles and incipient congregations. The trial proceedings record the plain speech, almost the *ipsissima verba* of dissidents as they gave blunt expression to deeply-held convictions and pent-up hatreds. Although the offending remarks of suspects like the cooper at Utrecht, cited above, were usually reported at secondhand, taken out of context and perhaps abridged by the clerk, a sufficient volume of dicta survives to show that the opinions held by these dissident artisans about, for example, the real presence and images, did not simply reflect the theology of the major Protestant reformers.

The Anabaptists of Holland were perceived, in the words of Mary of Hungary, as 'gens non letterez, povres, mécanicques'.[35] Likewise those who flocked to the open air services in 1566 were remembered (and belittled) as 'artisans la plupart, simple ignorans et aisez à séduire' and the image-breakers as 'scoundrels and vile persons with nothing to lose'.[36] Such stereotypes conveniently explained the apostasy of these 'gens de basse qualité'. Wittingly or not the authorities exploited deep-seated fears of social disorder to persuade the local magistrates of the need to take effective counter-measures and to drive a wedge between the heretics and their social peers.

The success of a stereotype depends on the verisimilitude of some element in the projected image, which by its demonstrable truth lends credibility to the whole. The contemporary descriptions of the dissidents as 'mechanics' were generally well-founded. The officers of the *Hof van Holland*, called on to suppress the Anabaptists around Amsterdam, cate-gorised the heretics put to death in 1531 as 'craftsmen such as fullers, weavers and the like'. A few years later they told Brussels that many of those carried away by the religious excitement were 'simple rustics ... of small intelligence'.[37] Scholarly research has generally confirmed these

---

[34] See below pp. 166–67.

[35] H. Pirenne, *Histoire de Belgique*, III (Brussels, 1923), p. 116.

[36] H. d'Outreman, *Histoire de la Ville et Comté de Valentienne ... illustreé et augmentée par le R.P. Pierre d'Oultreman* (Douai, 1639), p. 203; P.M. Crew, *Calvinist Preaching and Iconoclasm in the Netherlands, 1544–1569* (Cambridge, 1978), p. 8; see below p. 136.

[37] *DAN*, V, pp. 2, 21; A.F. Mellink, *De wederdopers in de noordelijke Nederlanden, 1531–1544* (Groningen-Djakarta, 1953), pp. 358–59. In 1561 the *Raad van Vlaanderen* described the majority of suspected heretics as 'povres gens idiotz ne scachans lire, ne scripre et ne voeullians soustenir quelques propos erronieux', E. de Coussemaker, *Troubles religieux du XVIe siècle dans la Flandre Maritime*, I (Bruges, 1876), p. 83.

contemporary impressions, although the Anabaptists did number among their followers a few wealthy and politically well-connected members.[38] Most dissidents made their living in and around Amsterdam as metal-workers, tailors, shoemakers, fishermen and mariners or were married to such. Their poverty readily persuaded the authorities that the Ana-baptists intended 'to lay their hands on the coffers of the rich'.[39] Rumours about the compulsory community of property at Münster and about Rothmann's call for the elect to wreak vengeance on the ungodly fed these instinctive apprehensions. The conduct of the Dutch Ana-baptists during 1534–35, however, scarcely justified such fears. When they hastened in March 1534 to prepare for the journey to Münster, they had indeed the assurance that they would find there 'goods enough for all the saints', but what counted was Münster's reputation as the New Jerusalem. Only there would they be safe when the Lord returned to judge the world.[40]

During the 1520s the new evangelical theology had found greatest favour among the clergy and those connected with the booktrade and education. The occupational profile of Anabaptism was quite different. Melchior Hoffman and his Dutch successors recruited above all from the 'non-intellectual classes'. Hostile contemporaries disparaged the Ana-baptists as *gens non letterez* because few of them knew Latin, not because they could not read. In fact they knew very well that a significant minority owned and read 'die nieuwe Evangelie boeckskens'.[41] The political and religious establishment insisted that weavers and furriers should 'remain at their trades' and not meddle in matters beyond their understanding.[42]

The recently-edited interrogations of suspected heretics at Amsterdam confirm the importance of Bible-reading among these *kleyne luyden*. Quite a few craftsmen had sufficient confidence and fluency to read passages of the scriptures aloud at their secret assemblies.[43] We hear of two linen weavers who used to spend the feastdays outside Amsterdam reading together and of small groups of Anabaptists, who travelled by

[38] L.G. Jansma, 'The Rise of the Anabaptist Movement and the Societal Changes in the Netherlands', *The Dutch Dissenters*, ed. I.B. Horst (Leiden, 1986), p. 95.

[39] Mellink, *Wederdopers in de noordelijk Nederlanden*, p. 363.

[40] Mellink, *op. cit.*, p. 31.

[41] Th. van Braght, *The Bloody Theater or Martyrs' Mirror* (Scottdale, 1951), p. 681. In the morality played directed against Hoffman's incarnational theology, his followers could both read and write. On literacy among the Anabaptists see also W.J. Kühler, *Geschiedenis der nederlandsche doopsgezinden* (Haarlem, 1932), p. 291. In 1545 the magistrates of Ghent, who most certainly could read, asked that the prosecution of religious offenders be the responsibility of the *gens lettrez et scavans en droist divin et humain* in the provincial court, see below p. 166–67.

[42] Van Braght, p. 686.

[43] *E.g.* a baker (*DAN*, V, p. 222); a maker of woolcards (V, p. 275); a merchant (II, p. 49); a basketmaker (II, p. 56); a sawyer (II, p. 158).

boat into the country, reading as they went.[44] Nor was the ability to read restricted to the menfolk. Claesgen Claesdr., we are told, 'took the New Testament (*evangeliebouck*), reading it and declaring from the gospel that the end of the world was at hand according to the signs contained in the gospel'.[45] Other women confessed to having read the New Testament on their own.[46] Quite a number of Anabaptists owned copies of the New Testament. A shipwright bought his in parts which he annotated so that he could more easily commit passages to memory and 'find the subject matter'.[47] The New Testament was, of course, the printed book most likely to be in the hands of these dissidents. It was, however, not the only book. Rem Peterssen, a furrier by trade, had a modest collection of four books at the time of his trial in 1535. Besides a New Testament, he had a copy of Bugenhagen's commentary on the Psalms, an imposing volume of some 300 folios, Oecolampadius's eucharistic liturgy and an un-identified 'book of the prophets'.[48] Works by Menno Simons and Dirk Philips figure only occasionally, though a tinker on Texel admitted in 1564 to having copies of Menno's *Van die wedergeboorte* and Dirk's *Van de geestelijcke Restitution*.[49] A master fuller had a manuscript version of a work by Dirk Philips.[50] An Anabaptist weaver, arrested near Breda in 1571, was found to have a New Testament, the martyrology *Het Offer des Heeren* and a copy of the letters of Jacob de Rore, who had been executed in 1569.[51] These examples of book ownership among dissidents, which could be readily multiplied, amply demonstrate the participation of craftsmen in the print culture of their time. The character of these books also provides a pointer to their everyday piety. It is noticeable that anti-Catholic polemic, though occasionally represented, was outweighed by works of devotion and spiritual edification.[52] This coincides with what is known about Dutch evangelical works in general. It finds confirmation in the range of suspect books offered for sale by two book-pedlars on trial in Amsterdam in 1560. When their stock of evangelical publications

[44] *DAN*, II, pp. 163–64; 103–4; 105.

[45] *DAN*, V, p. 189.

[46] *DAN*, II, pp. 79, 82, 157, 189.

[47] *DAN*, II, pp. 59–60.

[48] *DAN*, V, pp. 243–45. On the basis of his attack on image worship, which was recalled in the trial proceedings, the *boeck van den propheten* may be tentatively identified with the Dutch evangelical pamphlet *Van den Prophet Baruch*.

[49] Van Braght, p. 686.

[50] *DAN*, II, p. 254.

[51] K. Slootmans, 'Verhoren van wederdopers te Klundert gevangen genomen 5 augustus 1571', *Jaarboek van de oudheidkundige kring 'De ghulden Roos'*, XIII (1953), p. 34 fn.

[52] An Anabaptist on trial in 1555 had in his possession *De vall van der Roemsscher kercken*, a Dutch translation of an English Protestant attack on transubstantiation entitled *Faull of the Romyshe Churche*, *DAN*, II, p. 233; Johnston, 'Eclectic Reformation', pp. 310–11.

was impounded, it was found to contain religious song books, assorted works of consolation, simple catechisms and a compendium of scriptural passages.[53]

The *kleyne luyden* not only read, they also copied religious songs and texts.[54] No doubt the relatively high cost of books for such people explains the circulation of manuscripts. In the mid sixteenth century a master mason in Antwerp might earn between twenty-seven and thirty *stuivers* a day, but he was among the most highly paid of the craftsmen and a labourer-mason could expect only half as much. The cheapest pamphlets sold for only one *stuiver*, but publications of several hundred pages might cost eight, or even twelve *stuivers*. Complete Bibles too remained beyond the reach of most. A student at Leuven sold a Bible around 1540 for thirty stuivers and two tankards of beer.[55] It would seem that he did not drive a hard bargain for thirty years later an Anabaptist tailor at Klundert spent two *Philipsdaalders*, or seventy *stuivers*, on the purchase of a Dutch Bible.[56] The copyist could, by taking extracts from various sources, compile a work suited to his own religious needs. Otto Berentsz., a fuller at Amsterdam, composed his own evangelical commonplace-book, for he wrote down passages from 'many and various books and authors', as he told his interrogators in 1555.[57]

Although the repression prevented an outpouring of works by lay evangelicals, the *kleyne luyden* in the Low Countries did make original contributions to the stock of dissident literature. Quite the most remarkable proof of lay creativity came from the martyrs' 'epistles and confessions', written in prison. These letters, usually brimming with scriptural quotations, sometimes circulated in manuscript only being published after the Revolt.[58] Even during the persecutions enterprising evangelicals exploited the new technology which made possible the printing of simple pamphlets in the space of only a few days. In 1527 a shoemaker, filled with remorse about his abjuration, decided to declare his true religious convictions. 'Moved by the spirit', as he told his interrogator, he wrote two epistles addressed to the magistrates and inhabitants of his native town Dordrecht. Only four days elapsed between his delivery of the manuscript at the printing office at Antwerp and the distribution of

---

[53] *DAN*, II, pp. 265–68.

[54] *DAN*, II, pp. 162, 226.

[55] Johnston, 'Eclectic Reformation', pp. 27–28.

[56] Slootmans, 'Verhoren', pp. 19–20.

[57] *DAN*, II, p. 255.

[58] In 1570, an Anabaptist weaver from Breda had in his possession *Brieven van Jacob de Kersemaker* (Jacob de Rore) whose letters were first published in 1577, Slootmans 'Verhoren', p. 34 fn; N. van der Zijpp, *Geschiedenis der doopsgezinden in Nederland* (Arnhem, 1952), pp. 59–63. For bibliographical descriptions of such martyrs' epistles consult *Bibliographie des martyrologes protestants néerlandais*, I (The Hague, 1890).

the pamphlets in Dordrecht.[59] At about the same time a master tapestry worker arranged to have 400 copies of a manuscript 'containing several false and erroneous articles' printed at Cambrai for sale in his native Tournai.[60] The Reformation also prompted a rash of ephemerae – anticlerical satires, handbills, ballads and the like – which infuriated the targets of their insults before they passed into oblivion.

The process by which evangelicals within the Catholic church became Anabaptists or Calvinists was complex. For many separation from the church did not come easily. Jan Daelman, a Flemish evangelical, spoke for many such when he declared in 1557 'that the Roman church is the church of Christ, for all that religion there has been corrupted'.[61] But the forces pushing critics within the church towards schism and sectarianism were almost irresistible. The authorities endeavoured to winkle out the protestantising Catholics among the clergy. Where this policy succeeded – it was least effective in the northern and eastern provinces incorporated into the Habsburg Netherlands by Charles V – evangelicals found themselves in a state of perplexity. Should they attend the objectionable Roman mass or withdraw into sectarianism? Either course placed their souls in jeopardy. In 1531 a dispute broke out among the brethren in Antwerp, some of whom opposed the drift towards self-contained and exclusive conventicles. Bugenhagen had earlier advised that the brethren might meet privately to hear the gospel preached, but Luther opposed the administration of the sacraments in such 'house churches'.[62] The Anabaptist followers of Melchior Hoffman had no such misgivings. Indeed the 'covenanters', those *van de bont*, believed that their salvation depended on their standing apart from the world and separating themselves from the godless chaff. This imperative to create a gathered church did not diminish after Münster. Gillis van Aken con-

---

[59] *CD*, V, pp. 198–201; 202–3; see also J.G. de Hoop Scheffer, 'Cornelis Woutersz. van Dordrecht, een martelaar der hervorming, 1525–1529', *Kerkhistorisch archief*, IV (1866), pp. 1–22. The editors of *CD* give the date of the shoemaker's visit to the Antwerp printshop as *Sonnedaige, den sesten Marcii lestleden*, where De Hoop Scheffer read *Sonnedaige den lesten Marcii lestleden*. As 31 March 1527 fell on Sunday, I have followed De Hoop Scheffer's chronology. Because so many pamphlets had been printed, the shoemaker expected copies would still be around a hundred years after his death. Alas, none have survived.

[60] G. Moreau, *Histoire de protestantisme à Tournai jusqu'à la veille de la Révolution des Pays-Bas* (Paris, 1962), p. 61.

[61] Decavele, *Dageraad*, I, p. 383.

[62] G. Hammer, 'Die Streit um Bucer in Antwerpen' *Lutheriana: Zum 500. Geburtstag Martin Luthers von den Mitarbeitern der Weimarer Ausgabe* (Cologne-Vienna, 1984), p. 441; M. Luther, *Werke. Kritische Gesamtausgabe: Briefwechsel*, VI (Weimar, 1935), pp. 189–91. Luther's reply has not survived, but when a controversy arose among the Lutherans in the 1570s about the propriety of conventicles, the opponents of secret congregations alleged that Luther had refused to countenance them, J.W. Pont, *Geschiedenis van het lutheranisme in de Nederlanden tot 1618* (Haarlem, 1911), pp. 42–43.

tinued to preach on the need to leave the world and the Roman Church.[63] In the 1540s and 1550s the Calvinist offensive against Nicodemism led to the formation of 'churches under the cross' where a sharp distinction developed between those 'within' and 'without' the congregation. Quite apart from such doctrinal considerations, evangelicals in the Low Countries had to survive in a hostile environment. The cellular structure of Anabaptism and early Reformed Protestantism was well suited to this purpose. Within these underground congregations a small yet committed membership could lead an intense religious life.

During the winter of 1523–24 *secrètes assemblées*, in Dutch *heymelicke vergaderingen*, at Antwerp and Amsterdam first came to the notice of the authorities.[64] These met in private houses, alehouses and in the country-side. The social composition of the gatherings varied: craftsmen pre-dominated in the conventicles discovered at Antwerp in 1524 and at Veere c. 1529–31; painters, tapestry workers and their wives gave the tone to the more select gathering detected at Brussels in 1527. The degree of secrecy surrounding such activities also varied. The group at Veere posted someone outside to prevent informers from eavesdropping at the window,[65] but the Flemish villagers who met in the local taverns took few pains to disguise their activities.[66]

The size and frequency of such meetings determined relations within the group. The crowd of 200 who went on Easter Monday 1533 to hear a shearman expound the gospel in a village to the south of 's-Hertogenbosch presumably came out of curiosity.[67] By way of contrast the brethren in Antwerp, who wrote to Luther in 1531, had evidently met together for some years and, as a result, a sense of solidarity had developed even though they were not all of one mind.[68] When Mr. Claes van der Elst delivered a series of sermons during Holy Week 1527, he preached to between twenty and fifty persons, many of whom knew one another.[69] The conventicles at Veere seem to have gone on for several years before the authorities intervened. On occasion forty or fifty attended, though the numbers fluctuated sharply.[70] When the forbidden gatherings assumed a more exclusive character, the number of participants present at one time tended to decline. The Anabaptists in Holland, for example, rarely came together in groups larger than twenty persons,[71] and meetings

[63] *DAN*, II, p. 136.
[64] *CD*, IV, pp. 240, 257, 259–61.
[65] Hoop Scheffer, p. 513.
[66] Decavele, *Dageraad*, I, p. 269.
[67] L.J.A. van de Laar, 'De opkomst van de reformatie in 's-Hertogenbosch, c. 1525–1565', *AGKKN*, 20 (1978), p. 122.
[68] Luther, *Werke ... Briefwechsel*, VI, p. 190.
[69] Duverger, 'Lutherse predicatie', col. 224.
[70] Hoop Scheffer, p. 515.
[71] *DAN*, V, p. 13; II, p. 114.

of between ten and fifteen seem to have been customary.[72] The small size of such meetings made for greater intimacy, while also enhancing the authority of the leader. They were also less likely to attract unwelcome attention. When the Calvinist consistory at Antwerp decided in 1558 to divide the congregation of approximately 200 into sixteen or seventeen subgroups, each of which had eight to twelve persons, it did so partly to reassure wealthy well-wishers who hesitated to appear in the full assembly for fear of spies, but also for a practical reason: it would be easier to find suitable houses where small groups could come together inconspicuously. Although the ministers preached to two or three groups together, they gave instruction in the catechism to a single group at a time.[73]

The earliest conventicles arose spontaneously from the desire of those interested in the contemporary religious debate to search the scriptures. Very little is known about the conduct of such meetings or about the topics under discussion in the early years. The Bible-study meetings held in certain villages in Flanders began by someone reading a passage of scripture; the gathering then adjourned while the participants went off in pairs to consider the reading, after which they re-assembled in order to compare notes.[74] The discussions touched inevitably on controverted points of doctrine. When Mr. Claes van der Elst preached behind closed doors in Brussels in 1527, he criticised the mass, denied transubstantiation and taught how evangelicals should confess and communicate.[75] From the quarrel between a shoemaker, who belonged to a conventicle at Veere, and a priest in 1531 about 'freewill, namely that God had ordained whether we should be saved or damned', it would seem likely that this issue had been on the agenda of the study group, the more so as the shoemaker adduced a string of texts.[76] The conventicle provided a new forum for discussion; it also served as a vehicle of instruction in the new theology. Contemporaries described such illicit gatherings as *heymelicke schoelen* (secret schools) and it was said of the participants at the meetings at Brussels that they *ter scole gingen* (went to school).[77] When we look for an explanation why the same metaphors, crude arguments, proof texts and even anticlerical jokes recur, we should consider whether these might not have been disseminated through the conventicles, which functioned in effect as schools for nonconformity.

Those who took part in such meetings in the 1520s had no intention

---

[72] *DAN*, II, pp. 87, 92, 101, 130–31, 148; one hears too of groups with only three or four persons.

[73] *WMV*, Ser. III, deel ii (1e stuk), p. 77. In the 1560s a Reformed minister at Amsterdam also gave instruction in the catechism to a few at a time, Brandt, I, p. 315.

[74] Decavele, *Dageraad*, I, p. 269.

[75] Duverger, 'Lutherse predicatie', col. 227–28.

[76] Hoop Scheffer, p. 516.

[77] *E.g.*, Duverger, 'Lutherse predicatie', col. 225; Hoop Scheffer, p. 513 fn. 1; *CD*, V, p. 32; *DAN*, II, p. 49.

of creating self-contained congregations. The villagers who attended the Bible-study group in Flanders continued to go to mass, where some advertised their fashionable piety by taking copies of the New Testament to church instead of books of hours.[78] Even those who roundly condemned transubstantiation and refused to take communion at Easter may not have fully understood the implications of their dissent. Where clerics took part, as they often did in the 1520s, they might preach to the gatherings. The evangelicals at Antwerp had even been in the habit of celebrating the Lord's Supper at their meetings, although they had ceased to do so before 1531, perhaps because they could no longer call on the services of an obliging priest.[79] Despite the claims of some dissidents that they could consecrate the sacrament as well as any priest, there is no evidence that laymen did in fact administer communion at this time.[80] These evangelicals had not as yet withdrawn from the church; indeed the participants in the conventicles at Leuven in the 1540s still went to mass and to confession.[81]

The Anabaptist meetings were however radically different. In December 1531 the first Anabaptists to be put to death in Holland were executed in The Hague. Under interrogation they confessed that at the close of their Bible-study meetings, 'one of their number broke a loaf of bread which he distributed to everyone'.[82] Such communion services are well-attested in the subsequent trials of Anabaptists. A simple liturgy developed. On one occasion, after Gillis van Aken, an Anabaptist elder, had delivered an exhortation lasting two hours, several white loaves were placed on a table with a jug of wine, which he then distributed.[83] These gatherings were open only to those who had gained entry to the *verbont* (covenant), for which there was a well-defined procedure. Usually those who sought admission had to make certain declarations: they had to promise not to attend church, 'since what is done there is idolatry', not to drink, or to speak ill of others.[84] Later Gillis used to ask those who wanted to be baptised whether they believed Christ was the Son of the living God and then admonish them to live uprightly, not to swear or to curse.[85] By 1534 the Anabaptists operated a rudimentary system of poor relief and entrusted the task to 'deacons', who might be men or women.[86] Discipline was to become one of the major sources of controversy among the Dutch Anabaptists in the 1540s, but the first mention of excommunication

[78] Decavele, *Dageraad*, I, 268.

[79] Luther, *Werke ... Briefwechsel*, VI, p. 190.

[80] E.g., *CD*, V, p. 347; K.R. Pekelharing, *Bijdragen voor de geschiedenis der hervorming in Zeeland, 1526–1572* (Middelburg, 1866), p. 10; ORA Gouda, 147, fo. 79v.

[81] Johnston, 'Eclectic Reformation', p. 230.

[82] *DAN*, V, p. 19.

[83] *DAN*, II, p. 136; *cf.*, pp. 102, 114.

[84] *DAN*, V, p. 20; *cf.*, p. 90.

[85] *DAN*, II, p. 138.

[86] *DAN*, V, pp. 89, 111; II, pp. 137, 142, 222.

among the brethren at Amsterdam only occurs in 1548.[87] In every other respect the Anabaptists in that city constituted a separated brotherhood by the mid 1530s.

The self-awareness of the Anabaptists finds expression in the terminology they used of other dissidents in Amsterdam at this time. When the Anabaptists staged a coup d'état in May 1535, they called for the support of Lutherans and sacramentarians 'who loved the gospel'.[88] On other occasions they spoke of the other dissidents as being 'of the Word' and 'of the gospel'.[89] When they referred to themselves, they spoke about 'those of the covenant', 'the brotherhood' and the 'congregation of Christ' (*de ghemeente Christi*), which they contrasted with 'the world'.[90] In time the authorities distinguished between the sects. The *procureur-generaal* in Holland recognised that he was confronted by two 'sects': the Anabaptists and the *sacramentisten*.[91] The exclusiveness of the Anabaptists made these other groups of dissidents more conscious of their distinctive identities and therefore hastened the process of differentiation among Dutch evangelicals.

The records of the courts are particularly important for the study of lay dissident theology because they document anticatholic gestures and record the religious opinions of nonconformists about the Catholic church, more or less in their own words. At times the violent language of these dissidents seems far removed from the submissiveness and tender piety expressed in the 'epistles' in *Het Offer des Heeren*. This incongruity is more apparent than real. Many dissidents came before the courts because they had offended Catholic susceptibilities – they might have denied the real presence, derided the pious practices of their Catholic neighbours, or broken a statue. It was their hostility to the church and to the priesthood which therefore claimed the attention of the judges. Although that animosity is present also in the martyrologies, these were chiefly intended to console, encourage and to edify fellow believers. The trial proceedings cannot on their own provide a fair and balanced statement of nonconformist religious thought, but they can illuminate certain neglected aspects; of these I have chosen to explore their assault on the mass, and in particular on the real presence.

'Eat priests, shit monks and wipe your arse with canons'. This shocking and sensational graffito confronted visitors to the artillery yards at Amsterdam in March 1578, shortly before that city passed under the control of

---

[87] *DAN*, II, pp. 112, 130–31. The decision to discipline a member probably originated with the Amsterdam congregation.

[88] *DAN*, V, p. 261.

[89] E.g., *DAN*, V, pp. 277, 286, 287.

[90] *DAN*, V, pp. 20, 85, 277; II, p. 112.

[91] *DAN*, V, p. 120.

[92] *Dagboek*, II, p. 709. 'Eet papen, schijt monicken, veecht u naers met canonicken.'

the Dutch rebels.[92] The news saddened the Augustinian prior, Wouter Jacobsz., who recorded this bitter slogan in his diary, but as the prosecution of dissidents had by this time virtually ceased there was little chance that the perpetrators would be found. The prior could not however have been surprised. Though hostility to the clergy was less marked in the Low Countries than in Germany, the priesthood had been under attack for more than fifty years. Ever since the 1520s anticlericals of different sorts had jeered and even occasionally assaulted priests and religious in the towns and bands of vagabonds had periodically invaded religious houses. Though we may doubt the religious motivation of such anticlerical acts, there can be no question but that the Reformation weakened the rationale for the Catholic priesthood and the monasteries. Lay envy and suspicion of the first estate left the clergy in an exposed position at the time of iconoclastic riots in 1566. When the magistrates at Ghent, fearing an imminent attack on the churches, tried to recruit men to protect the clergy and church-buildings, they found that the great majority had not the slightest intention of raising a finger in defence of the priesthood.[93] When image-breaking threatened Middelburg, a magistrate told the council that he would protect his own house, but he would not fight to save the possessions of the clergy.[94] Even in Amsterdam, which served as a refuge for priests and religious forced to leave their native towns when the Beggars took control in 1572, the Catholic clergy did not always find a warm welcome. Wouter Jacobsz. tells of priests, who were unable to find lodgings, sleeping rough and of others, forced by poverty to earn a pittance by saying masses for money.

The priests owed their privileged position to their power, conferred at ordination, to absolve the sins of the laity and to celebrate mass. When the priests consecrated the eucharistic elements, to all intents and purposes he held Christ in his hands. A character in *Elckerlyc*, first printed at Delft *c.* 1495, put it thus: ' ... each priest can prepare/ with five words at the altar/ in the mass ... /God's true body, flesh and blood/ and holds the Creator between his hands/'.[95] Though anticlericalism was rife before the Reformation – Geiler of Kaysersberg spoke of 'the ancient hatred' between the clergy and laity – it lacked a theological justification. Critics of the late medieval clergy might denounce the hypocrisy, moral turpitude and avarice of many in holy orders, they might even include prelates and monks among the damned in their depictions of The Last Judgment, yet the laity depended for their salvation on the priests, who were alone empowered to administer the grace-conferring sacraments.

[93] M. Delmotte, 'Het calvinisme in de verschillende bevolkingslagen te Gent (1566–1567)', *TG*, LXXIX (1963), pp. 152–54.

[94] *Onderzoek van 's konings wege ingesteld omtrent de Middelburgsche beroerten van 1566 en 1567*, ed. J. van Vloten (Utrecht, 1873), pp. 103, 131, 156.

[95] Cited by D.P. Oosterbaan, *De Oude Kerk te Delft gedurende de middeleeuwen* (The Hague, 1973), p. 168.

When Luther taught that it was not ordination, or a tonsure, that made a man religious, but 'baptism, gospel and faith alone', he revolutionised the relationship between the clergy and laity. In the spiritual conflict between the two kingdoms, the faithful laity stood on equal terms with the evangelical clergy. There could then be no reason to deny the cup to the laity. Luther's repudiation of transubstantiation and his rejection of the mass as a sacrifice further reduced the significance of the priest. Although Luther upheld the need for an ordained clergy, more radical reformers glossed the notion that 'all men are priests before God' in such a way as to render a professional ministry redundant. They also transformed the sacrament of the altar into a commemorative meal. From that perspective the theological arguments for holding the priesthood in awe and for granting those in orders a privileged status disintegrated.

When such heady notions were adopted by those who had long resented the church's power and privileges, the reaction could be explosive. Outraged dissidents turned on the priests and accused these of having fabricated the church's teaching about penance, purgatory and the mass in order to line their own pockets. The Dutch anticlericals and dissidents had, as we know from the trial proceedings, a rich vocabulary of abuse. They denounced the clergy as 'soul-murderers', 'seducers of God', 'Judases', men who sold God for 'a doit' and 'god-guzzlers'.[96] At first the dissidents concentrated their fire on the 'deceits' practised by the clergy for their own financial benefit. Purgatory, a member of the conventicle at Veere claimed, only existed 'in the bottom of the priest's purse'.[97] Evangelicals used to joke about the mass. As the humour depends on a Dutch homonym – *misse* (mass); *mis* (awry); *mist* (dung) – the jest loses much of its force in translation. 'The mass', one version ran, 'has been well named, because everything there is amiss', and again, 'What's a mass/amiss? I often hear in my purse that it's amiss/ a mass'.[98] Before long all the practices of the church appeared to their opponents to have been conceived only to defraud honest men. When a priest took the sacrament to the sick at Venlo in 1566, a Calvinist shouted, 'You knave, haven't you gone round for long enough with your Judas purse?'[99] The money squandered to buy candles and to adorn the statues of the saints in the churches could be better spent on the poor, 'the living saints, who

[96] See above, p. 53; *CD*, V, p. 159; *Dagboek van gebeurtenissen opgetekend door Christiaan Munters, 1529–1545*, ed. J. Grauwels (Assen, 1972), p. 19; ORA Gouda, 147, fo. 80v; *Dagboek*, I, p. 56.
[97] Hoop Scheffer, p. 514.
[98] Duverger, 'Lutherse predicatie', col. 227; Hoop Scheffer, p. 514; cf., *BRN*, I, *Polemische geschriften der hervormingsgezinden*, p. 203; D. Coigneau, 'Literatuur en pennestrijd', *Het eind van een rebelse droom*, ed. J. Decavele (Ghent, 1984), p. 100.
[99] J.C.J. Kleyntjens, 'Stukken betreffende ketterij en beeldenstorm te Venlo', *BMHG*, LVI (1935), pp. 38, 42.

go naked and suffer from hunger'.[100] To a Calvinist at 's-Hertogenbosch the statues, saints, relics and the trappings of the mass seemed in 1566 so much 'merchandise', to be removed from the churches.[101] Easter itself was a 'fair' invented for the benefit of the clergy.[102]

Most evangelicals in the Low Countries rejected the real presence by the late 1520s and they reacted angrily to the notion that the consecrated host was in some sense special. They insisted that the host was ordinary bread, no different from that sold by the bakers of Amsterdam.[103] One dissident declared that the host was baked like ordinary bread between two irons and 'the priests eat it and shit it'.[104] They disparaged the host referring to it pejoratively as 'the breadgod', 'the mealgod', 'Brother Meal', 'the baked god', *Jan de Ronde* (Round John) and *Jan de Witte* (John White); the last on account of the brilliant white appearance of the consecrated bread, an effect, heretics alleged, achieved by the application of *hontsmeer* (dog fat). The Flemish Calvinists, if we may believe the satirical *Historie van Broer Cornelis Adriaensen* (1569–78), nicknamed the sacrament taken to the sick *joncker Melis inde halve mane* (Squire Meal in the Half Moon) because of the crescent-shaped pyx.[105] It did not end with namecalling. Dissidents committed deliberate acts of sacrilege which may be regarded as forms of ritual profanation. What had been consecrated for 'idolatrous' purposes had to be desecrated. When Anabaptists seized a monastery in Friesland in 1535, they made a point of immediately trampling the reserved sacrament underfoot.[106] In Limbourg, a small town to the east of Liège, a Calvinist woman allegedly urinated in the communion vessels in 1566.[107] Wouter Jacobsz. tells how, three days after Amsterdam passed under rebel control in 1578, the Calvinists ransacked the Heilige Stede (Holy Place), previously the focus of Catholic devotion in the town, and people tipped ordure on what had been the site of the holy sacrament.[108] Although it would not be difficult to

[100] *BRN*, I, p. 263; *cf.*, above p. 55; *DAN*, V, p. 55.

[101] *Documents pour servir à l'histoire des troubles religieux du XVIe siècle dans le Brabant septentrional: Bois-le-Duc (1566–1570)*, ed. P. Cuypers-van Velthoven (Brussels, 1858), p. 308; *cf.*, *Onderzoek ... omtrent de Middelburgsche beroerten*, p. 25.

[102] Hoop Scheffer, p. 514.

[103] *DAN*, V, p. 7; *cf.*, Decavele, *Dageraad* I, p. 598.

[104] *DAN*, I, p. 61.

[105] For nicknames see J.G.R. Acquoy, *Jan van Venray en de wording en vestiging der hervormde gemeente te Zalt-Bommel* ('s-Hertogenbosch, 1873), pp. 42–43; Van der Zijpp, *Geschiedenis der doopsgezinden*, p. 71; *Historie van Br. Cornelis Adriaensz.* (n.p., 1628), II, pp. 19–20, 23–24. For *hontsmeer* see A.C. Duke, 'An Enquiry into the Troubles in Asperen, 1566–1567', *BMHG* LXXXII (1968), p. 220. Most of these nicknames antedated the Reformation: English Lollards referred to the host in very similar terms in the fifteenth century.

[106] *DAN*, I, p. 30; S. Zijlstra, 'Blesdijk's verslag van de bezetting van Oldeklooster', *Doopsgezinde bijdragen*, n.r., X (1984), p. 67.

[107] F. Lemaire and A.L.E. Verheyden, 'Une enquête sur le protestantisme au duché de Limbourg en 1569', *BCRH*, CXVIII (1953), pp. 187, 193; *cf.*, *Dagboek*, II, p. 648.

[108] *Dagboek*, II, p. 727.

enumerate other acts of sacrilege, it would serve no useful purpose. It is more profitable to examine briefly the types of arguments deployed by the dissidents to refute the doctrines of transubstantiation and the real presence.

In the first place the dissident craftsmen appealed to the scriptures and cited in their support the store of texts built up by Protestant reformers in their polemics with the Romanists. They relied most heavily on John VI: 63; Acts VII: 48–50, 55–56; XVII: 22–24 and I Corinthians XI: 23–27.[109] Taken together these asserted the superiority of the spiritual over the fleshly; the infinite power of the Creator who did not dwell 'in temples made with hands'; the presence of the risen Christ at the right-hand of the Father; and the commemorative character of the Lord's Supper. We cannot be certain by what means the dissidents encountered these texts, whether from their own reading of the scriptures, from the evangelical literature or from the teaching they received in the conventicles. Certainly such passages were keenly discussed among the evangelical rank-and-file.[110] These scriptural arguments represent a simplification of doctrines elaborated by trained theologians. Yet the religious dissidents also devised their own refutations of the real presence. In February 1533 an argument broke out between Pieter Aemsz., a devout Catholic and a *schepen* of Amsterdam, and Adriaen Pietersz., who recklessly attacked the mass. The dissident cited the opening line of the Lord's Prayer in support of his belief that, since God was in heaven, He could not also be in the host.[111] From a strictly theological perspective the argument was seriously flawed: it confused the first and second persons of the Trinity. Yet the glib reasoning may have been more effective with a public accustomed to speak loosely about *God* being truly present in the sacrament. Indeed Pieter Aemsz. used just such language in this exchange.

This encounter reminds us that these lay dissidents employed arguments which would make the deepest impression on the religious sensitivities of those among whom they lived. Many years ago Huizinga drew attention to what he termed the 'naive religious conscience of the multitude' and in particular to their religious imagery 'both ultra-concrete and ultra fantastic'.[112] The age of eucharistic miracles and bleeding hosts might

---

[109] John VI: 63 *DAN*, II, p. 4: Acts VII: 48–50 *DAN*, V, p. 268, *DAN*, II, pp. 3, 40; Acts XVII: 22–24 *CD*, V, p. 140; Bezemer, 'Geloofsvervolging', p. 49; I Corinthians XI: 23–27 *DAN*, II, p. 4. Melchior Hoffman cited Acts VII: 48–50 in his quarrel with the Lutheran clergy of Schleswig-Holstein when he wanted to prove that 'the finite is incapable of holding the infinite', K. Deppermann, *Melchior Hoffman: Social Unrest and Apocalyptic Visions in the Age of the Reformation* (Edinburgh, 1987), p. 124.

[110] *E.g.*, Bezemer, 'Geloofsvervolging', pp. 47–49.

[111] *DAN*, V, pp. 8, 142; the same argument recurs in some later evangelical literature, Johnston, 'Eclectic Reformation', pp. 82–83.

[112] J. Huizinga, *The Waning of the Middle Ages* (Harmandsworth, 1955), pp. 166, 200.

have been in retreat by the sixteenth century, but one has only to read the journal of Christiaan Munters, a chaplain in Liège in the first half of the sixteenth century, to realise it was by no means dead. He included several stories about heretics who made feigned confessions of the Catholic faith. Although they deceived the priests, their double-dealing was revealed by an inability to swallow the host, which was retrieved intact from their tongues.[113] To counter the materialism of popular Catholic piety the nonconformists directly challenged, as we have seen above, the notion that the host possessed any miraculous properties. An image-breaker in Middelburg in 1566, who was trampling hosts on the ground, jested, 'What petty gods these people (*i.e.* the Catholics) have. If God were present (in the host), he might bite my toes off!'[114] Adriaen Pietersz. used an analogous argument when he offered to put the doctrine of the real presence to the test by piercing hosts to see if they bled.[115] Such arguments may strike us as naive and superficial, yet their effect in the sixteenth century was probably very different. Certainly the upholders of the old religion did not take such challenges lightly. Adriaen Pietersz. paid for his temerity with his life. There was much at stake. If the dissidents could demonstrate the impotence of the sacraments, they could show that the Roman Church was not only in doctrinal error; it also lacked the power to protect the community. As such it no longer deserved to enjoy the continued support of the people. In 1566 the parish priest in a village near Delft informed his parishioners midway through the mass that he had decided to adopt the Calvinist faith. The church was duly purged of images and the statue of St. George, the patron saint, was removed outside. Both the priest and his concubine ridiculed the statue in the hearing of their parishioners. On one occasion she was overheard saying, 'What a great god St. George is. He stands in the garden where he is unable even to keep away the sparrows!'[116] This incident was in effect a microcosm of a much broader conflict. The onslaught on the images, shrines and sacraments during the iconoclastic riots represented a trial of strength between the Catholic and Calvinist theologies.

Yet some dissidents who fiercely opposed those sacraments, shrines and statues were far from convinced that these were empty symbols. On the contrary, they attributed to them a demonic power. A Catholic questioned in Amsterdam in 1535 about her neighbour, then under suspicion of heresy, recalled a conversation with the accused. When the witness had told her about a pilgrimage she had made to a certain cross in the town, the latter retorted that, 'it was not God who had come to

---

[113] *Dagboek van ... Christiaan Munters*, pp. 23, 37–38.

[114] *Onderzoek ... omtrent de Middelburgsche beroerten*, p. 90.

[115] *DAN*, V, p. 40. Cited at length at the head of this essay.

[116] ARAB, RvB, 109 (113a) fo. 142.

her aid through that cross, it was the Devil'.[117] Again, when a Catholic, concerned to promote his faith, reminded a notorious heretic about the miracles daily wrought at the chapel of the Heilige Stede in Amsterdam, the dissident did not deny this or even argue that the priests deceived the people; he simply warned the Catholic that the Devil too performed miracles.[118] Moyses, the iconoclast at 's-Hertogenbosch who burnt the crucifix, believed that the Devil possessed Catholic images and symbols, which therefore had to be exorcised. To evangelicals the mass was a perverted form of religion. For that reason iconoclasts in 's-Hertogenbosch told some nuns to abandon the worship of their 'little gods' (the statues) and to cease the practice of 'witchcraft'.[119] If the Roman church were indeed the 'synagogue of Satan' its extirpation became an even more urgent business.

The state of research does not yet permit a considered assessment of the place of religion in the daily life of the Dutch dissidents in the second and third quarters of the sixteenth century. Nevertheless the judicial records, which are relatively plentiful on account of the repression, throw light on the dissident religious beliefs of the *non-letterez*. These *kleyne luyden* drew much of their theology, directly or indirectly, from Luther and the other leading reformers. Yet in their conflict with popular Catholicism, they also developed commonsensical arguments which were designed to refute the 'superstitions' with which they were daily confronted. The source of these remains largely unknown, though we may speculate that they owe something to pre-Reformation oral traditions of dissent. When exploring the 'people's Reformation' in the Low Countries it is necessary to analyse the language ordinary dissidents used when they spoke about the mass, images and pilgrimages. The learned scholastic theology against which Luther and the other reformers revolted touched them less directly than the beliefs and piety of their Catholic peers. By giving due weight to the witness of *le menu peuple* it may be possible to enter the religious world of these nonconformists.

---

[117] *DAN*, V, p. 191.
[118] *DAN*, V, p. 7.
[119] *Kroniek eener kloosterzuster ... over de troebelen te 's-Hertogenbosch in de jaren, 1566–1575*, ed. H. van Alfen ('s-Hertogenbosch, 1931), p. 3.

6

The Time of Troubles in the County of Holland, 1566–67

Most studies of the Troubles of 1566–67 have naturally concentrated on Flanders and Brabant, where the Reformed Protestants began holding their services and the iconoclastic disturbances were most intense.[1] The welter of events and the wealth of information make it extremely difficult to give a clear picture of this turbulent period, without doing violence to its kaleidoscopic character. For this reason it is perhaps worth turning our attention to Holland, where the slower pace of events allows easier appreciation of their disparate nature. A study of this region may also afford some insights into the Troubles in the Southern Netherlands: Holland was sufficiently close to the epicentre of the storm to register most of the shockwaves.[2]

Until May 1566 Holland preserved an outward calm, though beneath the surface faint traces of agitation were discernible. Early in April the *schutters* of Leiden had taken defensive measures against a possible incursion by Eric of Brunswick, whose conduct and troops in nearby Woerden they distrusted.[3] Towards the end of that month Morillon, faithful correspondent and informant of Granvelle, told his master that

---

[1] We wish to express our thanks to Aubrey Newman, Norman Ball, Rosemary Duke-Jones, Juliaan Woltjer and Ivo Schöffer who all gave generously of their time to suggest improvements to this article. The late Dr. H.A. Enno van Gelder, who acted as reader, provided useful advice. Naturally they cannot be held responsible for the opinions expressed here or for the omissions and shortcomings which remain.

[2] Roughly one-tenth of the persons summoned to appear before the Council of Troubles came from Holland: see A.L.E. Verheyden, *Le Conseil des Troubles: Liste des Condamnés* (Brussels, 1961). Though this list has been the subject of some criticism it remains the only general guide. For Holland see J. Marcus, *Sententiën en indagingen van den Hertog van Alba* (Amsterdam, 1735). This is based on the manuscript in the ARAG, Grafelijkheidsrekenkamer, 681 ter. Marcus rearranged the order of the entries.

[3] The Duke of Brunswick had been granted Woerden in 1558 as a cautionary town for services he had rendered to the Habsburgs. His military activities alarmed many people in the Netherlands in 1566 besides the *schutters* of Leiden. In July that year the Beggars in Amsterdam were concerned about his presence at Naarden and his conduct caused disquiet as far afield as Antwerp. Philip II also felt uneasy in May 1566 about the rumours then circulating, but later the government made him responsible for taking on troops in the Empire for service in the Netherlands.

the sole topic of conversation in Gorcum was of the 'tyrannie du Roi'.[4] In mid-April Hendrik van Brederode returned to Vianen from the South, where he had been the spokesman of the Beggars, as the members of the Confederation of the Nobility had become known. Brederode (1531–68) was by far the greatest landholder in the county: his manors, comprising almost one-twelfth of Holland, surpassed those of Hoorn, Egmont and Orange.[5] He owned extensive tracts around Ameide, elsewhere in the Alblasserwaard near Dordrecht, and in Kennemerland around Haarlem and to the north of Alkmaar. The cornerstone of his power was his position as the sovereign lord of Vianen on the Lek, where he had his own mint and high court of justice. Through his wife, Amelia von Neuenahr, he was connected with the Rhineland aristocracy, and the marriage of his sister to Thomas Perronet, seigneur de Chantonay, linked him with Granvelle and Burgundy. But for his father's presumptuous claim to the countship of Holland, the family would surely have stood higher in the royal favour.[6] After Reinoud's death in 1556, there was a partial reconciliation and in 1565 Hendrik was granted a royal pension.[7] Yet there remained something anomalous about the position of this great feudatory, three of whose brothers had died in the service of their liege-lord, for he was denied the honour and authority normally attendant on one of his standing.[8] Indeed the *stadhouderschap* of Holland or the governorship of Antwerp, which William of Orange may have wished to see conferred on Brederode, were the sort of offices a nobleman of his rank might have aspired to.[9] As the natural leader of the nobility in Holland, Brederode's choice in the coming struggle was bound to be crucial, for he could be expected to carry with him many of the country gentry as well as his own tenantry.

It is uncertain when Brederode joined the opposition, though as early as 1563 books of a heretical nature were being printed at Vianen,

[4] *Correspondance de Granvelle*, ed. E. Poullet and C. Piot (Brussels, 1877), I, p. 228.

[5] H.A. Enno van Gelder, 'De Hollandse adel in de tijd van de opstand', *TG*, XLV (1930), pp. 127–28.

[6] These claims were revived in 1566, for a coin was struck in Vianen that year bearing the arms of the count: See *NNBW*, X, p. 124. According to Van Haecht troops were recruited in Antwerp by Brederode in 1567 and the cry was that 'he was the lawful lord of Holland', *De kroniek van Godevaert van Haecht over de troebelen van 1565 tot 1574 te Antwerpen en elders*, ed. R. van Roosbroeck (Antwerp, 1929), I, p. 185. The Frisian nobleman Sjoerd Beyma also championed Brederode's title, (J.J. Woltjer, *Friesland in hervormingstijd* (Leiden, 1962), p. 149; as did a certain Claes Pens from The Hague, Marcus, *Sententiën*, p. 256.

[7] *Corresp. française Marguerite d'Autriche*, I, pp. 23–24.

[8] R.C. Bakhuizen van den Brink, 'Hendrik van Brederode en Willem van Oranje in 1566–1567', *Cartons voor de geschiedenis van den nederlandschen vrijheidsoorlog* (3 ed., The Hague, 1898), II, p. 24.

[9] Bakhuizen van den Brink, *op. cit.*, pp. 76–77. According to M. Dierickx, *Documents inédits sur l'érection des nouveaux diocèses aux Pays Bas* (Brussels, 1962), III, pp. 278–79. Brederode was a Knight of the Golden Fleece, but we can find no evidence to support this assertion.

presumably with his knowledge. Apparently he took only a minor part in the campaign against the Cardinal and he was absent from the meeting held at Spa in the summer of 1565. He was however among the first to put his name to the Compromise in December that year.[10] In January 1566 an investigation revealed that a printer at Vianen had a stock of forbidden literature and had himself published a Protestant martyrology.[11] By April 1566, when he presented the Petition to Margaret of Parma, Brederode had clearly emerged as one of the Beggars' leaders.

Defender as Brederode was of the Reformed Protestants in 1566, he did not openly commit himself to the new religion. Like so many of his estate he had long been bitterly hostile to ecclesiastics and by 1566 he was fiercely anticatholic.[12] Brederode's wife was Lutheran by upbringing, but his own religious convictions are harder to pin down. Enno van Gelder considers him a Protestant though he believes that it is impossible to decide whether he was a 'Lutheran' or a 'Calvinist'.[13] The library at his castle in Vianen contained, besides numerous histories, classics and romances, several Bibles and the odd work by Luther (possibly his wife's), Sleidan, Viret and Sebastian Franck. The most remarkable feature of his library was the almost total absence of the Catholic books of piety usually found in a collection of this size.[14] Unlike the Catholic members of the Confederation Brederode's religious loyalties were in harmony with his political standpoint, but he laid the emphasis on the latter. He perhaps deliberately avoided making a choice which could only cause offence: he had the support of the Reformed without embracing their religion and there was no point in alienating the lukewarm Catholics and the Lutheran princes of the Empire by choosing more often than was necessary, or before it was necessary.

The dissident gentry of Holland hitched their wagon to Brederode's star. Of the two hundred odd county families, no fewer than fifty-four belonged to the Confederation, although only thirty-eight may be regarded as Reformed or even tolerant of heresy.[15] The rest were Catholics, some

---

[10] M. Dierickx, 'De eerste jaren van Filips II', *AGN*, IV, p. 337. See also J. Kaufmann, *Über die Anfänge des Bundes der Adelichen und des Bildersturmes* (Bonn, 1889), pp. 20–31. Brederode knew that Louis of Nassau was at Spa in August 1565: see *Archives ou correspondance* (Leiden, 1841), I, pp. 396–98.

[11] H. de la Fontaine Verwey, 'Hendrik van Brederode en de drukkerijen van Vianen', *Het Boek*, XXX (1949–1951). See also the same author's, 'Over enige boeken te Vianen gedrukt tijdens het "Voorspel", *Opstellen ... aangeboden aan Dr. F.K.H. Kossmann* (The Hague, 1958).

[12] Bakhuizen van den Brink, 'De Adel', *Cartons* (3 ed., The Hague, 1891), I, pp. 72–74.

[13] H.A. Enno van Gelder, 'Bailleul, Bronkhorst, Brederode', *De Gids*, C (1936), pp. 368–71.

[14] J.J. Salverda de Grave, 'Twee inventarissen van het huis Brederode', *BMHG*, XXXIX (1918), pp. 1–172.

[15] H.F.K. van Nierop, *Van ridders tot regenten: De hollandse adel in de 16de en de eerste helft van de 17de eeuw* (n.p., 1984), appendix vii; Enno van Gelder, 'De Hollandse adel', *TG*, XLV (1930), p. 150 gives fifty-three.

of whom withdrew from the Beggars later in 1566. It was not then their faith which brought these men together, but their anxiety to safeguard their political and social position in the face of the encroachments of the Crown and the jurists. When they attacked the inquisition, they did so principally because it infringed their privileges and did not respect their feudal immunities.[16] Most of these gentry were men of slender means and circumscribed influence, whose only chance of power outside of the army was in the service of some great nobleman or as members of a town corporation. In some parts of the county the gentry had never counted for much, and this was especially so in the Gooi, West Friesland and Kennemerland. The gentry in these parts were often absentee landlords, strangers on their own manors: it is hardly surprising then that their political and religious inclinations counted for little with the inhabitants there.

After returning to Holland in April Brederode set about whipping up support for the Request. On 18 May he arrived in the vicinity of Haarlem, where he had a residence. News of his activity caused concern among the magistrates and Dirck Volckertsz. Coornhert, the town clerk, was sent to discover what was afoot. He and another official were quickly able to persuade 'le grant geu' to cease his canvassing in the town.[17] About a month later his presence was signalled in Amsterdam where he was on a similar mission.[18] For Brederode these weeks in Holland were pleasant ones, as he basked in an aura of popular acclaim. Excitedly he told Louis of Nassau that everyone there was 'geus et double geus',[19] and on 9 June, writing from Bergen, where he had been inspecting his new polder, he was still more ebullient: 'Je m'apercoys bien que ce bon Dieu est geu du tout ... Les geus sont par icy semé comme le sablon dullon de la mere'.[20] The events of 1567 would show that such optimism was misplaced, for, despite Brederode's endeavours, the Beggars failed to provide an acceptable leadership for the heterogeneous movements of protest.

Before Brederode left Holland early in July for Antwerp a government agent had informed Philip II that gatherings of heretics were taking place in Vianen, though it is by no means certain that such development had the Beggar's blessing.[21] During almost the whole of July he was

[16]   Enno van Gelder, 'Bailleul, Bronkhorst, Brederode', p. 374.

[17]   J. Kleijntjens and B. Becker, *Corpus Iconoclasticum: Documenten over den beeldenstorm van 1566 in de Bourgondische Monarchie*, I, *Haarlem* (Tilburg, n.d.), pp. 7–12.

[18]   'Anteykeningen van Broer Hendrik van Biesten: Nieuwe Mare dat geschiet is bynnen Amsterdam zedert dan Jaere 1534', *De dietsche warande*, VII (1866), p. 332. It was probably at this time that the *Oude Schutters* of Amsterdam joined the Confederation. The Confederation of the Nobility also sent three emissaries in June 1566 to Friesland where they tried, without much success, to gain support for their action, see J.J. Woltjer, *Friesland in hervormingstijd*, pp. 148–150.

[19]   *Archives ou correspondance*, II, p. 127.

[20]   *Archives ou correspondance*, II, pp. 130–31.

[21]   *Corresp. Philippe II*, I, p. 425.

occupied with the affairs of the Confederation at Antwerp, St. Truiden and Duffel, and when he returned home on 29 July he found that the mood in Holland had altered greatly in his absence.

Since May hedge preachers had been at work in the Flemish West-kwartier, publicly expounding the new doctrines; by mid-June assemblies several thousand strong were taking place outside Antwerp.[22] Further north on the Batenburg lands east of Den Bosch a heretical teacher had been active in the first days of the same month.[23] At Culemborg, on the Lek, Protestant services had been conducted since 2 June in the count's castle.[24] In Holland the decision to hold services in the fields was taken by a group of the foremost members of the Reformed congregation in Amsterdam on 8 July. Accordingly on Sunday 14 July Jan Arendsz., a basketmaker, who had ministered to the Reformed in Holland since 1559, preached in West Friesland before a crowd numbering several hundred, while the *schout* of Hoorn looked on disapprovingly from a nearby monastery.[25] A week later services were held on the outskirts of Haarlem and Alkmaar; and on the last day of the month the Reformed felt sufficiently confident to hold a service outside the gates of Amster-dam.[26] In the course of the next fortnight similar gatherings occurred across the IJ in Waterland.[27]

There is no firm evidence for services taking place elsewhere in the county before 18 August, when posters were discovered on the town-gates of Delft giving notice of a meeting to take place that afternoon at Rijswijk.[28] This was attended by many Delftenaars, some of whom went armed.[29] The service had probably been engineered by some of the Protestant nobility of The Hague, among them Diederick Sonoy, François

[22] Though the term 'hedge preacher' is unfamiliar in English, it is being used here on the analogy of 'hedge priest', which was a term of abuse in the sixteenth century and described an itinerant, unqualified and ignorant cleric. *Haagpredikant* also conveys the dual sense of an irregular preacher who travelled about the country and an ignorant fellow. It follows then that a 'hedge service' is a service conducted by such a person. See R. Fruin, 'Haagpreek', *Verspreide Geschriften* (The Hague, 1903), VIII, pp. 307–13.

[23] P. Cuypers-van Velthoven, *Documents pour servir à l'histoire des troubles religieux de XVIe siècle dans le Brabant septentrional*, I, *Bois-le-Duc* ('s-Hertogenbosch, 1858), p. 3.

[24] O.J. de Jong, *De Reformatie in Culemborg* (Assen, n.d.), p. 102.

[25] J.C. Breen, 'Uittreksel uit de Amsterdamsche gedenkschriften van Laurens Jacobsz. Reael', *BMHG*, XVII (1896), pp. 14–15; Brandt, I, pp. 315–19. *Corresp. française Marguerite d'Autriche*, II, pp. 308–9. See also *schout*'s deposition: ARAB, RvB, 109 (118), fo. 300–4.

[26] Brandt, I, pp. 319–28.

[27] ARAB, RvB 115 (125), fo. 241, 243v.

[28] Clandestine assemblies may have occurred earlier. The States of Holland heard on 6 July that there were indications that services were beginning in 'some parts of Holland'. On 15–16 June a renegade cleric had been refused permission to preach in Delft and there is a report of a service in Gorcum on 22 July. There are unsubstantiated reports about services near The Hague from 14 August. Meetings also took place at Sonoy's residence there.

[29] J. Smit, 'Hagepreken en beeldenstorm te Delft, 1566–67', *BMHG*, XLV (1924), pp. 212–13.

van Haeften and Cornelis van Wijngaarden: a number of the gentry from Voorburg and Den Briel were also there.[30] The first sermon near Leiden was preached out at Oegstgeest on 25 August. Here too the hedge services continued under the aegis of one of the local gentry, who escorted the minister.[31] That same Sunday a local priest at Den Briel asked leave to preach 'the true gospel of Christ' in the church there.[32] At Schoonhoven, where some of the burghers had been to service near Utrecht on 15 August,[33] the first Protestant assembly took place on 27 August.[34] But it was not until midway through September that a start was made in Rotterdam, by which time the *Accoord* had been published and several towns had suffered at the hands of the image-breakers.[35]

Before turning to the iconoclastic movement, there are a few observations to be made about the spread and character of the hedge services in the county. Originally confined to the lordships of the great nobility along the Lek, they then spread to the Noorderkwartier. At first sight this seems surprising, as this region figured hardly at all during the Troubles; in fact the impetus came from the Reformed congregation of Amsterdam, who had been persuaded by the draconian edict of 3 July to hold the first services away from that city. It is rather less easy to account for the late date at which such services were organised in the towns of South Holland. Brandt merely notes that representatives from Leiden, Delft and Utrecht came to Amsterdam to urge that such assemblies should be organised in their cities, for, so they claimed, the Governor was prepared to tolerate these, if they had begun before 21 August.[36] Probably the lack of suitable preachers hindered the Reformed. At this stage the burden was shared among Jan Arendsz., Pieter Cornelisz., Wouter Simons and Pieter Gabriel. As the supply of ministers increased, hedge services occurred throughout almost the whole county, with the significant exception of Gouda and Dordrecht.[37]

The organisers of these services were alert to the advantages to be gained by first holding these outside the jurisdiction of the towns. As the opening service in West Friesland took place in the district of the *schout* of Westwoud, the *schout* of Hoorn, the most important officer in the

---

[30] Marcus, *Sententiën*, p. 37; J.Smit, *Den Haag in den geuzentijd* (The Hague, 1922), pp. 31–35.

[31] D.H.A. Kolff, 'Libertatis ergo: De beroerten binnen Leiden in de jaren 1566 en 1567', *Leids jaarboekje* (1966), pp. 133–34.

[32] I.M.P.A. Wils, 'De reformatie en beeldenstorm in den Briel', *Haarlemsche bijdragen*, LVI (1938), p. 408.

[33] Marcus, *Sententiën*, p. 282.

[34] H. van Berkum, *Beschryving der stadt Schoonhoven* (Gouda, 1762), p. 512.

[35] H.C. Hazewinkel, *Geschiedenis van Rotterdam* (Amsterdam, 1940), I, p. 164.

[36] Brandt, I, p. 328. The *Accoord* was in fact signed on 23 August 1566.

[37] It was probably in the summer of 1566 that Jan Arendsz. endeavoured without success to conduct a service outside Dordrecht. See M. Balen, *Beschryvinge der stadt Dordrecht* (Dordrecht, 1677), p. 835.

region, was powerless to intervene. The earliest meetings around Haarlem and Alkmaar were held on the manors of Brederode. The Reformed took similar precautions at Edam, Leiden, and Delft. On each occasion the law officer of the nearby town was not competent to act. Margaret of Parma ruefully acknowledged that the plans had been carefully laid in the knowledge that the officials in the rural areas had no means of dispersing such gatherings.[38]

In addition to the brazen insolence of self-appointed preachers now retailing their doctrines from hastily improvised pulpits, alarming rumours continued to circulate. People said that the Spanish Inquisition was going to be introduced, that the government was raising troops in the Empire, that the Catholic clergy were to be massacred and the Protestants annihilated. One report in particular stalked Holland, causing great disquiet. It was alleged that those inveterate opponents of heresy, the Grey Friars, had compiled a *librum dictum sanguinarium* containing the names of Protestants and lukewarm Catholics.[39] Opinions differed as to their exact intentions, though all were agreed that these were nefarious. According to some the blacklist had been drawn up with a view to confiscating the property of the suspects, whereas others put a more bloodcurdling construction on the *bloetbouck*. In mid-August the matter was raised at a meeting in Schoorl attended by Brederode as well as some of the gentry and local dignitaries,[40] and at Hoorn worried citizens sent a deputation to Orange in Antwerp to make further enquiries.[41] Similar rumours were heard in Den Briel[42] and Delft.[43] Contemporaries saw the events of 1566 refracted through a prism of fear, which distorted the crisis and made them ready to believe the worst.

In this brittle atmosphere news of the image-breaking in Antwerp was sufficient to precipitate the storm in Holland. On the eve of the image-breaking there law and order was only being precariously maintained in the towns. In the face of a series of ambiguous orders from Brussels about the policy to be adopted towards heretics, town governments were confused and demoralised. With only paltry police forces and *schutterijen*

---

[38] *Corresp. française Marguerite d'Autriche*, II, p. 309.

[39] R. Fruin, *Uittreksel uit Francisci Dusseldorpii Annales, 1566–1616* (The Hague, 1893), p. 6. Dusseldorpius alleged that the rumour was deliberately disseminated by the Beggars for propaganda purposes.

[40] ARAB, RvB, 109 (110), fo. 9v.

[41] ARAB, RvB, 109 (118), fo. 303–3v, 311.

[42] Wils, *op. cit.*, pp. 412–13.

[43] J. Soutendam, 'Beeldstormerij te Delft in Augustus en Oktober 1566', *Bijdragen voor vaderlandsche geschiedenis en oudheidkunde*, n.r., IX (1877), p. 217. Smit, *Hagepreken en beeldenstorm te Delft*, pp. 218–19. See also report current in Middelburg about a roll of 300 burghers, classified as heretics, allegedly found in a religious house there, *Onderzoek van 's konings wege ingesteld omtrent de Middelburgsche beroerten van 1566 en 1567* (Utrecht, 1873), p. 125.

of dubious loyalty at their disposal they could not give a decisive lead. On hearing news of the destruction in the south the clergy of Amsterdam set about hauling down the images and carrying them out of the churches; and the same scene was repeated in other towns. Next day, 23 August, the first riot broke out in Amsterdam in the Oude Kerk, and though easily quelled, this set the pattern. During the next ten days outbreaks followed in Delft, The Hague, Leiden, Heenvliet,[44] Den Briel, and Alkmaar in that order. There were recurrences in Amsterdam in late September, and in Delft and Den Briel in October; elsewhere there was sporadic image-breaking. Such a bald summary however gives no inkling of the variety of iconoclastic activity.

The term *beeldenstorm* usually conjures up a scene of indiscriminate destruction with wreckers and looters running amuck in the churches. Such outbreaks were in fact comparatively rare in the northern Netherlands, yet because the image-breaking in Antwerp had taken this form with Europe looking on, the exception was taken for the rule.[45] In Holland the disturbances in Amsterdam, Delft, Leiden, and Den Briel conformed most closely to this pattern. Yet in The Hague, for example, the churches were stripped deliberately and methodically. Still more extraordinarily this was done with a semblance of legality. Two prominent members of the Reformed communities in The Hague and Delft informed the President of the *Hof van Holland* that they had a warrant to purge the churches. Without probing more deeply Mr. Cornelis Suys told them to proceed about their work 'without causing a commotion'; the twelve men so employed were paid out of the President's pocket.[46] Sometimes the images and trappings of the old religion were broken or taken down at the insistence of the nobleman on whose domain the churches stood. In mid-September the churches of Culemborg underwent just such an attack, with the count, Floris van Pallandt, lending a helping hand.[47] At Asperen the aged Wessel van Boetzelaer gave the order to strip the churches on 8 October.[48] The actual destruction was executed by his servants and overseen by two of his sons and Willem van Zuylen van Nijvelt, who brought several men-at-arms from Culemborg. The attack did not stop at images: altars were demolished, vestments destroyed, service books torn up and an organ smashed. A confessor attached to a nunnery was put out of the township and the religious were obliged to attend Reformed services in lay attire. Clearly the 'casting down' of the

---

[44] I.M.P.A. Wils, 'Beeldenstorm te Heenvliet', *Haarlemsche bijdragen*, LIV (1937), pp. 464–65.

[45] De Jong, *De beeldenstormen in de Nederlanden* (Groningen. 1964), p. 5.

[46] Breen, 'Uittreksel', pp. 32–33.

[47] De Jong, *De reformatie in Culemborg*, pp. 131–35.

[48] For Asperen see Marcus, *Sententiën*, pp. 130–41, which should be read in conjunction with A.C. Duke, 'An Enquiry into the Troubles in Asperen, 1566–1567', *BMHG*, LXXXII (1968), pp. 207–27.

churches in Asperen was intended to presage the introduction of Protestantism in this barony on the Linge. Unfortunately little is known of what took place in Vianen. Brederode ordered the images to be removed on 25 September; a week later the Reformed were allowed to hold their services in the parish church.[49] In both Vianen and Asperen, as in Culemborg, the decision to destroy or remove the images was taken by the nobleman despite opposition from below. In Asperen, for instance, the inhabitants begged Van Boetzelaer to allow them to hold mass during Lent 1567. Similar to this form of iconoclasm is that where priests had the images taken down: this happened in De Lier[50] and Woerden.[51] Once again there are signs that parishioners objected to these changes as Heer Arent Dircxz. Vos found out in De Lier. Another variant on this pattern is provided by those instances where a nobleman had an ancestral monument pulled down: Willem van Zuylen van Nijvelt had his family chapel at Aartsbergen demolished,[52] Herbert van Raephorst personally supervised the overthrow of two family altars in Wassenaar church;[53] a burgher of Rotterdam gave orders that a statuette which his forbears had donated to the church should be broken.[54] Finally one has to bear in mind the numerous isolated acts of iconoclasm in churchyards and along the roadside, where one is never certain whether the act was prompted by religious indignation or drunken bravado.[55] The heterogeneous character of the image-breaking makes it sometimes surprisingly difficult to determine whether a given town or village suffered or not. For example, Haarlem was one of the major towns in Holland to come through unscathed, yet in a letter of 27 August to Louis of Nassau Brederode described the town as seething, adding that not only had Egmond Abbey been menaced but that a religious house at Overveen, close to Haarlem, had been sacked.[56] When William of Orange visited Gorcum late in October he found that, though 'les autelz et ymaiges' had not been cast down, plans had been laid to do just that.[57] Zaltbommel

---

[49] J.W. te Water, *Historie van het Verbond en de Smeekschriften der Nederlandsche Edelen*, 4 vols. (Middelburg, 1776–96), IV, Bijlage QQ, p. 325.

[50] On De Lier see ARAB, RvB, 109 (113a), fo. 142–42v, 143–45v.

[51] See entry in *NNBW*, VIII, pp. 228–29, *s.v.* Erik van Brunswijk. The images in Woerden had been removed sometime before 18 September. Early in October the States of Holland received a petition from the townspeople alleging that Eric of Brunswick had wanted to bring in troops, because the images had been taken down and certain religious changes had occured. See *Resolutiën der Staten van Holland*, 1566, pp. 46–48.

[52] Marcus, *Sententiën*, p. 154.

[53] Kolff, 'Libertatis ergo', p. 120.

[54] Marcus, *Sententiën*, pp. 146–7.

[55] In mid-December Orange investigated a case of image-breaking in Amsterdam; it was found 'that this drunkard knew nothing of either religion or images', Breen, 'Uittreksel', p. 51; in January 1568 two drunken ruffians of Edam threw painted panels into the water there, ARAB, RvB, 115 (125), fo. 245.   [56] *Archives ou correspondance*, II, pp. 252–56.

[57] *Corresp. Guillaume*, II, p. 255. The impression given in Marcus, *Sententiën*, p. 27 is that the Franciscan house there was attacked at some stage.

3. 'Love not the World, neither the things that are in the world' (I John 2: 15). Engraving *c.* 1550–60 *(Stichting Atlas van Stolk, Rotterdam, FM 422)*

This denunciation of the Kingdom of the World derives from a drawing of Bernard van Orley, now in the Rijksprentenkabinet, Amsterdam. Popes, prelates, monks and priests have preferred worldly power, pomp and pleasure to seeking the Kingdom of God. They

join a procession of tyrants, idolaters and persecutors, who are being drawn unwittingly into the maws of Hell. The string of scriptural paraphrases, which have not been reproduced here, links the corruption in the Church with the Last Days. Antichrist enters the city and the mother of harlots, arrayed in a papal tiara, sits on the beast. On a hill outside the city Christ spurns Satan's offer of worldly dominion, while the persecutions of the saints demonstrate that the blood of martyrs is the seed of the true Church.

in Gelderland is another town where it is not easy to decide what happened; although there appears to have been no wholesale iconoclasm, desultory damage was done to images.[58] In the case of rural areas information is harder to come by. Nonetheless it is certain that the churches in De Lier, Warmenhuizen, Hem,[59] Heenvliet, Rugge,[60] and the chapel of a religious house at Noordwijk,[61] suffered from image-breaking of one sort or another; more detailed investigations would almost certainly uncover other cases. In Schoonhoven an attempt was made to invade the churches;[62] a similar move in Hoorn was only thwarted by the timely intervention of a group of resolute Catholics who drove off the would-be iconoclasts by pelting them with mud and dung.[63]

When one examines the iconoclastic movement in Holland, one becomes quickly aware not only of its protean nature but also that the groundswell of discontent covered a rather wider area than has hitherto been supposed: seemingly only Gouda and Dordrecht escaped. This raises the question as to why certain towns should have suffered in the way they did, whereas others remained relatively calm. While it would be foolish to expect a single or simple explanation, several possible causes suggest themselves for further investigation.

An essential prerequisite for iconoclasm in a town was the presence of Reformed Protestantism.[64] Little can be said here about the abomination images excited among Protestants, especially the radicals and the Reformed, but one has only to recall the attacks on churches in the 1520s in the Baltic towns and in Switzerland, the fierce iconoclastic outburst in Scotland in 1559–60 and on the eve of the civil wars in France to realise how inseparably the religious element was bound up with these disturbances. When social and economic factors are being discussed, it has to be remembered that the parish churches and religious houses bore the brunt, not the counting-houses of the merchants or the granaries of

---

[58] J.G.R. Acquoy, *Jan van Venray en de wording en vestiging der hervormde gemeente te Zalt-Bommel* ('s Hertogenbosch, 1873), pp. 34–41, where the author distinguishes between *beeldenstorm* and *beeldbreking*.

[59] ARAB, RvB, 109 (110), fo. 13–16. For the destruction at Hem, G. Brandt, *Historie van Enkhuisen. Historie der vermaerde Zee- en Koop-stadt Enkhuisen* (Hoorn, 1747), p. 134.

[60] Wils, *De reformatie en beeldenstorm in Den Briel*, p. 410.

[61] J. Kloos, *Noordwijk in de loop der eeuwen* (Noordwijk, 1928), p. 105.   [62] Marcus, *Sententiën*, p. 282.

[63] ARAB, RvB, 109 (118), fo. 319–19v. This shameful blot on the town's record was more or less hushed up, but the *schepenrol* for 21 October 1566 refers obliquely to the affair: see RANH, ORA, 4157. Both Velius and Snellebrand are silent on this matter, indeed they boast that the Reformation in Hoorn was not disfigured by such unseemly violence.

[64] This qualification is necessary because image-breaking in the rural areas was often the work of roving bands who had gone out into the countryside from the towns.   [65] The general impression is that whereas the leading theologians and university-trained pastors were opposed to unauthorised image-breaking, some of the lay preachers egged on their congregations to attack the churches. Some of the foremost members of the Reformed church such as Marnix van St. Aldegonde were prepared to defend the attack on the churches.

the corn hoarders. Yet although every town in Holland had its heretical cell by 1566, the presence of a Reformed community did not invariably provoke rioting. This was not surprising, for within Reformed Protestantism there were differences of emphasis and divisions of opinion: the issue of the forcible removal of images was one on which there was no unanimity.[65] Pieter Cornelisz., a former basketmaker turned preacher, took an active part in the onslaught on the Franciscan house at Alkmaar,[66] whereas his colleague and coreligionist Clement Martensz., a former priest, restrained the Protestants of Hoorn from following suit.[67]

Clearly social and economic tensions go far to account for the scale and ferocity of the image-breaking in some towns. In Leiden the decaying cloth industry had left a legacy of bitterness and widespread unemployment. At the same time the patriciate had become increasingly isolated from the community. No new industry emerged to take the place of cloth and the corporation was dominated by a tightly knit clique of drapers with a few brewers and rich merchants. Normally the isolation of the corporation was not serious, but in 1566, when the central government caved in, the members found themselves compelled to call on the assistance of the *schutters*, their potential rivals, to prevent the disorders getting out of hand.[68] At Delft, where the town's economy depended on beer, there was a serious rift between the large and small brewers, which had been widening since 1548. To protect the small producer a ceiling had been placed on the output of the large brewers, a restriction the latter found exceedingly irksome. In December 1564 the town corporation, on which many of the wealthiest brewers sat, passed a resolution allowing a greater degree of open competition. The ensuing conflict was fierce, but in September 1566 Brussels finally pronounced in favour of the big brewers.[69] As a result of their ill-concealed self-interest in this decision the magistrates alienated the townspeople; this hampered their efforts to keep order in 1566, as they frankly admitted afterwards.[70] Contemporaries were very conscious that the maintenance of law and order in the towns depended on there being political harmony.[71] Contemporary accounts of the riots abound with references to the image-

[66] H.E. van Gelder, 'Hervorming en hervormden te Alkmaar', *Alkmaarse opstellen* (Alkmaar, 1960), p. 60. First published in *Oud-Holland*, XL (1922).

[67] ARAB, RvB, 109 (118), fo. 314v.

[68] See Kolff, 'Libertatis ergo', p. 124.

[69] For this quarrel see Dirck van Bleyswijck, *Beschryvinge der stadt Delft* (Delft, 1667), p. 710 ff; also ARAH, Hof van Holland, 381, fo. 237 ff. and, most recently, J.J. Woltjer, 'Een Hollands stadsbestuur in het midden van de 16e eeuw: brouwers en bestuurders te Delft', *De Nederlanden in de late middeleeuwen*, ed. D.E.H. de Boer *et al.* (Utrecht, 1987), pp. 261–79.

[70] Smit, 'Hagepreken en beeldenstorm te Delft', p. 209.

[71] One of the questions put to witnesses appearing before the Council of Troubles in Gelderland concerned the relations between the magistrates and the community. See J. Kleijntjens, 'Stukken betreffende ketterij en beeldenstorm te Venlo', *BMHG*, LVI (1935), p.13.

breakers as *gens de basse sorte, het gemeyn volcksken* [the common people], *Heer Omnes* [Mr. Everyman], *boefkens* [young bully-boys], and *rabbauwen ende vyle personen die nyet te verliesen en hadden* [scoundrels and base persons with nothing to lose]. Time and again one encounters the fear that the rioters would turn from the churches to private property. Sometimes, as in Delft, the people looted the monastic cellars, taking away 'beer, meat, cheese, butter and whatever else was available',[72] and in Leiden and Amsterdam the churches were not only sacked but also plundered.[73] By bringing these features to the attention of historians in his book *Het hongerjaar*, Erich Kuttner has compelled them to acknowledge that many contemporaries, haunted as they were by the spectre of the *grauw* [mob], indeed considered that religion was no more than a pretext for an opportunity to steal. There are dangers in accepting too readily their judgment on the motives and social standing of the image-breakers, without first enquiring about the bias of such witnesses. Might not Catholics have used the time-honoured device of tarnishing their opponents' cause, by imputing to them the basest motives and labelling them collectively knaves and robbers? Often these opprobrious descriptions crop up in documents of an apologetic nature where the authorities are anxious to explain away their failure to keep order. In such circumstances the anonymous mob and the ubiquitous strangers furnished excellent whipping-boys. Many Protestants then, as later, were anxious to exculpate the new religion from these excesses, and so they too vilified the image-breakers.

Our suspicion that there is an element of caricature in the con-temporary view of the image-breakers as the *lie du peuple*, is confirmed when we discover that roughly half of those accused of storming the church in Alkmaar owned their own dwellings,[74] and at Leiden a fair sprinkling of independent artisans took part in the riot.[75] In the case of Culemborg a breakdown of the thirty-four iconoclasts reveals that 'three were comfortably off, five well-to-do, nine were persons of independent means, eight were simple people and nine earned their bread working for others or stood outside the main population'.[76] Though it remains

---

72 Smit, 'Hagepreken en beeldenstorm te Delft', p. 216.

73 Kolff, 'Libertatis ergo', p. 132; Breen, 'Uittreksel', p. 29.

74 ARAG, Staten van Holland vóór 1572, nr. 1203, Kohier van de Tiende Penning, 1562.

75 Kolff, 'Libertatis ergo', p. 132.

76 De Jong, *De Reformatie in Culemborg*, pp. 140–1. An investigation into the social structure of the Reformed in Ghent showed that one-third of those charged with iconoclasm owned their own dwelling. See M. Delmotte, 'Het Calvinisme in de verschillende bevolkingslagen te Gent, 1566–1567', *TG*, LXXVI (1963), pp. 145–76. On the other hand the most difficult persons to identify, and therefore to sentence, would be the riff-raff, for they would be unknown to the witnesses. It should be remembered that the Council of Troubles was probably more concerned to uncover the propertied heretic than his impoverished coreligionist. Nevertheless the presence of a large lumpenproletariat in the riots remains a matter of conjecture: it is not an established fact.

broadly true that the image-breakers were drawn from the lower end of the social scale, they were not wholly composed of the riff-raff as contemporaries supposed.

A phenomenon as many-sided as the image-breaking, involving a cross-section of the lower part of society, cannot be attributed to a single motive: it meant different things to different people. Whatever else it might be, it was an eloquent testimony to the widespread antipathy towards and often undisguised hatred of the clergy. As many of the plays put on by the *rederijkerskamers* had mirrored and exploited this anti-clericalism, it was appropriate that the iconoclastic riots in Leiden should be heralded by the local rhetoricians publicly ridiculing images.[77] Popular opinion was especially hostile to the Franciscans and the image-breakers singled out their houses in Alkmaar, Amsterdam, Delft, and Leiden. For the *gueux d'état* the onslaught on the churches may have been a way of venting discontent against the government in Brussels, for church and state were inextricably conjoined.

At the same time there can be no question that many of the Reformed felt deeply on the score of images; such people would have agreed with Sem Jansz. of Monnikendam that 'those who attack images and shatter them were doing God's will'.[78] For the Reformed there was another practical motive, which may have prompted them to break the images: the desire to get hold of a church for their own use. Such a church, it went without saying, had first to be purged of its popish trappings. As summer turned to autumn the need for a meeting place out of the weather became more urgent. There are numerous readily understood references in their petitions to the discomfort of attending services in the wind and rain. R.C. Bakhuizen van den Brink suggested long ago that the second bout of iconoclasm in October was caused by impatience at the procrastination on the part of the civic authorities in providing sheltered places for worship.[79] At Delft the corporation tried to ward off further disorders by having a barn built where the Reformed might meet out of the elements. It was a case of too little being granted too late, and on 5 October the Franciscan church there was sacked, everything abhorrent to the Reformed removed, the debris swept up and the church put in order for their services next day.[80] Sometimes then the removal of the images was simply the first step in making the churches suitable for

[77] Kolff, 'Libertatis ergo', p. 141.

[78] ARAB, RvB, 115 (125), fo. 234.

[79] Bakhuizen van den Brink, 'De Adel', *Cartons*, p. 70, fn. 1. In November Orange informed the Regent that it was difficult to prevent the services occurring inside towns, for it was winter and the countryside was inundated, *Corresp. Guillaume*, II, p. 283.

[80] 'Informatie van de schout', printed in the back of some copies of van Bleyswijk, *Beschryvinge*; Soutendam, 'Beeldstormerij in Delft', p. 221.

Reformed worship.[81]

In fact the Reformed only succeeded in acquiring a church building at Amsterdam, Asperen, Den Briel, Delft, Leiden, and Vianen. In a few village churches turncoat priests preached the gospel according to the Reformed religion, but they probably met with little success. Elsewhere the Reformed resorted to a variety of expedients. At Gorcum Orange gave them leave to build their own chapel, for which several wealthy members donated windows.[82] At Leiden the Reformed built their own barn for services,[83] and at Haarlem the town corporation even offered some financial assistance in its construction.[84] Occasionally the Protestants 'arranged' a service in the parish church. At Schoonhoven they staged the conversion of a prominent priest in the pulpit, who then proceeded to expound the new doctrines.[85] In the undefended town of Purmerend a Protestant service was held in the church but subsequently the heretics withdrew to a disused chapel-of-ease nearby.[86] At Overveen and in The Hague they could reckon on the hospitality of like-minded aristocratic followers. In many parts of Holland however the Reformed failed to gain any form of recognition. In the Noorderkwartier they never received leave to hold their services within the towns and so resorted to meeting in tents, in private houses and even in a salt factory.

Amid the upheavals of that autumn the Reformed in Holland started to organise themselves into congregations with consistories: in some parts one detects an embryonic *classis* emerging. These developments were suddenly halted when the central government clamped down in the spring of 1567. When the first consistory [*kerkeraad*] was established in Holland is not known, but almost certainly none existed before October 1566. In Brabant and Flanders a synodal network had been built up in the early 1560s and there are indications that even before the hedge services began a similar organisation existed on Walcheren.[87] Of course, a consistory was the culmination rather than the beginning of a process, the first stage of which was marked by the appearance of *aelmoesniers* [almoners]. Sometimes these were women as in Edam where Wendelmoet Thymans and Elberich Remmers were known by the Calvinists as 'mothers or distributors' [*moeders ofte wuytdeelsters*], because they took cheese,

---

[81] At Leeuwarden the preachers refused to conduct services in the churches in 1566 until these had been whitewashed; at Limbourg the church was also whitewashed and at Middelburg the ornaments were carefully removed under the supervision of the consistory and handed to the town council.

[82] Marcus, *Sententiën*, pp. 87–96.

[83] Kolff, 'Libertatis ergo', p. 140. The Reformed had used the Minderbroederskerk outside the town since mid-September, but following an agreement made on 25 January 1567, a '*geuzenhuis*' [Beggar's house] was constructed.

[84] Kleijntjens, *Corpus Iconoclasticum*, I: *Haarlem*, p. 137.

[85] Marcus, *Sententiën*, pp. 148–53.

[86] ARAB, RvB, 115 (125), fo. 279–87v.

[87] Van Vloten, *Onderzoek van 's konings wege*, p. 3.

butter and meat to the needy.[88] Collections were taken up during the services for the upkeep of the minister and for the poor. At Utrecht it was said that the Protestants used to bake bread for the paupers, and even distribute money.[89] Other people, known as *bewinthebbers* [leaders], arranged the services and provided a bodyguard for the preacher. In such inchoate groups, found throughout Holland, one discerns the beginnings of the diaconate and consistory. Occasionally one glimpses these informal bodies acting in concert. At Edam, for example, a notification of baptism was sent to the parish priest bearing, in addition to the child's name, the signatures of eight leading members of the Reformed community there.[90] These amorphous bodies are a reminder that the Reformed churches began perforce on a congregational basis and that the presbyterian framework came later, sometimes much later.

In addition to the sermons preached up and down the land in 1566, ministers also baptised, married and buried according to the rite of the 'new religion'. Communion services took place less commonly but they are recorded at Alkmaar,[91] Amsterdam, Den Briel, The Hague, and Leiden; in view of the sophisticated nature of the congregation in Gorcum, it is likely that communion also took place there. Little is known about how people were prepared for communion. In Amsterdam would be participants were first instructed in 'the fundamentals of salvation', though it is unlikely the whole congregation of 1,000 had been catechised,[92] for a few at least had come from outside the town.[93] At Leiden 284 communicated in the Minderbroederskerk on 5 January 1567.[94]

During the autumn full-fledged consistories were set up in several towns. On 11 January the Regent wrote anxiously to the *stadhouder* about this novel and treasonable development which, she understood, had begun to spring up in Holland.[95] In October 1566, when the Reformed in Amsterdam acquired a church, a body of elders and deacons was appointed,[96] and in Delft a consistory was installed around the same time, composed of at least eight elders and four deacons.[97] Similar

---

[88] ARAB, RvB, 110 (125), fo. 264.

[89] H. Brugmans, 'Utrechtsche kroniek over 1566–1576', *BMHG*, XXV (1904), p. 84.

[90] ARAB, RvB, 115 (125), fo. 274v–75.

[91] GA Alkmaar, Handschriften, A. 144 p. 202.

[92] Breen, 'Uittreksel', p. 49. See also account in *Anteykeningen van Broer Hendrik van Biesten*, pp. 337–38.

[93] ARAB, RvB, 115 (125), fo. 242.

[94] Kolff, 'Libertatis ergo', p. 139.

[95] *Corresp. Guillaume*, II, pp. 314–15.

[96] Breen, 'Uittreksel', pp. 45–46.

[97] In the report of the commissioners on the Troubles at Delft, ARAB, RvB, 109 (113a), fo. 137 ff., other members of the consistory were described as '*diaecken ofte ouderling*' [deacon or elder], which suggests that the distinction was not yet clear to outsiders. H.J.Jaanus, *Hervormd Delft ten tijde van Arent Cornelisz.* (Amsterdam, 1950), pp. 25–26.

bodies appeared in Den Briel, Gorcum, Leiden, Naaldwijk, The Hague and Alkmaar.[98]

With the setting up of the consistories the Reformed congregations of Holland were able to take a fuller part in the activities of the Reformed throughout the country. It was through the consistories that arrangements were made to collect for the 3,000,000 guilder request in Holland. Since the summer Gilles Le Clercq had been drawing up various schemes, whereby the Protestants would purchase their religious freedom from Philip II.[99] From the start it was whispered that the real intention was to raise money to recruit troops in the Empire, against the day when the King would use force to pacify the Low Countries. On 27 October the Request was handed over in Antwerp, after a meeting attended by representatives of 'all the churches in the Netherlands', including two from Amsterdam.[100] Less than a week later Dirk Volckertsz. Coornhert was shown 'a printed request ... concerning an offer [to the King] of three million carolus guilders', when he was in Schoonhoven for the assembly of the States of Holland, and he was asked to correct a Dutch translation of the original French.[101] In January petitions relating to this Request were handed over at Amsterdam, Leiden, and Delft and a similar document circulated in Den Briel. In Gorcum the sinister purpose behind this Request was known, for when one of the collectors was challenged as to what would be done with the money should the King reject the offer, he replied that 'they would then use the money to levy war against him'.[102] Another indication of the degree to which the Reformed churches were knitting together is a meeting held in Amsterdam in the New Year, attended by 'deputez des sectaires' from Antwerp, 's-Hertogenbosch, Tournai, Valenciennes, Harderwijk, Delft, Leiden, Edam, and other towns.[103] On another occasion the consistory of Antwerp sent a minister and two elders to reprimand their colleagues in Amsterdam for what they regarded as an erroneous opinion on the real presence.[104] Just as the congregations in Holland were groping their way towards a synodal system, the central government recovered, and by Easter 1567 the preachings had ceased almost everywhere, the barns where the Reformed had worshipped were levelled to the ground and

[98] Philip Cornelisz. was described as an 'elder' in Alkmaar. See N.J.M. Dresch, 'De rooftocht van Dirk Maertensz. van Schagen en zijn bende in 1568 in Noord-Holland', *BMHG*, XLVI (1925), p. 351.

[99] See J. Scheerder, 'Enige nieuwe bijzonderheden betreffende het 3,000,000 goudguldens rekwest', *Miscellanea Historica ... L. van der Essen*, 2 vols. (Leuven, 1947), I, pp. 559–66.

[100] Brandt, I, p. 395.

[101] Kleijntjens, *Corpus Iconoclasticum*: I: *Haarlem*, p. 20. Was this request printed in Vianen?

[102] Marcus, *Sententiën*, p. 89.

[103] *Corresp. Guillaume*, II, p. 329.

[104] Breen, 'Uittreksel', pp. 46–48.

their congregations scattered.[105]

With the collapse of the central authority in the summer of 1566 the centrifugal forces latent in the society of the Netherlands suddenly found themselves with an enlarged freedom of action. In consequence the local balance of political power was thrown haywire, especially in towns where the corporation had become dependent on Brussels. It is therefore important to look closely at the relations between the magistrate and the guilds and *schutterijen* to find out to what extent their interaction affected the course and character of the Troubles in the various towns.

In Holland the guilds had not attained the same political prominence as they had in Flanders and Brabant and their part in the Troubles was slight. In Rotterdam the Reformed clearly reckoned on support from among the guilds for on 3 October 1566 they asked the magistrate to consult with 'les confrères sermentez et les hooftmans [captains] des gildes' about what should be done if the [Spanish] Inquisition were introduced.[106]

Of greater moment in Holland were the *schutterijen*. Every town had one or more of such companies, composed of *poorters* [freemen] who usually had to meet a minimum property qualification. Their traditional task had been to keep the peace within the walls and to resist attack from without. Despite their officers being chosen by the magistrate they remained largely autonomous bodies. Yet these proud companies felt their influence in the towns shrinking as power became concentrated in the hands of the town government. The hiatus of 1566 afforded them an opportunity to recover some lost ground, since for a short space they provided the only guarantee of law and order.

It would be misleading to range the *schutterijen* with the Reformed in 1566 on the grounds that the two groups sometimes appear to run in harness, for their rivalry with the *vroedschap* antedated the Reformation; at heart they were more concerned about securing liberties than altering religion.[107] Already in mid-June the *Oude Schutters* of Amsterdam were giving one another the toast 'Vive les gueux': it was this guild which entered the Confederation in July, probably at Brederode's prompting.[108] The misgivings such slogans must have aroused among the staunchly

---

[105] For the survival of Reformed churches in Holland under Alva see below p. 201.

[106] Marcus, *Sententiën*, p. 144. See also H. ten Boom, *De reformatie in Rotterdam, 1530–1585* (n.p., 1987), pp. 112–13.

[107] This is not to say that the *schutterijen* of Holland did not have their share of heretics – on the contrary – but Protestantism could not provide a sufficiently broad base for the *schutters* as a whole. When the religious issue came to the fore, this sometimes led to dissension. For a recent discussion of the *schutterijen* see J.C. Grayson, 'The Civic Militia in the County of Holland, 1560–81: Politics and Public Order in the Dutch Revolt', *BMGN*, XCV (1980), pp. 35–63.

[108] *Anteykeningen van Broer Hendrik van Biesten*, p. 332.

Catholic city corporation were intensified when the *schutters* informed the town government 'that they were opposed to hindering the preachings which were held outside the town gates, though they would not allow these to take place inside the town walls'.[109] According to a contemporary Catholic observer this was because 'everybody had friends among those' who went to the services. Later the *schutters* were themselves divided over the issue whether or not to allow Protestant services inside the town, and some escorted the minister despite the protests of their colleagues.[110] During the riot of 23 August the *schutterijen* helped restore order, but shortly thereafter they advised the corporation to remove the images for the sake of peace.[111] On 27 August the magistrates approved the appointment of *oppercapiteynen* for the three *schutterijen*, with the task of keeping the corporation informed of the situation in the town.[112] After the second, and more serious, iconoclastic outburst on 26 and 27 September, an agreement between the corporation and the Reformed was drawn up according to which the Protestants promised to remain loyal to the government and the corporation pledged protection for *die van de religie*.[113] Significantly the newly elected captains of the *schutterijen* were party to this *Accoord*, an indication of their increased political influence. Apparently the *schutters* of Amsterdam continued to take an independent line, for in February 1567 they were forbidden to assemble and their confraternity was suspended because they had refused to take the new oath of loyalty.[114] Subsequently five of the six of the *oppercapiteynen* were banished for their part in the Troubles.[115]

The *schutterijen* of both Alkmaar and Schoonhoven were restive during 1566. In the former town proposals were put forward to enlarge the companies and to curb the merrymaking which went on among the *schutters*. These seemingly innocuous reforms originated with a group of *schutters* sympathetic to the new religion, among them one of the provosts, and the Catholic members withdrew in protest.[116] In the anxious days after the image-breaking there, the corporation even considered hiring men to guard the churches, presumably because they were uncertain of

---

[109] Breen, 'Uittreksel', p. 17.

[110] *Anteykeningen van Broer Hendrik van Biesten*, p. 534. The *schutters* refused to disperse the crowds attending the preachings because 'most were substantial burghers, their acquaintances, friends, relations, brothers and sisters', Brandt, I, p. 316; *cf.* the conduct of the *serment* at Tournai which also refused to hinder the services because their friends and relations attended, 'Extraits des registres des Consaux de Tournay', II (1559–1572), ed. L.P. Gachard, *BCRH*, XI (1846), pp. 408–9.

[111] Breen, 'Uittreksel', p. 30.

[112] Breen, 'Uittreksel', p. 30–31.

[113] Breen, 'Uittreksel', pp. 40–45. Margaret of Parma had declared an earlier agreement void on 1 September.

[114] *Corresp. Guillaume*, II, p. 353.

[115] Marcus, *Sententiën*, pp. 41, 123, 182.

[116] ARAB, RvB, 109 (110), fo. 51v-53.

the *schutters*' loyalties.[117] Later the companies were disbanded and only reinstated in 1569.[118] In Schoonhoven the *schutters* refused to accompany the procession of the Holy Sacrament on 25 August,[119] though it is not clear whether this followed from their reluctance to identify themselves too closely with a religious party, from their anticlericalism, or from Protestant sympathies, for some of these *schutters* at least were notorious heretics. In Dordrecht the *schutterijen* also refused to give way to the town government. In March 1567 the burgomasters wanted to let Eric of Brunswick into the town, but when the *schutters* were informed, they said: 'We will not have that papist, who is forever menacing us with the Spanish Inquisition', and they then took charge of the keys of the town. At the same time, however, they demonstrated their independence by refusing offers of help from Brederode.[120] In Leiden and Delft the evidence for the civic companies pursuing a policy independent of both the corporation and the Protestants is still clearer and it is to these towns that we now turn.

In Leiden the *schutters* had kept the watch at the town gates since the eve of the iconoclastic riots there.[121] Following these the corporation tried to enforce a new oath of allegiance on the companies, and on 5 October one of the burgomasters ordered that the keys of the city be kept at the townhall. The issue of the keys was crucial, for the Reformed had to pass outside the walls to attend their services and so ran the risk of being shut out, a prospect made all the less inviting by Duke Eric's armed presence in the locality. In reply to these demands the *schutters* insisted that the keys be given to them, for they suspected the burgomasters might deliver the town into the stranger's hands. Thereupon the magistrates complained that the town had become ungovernable and they asked William of Orange, as *stadhouder*, to visit the town. In January the *vroedschap* tried to regain the initiative, by paying off the *schutters* and replacing these with mercenaries. Once again the *schutters* successfully resisted and the gates remained in their control. At the same time they turned down offers of assistance in their duties from the Reformed, thus underlining their wish to stand aloof as a body from the religious conflict. In May 1567, only a few days before the town was occupied by outside forces and the *schutters* disarmed, they refused to wear their armour at a religious procession, so as to avoid giving the impression they were protecting the Sacrament.

In Delft some of the *schutters* had early shown their independent spirit

---

[117] GA Alkmaar, 2, Tweede Resolutieboek, 1565–1582, fo. 10.
[118] *Ibid.*, fo. 22v.
[119] Marcus, *Sententiën*, p. 281.
[120] *Kroniek ... Godevaert van Haecht*, I, p. 185.
[121] For a more detailed treatment and the sources see Kolff, 'Libertatis ergo', pp. 128–38.

when they escorted a Reformed minister in The Hague on 24 August,[122] but such conduct was probably uncharacteristic of the *schutterijen* as a whole. They quelled the riot on 25 August and a week later refused to admit a hedge preacher with his armed escort to the town. During the second round of image-breaking on 5 October, however, the split between the corporation and the *schutterijen* became clear for all to see. On that occasion the *vroedschap* had called in the *schutters* to restore order, but only a handful answered the appeal and the town government was reduced to seeking assistance from The Hague in bringing the companies to heel.[123] The corporation demanded a new pledge of loyalty to which the majority of the *schutters* replied by making the following counterdemands:

1) Henceforth each troop [*rot*] of twenty-five men would put forward the names of two or three persons, one of whom would be appointed captain [*hoofdman*] by the corporation.
2) In an emergency when the *schutters'* assistance was likely to be required, the companies had to be consulted beforehand in the butts [*doelen*].
3) Thereafter a unanimous decision would have to be reached by the town government with the *hoofdlieden* of the *schutterijen*.
4) The *schutterijen* would at all times have the right of free assembly, except in a dire emergency.[124]

Negotiations dragged on for a full week, when the corporation conceded the first two points, but steadfastly refused to allow the *schutters* more say in the town government, to which they retorted by alleging that their only obligation towards the city authorities was that of parading during the religious procession. At the same time they demanded a transcript of all the documents in the town archives pertaining to them. In addition they refused to prevent Protestant services occurring within the town, as that would make them appear to be 'partisan and hostile to divers many of the principal burghers, who though they were not members of the *schutterijen* belong nonetheless to the *corpus* of the town'. Lastly the corporation had to give in over the oath and the Reformed were left in possession of a church inside the walls since nobody could or would resist them.[125] Like the *schutters* at Den Bosch, who when asked to arrest a heretical preacher replied, 'Let those whose task it is to prevent the services, do so',[126] their colleagues of Delft refused 'to be executors of the royal placards'.[127]

[122] Smit, *Den Haag in den geuzentijd*, p. 38.
[123] Smit, 'Hagepreken en beeldenstorm te Delft', pp. 213–25.
[124] However roughly one-third of the *schutters*, associated with the 'party' of the *vroedschap*, disavowed this move; see also Grayson, 'Civic Militia', pp. 47–49.
[125] Soutendam, 'Beeldstormerij te Delft', p. 173 ff.
[126] Cuypers-van Velthoven, *Documents*, p. 22.
[127] Soutendam, 'Beeldstormerij te Delft', p. 199.

The attitude of these civic militias varied from town to town, but where the disturbances were fiercest, their importance as the traditional upholders of law and order was enhanced. At Hoorn the corporation was apparently master of the situation,[128] and at Haarlem relations between the militias and the town authorities were harmonious, thanks to the tact and moderation of one of the burgomasters.[129] In Alkmaar and Schoonhoven the religious question seems to have been of greater moment than in Amsterdam, Dordrecht, Leiden and Delft, where the *schutterijen* were especially conscious of their own traditions.

The last stages of the Troubles in Holland were dominated by Brederode.[130] On his return to Vianen at the end of July Coornhert was sent to seek his advice on how the preachings might be banned.[131] As yet Brederode was still regarded as a moderate. Soon afterwards he must have retired to the Noorderkwartier, where the atmosphere had grown more troubled since his triumphal visit in May. At Alkmaar a Franciscan had darkly forecast that Brederode would soon be brought to justice,[132] and on top of this came the issue of the sinister *bloetbouck* about which he was busily conferring with the local gentry and townspeople of Alkmaar in mid-August. Such problems paled before those which news of the riots in Antwerp and Flanders brought on 22 August. Already on that day Brederode had written to Orange to warn him of the explosive situation in Amsterdam, and now he wrote in haste to Orange's brother Louis of Nassau.[133] After expressing his disbelief at what he had been told, he went on to blame the Governor's stiff-necked attitude for precipitating the crisis. Only three weeks ago he had warned her that the people were restive and that, though they still looked to the nobility to give them a lead, things would have been much easier had the leaders of the Beggars been in a position to promise that the persecutions would cease, and that the Protestants might freely worship outside the towns until the States General had been consulted.[134]

On 26 August Brederode signed a warrant for the removal of all valuables from the churches on his manors in Kennemerland, thereby hoping to forestall a repetition of the disturbances then sweeping

---

[128] On 8 August 1566 the *vroedschap* abolished the property qualification for entry to the *schutterijen* and reverted to the practice whereby the burgomasters picked the men. At the same time the size of the *schutterijen* was increased. GA Hoorn Stadsarchief, 149, fo. 50. See also C. Chr. Sol, 'Reformatie en magistraatsbeleid in Hoorn, *circa* 1560–1573', *Holland*, XX (1988), p. 135.

[129] W.P.J. Overmeer, *De hervorming te Haarlem* (Haarlem, 1904), pp. 154–56.

[130] On Brederode's role see Van Nierop, *Van ridders tot regenten*, pp. 196–202.

[131] *Bronnen tot de kennis van het leven en werken van D.V. Coornhert*, ed. B. Becker (The Hague, 1928), RGP, Kleine serie, 25, p. 38.

[132] ARAB, RvB, 109 (110), fo. 38v-39. Brederode sent his steward to question the warden of the Grey Friars about this affair.

[133] *Archives ou correspondance*, II, pp. 232–33.

[134] *Ibid.*, pp. 233–36.

Holland.[135] About this time too he forbade the introduction of any 'novelties' in Vianen.[136] Though his steward in the Noorderkwartier interpreted this brief as a licence to indulge his own hatred of the clergy and carried it out in a manner calculated to offend good Catholics,[137] his conduct probably did not have his master's sanction. Indeed on 27 August Brederode wrote to Louis of Nassau in his idiosyncratic French telling him of his efforts to save Egmond Abbey; in the same letter, he said that he had expressly charged the forty or so 'jantylsomes' in his retinue 'ne s'avancer que an tout doulceur et aveq la modestie du monde: car il ne duyct nullement les user d'aulcune menace, ou aultrement on les incytroyt à plus grandes sédytyons, quy occasyoneroyt la perte et ruyne totalle des ses pays de par dessà'. At the same time he complained that the nobility were being treated like dogs,'comme sy jamés ne fust esté né de mère jans plus mechans'.[138] Undisguised as was his loathing for Morillon, Viglius, and 'leurs infectées satallystes', the overtone of the letter is one of wounded indignation, mixed with foreboding about the future.

From Egmond the party travelled to Hoorn, where they probably arrived on 28 August. On the way some of the gentry had caused a commotion in the church at Medemblik, even though Brederode himself does not seem to have been involved.[139] It was while in Hoorn that Brederode learnt from his secretary the terms agreed by the Regent and noblemen for the *Accoord*.[140] Although he had known discussions were afoot, and had himself urged the Governor to allow the Protestant to hold services outside the towns, news of the Confederation's dissolution stunned him.[141] Eye-witnesses later recalled how upset he was. In a poignant, almost pathetic letter to Louis on 3 September he expressed his shock on discovering that 'nostre Compromys est anychyllé antyérement'; had he not understood that the association was perpetual, he would never have joined it; now his men considered that they had been led like lambs to the slaughter, for the Compromise had been not only a means of putting pressure on Brussels but also of preserving their unity.[142] Brederode considered that the nobility had let themselves be outmanoeuvred: in their state of disarray the government would deal with them at will.

Brederode's conduct at Alkmaar on 1 and 2 September suggests that the news of the break up of the Confederation of the Nobility persuaded him to follow a more militant policy. While receiving the hospitality of

[135] ARAB, RvB, 109 (110), fo. 62.
[136] *Historie van het Verbond*, IV, Bijlage QQ, p. 325.
[137] ARAB, RvB, 109 (110), fo. 18–19.
[138] *Archives ou correspondance*, II, pp. 252–56.
[139] RANH, ORA, 5225, p. 7.
[140] ARAB, RvB, 109 (118), fo. 302v.
[141] *Archives ou correspondance*, II, p. 256.

the town, a report reached him that yet another Franciscan had alleged that 'le grant geu' would soon be strung up on the gallows.[143] Never one to suffer clerical insults gladly, and least of all at that moment, he flew into an ungovernable rage and demanded that the monk responsible be brought to justice and even threatened to kill him personally.[144] That afternoon he rode out of the town and within half an hour the image-breakers were on their way to the Franciscan house.[145] Before he left one of his company had been overheard saying that no great harm would come were all the monasteries cast down;[146] subsequently one of the image-breakers defended the attack on the grounds that it had been done at Brederode's behest.[147] Yet less than a week earlier he had been urging restraint on his followers and had himself intervened to save Egmond Abbey from destruction.

On 6 September the *vroedschap* of Haarlem was distressed to learn of rumours that Brederode had advocated the removal of the images in that town,[148] and soon after he told a deputation from Delft, sent to discover his attitude to the image-breaking, that while he strongly condemned the looting of churches, he could not regard the image-breaking in itself as sacrilege.[149] No wonder the town council of Leiden hesitated before allowing the lord of Vianen and his party to pass through the town at this time: the *schout's* comment that the visit had done nothing to help the cause of peace was probably a fair one.[150] It is his activities in Vianen which furnish the most telling evidence of his change of heart. On 16 September the first steps were taken to fortify the town and ten days later, when he began to enlist troops, the images were taken down. On 1 October the first Reformed service was held in the parish church of Vianen.[151]

Meanwhile delegates from the towns of Holland shuttled back and forth to Vianen. On 23 September Coornhert was there, on behalf of Haarlem, to discover what was going on,[152] for the council had received an invitation to come and discuss matters of general interest and ways of defraying the cost of the new defences.[153] On that occasion Brederode told the town secretary that Philip II was going to come in the spring at the head of an army and that the Regent could no longer be trusted.

---

[142] *Ibid.*, II, pp. 276–77.
[143] ARAB, RvB, 109 (110), fo. 44.
[144] ARAB, RvB, 109 (110), fo. 44.
[145] ARAB, RvB, 109 (110), fo. 36v.
[146] ARAB, RvB, 109 (110), fo. 42v-43.
[147] ARAB, RvB, 109 (110), fo. 51.
[148] Kleijntjens, *Corpus Iconoclasticum*: I: *Haarlem*, p. 13.
[149] Smit, 'Hagepreken en beeldenstorm te Delft', pp. 220–21.
[150] Kolff, 'Libertatis ergo', pp. 133–35.
[151] *Historie van het Verbond*, IV, Bijlage QQ, p. 325.
[152] Kleijntjens, *Corpus Iconoclasticum*: I: *Haarlem*, p. 19.
[153] *Historie, ibid.*

Among the towns represented at this unofficial meeting were Delft, Leiden, Amsterdam, Alkmaar, The Hague, Rotterdam, Schiedam, and Den Briel.[154] At the beginning of October Brederode was involved, with other nobles, in an unsuccessful attempt to seize control of Utrecht.[155] While Brederode was moving towards rebellion, he remained anxious to preserve a semblance of moderation: on 6 October he wrote to Margaret of Parma to assure her that the images had only been removed following anonymous threats to burn the town down, and it had been done in an orderly fashion. As for the Protestants holding services in the church, this was because the floods had made it impracticable for these to be conducted outside, where there was the additional hazard that they might fall in with 'ung tas de vagabondes' and seize Vianen.[156] Later Orange explained away Brederode's fortifications by claiming these were required against Eric of Brunswick. It all sounded very plausible, but for some time now the Duke had been raising troops in the Empire on behalf of Brussels.[157]

Throughout November and December a steady stream of distinguished visitors came to Vianen,[158] including some members of the German nobility. Later Brederode himself sent an embassy to the Palatinate, though its business is unknown. Then there were gentlemen from Artois and Hainaut, deputations from Antwerp and the towns of Holland, as well as noblemen like Louis of Nassau and Jean de Marnix, Sieur de Toulouse.

With Valenciennes under an interdict and Tournai subdued by Noircarmes, Margaret of Parma could act more decisively, but this new situation did not deter Brederode. The work of repairing the walls went on fitfully and on 2 January he received some artillery from William of Orange.[159] In January too the so-called *Concordantie van Vianen*, designed to unite Lutherans and Reformed under the Confession of Augsburg in the hope of persuading the German princes to intervene on their behalf, was printed in Vianen and distributed from there throughout the country.[160] In view of these developments, of which the Regent was apprised, it was not surprising that the government decided to unmask Brederode and to put an end to the charade. On 27 January Brederode was questioned by two commissioners, who asked him to take a fresh oath of allegiance. Predictably the Great Beggar replied that for a lifelong loyal subject of His Majesty such a step was unnecessary. Then

---

[154] *Bronnen tot de kennis*, pp. 39–42.
[155] A. van Hulzen, *Utrecht in 1566 en 1567* (Groningen, 1932), pp. 64–72.
[156] *Corresp. Guillaume*, II, p. 237.
[157] *Corresp. française Marguerite d'Autriche*, II, p. 368.
[158] *Historie van het Verbond*, IV, Bijlage QQ, pp. 326–27.
[159] *Ibid.* The inventory of his property lists some ordnance with the device 'Maintiendray'.
[160] H. de la Fontaine Verwey, 'Hendrik van Brederode', pp. 29–35; and *idem.*, 'Over enige boeken te Vianen', pp. 28–33.

the commissioners demanded explanations for the defensive works at Vianen, his recruiting of troops and the printing of heretical propaganda. On each count Brederode was evasive; his naive replies must have sounded very hollow indeed to anyone as well informed as the Governor.[161]

On 29 January Brederode attended a meeting of the greater nobility in Breda and then, from 2 until 16 February, he was in Antwerp raising troops. On 4 February the first detachment arrived in Vianen and the rest followed at their heels.[162] When Brederode turned northwards again Megen and Duke Eric were on the move: on 28 February, after storming Ameide, government forces occupied Utrecht.[163] Thwarted there, Brederode made a last effort to win control of a major city by withdrawing to Amsterdam on 26 February.

Despite his valiant efforts to breath new life into the rebellion, he was powerless to turn the tide now running so strongly in favour of the government. Ten days after the ragged forces under Jean de Marnix had been routed at Oosterweel on 13 March, Valenciennes surrendered. A fortnight later Noircarmes flushed Anthonie van Bombergen from Den Bosch. On 27 April Brederode bowed his head before the inevitable and fled to Emden, leaving his bewildered Walloon mercenaries to find their own salvation in the Noorderkwartier. Finally on 3 May Vianen capitulated to Brederode's arch-enemy Eric of Brunswick, by which time the government had started its extensive and thorough enquiry into the Troubles, which affords the student today an insight into those turbulent times in Holland.

Looking back on the Troubles in Holland one can discern three distinct geographical regions. The Noorderkwartier was the least affected by the events of that year: despite a precocious start in July 1566, when the Reformed Protestants of Amsterdam decided to hold their services there, the region north of the IJ remained comparatively calm. Few of the inhabitants joined the insurrection of Brederode and, when his demoralised troops retreated across the IJ in the last days of April 1567, they found little enthusiasm or even sympathy for the cause of the Beggars. In mid-Holland the towns dominated the scene. Old political rivalries between the *vroedschap* and the *schutterijen* revived: in the case of Amsterdam, the situation was complicated by a long-standing feud between the Dirkisten and the Doleanten, who represented different economic interests and who came, in time, to be identified with different religious positions. Long denied office the Doleanten gradually edged

---

[161] Bor, I, p. 147 [bk. III, fo. 104].

[162] *Kroniek ... Godevaert van Haecht*, I, pp. 174–87. Brederode apparently recruited mainly German troops and in quite small numbers; the many Walloons who went to Vianen had been sent by the Antwerp consistory, see Bakhuizen van den Brink, 'Derde rapport ... over onderzoekingen in buitenlandsche archieven', *Studiën en schetsen over vaderlandsche geschiedenis* (The Hague, 1913), V, pp. 161–62.

[163] A. van Hulzen, *Utrecht*, p. 106.

closer to the Protestants and, though they failed to make much headway in 1566, they returned in triumph in 1578.[164] At Leiden and Delft the presence of a large urban proletariat made the task of keeping order still harder. Further south, along the rivers, the nobility had more influence than elsewhere in the county and they led the reaction to the central government.

The emphasis here has fallen on the heterogeneous character of the Troubles. This is to be explained, in part, by the existence of what Ernst Kossmann, in a different though analogous context, has called a 'pyramide des conflits'.[165] In addition to the religious conflict the crisis was aggravated by political jealousies and tensions between competing economic and social interests.

Hendrik van Brederode was one of the few men in Holland who strove to transcend these narrow interests in a bid to form a broad-based opposition. In the nineteenth century Groen van Prinsterer and Motley judged Brederode severely, censuring him for his intemperate outbursts and his irresponsible conduct. Even though his admirers then and since have drawn attention to his contribution to the Revolt and his immense popularity in Holland, which surpassed anything accorded to William of Orange at that time, we are still inclined to dismiss him as a quixotic figure and a hothead, and to overlook his initial moderation and shrewdness.[166]

Although the insurrection of 1567 faded out almost before it had begun in Holland, it is tempting to compare what happened then with the events of 1572. It is, of course, true that the success of the Revolt in that year owed much to the hostility large sections of the population felt towards Alva's administration. Yet in 1566 relatively small groups of determined individuals had shown how easily they could seize the initiative and how difficult it was for unpopular town magistrates to oppose them, when the *schutterijen* were unreliable and the masses inclined to be anticlerical. The crucial part which the *schutterijen* of Dordrecht and Delft played in bringing these towns over to the side of the rebels in 1572 had been foreshadowed by their attitudes and conduct in 1566.[167]

During the Troubles the Reformed Protestants in Holland started to worship in public and even held communion services according to the rite of the 'new religion'. This marked a new departure, for until then

[164] J.E. Elias, *De vroedschap van Amsterdam, 1578-1795* (Amsterdam, 1963), pp. xxxv-xxxix; W. van Ravensteijn, *Onderzoekingen over de economische en sociale ontwikkelingen van Amsterdam gedurende de zestiende en het eerste kwart der zeventiende eeuw* (Amsterdam, 1906), pp. 169-86.

[165] E.H. Kossmann, *La Fronde* (Leiden, 1954), p. 138.

[166] For the debate between Groen van Prinsterer and H.C. van Hall see Bakhuizen van den Brink, 'Hendrik van Brederode en Willem van Oranje in 1566-1567', *Cartons*, II, pp. 1-26. For Motley's disparaging comments see *The Rise of the Dutch Republic* (London, 1883), pp. 332-33. A biography of Brederode is sorely wanted.

[167] Grayson, 'Civic Militia', pp. 55-58.

they had led a furtive existence. Distinct congregations also emerged in 1566, with rudimentary forms of organisation and, in some cases, a full consistory. When the Reformed Protestants returned to Holland in the summer of 1572 congregations and *classes* were set up with astonishing speed. Much of the credit for this achievement is due to the preparatory work carried out at the meeting held in Wesel in 1568 and at the synod of Emden in 1571, when plans for a complete presbyterian church structure were drawn up; it should be remembered that the basis for such a polity had already been laid in 1566.

7

Salvation by Coercion: The Controversy
surrounding the 'Inquisition' in the Low Countries
on the Eve of the Revolt

When the Protestant gentry behind the Compromise devised their programme late in 1565, they knew it had to appeal to their predominantly
Catholic compeers. So instead of a brusque demand for religious
freedom, which would have met with a bleak response, they called for
the abolition of the inquisition 'in whatever shape, open or covert,
under whatever disguise or mask it may assume'.[1] Fear and hatred of the
inquisition evidently provided the best hope of uniting political malcontents and religious dissidents, whose paths had been converging
since the Peace of Cateau-Cambrésis. The common policy still proved
too brittle to withstand the emotional shock of the image-breaking – but
an initially favourable response showed that the authors of the Compromise had accurately gauged the mood of anxiety. Nor was concern
about the inquisition confined to the 400 or so signatories of the
Compromise. The representative States of Brabant and Flanders had
registered quite separate protests in the spring of 1566, and the States of
Holland followed in July with a remonstrance that, in its original form,
bore an embarrassing resemblance to the request presented by Hendrik
van Brederode in April. That the inquisition was hated 'like the plague'
in the Low Countries is certain; it is less obvious why the suppression of
heresy should have aroused so much resentment in a society still over-
whelmingly Catholic, the more so since very few of those convicted of
heresy were tried by the inquisition proper.

Elsewhere in Europe north of the Alps the eradication of religious
dissidence, be it by Catholics of Protestants or by Protestants of Anabaptists, excited no such outcry, except of course from the victims.
Everywhere the severity of the repression was tempered by the inertia,
incompetence or connivance of those responsible for enforcing the law
and complicated by protracted wrangles between rival courts; but in the
Low Countries the measures taken against the heretics gravely strained
the loyalty of the aristocracy, lawyers and town magistrates to their
prince. This was not the first time the inquisition had helped foment a

---

[1] *Texts concerning the Revolt of the Netherlands*, ed. E.H. Kossmann and A.F. Mellink
(Cambridge, 1975), p. 60.

political storm in the Habsburg lands. In 1563 the Milanese had rioted when Philip II wanted to introduce the Spanish Inquisition and the nobles and burghers of the city of Naples had banded together when similarly threatened in 1547. On both occasions the King had yielded to these demands for the withdrawal of the Spanish Inquisition.[2] This turn of events did not go unnoticed in the Netherlands, and in the Compromise the example of Naples was expressly commended. In these Italian territories the fear had been that the inquisition would encroach on existing rights of ecclesiastical jurisdiction. The envy of established courts certainly contributed to the resentment against the inquisition in the Low Countries, though here the spread of the Reformation, especially in the maritime provinces, made the opposition more obstinate.

On 28 September 1520 Charles V signed an edict at Antwerp ordering the destruction of Luther's books in his hereditary lands in obedience to the Bull *Exsurge Domine*.[3] This was the first in a long series of placards of increasing complexity and severity, culminating in the notorious 'placard of blood' in 1550. To combat heresy Charles also instituted, probably on the advice of Alonso Manrique de Lara, his Spanish chaplain, a shortlived extraordinary tribunal in 1522, whose subordination to the prince was as complete as the royal-controlled inquisition he had lately come to know in Spain.[4] As Holy Roman Emperor, Charles V might on occasion be driven to reach an accommodation with the evangelical estates, but in the Habsburg Netherlands he took his oath to maintain the Catholic faith in deadly earnest. Addressing the States General in 1531 the emperor declared that were any member of his own family to become infected with the Lutheran sect he would consider him 'his enemy'.[5] Charles may have honoured Erasmus by making him a councillor – though as the Rotterdammer complained his salary was often in arrears – but in religion he aligned himself with the conservative theologians of Leuven and the mendicant opponents of Luther. The decision to prosecute 'heresy' so rigorously was momentous: it estranged many among the governing

[2] H.G. Koenigsberger, *The Habsburgs and Europe, 1516–1660* (Ithaca-London, 1971), pp. 52–53, 103; also *Corresp. Marguerite d'Autriche* (Gachard) II, p.95. The precedents of Naples and Milan were mentioned when Orange met members of the Compromise at Breda in late March 1566, *Mémoires de Pontus Payen*, ed. A. Henne (Brussels, 1861), I, pp. 121–22.

[3] L.E. Halkin, 'L'édit de Worms et la répression du lutheranisme dans la principauté de Liège' *Miscellanea historica in honorem Alberti de Meyer* (Leuven-Brussels, 1946), II, pp. 791–800.

[4] J. Scheerder, 'De werking van de inquisitie' *Opstand en Pacificatie in de Lage Landen* (Ghent, 1976), pp. 155–58; F. Walser, 'Alonso Manrique und Karl V: Ein Vorschlag für Einführung Spanischer Inquisitionsgerichte in den Niederlanden, 1520–1521', *ARG*, XXX (1933), pp. 112–18.

[5] *Resolutiën van de Staten van Holland*, 1531, p. 171 (7 October); cf. Hoop Scheffer, p. 610. Two of Charles' younger sisters, Mary of Hungary and Isabella of Austria moved in evangelical circles for a time in the 1520s. Charles's brother-in-law Christian II of Denmark also showed evangelical sympathies.

classes who, though in no sense formal heretics, did not share their prince's starkly simple world-picture of religion or accept that all varieties of heresy necessarily threatened traditional values and undermined political stability.

After 1530 the edicts almost invariably denounced the negligence of the police and the lenience of the judges towards suspects. In a memorandum from Philip II to his *stadhouders* and provincial councils in August 1559, just before he sailed for Spain, the King blamed the continued advance of heresy on the indifference, even malevolence, of those charged with the enforcement of antiheresy legislation.[6] These were sentiments echoed by all concerned about the maintenance of Catholicism in these provinces. Lindanus, who had served as ecclesiastical commissary to the provincial court of Friesland and later as inquisitor in Holland, thus declared in 1578: 'There is no doubt at all that Holland and Zeeland lapsed from the Catholic faith and rebelled against the King chiefly because the magistrates failed to do their duty. Everywhere they were either lax or corrupt in the administration of justice or sympathetic to the new doctrines or downright indifferent to religion ... Consequently the salvation of the Low Countries [*Salus Belgicarum*] requires that the magistracy be thoroughly renewed'.[7]

In Flanders, the inquisitor Pieter Titelmans energetically opposed the tide of heresy for more than twenty years with all the resources at his disposal, but by 1560 he was close to despair. Apart from threats made on his life by heretics, he suffered the anguish of knowing that the magistrates of the towns (even the *Raad van Vlaanderen*, which should have given him every help in his sacred mission) had often obstructed his work.[8] In February 1534, the two *commissarissen der luteriaensche secte* in the *Hof van Holland* asked that their burdensome and unpopular task should be shared by the other councillors: it was unfair that they should have been singled out 'to watch the misery of poor wretches under interrogation and torture and to preside in public while judgment was passed on them'.[9] This same college also rallied to the defence of the town corporations when these were reproached by Lindanus for being soft on heresy. In Friesland the provincial court virtually sabotaged the

---

[6] L.P. Gachard, *Collection de documens* [sic] *inédits concernant l'histoire de la Belgique* (Brussels 1833), I, pp. 332–39.

[7] Cited by P.T. van Beuningen, *Wilhelmus Lindanus als inquisiteur en bisschop* (Assen, 1966), p. 190.

[8] J. Decavele, *De dageraad van de reformatie in Vlaanderen, 1520–1565* (Brussels, 1975), I, pp. 26–31.

[9] J.S. Theissen, *De regeering van Karel V in de noordelijke Nederlanden* (Amsterdam, 1912), p. 274; cf. E.H. Waterbolk, 'Humanisme en de tolerantie-gedachte', *Opstand en Pacificatie*, p. 310. Jan Benninck, a member of the *Hof van Holland*, was alleged to have refused to vote in favour of the death sentence for heretics, A.F. Mellink, *Amsterdam en de Wederdopers* (Nijmegen, 1978), pp. 21–22.

Salvation by Coercion 155

repressive policy after 1557.[10] The reluctance of these *hoven van justicie* to execute the religious policy of the prince is especially remarkable because the central government had relied on these bodies of jurists to implement its policies in the provinces.

Though fervent Catholics certainly sat on these provincial councils, many of the jurists professed an undogmatic Catholicism. Perhaps as lawyers and judges they were more than usually aware how precariously order was maintained in society. 'Une foi, une loi, un roi' might remain the political ideal, but, after the Reformation, though the theologians continued to insist on doctrinal unity even when this threatened to provoke civil disorder, the lawyers were temperamentally disposed to look for pragmatic solutions.[11]

The familiar antagonism between the *gens de robe longue* and *de robe courte* has perhaps obscured the tension that often existed between the clergy and secular lawyers. In 1520 the mendicant Glapion reviled those judges prepared to hang some unfortunate wretch for stealing a few pence, yet did nothing about blasphemers, 'qui seront cause de la perdition d'ung peuple tout entier'.[12] Precisely the same charge was brought in 1533 by some conservatives, enraged by the indulgence shown towards alleged Lutherans in cosmopolitan Antwerp. The magistrates were accused of letting notorious heretics, who dishonoured God and the holy sacraments, go freely abroad, though they were prompt to bring any petty thief to trial.[13] The sympathy shown by the legal profession to Erasmus has received comment before. When Erasmus was uprooted by the Reformation in Basel in 1529, a Flemish Carthusian, Livinius Ammonius, invited him to settle at Ghent, where he was sure of congenial company because 'the whole Council of Flanders is devoted to you'. His testimony was corroborated by the president of the Council, who opposed the edict of 1529 against the 'Lutherans', declaring that he would rather be dismissed than enforce its savage provisions.[14] Significantly the Dominicans in the Low Countries forbade the reading of Erasmus's works in 1531, and the Crutched Friars in 1534; yet the provincial *Raad van Brabant* was critical when, in 1557, the theologians at

[10] J.J. Woltjer, *Friesland in hervormingstijd* (Leiden, 1962), pp. 116–22.

[11] See W.J. Bouwsma, 'Lawyers and Early Modern Culture', *American Historical Review*, LXXVIII (1973), pp. 303–27; J. Dewald, 'The "Perfect Magistrate": Parlementaires and Crimes in Sixteenth-Century Rouen', *ARG*, LXVII (1976), pp. 284–86.

[12] A. Godin, 'La société au XVIe siècle, vue par J. Glapion (1460?-1522), frère mineur, confesseur de Charles-Quint', *Revue du Nord*, XLVI (1964), p. 363.

[13] R. van Roosbroeck, 'Een nieuw dokument over de beginperiode van het lutheranisme te Antwerpen', *De gulden passer*, V (1927), p. 279.

[14] Decavele, *op. cit.* I, pp. 76–77. For the sympathy of the *Hof van Holland* towards Erasmus in 1519, see J. Trapman, *De summa der godliker scrifturen (1523)* (Leiden, 1978), pp. 112–13.

Leuven decided to ban his books.[15] Only a few years before Erasmus was put on the Index, Charles de Croy, *évêque-fainéant* of Tournai, had sharply attacked the younger set of jurists attached to the provincial courts for soliciting popular favour by mocking church ceremonies and insulting the clergy, bad habits the bishop ascribed to the 'colloques d'Erasme et autres livres plains de derisions'.[16] This blend of anti-clericalism and modish intellectual curiosity helps to explain why, in 1566, six of the lawyers belonging to the *Grand Conseil* at Mechelen and a dozen or so lawyers from the *Raad van Vlaanderen* openly patronised the Calvinist preachings.[17]

By 1500 humanist education had begun to modify the curriculum in the grammar schools. Alexander's *Doctrinale* was ousted by 1536,[18] and greater attention was being paid to Latinity, helped by the models of Cornelius Crocus of Amsterdam and, above all, Despauterius and Erasmus. In 1518 the *Collegium Trilingue* opened its doors at Leuven; that year also saw Greek being taught at Bruges, and in 1533 the corporation of Amsterdam sponsored a *Hebreeuwsche meester*. Publishing may be considered a rough guide to a society's intellectual and religious appetites. Between 1500 and 1540 approximately 4,000 titles poured from presses in the Low Countries, of which more than half were printed in Antwerp. About forty per cent of the books printed in this city had a religious character, including a significant scattering of heterodox works; thirty per cent concerned literature and pedagogy; and another eighteen per cent treated historical, geographical, scientific and medical subjects. Slightly more than half were printed in Latin.[19] Even if the governing classes and great merchants did not fully appreciate humanist scholarship, they were willing to patronise the authors and buy their books.

Religious observance among the burghers remained conventionally Catholic until the middle of the sixteenth century. Yet the patterns of spirituality had been changing well before the Reformation. By 1450 enthusiasm for monastic foundations had faded and few new religious

[15] *Acta capitulorum provinciae germaniae inferioris ordinis fratrum praedicatorum ab anno MDXV usque ad annum MDLIX*, ed. S.P. Wolfs (The Hague. 1964), p. 112; P. van den Bosch, 'De bibliotheken van de kruisherenkloosters in de Nederlanden vóór 1550', *Archief- en bibliotheekwezen in Belgie*, Extranummer XI, *Studies over boekenbezit en boekengebruik in de Nederlanden vóór 1600* (Brussels, 1974), p. 579; J. Tenret, 'La police des livres dans les Pays-Bas espagnols au XVIe siècle' (University of Brussels, *licence*, 1957–58), pp. 37–38.

[16] G. Moreau, *Histoire du protestantisme à Tournai jusqu'à la veille de la Révolution des Pays-Bas* (Paris, 1962), p. 134, fn. 1.

[17] E. van Autenboer, 'Het wonderjaar te Mechelen, 1566–1567' (University of Leuven *proefschrift*, 1952), pp. 235–36; Decavele, *op. cit.*, I, p. 105.

[18] R.R. Post, *Scholen en onderwijs in Nederland gedurende de middeleeuven* (Utrecht-Antwerp, 1954), p. 146.

[19] J.G.C.A. Briels, *Zuidnederlandse boekdrukkers en boekverkopers in de Republiek der Verenigde Nederlanden* (Nieuwkoop, 1974), pp. 4–5; L. Voet, *Antwerp in the Golden Age: The Rise and Glory of the Metropolis in the Sixteenth Century* (Antwerp, 1975), p. 395.

houses were established in the next fifty years. Instead the laity lavished gifts on parish churches, many of which were extensively rebuilt and embellished: indeed the majority of the great Gothic churches in the northern provinces received their final shape at the close of the middle ages. The laity also poured money into chantries and obits, endowed the singing of the divine office in the parish churches in the towns and created charitable foundations, the governors of which were responsible to the magistrates. This process of laicisation ought not to be interpreted as an expression of mistrust in the clergy, but when the haphazard provision for poor relief was channelled in Flanders into a *bursa communis*, the mendicants at Bruges denounced the reform as 'heretical'. The enlightened Catholicism characteristic of the leading families in the great towns of the Low Countries was regarded with suspicion by conservatives, apt to confound the religious stance of Erasmus or Cassander with the theology of Wittenberg. Nor were they entirely mistaken: certain magistrates and intellectuals in Tournai, Ghent, Bruges, Amsterdam and Antwerp did indulge in a sort of 'salon Protestantism', which could lead on to wholehearted commitment.[20] In the 1550s a supple Reformed minister like Adriaen van Haemstede in Antwerp, prepared to go discreetly to the houses of rich even though these were not yet ready to enter the 'church under the cross', could thus exert a great appeal.[21] Alternately, such people might dispense with dogmas and, while continuing to conform outwardly, cultivate the religion of the spirit that came to characterise the circle around the Antwerp printer Christopher Plantin. Whatever their own religious inclinations the town magistrates in the Low Countries had the delicate, sometimes disagreeable, task of accommodating their 'open' Catholicism with the rigid orthodoxy preached by the mendicants and prescribed by the placards.

The prevailing climate at Antwerp in the early 1530s is illuminated by the lament of certain conservatives that plain heresy masqueraded there as 'good and evangelical'; in their despairing view, nothing short of a full-blooded Spanish-style inquisition could turn the tide.[22] The Amsterdam town authorities had been reprimanded in the late 1520s for their lenience towards convicted heretics. Moreover some of the chaplains and schoolmasters appointed by the town had shown marked evangelical sympathies. The mood among the regents there is revealed in a comment made by one of the burgomasters in 1534. After some Anabaptists from Amsterdam had been executed in The Hague, he was overheard to say that the burgomasters would 'no longer deliver them to the butcher's block'. In the ensuing investigations, the *schout* was dismissed; he later fled rather than stand trial on heresy charges, and in

[20] Decavele, *op. cit.*, I, p. 322.
[21] A.J. Jelsma, *Adriaan van Haemstede en zijn martelaarsboek* (The Hague, 1970), pp. 49–53.
[22] Van Roosbroeck, *op. cit.*, p. 282.

1538 the moderates among the magistrates were ousted.[23]

No feature of the antiheresy legislation touched the *gens de lettres et de justice* more closely than the prohibition laid on the reading of certain books. Since 1529 the mere possession of forbidden literature – a category which by 1550 had been stretched to include many books an educated man might have in his library – had been made a capital offence. No wonder the *Hof van Holland* complained in 1531 that such a penalty was 'exorbitant', a view reiterated by the States of Friesland in 1554.[24] Even the *Conseil Privé* advised the *Raad van Vlaanderen* in 1549 that the penalty for reading forbidden books ought not to be imposed automatically. But with Charles V and Philip II insisting that the edicts be enforced literally, the position of the judges' discretionary powers was very uncertain.[25] When a Protestant pamphleteer, Gilles le Clercq, wanted in May 1566 to expose the grotesque and arbitrary cruelty of the placards, he pointed out that someone could be put to death in the Netherlands for having in his house a book which, though forbidden by the Leuven doctors, might have escaped the censure of the Sorbonne.[26]

Gilles le Clercq was probably thinking of the inconsistent rulings given by civil and ecclesiastical authorities about the standing of Erasmus and vernacular translations of the Bible. In effect he was calling attention to the problem of determining the boundary between 'orthodoxy' and 'heresy'. One reason for the antipathy felt towards the edicts on religion

[23] A.F. Mellink, *De wederdopers in de noordelijke Nederlanden, 1531–1544* (Groningen-Djakarta, 1953), p. 105; G. Grosheide, *Bijdrage tot de geschiedenis der anabaptisten in Amsterdam* (Hilversum, 1938), pp. 87–94. *DAN*, V, *Amsterdam 1531–1536*, ed. A.F. Mellink (Leiden, 1985), p. 257.

[24] Hoop Scheffer, p. 475, fn. 3; J.S. Theissen, *Centraal gezag en Friesche vrijheid: Friesland onder Karel V* (Groningen, 1907), pp. 493–94.

[25] Decavele, *op. cit.*, I, p. 35, fn. 120. For discussion about discretionary powers of judges in the sixteenth century, see E. Poullet, 'Histoire du droit pénal dans le duché de Brabant depuis l'avènement de Charles-Quint jusqu'à la réunion de la Belgique à la France, à la fin du XVIIIe siècle', *Mémoires couronnés et mémoires des savants étrangers publiés par l'academie royale ... de Belgique*, XXXV (1870), pp. 40–42; Gachard, *Collection*, I, p. 336. In 1561 the *Raad van Vlaanderen* asked how it should proceed in the case of a large number of suspects 'la pluspart povres gens idiotz ne scachant lire, ne scripre' for to have enforced the edicts strictly would have caused a terrible 'effusion de sang' leading to the depopulation of the region. Margaret of Parma agreed to pardon 'la commune tourbe seduicte et repentante' though the ringleaders were to be punished in strict accordance with the law. E. de Coussemaker, *Troubles religieux du XVI siècle dans le Flandre Maritime, 1560–1570* (Bruges, 1876), I, pp. 82–86.

[26] See his 'Remonstrance ofte vertoogh ... op de Requeste by den edelen', J.W. te Water, *Historie van het verbond en de smeekschriften der nederlandsche edelen*, 4 vols. (Middelburg, 1796), IV, pp. 110–11. This commentary on the Request was printed in May 1566; see Moreau, *op. cit.*, p. 165, fn. 4, and P.A.M. Geurts, *De nederlandse opstand in de pamfletten, 1566–1584* (Nijmegen, 1956), p. 17. Copies of the original French and Dutch versions of this pamphlet are recorded in *Belgica typographica, 1541–1600 ...* I, *Bibliotheca Regia Bruxellenis* (Nieuwkoop, 1968), no. 4125, 4130.

was the discrepancy between the religious conservatism of Charles V and the latitudinarianism of many gentry, lawyers and regents. It is important not to exaggerate the indulgence of the judges. Iconoclasts, Münsterites and Batenburgers received short shrift from the courts; indeed, the Anabaptists as a whole had little cause to extol the humanity and clemency of their judges. Dissidents among the *kleyne luyden* felt the law more severely than the rich and well-connected and, as Guicciardini noted, strangers to a town would be dealt with more harshly because they lacked the privileged protection enjoyed by the burghers.[27]

If the antiheresy legislation offended the tolerant susceptibilities of the high nobility and the practical good sense of the jurists, it also caused disquiet to the town corporations and representative estates because it threatened their privileges. Above all, the legal principles invoked by the edicts and the methods used to convict heretics were widely considered to infringe traditional notions of criminal justice.

Before a burgher 'de bon nom et de bonne renommée' could be arrested, the *schout* had first to investigate the credentials of the witnesses. Then having satisfied himself that a prima facie case had been established, he would seek the consent of the burgomasters to make an arrest. This preliminary enquiry, which resembles the true bill of English common law, was known as the *informatie precedente*. It gave some protection against arrests arising from frivolous or spiteful allegations, a clear risk where law enforcement often depended on informers for intelligence. Moreover, once capital charges had been laid the guilt of the accused was presumed: the object of the trial was to extract the confession of guilt from the accused, without which the death sentence could not be passed. By that confession made in open court the accused effectively signed his own death warrant, there being no appeal against a capital sentence for a self-confessed crime. In criminal law, only the prosecution had the right to seek revision of sentence.

For those whose chief concern was the preservation of the Catholic faith, the preliminary enquiry constituted a tiresome obstacle, for word of the investigation often came to the suspect's ear, and he then took refuge in flight. Ways were therefore devised to circumvent this procedure. When in 1534 the magistrates of the town of Limbourg had jurisdiction in heresy cases restored to them, they were warned to set aside privileges that postponed the arrest of suspects until after the *informatie precedente*; in matters touching God and the Faith such privileges were null.[28] Despite such endeavours to curtail the trial the preliminary enquiry remained an intrinsic part of the judicial process.

---

[27] On discrimination, see G. Moreau, 'La corrélation entre le milieu social et professionnel et le choix de religion à Tournai', *Bibliothèque de la revue d'histoire ecclésiastique*, XLVII: *Bronnen voor de religieuze geschiedenis van België* (Leuven, 1968), pp. 294–95; on Guicciardini, see E. Poullet, *op. cit.*, pp. 37–39.

[28] *ROPB*, III, pp. 453–54.

In 1546 the government therefore tried another tack. Under a new instruction the inquisitors were empowered to examine anyone. If they suspected that a layman had transgressed the placards on religion, they were to invoke the police to make the arrest, but – and this qualification is crucial – they were not obliged to disclose the grounds of their suspicion. When in 1557 an inquisitor duly called on the law officers of Delft to arrest a suspect without further ado, the States of Holland were promptly alerted because of the implied threat to their privileges. In the view of the States the inquisitors should only concern themselves with the canonical offence of heresy and leave the enforcement of the edicts to the civil authorities. Failure to distinguish between these two quite separate categories of offence made them very uneasy; ironically their disquiet was shared by some scrupulous inquisitors who now found themselves obliged to denounce to the civil courts suspects for crimes carrying the death penalty. When the States of Holland tried to persuade the other patrimonial provinces to join with them in making a collective protest, they failed to win their support, yet in both Flanders and Brabant the same anxiety was expressed.[29] In 1562 Antwerp drew the attention of Brussels to Article XV of the *Joyeuse Entrée* of Brabant: this stated that no one of good repute should be arrested 'sans précédente planière information'.[30] To the chagrin of 'honest fanatics' like Villavicencio and Titelmans, the magistrates of Bruges insisted the inquisitor should submit his evidence to them before making any arrests, a demand which was repeated in the remonstrance of the Four Members of Flanders in April 1566.[31] Gilles le Clercq returned to the issue in his *Remonstrance ofte Vertoogh*, when he protested against arrests based on 'dubious rumours or the delation of a single person'.[32] Behind such grievances lay more than a concern for simple justice. The burgomasters, as guardians of municipal privileges, had a duty to defend the burghers against improper proceedings by ecclesiastical as well as lay officers.[33] Were they to accede to the demands of the inquisitors, they would weaken their standing in the local community. Though they would continue to regard themselves as sincere Catholics, they did not necessarily accept that the removal of judicial safeguards was a justifiable price to pay for the suppression of 'heresy'.

Heresy was often hard to prove, even by the far from exacting rules of evidence applied by sixteenth-century courts. Evidence against suspects 'de qualité' was hard to obtain. In 1553 an erstwhile Anabaptist, who had already informed for profit on her coreligionists, told a zealous priest that Willem Bardes, the worldly-wise *schout* of Amsterdam, had been

---

[29] See note 64.

[30] *Corresp. Marguerite d'Autriche* (Gachard), II, p. 118.

[31] Decavele, *op. cit.*, I, pp. 178–90.

[32] *Historie van het verbond*, IV, p. 103.

[33] *Resolutiën van de Staten van Holland*, 1565, p. 20 (12 July).

rebaptised many years before. This sensational news confirmed the suspicions of the priest, long irked by the nonchalance of the *schout* towards the heretics. Eventually, after a most thorough investigation, Willem Bardes was cleared and his menial accuser burnt for giving false testimony. As for the priest, he was arrested in 1558, accused of having suborned witnesses, and finally banished from Amsterdam in 1562. Though later rewarded with a plum benefice in Brussels, his treatment by the civil courts was seen by Lindanus as further proof of how the fastidiousness of the judges had frustrated the campaign against heresy.[34] About this time, the magistrates of Gouda, Hoorn and Leiden also found themselves the targets of unfounded charges. After such disillusioning experiences the government in Brussels was inclined to discount information of this kind; so when a renegade Anabaptist listed several hundred heretics in Middelburg, Margaret of Parma refused to order their arrest unless more substantial evidence could be obtained.[35] But the suspicions the inquisitors had about the officers' and judges' zeal for the Faith naturally disposed them to take such reports seriously – and not without some cause. In 1566 Protestantism burst forth in localities alleged only a year or so before by their magistrates to be innocent of heresy. Probably the inquisitors had been right to suppose the authorities often connived at the activities of the dissidents.

The detection of heresy proper remained in the sixteenth century, as it had been in the middle ages, a matter for the ecclesiastical judge. As the Flemish *jurisconsult* Philips Wielant put it, 'heresy is punished by burning, with the ecclesiastical judge conducting the trial and the secular judge carrying out the sentence'. Yet the vast majority of so-called heretics were tried by the civil courts in the Low Countries. By the Edict of Worms cognizance had been expressly granted to the provincial and municipal courts in the Habsburg Netherlands, and the imperial mandate of 1529, concerning the prosecution of Anabaptists, made no mention of the ecclesiastical judge. For several reasons the government of Charles V had no wish to allow church courts a prominent part in the campaign against the religious dissidents. This may be attributable to the longstanding antagonism between the civil and ecclesiastical jurisdictions, but more to the point was the anxiety that, if prosecution were left to the ecclesiastical inquisitors and episcopal officials, the process would be unduly protracted by the desire to bring the miscreant to abjure his false opinions. Dissent on the large scale encountered in the Netherlands required summary trials and sharp punishments.

The crime established by the Caroline edicts was hybrid. According to these edicts it was a capital offence to possess forbidden books, to give

---

[34] J.J. Woltjer, 'Het conflict tussen Willem Bardes en Hendrick Dirckszoon', *BMGN*, LXXXVI (1971), pp. 178–99.

[35] *Corresp. française Marguerite d'Autriche*, I, p. 34.

lodging to heretics, to debate points of scripture with laymen and to neglect to denounce heretics to the police. Strictly these acts did not in themselves constitute heresy proper; they only gave cause for vehement suspicion of heresy. Thus far, the edicts may be held to have short-circuited the ecclesiastical inquisition, offenders being prosecuted in the civil courts. But in several respects the penal code recapitulated, sometimes verbatim, the medieval canon law on heresy.[36] The foremost notion of canon law to be incorporated into the Caroline edicts was that of heresy as a species of divine lese-majesty. This concept had gained acceptance in the late twelfth century and been introduced into imperial law by Frederick II between 1220 and 1239. In defence of the assimilation of heresy as treason, Aquinas had argued that the perversion of faith endangered men's souls, so that such an offence was more heinous than the counterfeiting of coin, a crime held under Roman law to be treasonable and punishable by death. A fortiori justice demanded that the stubborn heretic be put to death.[37] But whereas the church courts would commute the death sentence of misbelievers, prepared to renounce their false doctrines, to the penance of lifelong imprisonment, the civil judges in the Netherlands were denied any such latitude. Abjuration thus merely changed the mode of execution from the stake to the scaffold. In this respect offences against the edicts were treated as though they were crimes against the state. Accordingly there is a close parallel between the machinery Frederick II used against heresy in the kingdom of Sicily, and the means employed in the Habsburg Netherlands. In Sicily, too, heresy had been accounted high treason and prosecuted without resort to the ecclesiastical courts.[38]

No wonder civil courts in the Low Countries were bewildered. In 1527 the president of the *Grand Conseil* had to explain to puzzled deputies from Amsterdam that, though they should punish those who broke the edicts, they were not responsible for prosecuting those 'who *thought* ill of the doctrine and sacraments of the church'.[39] As the scope of the edicts widened, and the inquisitors became associated with the enforcement of those edicts, the mental crime of heresy proper became increasingly difficult to distinguish from offences against the placards of Charles V.

---

[36] For example, the judicial procedure laid down in Frans vander Hulst's instruction of 1522 echoed Boniface VIII's decretal of 3 March 1298; the notion that forfeiture occurred as soon as heresy was committed recurs in the edict of 22 September 1540.

[37] J. Lecler, *Toleration and the Reformation* (London, 1960), I, p. 85.

[38] On the legal notions informing the edicts of Frederick II, see E. Kantorowicz, *Kaiser Friedrich der Zweite* (Dusseldorf-Munich, 1963), I, pp. 238–48 and II, *Ergänzungsband*, pp. 109–12. I am indebted to Dr. E.O. Blake of the University of Southampton for drawing this parallel to my attention.

[39] *CD*, V, p. 207. In 1527 the magistrates of Lille consulted colleagues in nearby towns to discover how they should proceed against persons accused of 'ayant seme parolles Luteriennes'; M.P. Willems-Closset, 'Le protestantisme à Lille jusqu'à la veille de la Révolution des Pays-Bas', *Revue du Nord*, LII (1970), p. 199, fn. 5.

In imitation of the Roman law of treason the medieval inquisition held that an heretic's estate passed to the prince's treasury the moment he broke with the Catholic church. This notion duly appeared in the Edict of Worms, and more explicitly in the comprehensive edict of 1529. No part of the antiheresy legislation aroused more anxiety than the insistence that those who broke the placards should forfeit their property, as well as their lives. At first sight the indignation seems puzzling: after all, confiscation had been recognised in most provinces as a fitting punishment for treason long before 1500, and Wielant already considered heresy as a form of *crimen laesae maiestatis divinae*.[40] But heresy had been comparatively rare in the Low Countries during the fifteenth century, so that a legal theory, familiar to canonists and civilians, could still strike the town magistrates in the sixteenth century as newfangled.

Although the maxim 'qui confisque le corps confisque les biens' was widely known in the Low Countries and applied to certain crimes, the consequences for the legal heirs had been mitigated by local privileges, which fixed the maximum sum liable to forfeiture, at least for crimes other than treason, and exempted the dowries of Catholic widows. In the provinces more strongly affected by the *Sachsenspiegel* – namely Utrecht, Overijssel and Groningen – the estate of the executed criminal invariably passed to his heirs, and not to the prince. Willem van der Tanerijen, a Brabanter jurist of the late fifteenth century, also insisted that the sins of the heretical father should not be visited upon his orthodox children, who ought to succeed to his estate.[41] Clearly the placards on religion were deeply resented because the penalty of confiscation curtailed immemorial custom and authentic charters, and because it threatened the property of both *gens de petite estoffe* and *gens de qualité*.

At first the edicts respected the local privileges limiting confiscation, but already by the mid-1530s the towns in Holland and Zeeland had been forced to recognise that breaches of these edicts amounted to acts of divine lese-majesty. Where the sentences of the local courts limited confiscation in keeping with the privileges, the *procureur-general* succeeded in having these revised on appeal so that the entire estate of the executed Anabaptists passed to the fisc.[42] In French Flanders the towns and castellanies claimed they had always been exempt from confiscation, even for *crimen laesae maiestatis divinae*, and cited the sentence of certain heretics, condemned to death in 1429, when the magistrates of Lille had prevented confiscation.[43] When this privilege was scrutinised again in

[40] W. van Iterson, *Geschiedenis der confiscatie in Nederland* (Utrecht, 1957), p. 113.

[41] *CD*, II, p. 285.

[42] See ARAG Hof van Holland, 5654, fo. 1v-3, 21v-23. But in 1542 the provincial court upheld a local privilege of limited confiscation, when the *procureur-generaal* demanded total confiscation of a convicted murderer's estate; see fo. 97–98v and also Grosheide, *op. cit.*, pp. 259–72.

[43] *CD*, III, pp. 76–80, 121–22; also Van Iterson, *op. cit* p. 95. In 1545 the magistrates of Arras vainly insisted on their privilege of non-confiscation, Ch. Paillard, *Le procès de Pierre Brully* (Paris–The Hague, 1878), pp. 131–37, 158–69, 172–73.

1545 the *Grand Conseil* bluntly declared that heresy was an offence touching 'sa puyssance plainière et absolute selon laquelle icelle Sa Majesté ... peult tollir tous privilèges', including those of non-confiscation.[44] More ominous still was an ordinance of 1549, for this stated that confiscation for the crimes of lese-majesty 'divine et humaine' should be enforced 'nonobstant coustumes, privileges et usances pretendues au contraire par aulcunes villes ou pays'.[45] Valenciennes fought doggedly until 1564 to sustain this privilege, and several Flemish towns gained a respite until the arrival of Alva, while the States of Overijssel were still defending their 'old and immemorial freedom' from confiscation in 1571.[46]

Confiscation for heresy was enforced more strictly in the Habsburg Netherlands than elsewhere in the Empire. In Liège, where the antiheresy legislation closely resembled that in force in the Netherlands, the prince-bishop was forced to abandon the penalty of confiscation in 1545 because of the resolute opposition of the third estate.[47] In the free city of Cologne the property of convicted Anabaptists was not sequestered, and in the duchies of Jülich and Mark the children of Anabaptists succeeded to their parents' estate.[48] Anabaptists expelled from Hesse were even allowed to take their property with them, for as the landgrave said, he wanted 'weder irer leibe noch guts'.[49]

Because breaches of placards on religion were treated as treason, they were classified as 'cas privilégiés': consequently the provincial courts

[44] J. Verteneuil, 'Contribution à l'étude de la législation de Charles-Quint contre les hérétiques dans les Pays-Bas' (University of Liège *licence*, 1958–59), pp. 145–47. I am indebted to Professor G. Moreau for arranging for me to consult this and other unpublished theses of the University of Liège. For the fuller text of the legal opinion submitted by the *Grand Conseil* to Mary of Hungary see Paillard, *op. cit.*, pp. 155–57.

[45] *ROPB*, V, p. 577. Similar *non-obstante* clauses had been used against the privileges of non-confiscation claimed by Arras in 1460: *CD*, I, p. 460. For the opinion of jurists about such clauses, see J.H. Franklin, *Jean Bodin and the Rise of Absolutist Theory* (Cambridge, 1973), pp. 13–14. According to 'Remonstrance ofte vertoogh', *Historie van het verbond* IV, p. 122, the *Conseil Privé* had confirmed the privileges of non-confiscation on 13 September 1549.

[46] On Valenciennes, C. Paillard, *Histoire des troubles religieux de Valenciennes, 1560–1567* (Brussels, 1876), IV, pp. 42–69; on Flanders, Decavele, *op. cit.*, I, pp. 44–48; on Overijssel, Van Iterson, *op. cit.*, pp. 312–14, 403–4. In July 1566 the pensionary of Leiden persuaded the *vroedschap* to press for confirmation of the *ius de non evocando* and of the privilege which limited confiscation to sixty pounds. L. Knappert, *De opkomst van het protestantisme in eene Noord-Nederlandsche stad* (Leiden, 1908), p. 221.

[47] P. Harsin, 'De l'édit de Worms à la paix d'Augsbourg, 1521–1555: Étude critique de la législation liègeoise en matière d'herésie', *Bulletin de la commission royale des anciennes lois et ordonnances de Belgique*, XX (1959–60), p. 47.

[48] H.T.T. Stiasny, *Die strafrechtliche Verfolgungen der Täufer in der freien Reichsstadt Köln 1529 bis 1618* (Münster, 1962), pp. 154–55.

[49] H.W. Schraepler, *Die rechtliche Behandlung der Täufer in der deutscher Schweiz, Sudwest-deutschland und Hessen, 1525–1618* (Tübingen, 1957), pp. 72–6.

were entitled to act as courts of first instance, like the French *parlements*.[50] By the end of the middle ages, most local jurisdictions enjoyed privileges of *de non evocando* so that local inhabitants could not be cited before ecclesiastical or civil courts outside their place of residence, except for crimes infringing the *hoogheydt ende heerlijckheyt* of the prince. Such offences had been few, but prosecutions for heresy were, if not exactly two-a-penny, nevertheless fairly common. Naturally the towns and provinces strongly resisted this threat to their jurisdictional autonomy.

Holland, which had possessed a privilege of *de non evocando* since 1452, was compelled to defend that privilege in the first years of the Reformation. In 1523 the lay commissary with special responsibilities for heresy had a suspect conveyed outside the province, but the States protested so vigorously that Brussels henceforth respected the provincial privilege and instructed inquisitors at work in Holland on no account to try suspects outside the county.[51] This still left unresolved the status of the local courts in the matter of heresy.

As a rule the autonomy of the courts in the towns and bailiwicks and those seigneurial courts with criminal jurisdiction was secured by privileges of *de non evocando*. Judgments in these courts could only be overturned if the prosecution could prove that this sentence infringed the law, for, as already noted, the accused had no right of appeal once he had freely confessed to a capital crime. In practice, the provincial courts acted as a sort of judicial long-stop, intervening if the local forces of law were unequal to the occasion. The criminal cognizance of the provincial courts was chiefly concerned with matters reserved to the jurisdiction of the prince.

By the 1520s jurisdiction in heresy cases in Holland was already proving contentious. The States of Holland protested hotly at what they considered be the meddling of the provincial court, and during the summer of 1528 the States heard fighting words about the need to defend their privileges at any price.[52] The storm did not break at this time because in 1529 the sole competence in heresy cases was vested in special 'commissaires sur le fait des luthériens', and when the jurisdiction of the local courts in Holland was restored in 1534, the Anabaptist menace pushed the juridical

---

[50] For heresy as a 'cas privilégié' in France, see R.J. Knecht, 'Francis I, "Defender of the Faith"?, *Wealth and Power in Tudor England: Essays presented to S. T. Bindoff*, ed. E.W. Ives, R.J. Knecht and J.J. Scarisbrick (London, 1978), p. 110.

[51] Hoop Scheffer, pp. 155–61, 174–99; for an inquisitor's commission, see ARAG Hof van Holland, 37, fo. 37v-40v.

[52] *CD*, V, p. 344. On this occasion the deputies to the States from Delft remarked that 'they should assist one another in all privileges, even if they had on that account to travel down to Spain [al soudt men daeromme in Spangen sacken]'.

argument into the background. By 1544, however, that threat was at an end, and the earlier controversy revived when the *procureur-generaal* had an heretic removed from Amsterdam to stand trial in The Hague. The towns reacted by demanding from the Governor, Mary of Hungary, an unequivocal confirmation of their privileges of *de non evocando*. To their dismay Mary replied that, though it had never been intended to diminish the jurisdiction of the local courts, the alleged offence of heresy was akin to lese-majesty, and therefore properly belonged to the provincial court.[53] For all their indignant bluster the States could adduce no solid counter argument. Although the local courts continued to try most cases of heresy until the Council of Troubles was set up in 1567, they did so only on the sufferance of the government.

This reverse continued to worry the States. In 1548 they claimed that if the privileges of *de non evocando* could be subverted, then 'all the other privileges might easily be called into question, and the province stripped of these'.[54] For that reason the States began to organise their records, to study their privileges more carefully and to gather precedents. At that time the government was not planning any general assault on privileges, but the experience of the States in the affair had been thoroughly frustrating, and served to remind them how limited was the protection given by such privileges, and how impotent they were to defend those privileges. By as it were rewriting the rules of the game, the government had notionally withdrawn a whole range of offences from the purview of the local courts. All the States of Holland could do, as the guardians of those privileges, was to remind the provincial council of its duty to ensure that edicts published in the county did not violate the privileges.

In the other patrimonial provinces this particular privilege does not seem to have stirred the same passions. In Flanders, for example, the sheer volume of business created for the courts by the antiheresy legislation required the continued employment of the magistrates. When jurisdiction in heresy cases was transferred in 1529 to the special commissions, the States of Flanders protested and the jurisdiction of the local courts was promptly restored.[55] Indeed after the *schepenen* of Ghent had been forbidden to try heretics in 1540, it was the provincial court that urged the restoration of the municipal court's jurisdiction in 1545. Instead of welcoming this, the magistrates of Ghent would have been content to leave the whole burdensome and disagreeable business to the jurists of the provincial court, the 'gens lettrez et scavans en droist divin

[53] Grosheide, *op. cit.*, pp. 276–81.
[54] *Resolutiën van de Staten van Holland*, 1548, p. 12 (27 February).
[55] Decavele, *op. cit.*, I, p. 33.

et humain'.[56] Under a privilege granted in 1290 the burghers of Valenciennes claimed exemption from examination under torture; but this was disputed by Brussels in 1562, on the by now familiar grounds that such a privilege did not cover the 'crime de lèse Majesté divine et humaine'. Eventually the town conceded the substance and agreed to 'desbourgeoiser' prisoners accused of heresy.[57]

In Gelderland and Groningen the debate about the antiheresy measures took place in a quite different political and constitutional setting. Together they composed what Margaret of Parma could still describe in 1560 as the 'pays ... de nouvelle conqueste' to indicate their untried loyalty to the Habsburg dynasty, and their aloofness from the hereditary provinces.[58] For that reason Brussels treated them with special delicacy. These provinces also differed in two other respects. First, they were not subject to the antiheresy legislation in force elsewhere in the Netherlands: offences carrying the death penalty in the patrimonial lands were punished by a scale of fines in Groningen and Gelderland.[59] Secondly, the growth of confessional consciousness was markedly slower here than in the provinces to the south and west. Gelderland, especially, had been affected by the eirenicism fashionable in the duchy of Cleves and by the evangelical reforms inspired by Hermann von Wied. In Gelderland the provincial court, set up after the duchy had been incorporated into the

---

[56] *Ibid.*, pp. 37–38; Verteneuil, *op. cit.*, pp. 142–44. For the reluctance of the local courts to sentence persons accused of offences against the antiheresy edicts see Th. Sevens, *Handvesten rakende de wederdoopers en de calvinisten der XVIe eeuw in de voormalige kastelnij van Kortrijk* (Kortrijk, 1925), pp. 14–15. In 1569 a Flemish *baljuw* recommended that certain heretics be tried by the provincial court since the local magistrates were in such matters 'very perplexed' being simple tenants [*mannen van leene*] and country folk, De Coussemaker, *Troubles religieux*, I, p. 69. The *schout* of Niedorperkogge complained in 1571 that the local *schepenen* refused to convict a heretic, 'alleging that they have never dealt with such a sentence, hoping always that a better pardon will come', A.C. Duke, 'Nieuwe Niedorp in hervormingstijd', *NAK* n.s., XLVIII (1967), p. 67. The local courts in Franche Comté were also reluctant to exercise their jurisdiction in cases of heresy; see L. Febvre, *Notes et documents sur la réforme et l'inquisition en Franche-Comté* (Paris, 1912), pp. 42–45.

[57] Paillard, *op. cit.*, IV, pp. 35–42. During the interrogation of two heretics of Mechelen in 1555 the schout declared that since these were no longer burghers, he would examine them under torture, [A. van Haemstede], *Geschiedenis der martelaren* (Arnhem, 1868), p. 423.

[58] *Corresp. Marguerite d'Autriche,* (Gachard), I, p. 540; see also *Historie van Groningen: Stad en land,* ed. W.J. Formsma *et al.* (Groningen, 1976), p. 216.

[59] See C.H. Ris Lambers, *De kerkhervorming op de Veluwe, 1523–1578* (Barneveld, 1890), pp. x-xiii; *DAN*, I, *Friesland en Groningen, 1530–1550,* ed. A.F. Mellink (Leiden, 1975), pp. 139–41, 163–65. During the early summer of 1566 anxiety about the 'secret and pernicious inquisition' spread in Gelderland, G. van Hasselt, *Stukken voor de vaderlandsche historie,* I (Arnhem, 1792), pp. 66–67, 69–72, 76, 78, 80–83. Margaret of Parma remarked however that the States of Gelderland had less cause for concern in this respect than any other provincial States, 'n'ayants ni l'inquisition ny placcartz telz que aultres', *Briefwisseling tusschen Margaretha van Parma en Charles de Brimeu, graaf van Megen, stadhouder van Gelderland, 1560–1567,* ed. J.S. van Veen, (Arnhem, 1914), p.199.

Netherlands in 1543, rather than the heresy edicts themselves, stood at the heart of the controversy. Nevertheless the States displayed an allergic sensitivity, particularly when the provincial court claimed the right to gather information on suspected heretics in the towns. They saw in such commissions an inquisition in another guise.[60] In Groningen, too, 'inquisition' was used in this way. In 1556 the *stadhouder* warned the burgomasters of the provincial capital that, unless effective steps were taken against the sectaries, he would fetch a special commission and 'even conduct an *inquisitie*'.[61] Similar inquisitorial commissions were sent to Tournai and Valenciennes in 1554 and again in 1561 to sit alongside the local judges, when it seemed that they were no longer willing or able to enforce the edicts against heretics.[62]

When in 1560 Groningen refused to issue an edict against the heretics, it argued that since the towns and provinces enjoyed different privileges, the new edicts could not be implemented uniformly. Instead these should be tailored to the local constitutions.[63] But these disparities between and within the provinces hampered cooperation in the defence of the privileges. When at the States General of 1557–58 Holland tried to persuade the other provinces to combine in order to reduce the powers of the inquisitors to conform to canon law, their proposal was rejected by other provinces. Brabant objected on the grounds that the duchy knew nothing of any ecclesiastical inquisition, and Hainaut demurred lest recognition of a canonical inquisition should prejudice the provincial privilege of non-confiscation. At the same assembly Tournai proposed that a bargain be struck with the King who, in return for a subsidy, would grant all the patrimonial provinces exemption from confiscation. This too came to nothing, because some provinces saw no point in paying for a privilege they already enjoyed.[64] Moreover the States General could not

[60] Ris Lambers, *op. cit.*, pp. lxviii-lxix; A. Zijp, *De strijd tusschen de Staten van Gelderland en het Hof, 1543–1566* (Arnhem, 1913), p. 144.

[61] *Diarium van Egbert Alting, 1553–1594*, ed. W.J. Formsma and R. van Roijen (The Hague, 1964), RGP, Grote serie, 111, p. 63. For parallel usage in Cleves, see I.G. Sardemann, 'Der Landtag zu Essen und die Inquisition', *Zeitschrift des bergischen Geschichtsverein*, I (1863), pp. 201–14.

[62] Moreau, *Histoire du protestantisme à Tournai*, pp. 176–82, 230–39; C. Muller, 'La réforme à Valenciennes pendant la Révolution des Pays-Bay, 1565–1573' (University of Liège *licence*, 1973–74), pp. 1–2, 19–20. In 1561 the *Raad van Vlaanderen* proposed 'une inquisition générale par forme de grandz jours', but this was rejected because such extraordinary commissions were unknown in the Habsburg Netherlands; Decavele, *op. cit.*, I, pp. 39–40. In the prince-bishopric of Liège, however, *enquêtes-générales* took place in 1559, 1560 and 1562 in an endeavour to unmask suspected heretics, see W. Bax, *Het protestantisme in het bisdom Luik en vooral te Maastricht, 1557–1612* (The Hague, 1941), pp. 15–17.

[63] J.A. Feith, 'Eene mislukte poging tot invoering der inquisitie in Groningen', *Historische avonden*, I (1896), p. 173.

[64] 'Notulen en generaal advies van de Staten Generaal van 1557–1558', ed. P.A. Meilink, *BMHG*, LV (1934), pp. 276, 311; G. Griffiths, *Representative Government in Western Europe* (Oxford, 1968), pp. 359–60.

speak for the newly-incorporated provinces, who neither were, nor wished to be, represented at these meetings.

After 1559 common fears helped to draw the aggrieved groups in the provinces closer together. With the wars ended, Philip was more than ever eager to enforce the rigid religious policy inherited from his father. This repressive policy coincided with the introduction of Protestant church orders in Sedan, Scotland and, above all, England. In France, too, the Huguenot star was in the ascendant, as was shown by the Colloquy of Poissy and the Edict of January (1562).[65] To the King these alarming alterations only seemed to underline the necessity to root out heresy in the Low Countries. In vain Margaret of Parma tried to deflect royal policy from a procrustean orthodoxy, suitable for Spain 'fermez de mer et de montagnes', but plainly impractical for a small trading country like the Netherlands, hemmed in on all sides by heretical neighbours.[66] Many of the gentry, magistrates and jurists had, for example, never wholeheartedly endorsed a policy of indiscriminate repression.[67] Their disquiet led to the severity of the edicts unofficially being moderated, first in Holland and Friesland, and after Granvelle's departure in 1564 also in the southern provinces. Proposals for a drastic reform of diocesan organisation provoked an outcry from politically influential chapters and abbeys, whose privileges were thereby curtailed. The increased number of bishops intensified apprehension about the inquisition, henceforth mistakenly, but damningly, confounded with its Spanish namesake. Like the controversial decision to publish the Tridentine decrees in July 1565, the scheme for the new dioceses showed how little protection the privileges gave when the King had made up his mind. Nevertheless, the moderates could console themselves with the hope that Granvelle's recall, and the return of the high nobility to the *Conseil d'État* in 1564, heralded a change of policy. Such optimism was shown to be without foundation in December 1565, when the King made it plain that on the matter of religion he stood where he had always stood, foursquare behind his inquisitors. For the small Protestant lobby behind the Compromise this reminder of royal intransigence could not have been more timely.

[65] An earlier French edict on religion attracted the attention of Dutch Protestants in London, for in February 1561 Jan Utenhove undertook to translate it into Dutch, A.A. van Schelven, *Kerkeraads–protocollen der nederduitsche vluchtelingen-kerk* (Amsterdam, 1921), p. 121.

[66] *Corresp. Marguerite d'Autriche* (Gachard), III, pp. 462, 542.

[67] In 1564–65 a Walloon gentleman Balthasar Rolin dict Aymerie found himself under investigation by the inquisition following certain malicious accusations. The procedures of the inquisitors provoked indignation among other gentry, see *Corresp. Marguerite d'Autriche* (Gachard), III, pp. 509–11, 516–17, 563–64; *Corresp. française Marguerite d'Autriche*, I, pp. 10, 37, 45, 57; II, p. 60. For another instance of concern among the nobility concerning the investigation of one of their number by the inquisitors at this time, see H.A. Enno van Gelder, 'Bailleul, Bronkhorst, Brederode', *De Gids*, C (1936), pp. 373–74.

To prevent damaging disputes about the privileges, such as had taken place at the States General some years earlier, the Compromise refrained from making precise demands. Signatories bound themselves to prevent the introduction of 'this inquisition in whatever shape ... whether bearing the name of inquisition, visitation, edicts or otherwise'. Such a protean inquisition could be taken in Flanders and Holland to refer to the ecclesiastical inquisition headed by Titelmans and Lindanus, and in the Walloon towns and Gelderland to mean the government commissions that had overridden local jurisdictions in the pursuit of suspected heretics. Again the inquisition was, as Granvelle's correspondent Morillon complained in February 1566, equated by some with the placards of Charles V;[68] in its Spanish guise it conjured up, especially in Antwerp, the nightmare of paid informers, anonymous delations and secret trials.

In an essay on the causes of the Revolt the nineteenth-century man of letters Bakhuizen van den Brink remarked, somewhat disparagingly, on the 'heady power' the word privileges then possessed. Plainly the publicists of the Revolt exaggerated when they pretended the *Joyeuse Entrée* of Brabant justified taking up arms against their lawful prince. Yet the antiheresy legislation had created a tension between the prince, who bore 'le soing principale de garder et de faire observer ladicte religion catholique',[69] and his subjects, who thought their judicial and property rights had been secured by privileges. Usually comprehensive edicts were sent to the provincial courts for registration and allowance was made for custom, usage and the privileges. To some degree this continued to be the practice until 1567, even with the placards on religion. Charles V intended, however, that much of the criminal legislation should be enforced uniformly, at least in the patrimonial provinces,[70] hence the controversial *non obstante* clauses inserted in certain edicts. Provided the governing class accepted the necessity for such measures all was reasonably well; with the edicts against heresy this consensus was often conspicuously lacking. These edicts created an offence that exposed the upper reaches of society to prosecution. The magistrates found themselves not only passing capital sentences on 'gens de basse sorte', the staple diet of the courts, but also on skilled craftsmen, schoolmasters, merchants, lawyers and even gentry.[71] Because a breach of these edicts was treated as heresy and classified as a 'delit du cas privilégié', an accused could not invoke

---

[68] *Archives ou correspondance*, I, p. 439.

[69] *ROPB*, V, p. 576. For the statements by Don John of Austria and Requesens concerning the fundamental duty of the prince to uphold the Catholic faith see *Archives ou Correspondance*, V, p. 475.

[70] Johannes Junius de Jonghe, who argued in 1574 that the provinces of the Netherlands made up a single political body, rested part of his case on the fact that Charles V and Philip II had issued edicts concerning religion 'in all provinces in general', *Texts Concerning the Revolt*, p. 123.

[71] For concern on these matters among the high nobility, see *Mémoires de Viglius et d'Hopperus*, ed. A. Wauters (Brussels, 1858), p. 141.

privileges which otherwise would have spared him examination under torture and permitted his estate to descend to his lawful heirs.

In a *Ständestaat* like the 'seventeen Netherlands' it was difficult to reconcile the privileges with the legislative initiative of the prince. Groningen was uniquely well-placed to defend its constitution: here edicts detrimental to the privileges were not published and the provincial States could meet freely.[72] Although the representative bodies of Gelderland and Utrecht also claimed the right to convoke themselves, in practice the consent of the *stadhouder* was required. In 1565 the States of Holland tried to argue that privilege and 'good usage' entitled the *landsadvokaat* or the towns to summon the States. At that time William of Orange, who was *stadhouder*, rejected this claim; ironically it was this assertion that gave a semblance of legality to the meeting at Dordrecht in July 1572, at which William was recognised as the legitimate *stadhouder* of Holland and Zeeland.[73] Although the States were guardians of the privileges, they could only defend them indirectly, by withholding consent to subsidies and by calling on the provincial councils to ensure the edicts were in keeping with the privileges. In 1554 the States of Friesland denied that the prince could make law as he pleased, irrespective of their treaties and privileges, but Charles V resisted their demand to be allowed to examine the edicts before these were published: the right to issue placards belonged to the prince alone. Rather than push the general constitutional argument too far, the States backed down, preferring to seek remedies for specific grievances.[74] Relations between the prince and the States were often strained by demands for subsidies; but sooner or later a balance of sorts would be struck between the need for supply and redress of grievances. The edicts against heresy did not provide the same scope for compromise, especially because Charles V and Philip II took their supreme obligation to uphold the Catholic faith seriously, and interpreted 'orthodoxy' so narrowly. In 1562 the States of Brabant protested that the incorporation of certain abbeys to endow the new bishoprics overrode 'ancient customs, usages and immemorial rights'. In his reply the King explained that even well-founded privileges ought not to obstruct measures taken for the good of the church. In support he cited two tags: *cum summa sit ratio quae pro religione facit et salus populi suprema lex sit*. The first, which made the benefit of religion the highest

---

[72] According to H. de Schepper, 'De burgerlijke overheden en hun permanente kaders 1480–1579' (Nieuwe) *AGN*, V, p. 325, only the Four Members of Flanders [Ghent, Bruges, Ieper and the Brugse Vrij] among the patrimonial provinces successfully upheld the right to convoke themselves.

[73] See *Resolutiën der Staten van Holland* between 14 September 1565 and 27 January 1566.

[74] Woltjer, *Friesland*, p. 36; Theissen, *Centraal gezag*, p. 406. The States of Overijssel claimed in 1552–53 to have the right to inspect the edicts to ensure that these conformed with the liberties and customs of the province, J. de Hullu, 'Bijdrage tot de geschiedenis der hervorming te Deventer', *Archief voor de geschiedenis van het Aartsbisdom Utrecht*, XLIII (1917), pp. 268–69.

concern, may be medieval in origin; the second maxim derives from Cicero's *De Legibus*, and had become a commonplace in the middle ages, when *salus* often embraced both the notion of 'salvation' and 'well-being'.[75] What precisely Philip II had in mind is uncertain, but he certainly felt a heavy responsibility for the souls of his people.

In 1566 two separate, though related, solutions to the constitutional problem were being advanced. Gilles le Clercq concluded his *Remonstrance ofte Vertoogh* by advocating freedom of conscience, which implies that the prince relinquish his role as defender of the faith. Another way out of the impasse was also proposed by a Protestant who was closely involved with the Compromise. Thus Nicholas de Hames asserted in February 1566 that the evils in the commonwealth could be remedied by the States General, for they were empowered to take the initiative and convoke themselves.[76] Both the Request of April 1566 and the remonstrance of the States of Holland, before it was diluted to spare embarrassment, wanted a new religious policy to be framed with the 'advice and *consent*' of the States General. In 1566 the notion of the prince as legislator was still intact, though the great majority of the edicts were devised in answer to petitions from towns, guilds, provincial courts and the States. The antiheresy legislation had, however, been directly inspired by the prince, though the States General had been consulted on one previous occasion in 1531.[77] Probably the petitioners of 1566 sought to extend the principle of consultation so that it covered edicts on religion.

Philip II utterly rejected collaboration with the States General on this matter, and the constitutional debate petered out when the government suppressed the insurrections in 1567. The defection of the towns in Holland and Zeeland to William of Orange in 1572 pitched those provinces into an unforeseen constitutional predicament. Willy-nilly – and the 'rebels' began by trying hard to conceal the fact from themselves – sovereignty passed to those towns with votes in the provincial States. Before the Revolt the corporations of such towns had claimed to 'represent' the interests of the wider, though disfranchised community – the *corpus*.[78]

---

[75] *Corresp. Marguerite d'Autriche* (Gachard), II, p. 143.

[76] Griffiths, *op. cit.*, pp. 406–7. The claim was probably based on the *Grand Privilège* of 1477, but this had been repudiated by Philip the Fair in 1493.

[77] J. Gilissen, 'Les Etats Généraux des pays de par deçà, 1464–1632', *Assemblées d'Etats* (Leuven–Paris, 1965), pp. 309–10. When William of Orange prepared his *Verantwoordinge* in 1568 he recalled the occasion when Charles V had consulted the States General in 1531.

[78] P. Geyl, 'An Interpretation of Vrancken's *Deduction* of 1587 on the Nature of the States of Holland's Power', *From the Renaissance to the Counter-Reformation: Essays in Honour of Garrett Mattingly*, ed. C.H. Carter (London, 1966), pp. 230–46. The 'representative' character of the town corporations had been proclaimed well before the Revolt. For example the *schepenen* of Westzaan, Krommenie and Krommeniedijk described themselves in 1534 as representing ' 't corpus vande selven dorpen', ARAG, Stukken afkomstig van ambtenaren van het centraal bestuur, 92, no. 24 and the burgomasters of Gouda likewise considered themselves as 'representerende 't corpus van de stadt', GA Gouda ORA, 175, letter dated 19 December 1571.

The same notion applied to the provincial States: the States of Friesland described themselves under Charles V as 'being the *corpus* of the province'.[79] The rebel publicists harked back to the same theme in order to justify their resistance to the tyranny of Alva. God had appointed such bodies to defend 'the privileges, rights and freedoms of the common people whom they represent in the three estates of the clergy, nobles and towns'.[80]

E.H. Kossmann has shown how the concept of sovereignty shifted during the sixteenth century so as to correspond more closely with the enhanced power of the state. Whereas the task of the 'sovereign' had been traditionally to protect the constitution and to uphold an unchanging system of law, the 'sovereign' appeared in Bodin's analysis as a dynamic law maker.[81] In the case of the young Dutch Republic this sovereignty came to be vested in the provincial States, but insofar as these, together with the town corporations, now had the power to make the laws to meet their needs, they no longer had the same overriding concern to uphold the privileges.

Paradoxically the Revolt, justified on the basis of the privileges of *de non evocando* and non-confiscation and partly undertaken in their defence, gave birth to a state where such privileges lost much of their *raison d'être*, at least for those with political power. The anomalous character of the new constitution was too perplexing for this to be grasped at first. Indeed, after the eloquent defences of privileges in general, the new state could scarcely abandon its faith in their necessity, especially as long as there was a possibility of the King resuming some sort of loose suzerainty over the rebellious provinces. The urban privileges, which entitled towns to freedom from tolls, right of staple and all the other privileges characterised by Huizinga as the 'I may do what you may not do' variety, retained their local significance.[82] Eventually the exigencies of war prompted a muted criticism of these local privileges in the 1580s: too rigid an adherence to 'pretended privileges' could damage the common weal. Whereas the preamble of the Act of Dismissal asserted that 'the prince is created for the subjects', six years later a convinced Calvinist and strong supporter of Leicester warned that 'the privileges are there for the sake of the people, the people do not exist for the sake of the privileges'.[83] Although the spokesmen of the common people long

[79] Theissen, *Centraal gezag*, p. 338.

[80] *Texts Concerning the Revolt*, p. 139.

[81] E.H.Kossmann, 'Popular Sovereignty at the Beginning of the Dutch Ancien Regime', *Acta Historiae Neerlandicae*, XIV (1981), p. 1–28.

[82] J.J. Woltjer, 'Dutch Privileges, Real and Imaginary', *BN*, V *Some Political Mythologies*, ed. J.S. Bromley and E.H. Kossmann (The Hague, 1975), pp. 19–35, cit. p. 21.

[83] *Texts Concerning the Revolt*, p. 272. When Marnix defended Orange's radical alteration of Leiden's constitution in 1575, he stated that, 'les loix et polices sont faict pour le bien, repos et soulagement du peuple, et non pour le lier et détenir...en servage', R. Fruin, *Verspreide geschriften* (The Hague, 1900), II, p. 485 fn.2.

4. The Tyranny of Alva. Engraving *c.* 1569 *(Stichting Atlas van Stolk, Rotterdam, FM 409)*

Cardinal Granvelle advises Alva, 'the scourge of God', to persecute the 'evangelicals' still more savagely. The Devil stands behind, ready to reward the Cardinal with a papal tiara and the Duke with a royal crown. A group of inquisitors and churchmen attend Alva. The 'seventeen Netherlands' kneel in chains before the Duke, their privileges in shreds, though one holds the Bible. On the extreme right magistrates look on, but because they did not dare to protest for fear of losing their possessions, they have been changed into

stone pillars. A cardinal scoops confiscated property up from the 'red sea' fed by the blood of innocent evangelicals. Alva's cruel treatment of the Protestants, who are tortured and put to death, and the execution of Egmont and Hoorn complete the indictment.

The rebels hoped to rally Protestant opinion in Germany with this propaganda. The theme proved popular and several paintings on the subject were made in the early seventeenth century.

continued to employ the rhetoric of the privileges, which acquired a more or less mythical character, some Calvinists recognised that their interests would be better served by the election of 'God-fearing men' to these corporations: in other words, giving these bodies a more democratic character.[84]

If the constitutional privileges ceased to fulfil the same role in the United Provinces which they had performed before Philip's authority had been forsworn in 1581, the religious disposition of the ruling classes did not change fundamentally as a consequence of the Revolt. Of course many town regents and gentry now attended sermons delivered by the *predikanten* in churches whose austerity was relieved by their hatchments and imposing box-pews but, as a body, the *Heren* showed no eagerness to become professed members of the Reformed church. Indeed they remained distinctly wary, lest the discipline of this church should give rise to a 'new monkery'. Those who had once feared that they would become 'miserable and everlasting slaves of the inquisition' had no intention of exchanging 'l'inquisition d'Espaigne' for 'de Geneefsche inquisitie'. For that reason the Union of Utrecht laid down the principle that each individual should enjoy freedom of conscience.

[84] *Texts Concerning the Revolt*, pp. 231–34; see also G. Griffiths, 'Democratic Ideas in the Revolt of the Netherlands', *ARG*, L (1959), pp. 50–63.

8

From King and Country to King or Country?
Loyalty and Treason in the Revolt of the Netherlands

The 'seventeen Netherlands' owed their existence largely to the energies of their rulers.[1] Until 1548, when this hotchpot of duchies, counties and lordships was united in the Burgundian circle of the Empire, the boundaries of the Low Countries had expanded or contracted according to the military and diplomatic fortunes of their princes: there was nothing natural or inevitable about them. Charles V had, for example, threatened to annexe the prince-bishopric of Münster in 1534–35, as he had added Utrecht only a few years earlier.[2] Nor can the incorporation of the duchy of Gelre in 1543 be considered the outcome of an ineluctable historical process. Since the late fifteenth century the rulers in the Low Countries had sought to assert their control over the duchy. Yet there had been times when it seemed as though Gelre, which looked Janus-faced both up and down the Rhine, might, in combination with Jülich and Cleves, have constructed a formidable anti-Habsburg constellation into whose orbit a large part of the northern Netherlands would be drawn.[3]

Each province stood in a special relationship to the prince. Philip was duly recognised in 1555 as duke of Brabant, Limburg, Luxemburg and Gelre, count of Flanders, Artois, Hainaut, Holland, Zeeland and Namur and as lord of Friesland, Mechelen, Utrecht, Overijssel and Groningen. The precise nature of this bond was defined by chartered privileges which the prince swore to observe when he made his state entry. It was the duty of the provincial states to resist any breach of these privileges. In Friesland and Gelre, which as latecomers to the Habsburg Netherlands were especially sensitive about their privileges, the States appointed

---

[1] This paper was originally read at the Royal Historical Society's Conference on 10 September 1981 and revised for publication. I wish to acknowledge my debt to Professor Dr. K.W. Swart for his many helpful suggestions, and to the members of the conference for their comments. Mr. P.J. Regan of the University of Southampton is presently preparing a doctoral dissertation on the sources of patriotic sentiment in the Low Countries in the early modern period.

[2] A. Mellink, *Amsterdam en de wederdopers in de zestiende eeuw* (Nijmegen, 1978), pp. 54–56.

[3] F. Petri, 'Die früheren Habsburger in der niederländischen Geschichte', *BMHG*, LXXII (1958), pp. 29–34; W. Jappe Alberts, 'Gelderland van 1543–1566', *Geschiedenis van Gelderland, 1492–1795*, ed. P.J. Meij, *et al.* (Zutphen, 1975), pp. 82–85.

standing committees to watch over these.[4] As a rule edicts were examined by the provincial councils, which acted on the prince's behalf – not by the provincial states – and were modified to conform with local privileges and custom before they were published. When the town of Groningen refused to issue an edict concerning heresy in 1560, the magistrates insisted that as towns and provinces enjoyed dissimilar rights, new laws should be tailored accordingly.[5] Between the prince's solemn obligation to uphold the privileges and the imperative to standardise legislation and legal practice in the interests of efficient government there remained an unresolved and, in the end, irreconcilable tension.

Charles V, like his Burgundian predecessors, gave a semblance of coherence to his fragmented territories by involving the score or so great noble houses in their government. These gave counsel on matters of state and served the dynasty as provincial governors and captains of the military companies, while a few held high office in Spain or Italy. Their sense of belonging to a *corps d'élite* was enhanced by admission to the order of the Golden Fleece, whose insignia was sported by a sprinkling of minor princes as well as an impressive array of Spanish grandees.[6] Aside from the maverick house of Brederode, whose treasonable claims to the countship of Holland Charles treated with surprising lenience, and the more tiresome insubordination of the margraves of Baden in Luxemburg during the 1520s, the nobility remained conspicuously loyal to their Habsburg prince.[7]

The magnates of the Low Countries had not always been distinguished by their fidelity. When open war broke out between Burgundy and Valois in the second half of the fifteenth century, several prominent nobles at the Burgundian court embraced the party of the French king, partly because he was their feudal superior, but prompted too by a natural desire to save their possessions in France from forfeiture. The constancy of the Netherlands nobility under Charles V appears the more remarkable because a style of government, later associated with the hated Granvelle – namely, the pervasive influence of jurists in the collateral councils and the restrictions placed on the *stadhouders* in their governments – may be traced back to the regency of Mary of Hungary.[8] Yet those nobles who yearned in the dark days of Alva and Requesens for a return to the time

[4] A. Zijp, *De strijd tusschen de Staten van Gelderland en het Hof, 1543–1566* (Arnhem, 1913), pp. 145–46; J.J. Woltjer, *Friesland in hervormingstijd* (Leiden, 1962), p. 18.

[5] J.A. Feith, Eene mislukte poging tot invoering der inquisitie in Groningen, *Historische avonden*, I (1896), p. 173.

[6] Thierry de Limburg Stirum, *Het Gulden Vlies: Vijf eeuwen kunst en geschiedenis* (Bruges, 1962), pp. 38–41.

[7] P. Rosenfeld, 'The Provincial Governors in the Netherlands from the Minority of Charles V to the Revolt' (unpublished Columbia University Ph.D. thesis, 1959), pp. 136–37, 202–6.

[8] See Rosenfeld, 'The Provincial Governors'; M. Baelde, 'Edellieden en juristen in het centrale bestuur der zestiende-eeuwse Nederlanden', *TG*, LXXX (1967), pp. 39–51.

of Charles V were not entirely deceived. The Emperor had governed with their advice and he had rewarded them richly, loading them with pensions, perquisites and honours, raising their baronies to the rank of counties and preferring their younger sons to high ecclesiastical office.[9] Above all, Charles had paid them the compliment of sending as governors-general members of his family, whose modest households compensated in some degree for the long absences of the far more splendid imperial court. Those present at the ceremony in Brussels on 25 October 1555, when Charles V renounced his overlordship of the hereditary Netherlands in favour of Philip, could have been in no doubt about the affection of the nobles for their prince.[10]

In the States General, represented on that occasion by deputations from all save one of the provincial states, the Low Countries ostensibly possessed an institution capable of articulating the political identity of the country. In fact the States General was by virtue of its composition and traditions quite unfitted to transcend provincial particularism. The provinces incorporated under Charles V, the *pays de nouvelle conqueste*, declined to enter a wider political union lest their privileges should be infringed.[11] Consequently these provinces, as well as Luxemburg, usually kept aloof from the States General until after the Pacification of Ghent, preferring to treat directly with the prince or his viceroy. Even the patrimonial provinces, which had acknowledged the same dynastic head since the early fifteenth century, were reluctant to countenance any changes that might weaken the power of the provincial states. The embassies sent to the meetings of the States General were only empowered to hear and report back the propositions of the government, which would then be relayed to the constituent parts of the provincial states. In the case of Brabant no decision could be reached until unanimity had been secured within and between the towns with a vote in the third estate. So cumbrous a procedure exasperated the central government, yet it refrained from any drastic reform lest, in a more coherent States General, those who were opposed to some aspect of royal policy might combine to thwart it more effectively. Usually the governor-general would employ 'stick-and-carrot' tactics, patiently playing off one province, or one order within the States, against another. In this game the disparities between the provinces provided the government with useful leverage. Though the States General was sufficiently vigorous to prevent schemes for permanent taxation in 1535 and again in 1569, and so avoid the fate

[9] Rosenfeld, 'The Provincial Governors', pp. 127–31; H. Pirenne, *Histoire de Belgique* (3rd edn., Brussels, 1923), III, p. 193.

[10] *E.g.* Report by John Mason from Brussels on 27 October 1555 in *Relations politiques*, I, pp. 1–3.

[11] J.S. Theissen, *Centraal gezag en Friesche vrijheid: Friesland onder Karel V* (Groningen, 1907), p. 261; A. Zijp, *De strijd tusschen de Staten*, pp. 58–59.

of its moribund counterpart in France,[12] it remained, at least until 1576, a defensive body, 'intended', as a Belgian historian has said,'to secure local privileges against the encroachments of the sovereign'.[13]

The differences which hampered the growth of a Netherlandish political community reflected the several distinct and dissimilar societies to be found cheek by jowl in the seventeen provinces. The bonds of loyalty to the prince and the degree of participation in the wider community greatly varied. Even the character and political power of the nobility differed widely between one part of the country and another.[14] In the mainly agricultural provinces of Hainaut and Artois the Reformation made little headway outside a few large towns. In this region of corn and numerous small villages, the *noblesse* still dominated society. Through the work of the French social historian Muchembled, the world-picture of the minor gentry in Artois can be reconstructed from the letters of a certain François de Boffles.[15] Like many of his rustic compeers, the routine of Sieur de Boffles scarcely set him apart from the better-off peasants among whom he lived. However, through his assiduous correspondence he remained in touch with some of the most influential county families and these, in turn, gave access to the more rarified society of the upper nobility. These ties were indispensable if de Boffles were to arrange the *bonnes alliances* for his children, on which he lavished, so much attention. Such gentry might live close to the soil, but in their daydreams they inhabited the world of the nobility, as they exchanged news about tournaments and duels of honour, even if few of them entered the lists.[16] Despite the enormous disparities in wealth between the noble house of Croy and the Sieur de Boffles, they were at one in their esteem for the chivalric conventions,[17] in their instinctive and unshakeable Catholicism and their political conservatism. From the *petite*

---

[12] C. van de Kieft, 'De Staten-Generaal in het bourgondisch-oostenrijkse tijdvak (1464–1555)', *500 jaren Staten-Generaal in de Nederlanden: Van statenvergadering tot volksvertegenwoordiging*, ed. S.J. Fockema Andreae and H.Hardenberg, (Assen, 1964), pp. 25–26. After 1585 the States General withered away in the southern Netherlands, meeting for the last time in 1632–34.

[13] G. Malengreau, *L'esprit particulariste et la révolution des Pays-Bas au XVIe siècle (1578–1584)* (Leuven, 1936), p. 159.

[14] C.A.J. Armstrong, 'Had the Burgundian Government a Policy for the Nobility?', *BN*, II, ed. J.S. Bromley and E.H. Kossmann (Groningen, 1964), pp. 9–10.

[15] R. Muchembled, 'Publication du "Registre secret de François de Boffles", seigneur de Boffles: Introduction à l'étude des mentalités de la noblesse artésienne' (Thèse de doctorat de IIIème cycle, Université de Paris I, 1973).

[16] Muchembled, 'Registre secret de François de Boffles', I, pp. 97–102; II, pp. 141–42, 253–55.

[17] Muchembled, 'Registre secret de François de Boffles', II, pp. 382–86; L.P. Gachard, *La Bibliothèque Nationale à Paris: Notices et extraits des manuscrits qui concernant l'histoire de Belgique* (Brussels, 1875), I, pp. 464–65.

[18] H.L.G. Guillaume, *Histoire des bandes d'ordonnances des Pays-Bas* (Brussels, 1873), pp. 65–97, 108–9, 143–44.

noblesse of the Walloon provinces were recruited men-at-arms and archers for the *bandes d'ordonnances*; they demonstrated their devotion to the prince by fighting in France and quelling rebellion at home.[18] Almost to a man they despised and feared heresy, which seemed to threaten not only the Catholic church but the dominant place held by the nobility in the local political and social hierarchy.[19]

By comparison the nobility of Holland made an altogether more modest impression. Barely 200 families were ranked as noble by the mid sixteenth century and, apart from the lords of Brederode, none of the high nobility maintained their households in the vicinity. Sometimes outsiders wondered whether a nobility worthy of the name existed at all. An English agent once remarked that, when support for William of Orange was under discussion by the Queen's privy councillors, they 'would looke with what great personages they should dele [in Holland]. And then seinge none but townsmen ..., yt would hinder the good entent, even for lack of cowtenance'.[20] In 1588 a Dutch supporter of Leicester mocked the pretentious title of 'sovereign lords' assumed by the members of the States whom he ridiculed as 'Hans Crap-pepper, Hans Pedlar, Hans Brewer, Hans Cheesemonger and Hans Miller'.[21]

Though the *landadel* set great store by their noble birth and preserved their separate identity by practising endogamy,[22] the legal and fiscal distinctions between noble and commoner had been virtually effaced by the early seventeenth century.[23] In the States of Holland the voice of the nobility was heard with respect, but it was the regents in the towns who set the tone, while even in the countryside self-reliant communities of free peasants diluted the influence of the nobility. The links between fiefs and military service had long since been broken and the *landadel* of Holland rarely went to court, or served in the army. Instead they remained in the county, holding positions as bailiffs and foresters, which offices they leased, or sat in the provincial council in The Hague or the boards of the *heemraadschappen* [drainage authorities].[24] For these

[19] The handful of avowed Protestants among the gentry of Artois and Hainaut belonged significantly to two or three families. Pontus Payen had the deepest contempt for such men, but he made an honourable exception for the witty and well-read Jean le Sauvaige, who, however, redeemed himself because he died 'détestant les erreurs de Calvin', *Mémoires de Pontus Payen*, ed. A. Henne (Brussels, 1861), I, pp. 33–35, 338–40.

[20] *Relations politiques*, VIII, p. 246.

[21] Bor, III, p. 205 [bk. 24, fo. 42].

[22] H. van Nierop, ' "Het Quaede Regiment": De Hollandse edelen als ambachtsheren, 1490–1650', *TG*, XCIII (1980), p. 435.

[23] H. Grotius, *The Jurisprudence of Holland*, ed. R.W. Lee (Oxford, 1926), pp. 59–61.

[24] H.A. Enno van Gelder 'De Hollandse adel in de tijd van de opstand', *TG*, XLV (1930), p. 150. On the weakness of seigneurial institutions in Holland see J. de Vries, *The Dutch Rural Economy in the Golden Age, 1500–1700* (New Haven, 1974), pp. 36–37, 39–41, 55. When Holland was incorporated into the Burgundian Netherlands, certain Germanic customs and institutions in respect of justice survived, see H.P.H. Jansen, 'Modernization of the Government: the Advent of Philip the Good in Holland', *BMGN*, XCV (1980), pp. 255–56, 263.

reasons they had less cause than their southern compeers to look to the higher nobility and the central government for advancement but, by the same token, they were under considerable pressure to reach an accommodation with the new political and ecclesiastical order established in the county after 1572, though few of them wholeheartedly welcomed either the Beggars or the Reformed church.

In Friesland the absence of effective lordship and a feudal nobility permitted the growth of a kind of territorial, even tribal, loyalty: the cry 'Free and Frisian' was already heard in the mid-fifteenth century, while the belief 'that a Frisian should have no lord save God alone', still found advocates in the 1520s.[25] By the terms of the treaty made between Charles V and Friesland in 1524 the prince was entitled to nominate the chief officials in the rural administration. In practice the vigilance of the provincial states in defence of the privileges and the inclination of provincial court to adapt itself to its Frisian surroundings severely curtailed the central government's freedom of action.[26] Consequently incorporation into the Habsburg Netherlands made little difference to the local nobility, who continued to administer justice and dominate the political life of province, as they had done before 1524. Opportunities for Frisians outside the province were limited, though the brilliant careers of Viglius and Hopperus suggest that the often well-educated Frisian nobles might in time have derived benefit from the province's closer association with the Habsburg dynasty.[27] Throughout the sixteenth century Friesland remained physically and politically remote, almost unruffled by the controversies raging elsewhere in the Low Countries. This isolation accounts for the cool reception the local nobility initially gave the Compromise in 1566. When in 1577 Frisian deputies finally joined the States General, their parochial demands showed scant understanding of the political situation in the south. For much of the 'revolt against Spain', Friesland was absorbed by local political issues.[28]

More than once Margaret of Parma complained to Philip about 'la liberté si grande' in the newly-acquired provinces. The government in

---

[25] Theissen, *Centraal gezag*, pp. 258–59, 284.

[26] Woltjer, *Friesland*, ch. II.

[27] *Vigliana. Bronnen, brieven en rekeningen betreffende Viglius van Ayatta*, ed. E.H. Waterbolk *et al.* (Groningen, 1975), pp. 6–15. On the good education of the Frisian élite, see E.H. Waterbolk, 'Aspects of the Frisian Contribution to the Culture of the Low Countries in the Early Modern Period', *BN*, IV, ed. J.S. Bromley and E.H. Kossmann (The Hague, 1971), pp. 118–20. Friesland did not undergo feudalism. Consequently the so-called Frisian *adel* had neither the political privileges nor the seigneurial rights enjoyed by most European aristocracies. In Friesland the term 'noble' was applied to those families who, because they lived off the income from their property, had more time to devote to local government. They therefore exercised a considerable political influence, Woltjer, *Friesland*, p. 45.

[28] J.J. Woltjer, *Friesland*, pp. 148–50, 248–50. In 1570 several gentry from Groningerland offered their service to Orange, though they had never been invited in 1566 to enter the Compromise, Bor I, p. 311 [bk. 5, fo. 224].

Brussels feared it would be especially hard to enforce royal policy in Groningen after the Spanish army departed in 1561.[29] Evidently these provinces had no wish to develop closer political links among themselves, or with the patrimonial lands.[30] Because their loyalty to the dynasty was yet untried, they were treated with circumspection by the central government, which hesitated to accelerate their integration. This may explain why Charles's new subjects were not made very welcome in the *bandes d'ordonannce*.[31] In these provinces the prince remained an abstract and ambivalent figure, at once upholding and threatening their liberties. Ironically the very particularism that prevented their assimilation also served to insulate them from the political and religious distempers which afflicted the core of the Habsburg Netherlands after 1559.

Only in the Walloon provinces did conditions allow the nobility, in the words of Bodin, to function as 'la principale liaison' between the prince and his people.[32] Although the government of Charles V tried to build up support by the distribution of patronage and pensions elsewhere, the 'chains of command' running between the centre and the outlying provinces were defective, and Brussels was obliged to rely on the provincial courts, which came to be greatly resented in Utrecht, Friesland and Gelderland. In the towns Charles V tried, whenever the opportunity occurred, to suppress the political power of the guilds and civic militias and to encourage the formation of dependable urban oligarchies in the belief that these could be supervised more effectively.[33] How durable the loyalty of the nobility, gentry and town corporations to the prince would prove, once the governing classes in the patrimonial provinces lost their confidence in the political and religious policies advocated by Philip and his ministers, remained to be seen as did what alternative foci of loyalty would emerge to take, if need be, the place of the prince.

The sense of national awareness among the governing classes in the Burgundian Netherlands was, as Huizinga showed in his famous essay on the subject, inseparable from their devotion to the ruling dynasty.[34] The growth of a Netherlandish consciousness among the nobility had been retarded by the equivocal relationship between the Valois dukes and

[29] *Corresp. Marguerite d'Autriche* (Gachard), I, pp. 257–58, 478–79, 540.

[30] Theissen, *Centraal gezag*, pp. 260–62.

[31] *Corresp. Guillaume*, I, pp. 43–47.

[32] G. Griffiths, *Representative Government in Western Europe in the Sixteenth Century* (Oxford, 1968), p. 505.

[33] *E.g.*, Tournai (1522), Utrecht (1528), Ghent (1540). An anonymous memorandum, probably composed in 1567–68, advised Philip II, among many other things, to suppress the *Breeden Raedt* in the towns as this general council was considered a cause of political instability, *Archives ou correspondance*, IX, 74*-75*.

[34] J. Huizinga, 'Uit de voorgeschiedenis van ons nationaal besef', *Verzamelde Werken* (Haarlem, 1948), II, pp. 97–160. This essay was first published in 1912.

[35] W. Obert, *Discours en bref des choses mémorables advenues en ces Pays-Bas ... signamment de ce qui s'est passé en la ville d'Arras*, ed. A. d'Héricourt (Paris, n.d.), p. 47.

their feudal superiors, the kings of France. Under the Habsburgs certain obstacles to the formation of a sturdier sense of national identity disappeared. From the accession of Louis XI until the peace of Senlis in 1493, and for much of the first half of the sixteenth century, there was open war between the rulers of the Low Countries and France. In its wake anti-French sentiment developed, especially in the border provinces of Artois and Flanders. Indeed this legacy of francophobia was sufficient to damn William of Orange's projected alliance between the States General and Anjou. The States of Artois, haunted by the fear of French domination, recoiled in horror from the idea that a Valois prince should be received in 1578 as 'protector and defender of the Netherlands liberties against the Spanish tyrant';[35] many 'patriots' in Flanders believed their cause had been defiled by its association with Anjou.

The constitutional position of the Low Countries within the Holy Roman Empire was redefined in 1548. According to the treaty of Augsburg concluded that year, all the hereditary lands of the Habsburgs in the Low Countries and Burgundy were brought together in the Burgundian Circle. The members of this circle made a contribution to the Reich in return for enjoying its protection, but wer : henceforth exempt from the jurisdiction of the imperial court of appeal.[36] The significance of the imperial connexion varied from one part of the Low Countries to another. In Brabant it was no more than a dim memory, though revived in the 1560s for polemical purposes. In the northern and eastern provinces, which had formerly belonged to the Westphalian Circle and whose towns still prized their membership of the Hanse, the links remained strong and sincere.[37]

Of course the Habsburg princes had never intended to foster a specific and exclusively Netherlandish consciousness. Convenience had obliged the rulers of Burgundy and the Low Countries to administer these territories separately. Nor did Charles depart from the Burgundian practice of appointing natives of Franche-Comté to office in the central government of the Netherlands. Granvelle, himself a Burgundian, stood in this tradition when he advised Philip II to confer commanderships in the Spanish military orders on the higher nobility of the Netherlands. Even after his rupture with Orange, the Cardinal urged the King to make

---

[36] P.L. Nève, *Het rijkskamergerecht en de Nederlanden* (Assen, 1972), pp. 121–27, 518–22.

[37] For the imperial connexion in Brabant, see P.J. van Winter, 'Een apocriefe tekst van het verdrag van Augsburg van 1548', *Verkenning en onderzoek* (Groningen, 1965), pp. 77–81; L. Metsius, 'Sur les causes, l'origine et le progrès des troubles des Pays-Bas', *Corresp. Philippe II*, IV, 740; for the newly incorporated provinces, see Theissen, *Centraal gezag*, pp. 385–97; *Uittreksels uit het dagboek van Arent toe Boecop* (Deventer, 1862), pp. 75–82; J.C.H. de Pater, 'Leicester en Overijsel', *TG*, LXIV (1951), pp. 256, 266. See also R. Glawischnig, *Niederlande, Kalvinismus und Reichsgrafenstand, 1559–1584: Nassau-Dillenburg unter Graf Johann VI* (Marburg 1973), pp. 169–70.

the Prince viceroy of Sicily.[38] By such means the Granvelle hoped to deliver the spendthrift nobility from their creditors and, more important, reconcile them to the changed nature of the Habsburg monarchy, whose centre of gravity had indisputably shifted to Castile.

It was precisely the Spanish character of the ruling dynasty after 1555 that the nobility of the Low Countries found hardest to stomach. According to the report of a Venetian ambassador in 1557 the native nobility took a strong dislike to Philip because he preferred the Spanish way of life and took counsel only from Spaniards.[39] There was, of course, nothing sinister about their presence for they were in attendance to advise the King about the affairs of Castile and Aragon. The Netherlands nobility seem to have been unusually sensitive about the supposed influence of foreigners at this time. In 1553 they complained that the Duke of Savoy, the commander of the Habsburg army, had filled his council of war with Spanish and Italian commanders.[40] A few year later Charles de Lalaing denounced Granvelle as 'an enemy of the Low Countries, a foreign intruder'.[41] To add insult to injury Philip's court at Brussels swarmed with Spaniards: according to the Venetian ambassador nine in every ten members of this vast company of well over 1,000 were Spaniards.[42] In the 1520s Margaret of Austria had offended the native nobility by surrounding herself with courtiers from Savoy and Franche-Comté,[43] but after 1555 the nobility of the Low Counties felt excluded from access to their prince in their own country. At this time too, Lalaing, Orange and Hoorne protested vigorously against dynastic policies they considered harmful to the prosperity of the Low Counties. So, when war with Scotland seemed imminent in the autumn of 1557, one nobleman advised Philip to wage it 'not as prince of the *pays de pardeça* but as *roi d'Angleterre*'.[44] Only a few days before Philip sailed for Spain in 1559, the French ambassador observed that the spirits of the nobility would revive once the King was out of the country.[45] The desire of the high nobility to be quit of their prince is a remarkable testimony to their estrangement

[38] *Corresp. Philippe II*, I, pp. 239, 260; Renon de France, *Histoire des causes de la désunion, révoltes et altérations des Pays-Bas, 1559–1592*, ed. C. Piot (Brussels, 1886), I, p. 29.

[39] L.P. Gachard, *Relations des ambassadeurs vénitiens sur Charles-Quint et Philippe II* (Brussels, 1856), p. 87.

[40] Rosenfeld, 'The Provincial Governors', pp. 243–44.

[41] M. van Durme, *Antoon Perronet, bisschop van Atrecht, kardinaal van Granvelle, minister van Karel V en van Filips II (1517–1586)* (Brussels, 1953), p. 159.

[42] Gachard, *Relations des ambassadeurs vénitiens*, pp. 42–43. Badoaro's impression receives confirmation from the *Estat du roy d'Espaigne ... en l'an 1558* published with *Relations*, pp. 251–70.

[43] Rosenfeld, 'The Provincial Governors', pp. 199–200.

[44] *Relations politiques*, I, pp. 101–2. See also A. Louant, 'Charles de Lalaing et les remonstrances d'Emmanuel-Philibert de Savoie (juillet et novembre 1556)', *BCRH*, XCVII (1933), pp. 255–69.

[45] Gachard, *Relations des ambassadeurs vénitiens*, p. 87, fn. 1.

from the dynasty. But if they expected, in the King's absence, to govern the Low Countries, they were to be swiftly disappointed by the high value Margaret of Parma placed on the advice of Granvelle and Viglius.

In one respect the high nobility seemed ill-fitted to champion the interests of the Low Countries against 'foreigners', for not a few of them were related by blood or marriage to the German aristocracy: Brederode, Floris van Pallandt, Willem van den Bergh, Egmont and Hoorne had all taken German consorts, while both William of Orange and Peter Ernst of Mansfeld were German by birth. In 1562 Margaret of Parma commented with asperity on the inconsistence of those who demanded the removal of Burgundians from office in the Low Countries, yet regarded men born outside the King's dominions as natives.[46] Orange, who never concealed his German origins, subsequently sought to refute the charge that he was a stranger by emphasising his credentials as the scion of a family whose members had loyally served the rulers in the Netherlands, and whose connexions with the provinces had begun more than 200 years earlier.[47] In this sense Orange was justified in considering himself to be a compatriot Netherlander, whereas Granvelle remained a foreigner. Yet, as the States of Holland privately acknowledged in 1587, the King would be disinclined to regard his subjects in Italy and Spain as foreigners in the Low Countries.[48] Despite their affinities with the nobility of the Empire and France, the Netherlands magnates, whose fiefs lay scattered through the patrimonial lands, naturally developed a sense of responsibility towards the Low Countries by virtue of their obligations as members of the *conseil d'état* and as captains of the *bandes d'ordonannce*, concerned with the defence of *nostre patrie*.[49]

Of course the notion of service to the *patrie* was indivisible from the feudal loyalty they owed the King as their liege. The authors of the Request submitted to Margaret of Parma in April 1566 naturally coupled

---

[46] *Corresp. Philippe II*, I, pp. 224, 231.

[47] *Corresp. Guillaume*, II, p. 74; *The Apologie of Prince William of Orange against the Proclamation of the King of Spaine*, ed. H. Wansink (Leiden, 1969), pp. 48–51; see also *Texts Concerning the Revolt of the Netherlands*, ed. E.H. Kossmann and A.F. Mellink (Cambridge, 1974), p. 117.

[48] Bor, III, p. 139 [bk. 23, fo. 96]. The King's commissioners at the peace negotiations held at Breda in 1575 were instructed to tell the rebels that 'les Espaignols ... estans subjectz naturelz du Roy comme eulx, ne peuvent estre tenuz pour estrangers', *Corresp. Philippe II*, III, p. 586. In practice contemporaries acknowledged that there were different degrees of 'foreignness'. In Holland natives of Brabant could not hold office on the grounds that they were *uytheemschen* and the States of Holland were reluctant to make an exception even for the *stadhouder* for fear the prince might appoint 'a Spaniard or an Englishman', *Resolutiën van de Staten van Holland* (1555), pp. 12, 14, 33. As the above extract testifies, the King drew the sharpest distinction between those born (or brought up) within his various dominions and those born outside. Granvelle considered himself no more a Netherlander than a Italian: 'je suis de partout et ma fin est procurer de faire mes affaires et d'employer en ceux du Maitre et du public', Van Durme, *Antoon Perronet*, p. 338.

[49] Rosenfeld, 'The Provincial Governors', pp. 137–39.

the two notions together.[50] Philip thanked Aarschot for the services he had rendered both the King and his country,[51] and Margaret of Parma declared that Orange would perform a 'great service to God, Your Majesty and his *patrie*' if he succeeded in enforcing an agreement reached with the confederate nobility on religion.[52] Such an association of ideas occurred as readily to the acquaintances of de Boffles,[53] as to the Calvinist ministers at Valenciennes, who insisted in 1566 that they were 'faithful and loyal servants of His Majesty and loved their country'.[54]

The high nobility had, as faithful vassals, a clear duty to give the King frank advice in order that he might enjoy his inheritance in tranquillity. When certain of the nobility complained to Philip in 1563 about Gran-velle's policies, they couched their appeal in precisely these terms.[55] The Compromise, which was composed late in 1565, employed similar language when it described the nobility, 'as His Majesty's helpers whose function it is to maintain his authority and greatness by providing for the prosperity and safety of the country through our prompt and willing service'.[56] The duty of the high nobility towards both the King and the people is evident in yet another document from this time, when they refer to themselves as 'humble servants of His Majesty, protectors of the nobility, the country and the entire people'.[57] But when the interests of the King and the community appeared to come into conflict, there would be those in the Low Countries who expected the nobility to stand by the privileges.[58] The Dutch scholar Oudendijk has demonstrated that William of Orange, in his double capacity as the King's chief vassal and as the foremost member of the States General, maintained until 1580 that he had a sacred obligation to protect the Low Countries against the King's evil ministers on behalf of the King.[59]

Outside the ranks of the nobility, *patrie* continued to denote, as it had during the middle ages, one's native town or province. Erasmus, for example, once declared, 'My *patria* is Holland and Holland is its name', though the *patria* remained for that much-travelled humanist a protean notion, capable on occasion of signifying the old Burgundian

[50] *Texts Concerning the Revolt*, p. 63.

[51] E. Dony, 'Lettres de Philippe II et de Marguerite de Parme à Philippe de Croy, troisième duc d'Aerschot, 1558–1593', *BCRH*, LXXXI (1912), pp. 435–36.

[52] *Corresp. Guillaume*, II, p. 400. For other examples, see pp. 231, 295, 305.

[53] Muchembled, 'Registre secret de François de Boffles', II, pp. 42, 64, 85.

[54] L.A. van Langeraad, *Guido de Bray, zijn leven en werken* (Zierikzee, 1884), p. cviii.

[55] *Corresp. Guillaume*, II, pp. 35–39; see also the *Corresp. Philippe II*, I, p. 259.

[56] *Texts Concerning the Revolt*, p. 60.

[57] *Archives ou correspondance*, II, p. 470.

[58] See the petition addressed to Brederode by three Protestant prisoners in July 1566 in *Archives ou correspondance*, II, pp. 143–44.

[59] J.K. Oudendijk,'"Den Coninck van Hispaengien heb ick altijt gheert"', *Dancwerc: Opstellen aangeboden aan Prof. Dr.D.Th. Enklaar* (Groningen, 1959), pp. 264–78.

Netherlands with Brabant at its heart, or the entire universe.[60] A dictionary published at Antwerp in 1562 glossed *patria* as 'everybody's country, fatherland, the town, village, hamlet or any other place where one is born'.[61] In France a rough-and-ready distinction had emerged by the early sixteenth century between *patrie,* meaning the whole kingdom, and *pays,* which denoted a region.[62] Such an evolution was impeded in the case of the Low Countries by this region's ambivalent relationship with *Germania* and *Gallia,*[63] the incoherence of their political organisation and the absence of any sense of community between the Burgundian and the newly incorporated provinces. Until well into the seventeenth century the emotional attachment was to the province. Protestant exiles from the southern Netherlands resident in the United Provinces or abroad spoke nostalgically of Flanders as their *vaderland,* and where Christiaan Huygens' own country was unmistakably Holland, Oldenbarnevelt referred to Utrecht as his 'fatherland'. [64]

In medieval Dutch *vaderlant* only connoted heaven, man's eternal abode, but when Luther's Bible was translated into Dutch, the translators

[60] J.J. Poelhekke, 'The Nameless Homeland of Erasmus', *Acta Historiae Neerlandicae,* VII (1974), pp. 54–87. Quotation on p. 55.

[61] S. Groenveld, 'Natie en nationaal gevoel in de zestiende-eeuwse Nederlanden', *Nederlands Archievenblad,* LXXXIV (1980), p. 376. I am obliged to the author for giving me an offprint of his stimulating article so soon after publication. For contemporary examples of the versatile usage of *patria* before the Revolt: Gnapheus described the Protestant Pistorius, put to death in 1525 as 'natione Hollandus, patria Wordenas', *CD,* IV, p. 408; Van Haemstede wrote of Angelus Merula having been removed 'from his "fatherland" [Holland] to Brabant', *Historie der martelaren* (Arnhem, 1868), p. 559; Viglius, writing from Ingolstadt in 1541, used *patria* to denote the Habsburg Netherlands as a whole, F. Postma, *Viglius van Aytta als humanist en diplomaat, 1507–1549* (Zutphen, 1983), p. 85 and fn. 266; the first Dutch translation of Erasmus's *Querela Pacis* (1567) included an introduction which referred to 'Nederlandt, ons eyghen vaderlandt', S.W. Bijl, *Erasmus in het nederlands tot 1617* (Nieuwkoop, 1978), p. 263.

[62] G. Dupont-Ferrier, 'Le sens des mots "patria" et "patrie" en France au moyen-âge et jusqu'au début du XVIIe siècle', *Revue Historique,* CLXXXVIII (1940), p. 95.

[63] Poelhekke,'The Nameless Homeland', p. 58. Pontus Payen writes of 'nostre Gaule Belgique' when referring to the southern Netherlands, *Mémoires,* II, pp. 190–91. In the late sixteenth century some parts of the northern Netherlands still felt a sentimental attachment to the German Nation. In 1578 the subjects of the Count of Culemborg swore to render no aid to Don John and his followers because they were 'dootsvyanden ende vertreders onses Vaderlants ende der geheelen Duytscher Nation', A.P. van Schilfgaarde, *Het Huis Bergh* (Maastricht, 1950), p. 194.

[64] R. van Roosbroeck, *Emigranten: Nederlandse vluchtelingen in Duitsland (1550–1600)* (Leuven, 1968), pp. 349–51. Exiles from the south occasionally had inserted into their contracts a condition releasing them, should political and religious circumstances permit them to return to their 'vaederlicke stadt' or their 'vaderlant vlaenderen', *e.g.* J. Briels, 'Zuidnederlandse onderwijskrachten in Noordnederland, 1570–1630', *AGKKN,* XIV (1972), p. 280; KA Enkhuizen, 10a Kerkeraadsnotulen, 23 May 1585. For similar usage in the seventeenth century see E.H. Kossmann, 'The Dutch Case: A National or a Regional Culture?', *Transactions of the Royal Historical Society,* 5th series, XXIX (1979), p. 165; H. Gerlach, *Het proces tegen Oldenbarnevelt en de 'Maximen in den staet'* (Haarlem, 1965), p. 466.

availed themselves of the profane sense, which *Vaterland* had already acquired in late medieval German, in order to render the notion of one's country.[65] But since *vaderland* was commonly equated with the local *patria*, there was a clear need for a concept capable of embracing the sum of the *patriae* which made up the 'seventeen Netherlands'. The obvious solution was to refer to the whole as *het gantsse vaderland, het gemeyne vaderlant* or the *universa patria*. By the late thirteenth century French jurists had begun to distinguish between the *communis patria*, in other words the kingdom of France, and the more limited *patria* or *pays*.[66] An exact parallel may be found in German legal circles in the early sixteenth century,[67] and by the mid century Calvinist exiles from the Low Countries, also employed this concept. The Flemish Reformed minister Marten Micron began his London church order of 1554 by wishing 'all who loved everlasting salvation and truth throughout the entire Netherlands [*de gansche Nederlanden*] peace, grace and mercy'.[68] When after 1567 William of Orange corresponded with German princes about the affairs of the Low Countries, he wrote of *desz gemeinen vatterlandts*.[69] The commissions, instructions, pamphlets and official correspondence emanating from the circle around Orange are also littered with references to 'the whole Netherlands', 'our fatherland' 'our dear fatherland'.[70] A similarly all-embracing patriotism inspires the fighting songs composed at this time, of which the *Wilhelmus* and *Ras seventhien provincien* are the best known.

The Calvinists and rebels, who had fled the country at the approach of Alva, warmed to this sort of rhetoric. In exile they drew together, uniting in strident hispanophobia. Besides, the stranger-churches, which provided both a sense of security in unfamiliar surroundings and spiritual consola-

[65] *Woordenboek der Nederlandsche taal*, ed. M. de Vries, L.A. te Winkel *et al.* (The Hague, 1958), XVIII, col. 176; *Middelnederlandsch Woordenboek* ed. E Verwijs and J. Verdam (The Hague, 1916), VIII, col. 1140. Veluanus states in 1554 that a Christian may fight with a good conscience 'vor hoir vaderlant', *BRN*, IV, p. 357

[66] E.H. Kantorowicz, *The King's Two Bodies: A Study in Political Theology* (Princeton, 1957), pp. 246–48.

[67] H.H. Jacobs, 'Studien zur Geschichte des Vaterlandsgedankens in Renaissance und Reformation', *Die Welt als Geschichte*, XII (1952), p. 94.

[68] M. Micron, *De christlicke ordinanciën der nederlantscher ghemeinten te Londen, 1554*, ed. W.F. Dankbaar (The Hague, 1956), p. 35.

[69] *E.g. Archives ou correspondance*, III, p. 143; J.B. Drewes, *Wilhelmus van Nassouwe: Een proeve van synchronische interpretatie* (Amsterdam, 1946), pp. 64–65. Groenveld ('Natie en nationaal gevoel', pp. 377–80) believes that the concept of the 'common fatherland' occurred as the horizons of the political nation extended outwards from the local urban or rural community to encompass the whole province, or, in the case of the high nobility, the whole country. The *Grand Privilège* (11 February 1477) used *onsen ghemeenen landen* to mean the Burgundian Netherlands, see *Klein plakkaatboek van Nederland*, ed. A.S. de Blecourt and N. Japikse (Groningen-The Hague, 1919), pp. 4–6.

[70] For numerous examples see *Corresp. Guillaume*, II; *La correspondance du prince Guillaume d'Orange avec Jacques de Wesenbeke* (Utrecht-Amsterdam, 1896) and P. Fredericq, *Het nederlandsch proza in de zestiendeeuwsche pamfletten uit den tijd der beroerten met eene bloemlezing (1566–1600)* (Brussels, 1907), pp. 23–51.

tion, served to bring French and Dutch-speaking exiles together, as well as linking them with their compatriots and coreligionists, scattered through the towns of the Rhineland, northern Germany and south-eastern England. It would, however, be foolish to suppose that a sense of Netherlands nationality matured overnight. Within the churches, distinctions were still made between Hollanders, Brabanters and Walloons. More seriously, there were divisions of opinion, which tended to coincide with provincial groupings, between those who were above all concerned to advance the cause of the gospel and those who were intent, as they said, on 'the rebuilding of the Netherlands'.[71] Yet it was in exile that a sense of national awareness, more or less divorced from the King, developed in close association with the Reformed faith.[72]

The cautious oligarchies in the towns of Holland, who had remained in office under Alva, found this combination of Netherlandish patriotism and Protestantism thoroughly uncongenial. Yet, despite their small zeal for 'the religion' and their distaste for garrisons and the financial burdens brought by the war, most of them gave their qualified support to Orange. He in turn acknowledged the justice of their grievances against the unruly Beggars, when in January 1573 he dismissed his hated Liègeois lieutenant Guillaume de la Marck. To outward appearances the constitutional proprieties were still observed, for the States of Holland recognised Orange in 1572 as 'the governor general and lieutenant of the King'. But the sense of loyalty to the King in Spain weakened as hatred for the Spaniards fighting in Holland mounted, so that by the autumn of 1575 the States of Holland resolved, in the words of a well-informed English agent, to 'renounce the King and his jurisdictions in all conditions, deface his armes in their townes and extinguish all memory that may be of him'.[73] Perhaps because Holland, the least Burgundian of the patrimonial provinces, had preserved a large measure of political autonomy, the governing classes there could contemplate secession from 'the crowne of Spayne' with greater equanimity. Who or what should take Philip's place remained obscure. The States had invested Orange with the 'absolute power, authority and sovereign command' for the duration of the war,[74] and there was a proposal that Elizabeth of England should

---

[71] *WMV*, ser. II, ii p. 5.

[72] A synod held at Bedburg in July 1571 called on everyone to do his utmost to advance 'the foundation of the church and the deliverance of the fatherland', *ibid.*, p. 6. The comprehensive patriotism in Reformed circles found eloquent expression in 1578 when the national synod refused to allow Flemish ministers to desert their congregations in Holland in favour of a call to their native province 'since the entire Netherlands is our universal fatherland' [het gheheele nederlant onse alghemeyne vaderlant is], *WMV*, ser. II, iii p. 265.

[73] *Relations politiques*, VII, p. 590. In August 1575 the States of Holland minted a *leeuwendaalder* which significantly made no allusion to the King, H. Enno van Gelder, *De nederlandse munten* (Utrecht-Antwerp, 1965), p. 79.

[74] *Texts Concerning the Revolt*, p. 38.

assume the title of Lady and Countess of Holland and Zeeland.[75] After the failure of negotiations at Breda, and with Hierges threatening Dordrecht and Rotterdam, seasoned observers as well as the Dutch themselves concluded that the rebels must enlist support from either England or France; otherwise their cause would fail.[76]

The isolation of those towns in Holland and Zeeland, which Orange still held *à sa dévotion* by the summer of 1576, ended abruptly when a wave of mutinies in the royalist armies compelled the States General to seek an end to the fighting with the rebels and the withdrawal of all foreign soldiers from the soil of the Low Countries. Orange's vision of 'the whole Netherlands' working together to expel the foreign tyrant seemed on the point of fulfilment. An impressive flood of pamphlets and apposite political engravings celebrated this new-found solidarity between the provinces, as though they were striving by their sheer number to conceal how little support there was for the union outside Holland, Zeeland and Brabant.[77]

During the summer of 1576 the defence of Brabant and Flanders preoccupied the Council of State. Late in July the Council declared the mutineers, who had seized the Flemish town of Aalst, to be 'enemies of the King and the *patrie*'.[78] The threat posed by the mutinies of German and Spanish forces concentrated attention on the protection of the *patrie*. When in early September the members of the Council of State were placed in custody, this was said to have been the work of men imbued with a passionate zeal for *la patrie*.[79] Writing to the French king in October, the States General professed their sincere concern for 'the defence and preservation' of our *patrie* against the Spaniards'.[80] From the security of Antwerp Jeronimo de Roda, the one man then in the Low Countries still to enjoy the confidence of the King, sneered at the loyalists, who now hastened to enter into negotiations with Orange, out of some supposed concern for the good of the country.[81] And indeed Walloon nobles with impressive records of service to Philip, notably Hierges and François de Hallewyn, now made a point of affirming their

---

[75] C. Wilson, *Queen Elizabeth and the Revolt of the Netherlands* (London, 1970), p. 35.

[76] *Relations politiques*, VII, pp. 557, 572–73, 597–99.

[77] Even in Flanders the Pacification was initially received with little enthusiasm by the provincial authorities, though the Eternal Edict (12 February 1577), by which Don John ratified the Pacification in return for an undertaking that the States General would maintain the King's authority and the Catholic religion, was greeted more warmly, P. van Peteghem, 'Vlaanderen in 1576: revolutionair of reactionair?', *TG*, LXXXIX (1976), pp. 335–57.

[78] P. Genard, *La furie espagnole: Documents pour servir à l'histoire du sac d'Anvers en 1576* (Antwerp, 1876), p. 13.

[79] *Ibid.*, p. 109.

[80] *Actes des états-généraux des Pays-Bas, 1576–1585*, ed. L.P. Gachard (Brussels-The Hague, 1861), I, p. 27.

[81] Genard, *La furie espagnole*, p. 305.

desire to serve their country.[82] Evidently the brutal misconduct of the mutinous foreign troops aroused these patriotic sentiments, but they were almost invariably coupled with asseverations of loyalty to the King and the Catholic Faith. In marked contrast the patriotism evolving in the towns of Holland began acquiring a faintly republican and Protestant veneer.

As the acknowledged leader of the revolt and the preeminent noble in Brabant, William of Orange took the keenest interest in events in the duchy during 1576.[83] To demonstrate his solidarity with the measures taken by the States of Brabant, and later by the States General, against the mutineers, Orange began during early October to employ a new form of signature in his correspondence with these bodies. For the customary 'vostre très-affectioné à vous faire service', he substituted the formula 'vostre très-affectioné et patriot' or, on occasion, 'vostre amy et vray patriote'.[84] By describing himself as a *patriot*, Orange reaffirmed his political connexions with Brabant, the *patrie* of the house of Orange-Nassau, from which he had been cut off since his flight in 1567. In other words Orange was reminding the provincial states that he was their compatriot.[85] At a time when the defence of the *patrie* was uppermost in the minds of the governing classes in Brabant, Orange's claim to be a fellow countryman could also be interpreted as a claim to be a true friend of the *patrie*, a patriot in the sense of one who loves his country. The Orangists in Brussels and elsewhere in the southern provinces seized upon the notion and began to call themselves *vrays patriots* or, more commonly, *bons patriots*.[86] Whether this appellation was arrived at by accident or design, it was a masterstroke. The iconoclastic riots and the insurrections of 1566–67 had given the *gueux* an evil reputation in the southern provinces. By appropriating the title of *bons patriots*, the Orangists were able to turn the patriotic mood to their account and to present themselves as the undoubted champions of the *patrie* against the mutineers and the perfidious Don John.[87] The term *bons patriots* overcame, or more accurately sidestepped, a delicate problem of nomen-

---

[82] *Ibid.*, p. 307; *Relations politiques*, IX, pp. 96–97.

[83] *E.g.*, Letters in *Corresp. Guillaume*, III, pp. 106–13.

[84] *E.g.*, Genard, *La furie espagnole*, p. 138. *Corresp. Guillaume*, III, p. 120. Orange evidently ceased to use this formula in 1580 (*Ibid.*, IV, p. 253).

[85] *E.g.*, *ibid.*, IV, pp. 181–85. Metsius, the bishop of 's-Hertogenbosch, who sat in the States of Brabant, remarked on Orange's formula; he saw it as a device to win over his correspondents, *Corresp. Philippe II*, IV, p. 74.

[86] *Corresp. Philippe II*, IV, p. 752; De Lumbres used the formula *vray patriot*, when writing to the States-General in October 1577, *Documents concernant les relations entre le duc d'Anjou et les Pays-Bas (1576–1584)*, ed. P.L. Muller and A. Diegerick (Utrecht, 1889, I, pp. 68–9). In the summer of 1577 English agents in the southern provinces referred in their despatches to 'the best patriotes and lovers of their countrie', 'the best patriotes' and 'wise discreete and good patriots' *Relations politiques*, IX, pp. 333, 393, 427. Even Don John styled himself in a letter to the States General of 27 July 1577 as 'een oprecht Compatriote', Bor, I, p. 836 [bk. 10, fo. 259].

clature. Patriotic Frenchmen were proud to call themselves *bons francoys*, but how should patriotic inhabitants of the 'seventeen Netherlands' describe themselves? *Bons patriots* conveniently left open the precise geographical location of the *patrie*.[88]

Hitherto patriots in the modern sense had been clumsily periphrased as *amateurs de la patrie* and *liefhebbers van 't vaderland*. Though this long-winded expression persisted for some time to come, partly no doubt because 'patriot' carried with it factional undertones, there was a tendency after 1577 to equate the *bons patriots* with those altruists who placed country before party or personal interest. For example, an English agent reported in June 1577 that Granvelle's brother, Champagney, 'joyneth harde with them that are thought to bee the best patriotes and lovers of their countrie' and a pamphlet of 1578 speaks of 'tous bons patriots et amateurs de la republicque'.[89] Naturally the opponents of the Orangists hotly disputed this claim and they sought by all possible means to blacken the name of the patriot party, impugning their motives and regarding them as apostates, insolent upstarts, criminals and bankrupts.[90]

[87] The Augustinian prior Wouter Jacobsz. noted in his journal on 6 October 1576 that the rebels 'perceived that the name of the Beggars had become very odious to men of discernment because of the boundless villany of these ... so it suited them to change this name into the name of the States, believing they could thus better advance their mischief, the more so since they now made themselves out to be saviours [*reformatoors*] of the country and protectors of the Catholic religion.' *Dagboek*, II, p. 600.

[88] For the usage of *patriot* I have consulted E. Huguet, *Dictionnaire de la langue française du seizième siècle* (Paris, 1961), V, p. 685; P. Robert, *Dictionnaire alphabétique et analogique de la langue française* (Paris, 1962), V, p. 191, and E. Littré, *Dictionnaire de la langue française* (n.p., 1957), V, pp. 1561–62. Until *c.* 1560 *patriot* seems only to have been used in the sense of compatriot. Catherine de Medici however used *patriot* to mean a disinterested lover of one's country when she wrote to Cardinal Châtillon on 10 April 1562: 'Pour se, vous qui avés tousjours fayst profésion de bon patri [ote], monstré à set coup que vous et vos frères ne volés pas aystre cause de la rouine de vostre patrie mès au contrère de la conservation', *Lettres de Catherine de Médicis*, ed. H. de la Ferrière (Paris, 1880), I, p. 293. Prof. K.W. Swart generously supplied this reference. According to the French lexicographers *patriot* came to mean one who loves his country during the late 1570s. Significantly many of their earliest examples are taken from the French writings of Marnix. According to the *Oxford English Dictionary* 'patriot' was not current in English before 1605.

[89] *Relations politiques*, IX, p. 333; see also petition submitted in June 1578 to the Archduke Matthias by certain Protestants, cited in 'Mémoires des choses passées au Pays-Bas depuis l'an XVc septante-six jusques le premier de may 1580', *La Bibliothèque Nationale à Paris: Notices et extraits des manuscrits qui concernent l'histoire de Belgique*, ed. L.P. Gachard (Brussels, 1875), I, p. 190.

[90] *E.g.*, Jan de Pottre, a Catholic inhabitant of Brussels, accused the States' soldiers of being 'patryotten in de kiste ... maer niet patryotten van huerlieder vaederlant', *Dagboek van Jan de Pottre, 1549–1602*, ed. Baron de S. Genois (Ghent, 1861), p. 85. For Pontus Payen's bitter remarks, see his *Mémoires*, II, pp. 76, 183–85; Johannes Lensaeus, a professor at Leuven, wrote an *Oratio contra pseudopatriotas, hoc est, Romanae Ecclesiae Desertores, qui se solos patriae veros amatores esse falso iactitant* (Cologne, 1580), see B.A. Vermaseren, *De katholieke nederlandsche geschiedschrijving in de XVIe en XVIIe eeuw over den opstand* (Maastricht, 1941), p. 46.

In this they anticipated Doctor Johnson's dictum that 'patriotism is the last refuge of a scoundrel'.[91]

Patriotic fervour gripped Brussels in the summer of 1577 after Don John had seized Namur in July. The climax came on 23 September when Orange entered Brussels to be saluted with *tableaux vivants* representing the histories of those heroic saviours of the people of Israel, Joseph, Moses and David.[92] None of those present could have failed to understand that Orange had joined the pantheon of those who had delivered their country.[93] The classical conceit of the *pater patriae* was familiar enough in the sixteenth century, but usually this extravagant compliment was paid to ancient heroes like Arminius or ruling princes like Philip the Good and Louis XII.[94] At Brussels the recipient of these tributes was neither a legendary figure from the remote Teutonic past nor a successful ruler, but a nobleman who, for all his sovereign title, appeared in the eyes of his King doubly damned as a rebel and an heretic. Few who watched William's triumphant entry could have doubted that the King had forfeited the affections of his subjects in Brussels.

If patriotism was in vogue, the most odious crime in the popular mind was the betrayal of the *patria*. Since 1568 the notion had been gaining ground in Orangist circles that native Netherlanders, who denied the prince their support, were guilty of deserting their country and forsaking God.[95] In the aftermath of the mutinies of 1576 there was a groundswell

---

[91] By virtue of these antecedents *patriot* became associated in the late sixteenth century with a complex of ideas that could not always be reconciled. These included the fight against Spain, the causes of both Protestantism and Liberty and the party of William of Orange. Even before 1600 'patriot' denoted a non-Calvinist in Holland: it was decided in 1597 that two names should be proposed for each vacancy in the Rotterdam *vroedschap*, of whom one should be a member of the Reformed church and the other 'one of the good patriots or politiques', A.Th. van Deursen, *Bavianen en slijkgeuzen: Kerk en kerkvolk ten tijde van Maurits en Oldenbarnevelt* (Assen, 1974), p. 91, fn. 53. During the internal political conflicts in the seventeenth century, the States Party annexed the title of *patriot*, though the Orangists fiercely contested their claim and tried to distinguish between old-style patriots and the rest. Because *patriot* then acquired republican resonances, it commended itself to those who wished to reform radically the Dutch ancien regime at the close of the eighteenth century. For more details see E.H. Kossmann, *In Praise of the Dutch Republic: Some Seventeenth-century Attitudes* (London, 1963), pp. 8–11; *Woordenboek der nederlandsche taal*, XII, i, col. 804–10.

[92] *Relations politiques*, IX, pp. 538–40.

[93] In fact Orange had been called the 'father of the fatherland' by several writers before 1577; *e.g.* in 1571 by Geldorp (see *Texts Concerning the Revolt*, p. 92). In 1572 he was described as the 'redeemer of the freedom of the Netherlands', *ibid.*, p. 93, and as 'the patron of the fatherland and champion of freedom', *ibid.*, p. 97.

[94] For Arminius, see *Trübners Deutsches Wörterbuch*, ed. A. Gotze and W. Mitzka (Berlin, 1956), VII, p. 366; for Philip the Good, see *Texts Concerning the Revolt*, p. 121 and *Verhandelingen en onuitgegeven stukken betreffende de geschiedenis der Nederlanden*, ed. J.C. de Jonge (Delft, 1825), I, p. 121; for Louis XII see *New Cambridge Modern History*, ed. G.R. Potter (Cambridge, 1961), I, p. 293.

[95] *Archives ou correspondance*, III, p. 203.

of support for Orange in Brabant, and those who opposed peace negotiations with him were reviled as enemies and traitors of their country.[96] Similarly, when Champagney visited Ghent in August 1578, he had to endure shouts of 'there goes the traitor to his country (*lands verraeder*)' and 'death, death to the traitors'.[97] This sentiment was not confined to the streets. During the siege of Leiden, when defeatism was pervading the town corporation, Johan van der Does roundly declared that those magistrates who agreed to surrender the city to the Spaniards would be considered as 'men without honour, perfidious traitors to their country and oath-breakers'.[98]

Lese-majesty remained the essence of treason, but gradually, *maiestas* came to be identified with the abstract corporate body represented by the King, *i.e.* the state or the *patrie*, rather than with the person of the monarch.[99] From the perspective of the States General the supporters of Don John and the Malcontents appeared as traitors to their country. Following Don John's volte-face in July 1577, the Walloon nobles, who had escorted the governor-general, were ordered by the States General to return to Brussels at once, on pain of being 'proclaymed traytors and rebells to their countrie'.[100] In March 1579 Valentin de Pardieu, who acted as Farnese's agent in the negotiations leading to the reconciliation of Montigny, was declared by the States General to be an enemy 'à la patrie'.[101] The notion of treason as the betrayal of one's country was applied by the courts in the provinces belonging to the Union of Utrecht after these had repudiated Philip's authority in July 1581. During the next decade several people, including Petrus Dathenus, Willem van Blois van Treslong and Jacques Reingout, were accused of having acted contrary to the interests of their country.[102] At the same time office-holders

---

[96] *Corresp. Philippe II*, IV, p. 749.

[97] G. Renson, *Frederik Perronet, Heer van Champagney en zijn strijd met Willem van Oranje (1574–1584)* (Antwerp, 1949), pp. 43, 45.

[98] L.G. V[isscher], 'Over de belegering van Leiden en het kapiteinschap van Johan van der Does, 1574', *Kronijk van het historisch genootschap*, II (1846), p. 154. Bartold Entens inveighed against the States of Holland in 1573, when they failed to pay and feed the soldiers and called them *verraders des lands* Bor, I, p. 424 [bk. 6, fo. 310].

[99] In 1575 Sonoy had to defend his repression of Catholics in the Noorderkwartier who had been accused of treason. He asserted that Hoorn's attempt to frustrate the trial of its burghers on the grounds of its privileges was unacceptable: other towns with greater privileges had set these aside because the case involved *crimen laesae patriae*. Bor, I, p. 633 [bk. 8, fo. 113]. Professor K.W. Swart kindly drew my attention to this passage.

[100] *Relations politiques*, IX, p. 442.

[101] *Correspondance de Valentin de Pardieu, Sr. de la Motte, 1574–1594*, ed. I.L.A. Diegerick (Bruges, 1857), p. 37; for Dutch text, see Bor, II, p. 46 [bk. 13, fo. 99].

[102] For Dathenus, see Bor, II, p. 518 [bk. 19, fo. 48]; for Blois van Treslong, see *ibid.*, II, pp. 570–94 [bk. 20, fo. 12–30]; for Jacques Reingout, *ibid.*, II, pp. 777, 910 [bk. 21, fo. 70; bk. 22, fo. 40].

and, in some towns, burghers, were required to swear their allegiance to the United Provinces and its institutions and to have no dealings with 'the enemies of the fatherland'.[103]

To the Walloon nobility, reared in obedience to the *prince naturel*, the act of rebellion was hard to understand, let alone support. In their eyes service to the *patrie* remained synonymous with the King's service: apart from the King, the nobility knew no *patrie*. As devout Catholics and royalists, they found the heretical and even republican associations of *vaderland* alien and repugnant.[104] Some at least had only endorsed the Pacification with Orange because they had been told this would end the rebellion and lead to the restoration of Catholic worship in Holland and Zeeland.[105] When instead Protestants re-appeared in Brabant and Flanders in 1578, they were shocked, and the Walloon provinces repudiated the policy of religious peace, advocated by the Archduke Matthias and Orange, as a gross violation of the Pacification. In the face of the apotheosis of Orange at Brussels in 1577 and the political and religious radicalism espoused by Ghent, the nobility felt threatened and humiliated. After the army of the States General, which they commanded, had been routed by Don John in January 1578, many Walloon nobles came to believe that Orange had deliberately sought to destroy their credit with their regiments by withholding the money, which alone could prevent the disintegration of these.[106]

The new willingness of the Habsburg monarchy, now skilfully represented by the new governor-general Farnese, to redress the grievances the high nobility had voiced about the style of government as long ago as 1555 and to resume its accustomed role as the fount of patronage, could not have been more timely. Contemporary Orangist publicists as well as

---

[103] For the oath to be taken after the dismissal of Philip's authority, see Bor, II, p. 280 [bk. 16, fo. 38]; see also the oath sworn by the captains of the militias and the burghers of Utrecht in 1586, *ibid.*, II, 734 [bk. 21, fo. 39]. A similar oath was imposed on the subjects of the count of Culemborg in 1578 (see fn. 63).

[104] The Swiss constitution was held up by some patriots as a model for the Netherlands *c.* 1577, see *Corresp. Philippe II*, IV, p. 769; E.O.G. Haitsma Mulier, *The Myth of Venice and Dutch Republican Thought in the Seventeenth Century* (Assen, 1980), p. 64, fn. 199.

[105] M. Baelde and P. van Peteghem, 'De pacificatie van Gent (1576)', *Opstand en Pacificatie in de Lage Landen* (The Hague, 1976), pp. 30–31; H. Demeester, 'De katholieken en de pacificatie van Gent', *ibid.*, p. 152; P. van Peteghem, 'Vlaanderen in 1576', pp. 346–47.

[106] For the fears of the Walloon nobility about the break up of their regiment, see *Mémoires sur Emmanuel de Lalaing, Baron de Montigny*, ed. J.B. Blaes (Brussels, 1862), pp. ix–xi, 4–8, 10; 'Memoires des choses passees', p. 188. Valentin de Pardieu was for ever demanding money to pay the troops under his command, see *Correspondance de Valentin de Pardieu, passim.* Farnese acutely sized up the plight of these Walloon nobles when he provided funds for the payment of their mutinous troops by the treaty of Mont St. Eloy (6 April 1579).

later patriotic Dutch and Belgian historians all raged against the apparent duplicity and venality of the aristocracy, who appeared to these to place their private ambitions before their country,[107] quite overlooking the ties of interest and sentiment which bound the nobility to the monarchy. There was nothing specially novel about *la politique de douceur* practised by Farnese. Charles V had known how to retain the fidelity of his nobility and Philip was prepared after 1578 to make amends for his earlier negligence. In France Henry IV would condemn the treason of the aristocratic Ligueurs but he often rewarded the traitors;[108] Richelieu adopted similar tactics to detach the Protestant high nobility from the defiant Rochelais in the 1620s.[109] Perhaps the Walloon nobility might have been induced to stand by the States General, if an acceptable alternative prince had been in prospect. Anjou was suspect in their eyes as a French prince; he lacked the support of Henry III, which might have made him a serious candidate; and Elizabeth had no wish to be drawn more deeply into the Netherlands. Nor were the Walloon nobles alone in seeking to reach an understanding with the King after 1578. A select company of incorruptible and stalwart Calvinists were still prepared in the mid 1580s to advocate a general peace with the King, provided the Protestants were granted a measure of religious freedom. Such was the position of Petrus Dathenus at Ghent in 1584 and Marnix van St. Aldegonde at Antwerp in 1585.[110] In Marnix's opinion 'the purpose of the war was', as he told the States of Artois in 1578, 'to obtain liberty of conscience'.[111] If that were conceded, then he and other good Calvinists were prepared to be loyal subjects of the King. In essence this had been the standpoint of Guy de Brès in 1561, when he composed his appeal from the Christians in the Low Countries to Philip.[112] Ever since the early 1560s some Protestants had opposed the use of force against the ordained authorities as unscriptural and though this opinion was not widely shared, it was still being advanced, especially in Lutheran circles,

---

[107] In 1587 Gerard Prouninck van Deventer published a pamphlet in which he sought to mitigate the wave of anti-English sentiment in the Union of Utrecht after William Stanley and Roland York's treachery at Deventer by listing the Netherlands nobles, who had 'betrayed' the towns and provinces entrusted to their care, Bor, II p. 883 [bk. 22, fo. 22].

[108] R. Dallington, *The View of France, 1604*, ed. W.P. Barrett (London, 1936), sig. G.

[109] D. Parker, *La Rochelle and the French Monarchy* (London, 1980), ch. IV.

[110] For Dathenus, see T. Ruys, *Petrus Dathenus* (Utrecht, 1919) pp. 183–89; for Marnix, see L. van der Essen 'Marnix en de verdediging van Antwerpen, 1584–1585', *Marnix van Sinte Aldegonde: Officieel gedenkboek* (Brussels, 1940), pp. 51–70; C. Kramer, *Emmery de Lyere et Marnix de Sainte Aldegonde* (The Hague, 1971), pp. 57–67.

[111] *Correspondance secrète de Jean Sarrazin, grand-prieur de Saint-Vaast avec la cour de Namur*, ed. C. Hirschauer (Arras, 1912), p. 17.

[112] J.N. Bakhuizen van den Brink, *De nederlandse belijdenisgeschriften in authentieke teksten* (Amsterdam, 1976), pp. 62–69.

more than twenty years later.[113] The Lutheran minister at Woerden so vehemently denounced the dismissal of the King's authority as unchristian that the States of Holland ordered him out of the country early in 1582.[114] When the States proposed to offer Elizabeth the sovereignty in 1585, the burgomasters of Deventer objected on the grounds they were bound to consider Philip as their lawful prince, even as David had continued to acknowledge Saul as the Lord's anointed, despite being persecuted by him.[115]

With the assassination of William of Orange and the debacle of his French alliance, voices were again raised in Holland in favour of re-opening negotiations with Philip in search of the honourable peace, which had eluded the parties at the discussions in Cologne in 1579. The 'bloody civil war' was sapping the will to resist, while the prospect of toleration for the Protestants, which Parma still dangled before the rebels, seemed to remove the need for resistance.[116] Small wonder the war-weary magistrates of Gouda urged the States of Holland in 1588 to see whether honourable terms could now be secured.[117] The endless discussions over local privileges, the feuding between pro- and anti-Leicester factions in Utrecht and Leiden, and the separatist tendencies in West Friesland caused an experienced politician like Aggaeus de Albada, who had been present at the fruitless negotiations in Cologne, to prefer 'a tolerable peace' with Philip to yet another alliance for the continuation of the war.[118] Both foreign observers and Dutch politicians were convinced that, in the absence of some sovereign head, the centrifugal forces could not be kept in check. 'Nothing has been more damaging to the Dutch and their allies', Hessel Aysma, the zealous Calvinist president of the Frisian court wrote in 1587, 'than the lack of authority', and Gerard Prouninck, the like-minded burgomaster of Utrecht, to whom

[113] On the debates in the 1560s, see P.M. Crew, *Calvinist Preaching and Iconoclasm in the Netherlands, 1544–1569* (Cambridge, 1978), pp. 43–50, 66–70, 128–34. That the debate continued may be surmised from Geldorpius' contemptuous remarks in 1571 about 'those heretics who loudly proclaim that the clattering of arms does not accord with the Gospel', *Texts Concerning the Revolt*, p. 91. See also the reply of a Dutch minister to a colleague at Emden, who had evidently deplored the Reformed Protestants' involvement in the revolt in Holland after 1572, A.A. van Schelven, 'Emden in niederländischer Beleuchtung aus dem Jahre 1573', *Jahrbuch der Gesellschaft für bildende Kunst und vaterländische Altertümer zu Emden*, XX (1920), pp. 174–93. For the Lutheran standpoint see following note.

[114] J.W. Pont, *Geschiedenis van het lutheranisme in de Nederlanden tot 1618* (Haarlem, 1911), pp. 373–76.

[115] J.C.H. de Pater, 'Leicester en Overijsel', *TG*, LXIV, pp. 265–66.

[116] A.M. van der Woude, 'De crisis in de opstand na de val van Antwerpen', *BGN*, XIV (1959–60), pp. 50, 53.

[117] C.C. Hibben, *Gouda in Revolt: Particularism and Pacifism in the Revolt of the Netherlands 1572–1588* (Utrecht, 1983), pp. 232–39.

[118] See K. van Berkel, 'Aggaeus de Albada en de crisis in de opstand, 1579–1587', *BMGN*, XCVI (1981), pp. 1–25. Albada was also distressed by the spiritual and moral decadence of the governing classes in Holland.

Aysma wrote, would have wholeheartedly concurred.[119] Whereas Aysma and Prouninck looked to Elizabeth to provide that authority, the Walloon nobility turned again to Philip.

Such unity and coherence as the 'seventeen Netherlands' possessed derived from common loyalty to the prince; many doubted whether the union could survive the repudiation of Philip's authority, let alone the absence of any prince. In the event it did not survive intact. The Union of Utrecht, which slowly took shape after 1579, was composed of the two patrimonial provinces least well integrated into the Habsburg-Burgundian Netherlands, together with the newly incorporated provinces. By reason of their remoteness, their peculiar social structure and independent political traditions, these could more easily detach themselves from the King. By the same token, their particularism continued unabated and their loyalty to the United Provinces qualified. As the armies of the Union slowly encircled Groningen after 1589, that town considered, apparently with the encouragement of Oldenbarnevelt, the *landsadvocaat* of Holland, placing itself under the authority of the house of Saxony rather than suffer incorporation in the United Provinces.[120] In the longer term the indispensable authority in the Union was provided not by a prince but by the political dominance of Holland, while a grudging loyalty to the Generality was secured by the seven sovereign provinces' struggle for survival in a hostile world.[121]

---

[119] Bor, III, p. 107 [bk. 23, fo. 73]; see also *Texts Concerning the Revolt*, pp. 35, 44, 270, and above fn. 73.

[120] W.J. Formsma, 'De aanbieding van de landsheerlijkheid over Groningen aan de hertog van Brunswijk in de jaren 1592–1594', *BMGN*, XC (1975), pp. 11–14; C.P. Hooft doubted the sincerity of Groningen's commitment to the Union, *Memoriën en adviezen* (Utrecht, 1871), I, pp. 143–44.

[121] G. de Bruin, 'De souvereiniteit in de republiek: een machtsprobleem', *BMGN*, XCIV (1979), pp. 27–40.

Within the image:
TIS·AL·VERISREN·GHEBEDN·OFT·GHESCHETEN
ICK·HEB·DE·BESTE·CANSE·GHESTREKEN
1566

LÆT ONS WEL BIDDEN SONDER OPHELDEN | LÆT ONS RAS KEREN EN WORDEN NIET MOE
OCH DAT ONS HEILCDOM TE MEER MACH GEIDEN | WANT ÆLIB DEES CREMEKIE HOORT DEN·DVYEL TOE

5. Triumph of the Iconoclasts. Satire on the Catholic Church (*c.* 1566)
(Amsterdam, Rijksmuseum, Rijksprentenkabinet, FM 479-A)

While imagebreakers haul down a statue of the Virgin above the church door, Beggar soldiers energetically sweep up chalices, patens and pyxes, explaining that 'all this merchandise belongs to the devil'. Meanwhile prelates and priests call on the seven-headed beast of Revelation, who carries the pope as Antichirst, lest worse befall their sanctuary; but the devil flies off, clutching liturgical ornaments, for he knows that the game is up.

9

Towards a Reformed Polity in Holland, 1572–78

In 1587, fifteen years after the Beggars had given the Revolt a territorial base in Holland, fewer than one in ten of the inhabitants belonged to the Reformed church.[1] Though this much quoted estimate of the Reformed following in Holland is ambiguous – the fraction described as 'van de Gereformeerde Religie' could refer to the professed membership or embrace all who went to Reformed services – it is significant that the group of leading ministers did not rebut the allegation made by the States of Holland. By showing the partial and piecemeal acceptance of the Reformed church in the United Provinces, Geyl disposed of the myth that the northern provinces had naturally and spontaneously chosen 'Calvinism'.[2] This sparked off a lively exchange between historians concerning the means used to wean the North from Catholicism. According to Geyl Reformed Protestantism was imposed from above on a reluctant population and Enno van Gelder subsequently charted the course of the *revolutionnaire reformatie.*[3] Rogier was however the first to offer a credible explanation for the patchwork character of the contemporary confessional map of the Netherlands. For Reformed Protestantism to triumph certain preconditions had to be fulfilled: Catholicism had to be corrupt at the parochial level, the civil authorities had to give vigorous support to the new religion and there had to be a prolonged interruption of the Catholic cure of souls.[4]

[1] We wish to thank the late Dr. J.P. van Dooren and W. Veerman for facilitating the consultation of the local records of the Nederlandse Hervormde Kerk. In 1972 the Research Board of Reading University and the 'Twenty-Seven Foundation' gave grants to Rosemary L. Jones for the gathering of material used in this article. Bor, II, pp. 975–76 [bk. 22, fo. 88]; *cf. Archives ou correspondance*, V, pp. 69–70, where Groen van Prinsterer reviews the contradictory evidence about the support for Calvinism in Holland.

[2] P. Geyl, 'De protestantisering van Noord-Nederland', *Leiding*, II (1930), pp. 113–23.

[3] H.A. Enno van Gelder, *Revolutionnaire reformatie: De vestiging van de gereformeerde kerk in de Nederlandse gewesten, gedurende de eerste jaren van de opstand tegen Filips II, 1575–1585* (Amsterdam, 1943).

[4] L.J. Rogier, *Geschiedenis van het katholicisme in Noord-Nederland in de zestiende en zeventiende eeuw* (Amsterdam-Brussels, 1964), II, pp. 334–49; *idem.*, 'De protestantisering van het Noorden', *AGN*, V, pp. 327–34.

Rogier, like Geyl, believed that without these handicaps, Catholicism would have retained the loyalty of the great majority. Though Rogier's approach to the protestantisation of the northern Netherlands was widely recognised as a notable advance his thesis did not command complete support: even at the time he was criticised for having underestimated the religious appeal of Protestantism.[5] More recent scholarship has underlined the range and diversity of religious belief in the sixteenth century. Consequently Rogier's assumption about the vitality of Catholicism seems less plausible now than when he was writing thirty years ago. The hold of the church over a substantial part of the population, especially in the towns, had been loosened long before 1572. Allegiance to the traditional religious values had been weakened by the spread of humanism, the extension of education to the urban middle classes, anticlericalism and, of course, Protestantism. Those estranged from the church were rarely, 'Calvinists', but to a greater or lesser degree, they found the sermons of the mendicants stale and uninspiring and the speculative theology of the later middle ages irrelevant: above all they feared and hated the inquisition.[6] Secondly the civil authorities, even in Holland, rarely stood four-square behind the Reformed church. Insofar as the provincial States and town corporations had an explicit religious policy, it was 'de-Catholicisation' by degrees rather than 'Calvinisation' by edict.[7]

In this debate surprisingly little use has been made of the local records of the Reformed churches in Holland. Most participants have been content to quarry the voluminous records of the provincial and national synods published at the end of the last century. Tukker's study of the *classis* of Dordrecht, based on the archives of that body, demonstrated how a knowledge of the local Reformed churches could enrich our understanding of protestantisation.[8] But he was chiefly concerned to show how the *classis* worked and its relations with the civil authorities. Apart from an account of the evolution of the classical boundaries Tukker was not especially concerned with the fortunes of the Reformed church during the earliest years of the Revolt.[9]

Hitherto the upbuilding of a Reformed polity in Holland in the years

[5] R.R. Post, 'Een belangrijk boek over de geschiedenis van het katholicisme in Noord-Nederland in de eeuwen van overgang', *BGN*, I (1946), pp. 230–41.

[6] H.A. Enno van Gelder, 'Nederland geprotestantiseerd?', *TG*, LXXXI (1968), pp. 445–64; *idem.*, *Erasmus, schilders en rederijkers*, (Groningen, 1959); J.J. Woltjer, 'Inleiding', *Catalogus: Opstand en onafhankelijkheid: Eerste vrije statenvergadering Dordrecht, 1972*, (n.p., 1972), pp. 5–28.

[7] H.A. Enno van Gelder, *Getemperde vrijheid* (Groningen, 1972); O.J. de Jong, 'Is Nederland geprotestantiseerd?', *Rondom het woord*, IX (1967), pp. 65–67.

[8] C.A. Tukker, *De classis Dordrecht van 1573 tot 1609* (Leiden, 1965).

[9] For an excellent example of the way classical and consistorial archives can be used to put a new perspective on church history see A.Th. van Deursen, *Bavianen en slijkgeuzen: Kerk en kerkvolk ten tijde van Maurits en Oldenbarnevelt* (Assen, 1974), but, as the title explains, the author pays most attention to the period after 1590.

immediately after the seizure of Den Briel has been studied from the standpoint of particular congregations or through the lives of prominent ministers. The purpose of this essay is to set the growth of the Reformed churches against the background of the fighting in Holland: in other words to bring together the Reformation and the Revolt. While the starting date needs no explanation, 1578 has been chosen as the *terminus ad quem* because in February that year Amsterdam finally acknowledged the Prince as *stadhouder* and the civil war ended in Holland. As the *Gecommitteerde Raden* of the Noorderkwartier put it in May 1578: 'Now by the grace of God the towns of Holland have been reduced to a single body and are obliged and bound to one another.'[10] With the Revolt safeguarded in Holland, the Reformed there could look ahead with more assurance, especially with the prospect of the Reformation breaking through again in Flanders and Brabant and the opening up of Friesland, Utrecht and the towns of Zwolle, Deventer and Kampen to the 'true Reformed religion'.

When 'the first freedom of the Netherlands' dawned in 1566 none of the towns in Holland could boast a Reformed consistory, or even a permanent minister, though in 1559 Jan Arentsz. Mandemaecker had received a roving commission from Emden to serve the Reformed in the county. But soon after the image-breaking full-fledged consistories came into being at Amsterdam, Delft, Den Briel, Gorcum, Leiden, Alkmaar, The Hague and Naaldwijk; elsewhere informal organisations developed. By early 1567 the Reformed congregations in Holland were beginning to collaborate more closely.[11] But following the defeat of the insurrections in the Westkwartier of Flanders and the surrender of Valenciennes and 's-Hertogenbosch in March 1567 the opposition to Brussels in Holland collapsed and with it the newly-formed Reformed congregations.

Despite the flight of most ministers and *consistoriaulx* in the spring of 1567, a vestigial Reformed presence was maintained in some localities. In the remoter parts of the Noorderkwartier apostate clergy lingered on: in November 1567 the *baljuw* of Kennemerland made a vain attempt to arrest some turncoat clergy skulking in the villages of Schoorl and Callantsoog.[12] When commissioners of the *Raad van Beroerten* took evidence in Waterland in 1568, the new incumbent at Ilpendam testified that his heretical predecessor was still in the offing. Some villagers were contributing to the upkeep of the former priest, presumably in return for his ministrations.[13] Elsewhere itinerant preachers remained at work.

[10] RANH, Archief van Gecommitteerde Raden van de Staten van Holland ... in West-Friesland en het Noorderkwartier, 13ii fo. 124.

[11] See above p. 140

[12] ARAG, Grafelijkheidsrekenkamer, Rekeningen 3721, fo. 18–18v.

[13] ARAB, RvB, 115 (125), fo. 313. According to Bor, I, p. 323 [bk. 5, fo. 233], 'noch vele conventiculen en vergaderingen der Gereformeerden' were held in the Noorderkwartier during Alva's regime.

A certain Hermannus Geldorpius taught in several towns 'under the cross', including a stint at Amsterdam around 1567.[14] At Delft, where the Reformed were served by several preachers in these dark days, a consistory of sorts survived.[15] In 1568 Emden was solicited by the 'church [*gemene*] of Haarlem' to persuade Sixtus to prolong his ministry with them, but in vain for this former priest succumbed to the plague later that year in the East Frisian town.[16] At Enkhuizen Andries Dircksz. had been recalled in 1566 to serve in the town where he had once been a parish priest. After being chosen by 'all favourers [*liefhebbers*] of the gospel with a show of hands' in Enkhuizen he agreed to serve. When the persecutions resumed in 1567 he was a marked man and a liability and he therefore took formal leave of the congregation. In his place came Rijckert Claesz., a local lay preacher, who could serve the church there 'more quietly'[17]. Whether Rijckert remained in West Friesland is uncertain, though he acted as an Orangist agent in those parts.[18]

The degree of continuity should not be exaggerated. With few exceptions the congregations disbanded in 1567 and the Reformed had to start almost from scratch in the summer of 1572. Of a classical framework before that year there is not a shred of evidence: indeed the vagueness of the classical divisions proposed at the national synod of Emden in 1571 shows that no supra-consistorial organisation then existed.[19]

What had been envisaged at Emden in 1571 came a step closer to reality after the Beggars had ensconced themselves in the towns of Holland during the spring and summer of 1572. Alva, having flushed Louis of Nassau from Mons and suppressed the revolt in Gelderland and Friesland, entered the county towards the close of 1572 to crush the insurrections there. For the next four years Holland, together with Zeeland, was to be the battleground with Hollanders on both sides in the conflict. The war left an indelible mark on religious developments at this time: both the proscription of Catholicism and the slow advance of the Reformed church need to be seen against this background.

---

[14] RV, II, p. 182. His widow gave a brief account of his services to the Reformed church when she petitioned the synod in 1579 for a pension. Apparently he had been active 'in de laetste troublen' (1572?) at Delft, Gouda, Abbenbroek and occasionally Dordrecht. He was certainly preaching at Schiedam in October 1572 and he appears as a minister at Abbenbroek in 1574. He may be identical with Hermannus 'geweest hebbende pastoir omtrent Amsterdam' who preached at Schagen in 1566–67 and conducted the marriage of Sybrant Jansz., ARAB, RvB, 2, fo. 26.

[15] H.J. Jaanus, *Hervormd Delft ten tijde van Arent Cornelisz (1573–1605)* (Amsterdam, 1950) pp. 24–27, 55–56.

[16] Emden 329/2, fo. 210v, 215, 218v; 329/3, fo. 5. Sixtus or Sytthie Abbesz. had been a priest in Leeuwarden in 1566 until his apostacy. Early in 1567 he worked around Beverwijk before fleeing to Emden.

[17] KA Enkhuizen, 10a, Kerkeraadsnotulen, 15 November 1589.

[18] Bor, I, p. 323 [bk. 5, fo. 233]; *Corresp. Guillaume*, III, pp. 38–39.

[19] *WMV*, II, iii, p. 61.

In 1572 William of Orange worked for a *modus vivendi* between Catholics and Protestants, as he had done in 1566 and would do so again after 1578. His instructions issued to Sonoy on 20 April 1572 stipulated that the Word of God should be preached in the region under his care, 'without nevertheless suffering those of the Roman church in any way to be molested or likewise hindered in the exercise of their religion until such time as we have otherwise ordained or that necessity and exigency should otherwise require'.[20] At the meeting of the provincial States in July Orange reiterated his wish for 'freedom of religion for both the Reformed and Roman religions'.[21] The same point was made in the placard of 23 August 1572, which sharply condemned the maltreatment of Catholic clergy by rebel soldiers.[22] Protection of the priests and the church buildings was also guaranteed by the local agreements concluded that summer at Dordrecht, Haarlem, Gouda and Schoonhoven.[23]

This *religievrede* was broken almost as soon as it was published. The Beggars were scarcely installed in Den Briel than they burnt a religious house at Rugge and soon after that ransacked the churches of Maasland, De Lier, Naaldwijk and 's-Gravenzande.[24] If Barthold Entens were responsible for the damage suffered by the church at Schiedam,[25] Lumey was to blame for the destruction done at Haarlem, Leiden, Gouda and Schoonhoven.[26] Such conduct must have sapped Catholic confidence in the new order, but worse was to come with the summary execution of five Franciscans at Enkhuizen in late June and the nineteen 'martyrs of Gorcum' shortly afterwards. Whether Orange's presence could have prevented these excesses is doubtful, for troops under his command killed more than a score of clergy at Roermond.[27] The fanatical hatred

---

[20] Bor, I, p. 375 [bk. 6, fo. 276]. Sonoy's instructions follow closely those drawn up by Orange in November 1570, *Correspondance du prince Guillaume d'Orange avec Jacques de Wesenbeke*, ed. J.F. van Someren (Utrecht, 1896), pp. 148–53.

[21] Bor, I, p. 389 [bk. 6, fo. 283].

[22] Bor, I, p. 399 [bk. 6, fo. 290].

[23] Agreements for Dordrecht and Haarlem in Bor, I, pp. 379–80 [bk. 6, fo. 276]; for Gouda see L.A. Kesper, 'De Goudsche vroedschap en de religie', *Bijdragen voor vaderlandsche geschiedenis en oudheidkunde*, 4e reeks, II (1902), pp. 392–93; for Schoonhoven H. van Berkum, *Beschryving der stadt Schoonhoven* (Gouda, 1762), p. 515 and W.J. Verwer, *Memoriael-bouck: Dagboek van gebeurtenissen te Haarlem van 1572–1581*, ed. J.J. Temminck (Haarlem, 1973), p. 14.

[24] P.J. Goetschalkx, 'Invoering van de hervorming te Naaldwijk, Honsholredijk en andere plaatsen rond de stad Delft', *BBH*, XXVII (1903) pp. 341–42.

[25] K. Heeringa, 'Bijdragen tot de geschiedenis van de hervormde kerk te Schiedam', *NAK*, n.s., IX (1911), p. 192.

[26] For Haarlem, Verwer, *Memoriaelbouck*, p. 12; Leiden, R.L. Jones, 'De nederduitse gereformeerde gemeente te Leiden in de jaren 1572–1576', *Leids jaarboekje*, LXVI (1974), p. 128; Gouda, Kesper, 'Goudsche vroedschap', pp. 404–5; Schoonhoven, Van Berkum, *Beschryving.*, p. 516.

[27] P. Opmeer, *Martelaarsboek ofte historie der hollandsche martelaren*, II (Antwerpen, 1700) lists forty-nine Catholics killed by the Beggars in 1572.

of everything savouring of popery was too deeply ingrained in the Beggars to be put aside now that they were masters of towns and no longer freebooters. Their slogans had a Protestant ring and their ostensible ambition was the restoration of 'true religion' in the Low Countries, but their hatred of Catholicism was stronger than their attachment to Reformed Protestantism. For all their regulations about attendance at divine service on board, Dolhain, who knew the Sea Beggars well, described them as men 'sans religion' and the Reformed churches in exile regarded them with dismay.[28]

The Beggars were not alone in threatening the *religievrede*. Orange's instructions to Sonoy also included an order enjoining him to inventory all valuables 'whether they be money, gold and silver, both worked and worked, hallowed, consecrated or unconsecrated [belonging to] the churches, religious houses or other such like chapels'.[29] Though not directed against the Catholic religion, such a measure must have perturbed many Catholics. Orange here found himself in a quandary. To finance the war without imposing unpopular taxes the Prince was forced to avail himself of any readily available source of supply, including the sale of redundant church silver.[30] Yet this act of impropriation ran counter to the policy of religious peace proclaimed in the same instructions. In the face of these insults the Catholic reaction was remarkably muted. Many of the priests, who might have given a lead to their parishioners, slipped quietly away to Amsterdam or Utrecht, leaving the Beggars in control. The journal kept by the Augustinian prior, Wouter Jacobsz. during his exile at Amsterdam shows how diffident and bemused were the Catholics in his circle. His account of events, written more in sorrow than in anger, bears no trace of the belligerence associated with Tridentine Catholicism. In 1572 confessional consciousness was less acute north of the rivers and, consequently, Catholics in Holland were mentally ill-prepared to counter

---

[28] J.C.A. de Meij, *De watergeuzen en de Nederlanden, 1568–1572* (Amsterdam-London, 1972), pp. 164–81. De Meij is inclined to give greater credence to the religious motives of the privateers though he acknowledges their rabid hatred of popery. Sonoy is an example of a Sea Beggar who was a convinced Reformed Protestant. A member of the church at Alkmaar, he promoted the Reformed religion in the Noorderkwartier. For Dolhain's remark see B. Dietz, 'Privateering in North-West European Waters 1568 to 1572', (Unpub. London Ph. D. 1959) p. 268; De Lumbres too complained about the Sea Beggars' 'unordentlichen gottlosen Leben', P.J. van Herwerden, *Het verblijf van Lodewijk van Nassau in Frankrijk: Huguenoten en Geuzen, 1568–1572* (Assen, 1932), p. 164.

[29] Bor, I, p. 376 [bk. 6, fo. 273].

[30] For the implementation of this policy at Hoorn, T. Velius, *Chronyk van Hoorn*, (Hoorn, 1740), p. 345 and Gouda, Kesper, 'Goudsche vroedschap', p. 400. This policy met stiff opposition at Delft, J.H. van Dijk, 'Bedreigd Delft', *Bijdragen voor vaderlandsche geschiedenis en oudheidkunde*, VI (1928), p. 184. For the decision of the provincial States see R.C. Bakhuizen van den Brink, 'Eerste vergadering der Staten van Holland 19 Juli 1572', *Cartons voor de geschiedenis van den Nederlandschen vrijheidsoorlog*, 3e druk, II (The Hague, 1898), p. 200.

the propaganda and tactics of the Calvinists.[31]

On the other hand the local agreements between the Beggars and the magistrates in 1572 fell far short of what the Reformed required or had expected. Though freed from the fear of persecution, the concessions they extracted initially were sometimes little better than those obtained in 1566. Only rarely were they granted a church, though in Leiden and Delft they had demanded 'the chief church'.[32] Moreover no financial provision was made for the new church. The Reformed acquiesced, but they did so with bad grace and they remained as determined as ever to root out superstition and implant the true religion. For the zealots among the Reformed this *religievrede* represented an unsatisfactory compromise and they were not prepared to work for its continuation.

The insecurity felt by the small Reformed groups helps to explain the disorders in the towns after the *overgang*, as these strove to consolidate their legally anomalous and politically precarious position. In those towns which accepted the Prince in 1572 as the King's *stadhouder*, the Catholic corporations survived largely intact. Here and there Orangists returning from exile and the occasional professed member of the Reformed church replaced *glippers*, as the Catholic fugitives were known, but drastic purges, such as occurred when Amsterdam joined the Revolt in May 1578, were out of the question. No wonder requests from Reformed congregations for the use of churches and for financial assistance received evasive answers from the unpurged magistracies. At Schiedam the Reformed had been promised the parish church in the summer of 1572, but the town corporation refused to cooperate. Despite a sympathetic reply from the Prince, to whom the Reformed had appealed in December, they had still received no satisfaction a few months later. The reason was not far to seek: '... the burgomasters, *kerkmeesters* and the administrators of the aforesaid [ecclesiastical] property showed utter contempt and disaffection for the Christian religion and the common cause'.[33] It was no different at Purmerend and Warmenhuizen, where the Reformed,

[31] For the different tempo of development in Flanders and Brabant on the one hand and Holland and Zeeland on the other see J.J. Woltjer, *Kleine oorzaken, grote gevolgen*, (Leiden, 1975).

[32] For the demands of the Beggars at Leiden, GA Leiden, Stukken betreffende het Beleg 1574, nr. 52. Identical demands were presented at Delft, see A. Kluit, *Historie der hollandsche staatsregeering tot het jaar 1795* (Amsterdam, 1802), I, p. 518. Verwer, *Memoriaelbouck*, p. 6 tells of the Beggars coming to Haarlem on 4 July 1572 with 'zeeckere voer gemaect accoerde'. The Calvinists demand for the chief church made it very difficult to maintain a religious balance in the towns, as we may see from the arguments advanced by Catholics and Calvinists for the exclusive use of the parish church at Nijmegen in 1579, R.J. Kolman, *De reductie van Nijmegen (1591): Voor-en naspel* (Groningen, 1952), pp. 34–35. When the Reformed at Kampen demanded the parish church in 1572, the magistrates offered instead the friars' church 'situated in the centre of the town ... being the most convenient for preaching as it had few pillars', *Uittreksels uit het dagboek van Arent toe Boecop* (Deventer, 1862), p. 132.

[33] Heeringa, *Bijdragen*, pp. 192–93, 195–202.

unable to obtain 'the exercise of their new religion', appealed over the heads of the magistrates to Sonoy.[34]

In the latter part of 1572 churches in Haarlem, Leiden, Gouda and Dordrecht were repeatedly damaged by Protestant invaders.[35] To forestall further disturbances the magistrates of Leiden and Gouda closed all the parish churches for a while. The Catholics suffered more from this step, which usually heralded the complete ban on Catholic worship in a town. In a bid to reopen the parish church at Gouda for Catholic services without jeopardising public order, the conservative magistrates urged the parish priest to resume preaching 'the Word of God on all festivals'. Their endeavours foundered, however, on the intransigence of the priest, who in January 1573 insisted that he should also be permitted to celebrate mass. Evidently the *vroedschap* had proposed a modified version of the liturgy such as may then have been employed in 'two of the chief towns of Holland'.[36]

With the return of the royalist army to Holland at the end of November 1572 the future of the Revolt looked bleak: Mons, Mechelen, Zutphen and Friesland had been pacified and Naarden capitulated on 1 December. The mood in the rebel-held towns was so volatile that both Beggar successes and defeats could provoke anticatholic demonstrations. For example the capture of Schoonhoven by Lumey in October 1572 was celebrated by an onslaught on the churches at Dordrecht,[37] while the onset of the siege of Haarlem was marked by image-breaking in the cathedral there and the callous murder of Father Cornelius Musius in Leiden. The *religievrede* was also a casualty. In January 1573 Orange dismissed Lumey and tried to restore the mass in Delft, where Catholics had apparently been unable to celebrate Christmas.[38] According to a correspondent

[34] For Purmerend RANH, Collectie Aanwinsten, 705, fo. 67–67v; for Warmenhuizen, RANH, Warmenhuizen, 105. By calling on the assistance of the military governors, several of whom warmly supported the new religion, the Reformed may have antagonised the local magistrates.

[35] For Haarlem see Verwer, *Memoriaelbouck*, pp. 6, 10, 12, 14–15, 55, 61; B.M. de Jonge van Ellemeet, 'Uit de geschiedenis der Haarlemsche St. Bavo-kerk tijdens de Reformatie en de scheiding van kerk en staat', *NAK*, n.s., XXVII (1935), p. 6; Leiden see Jones, 'Nederduitse gereformeerde gemeente', pp. 126, 128; Gouda, Kesper, 'Goudsche vroedschap', p. 396; Dordrecht, G.D.J. Schotel, *Kerkelijk Dordrecht* (Utrecht, 1841), I, pp. 60–61, 74–75.

[36] For this matter GA Gouda, 45, fo., 24v-25; Kesper, 'Goudsche vroedschap', pp. 410–23. Liturgical compromises were tried elsewhere in the northern Netherlands, for example, at Utrecht under Duifhuis and at Amersfoort in 1579–80, C.A. van Kalveen, ' "Een vast gelove, ende Christus vrede sij met ons ende alle onsen vianden mede": De definitieve vestiging van de reformatie te Amersfoort, 1579–1581', *NAK*, LXII (1982), p. 38.

[37] Schotel, *Kerkelijk Dordrecht*, pp. 74–75.

[38] *Dagboek*, I, p. 196. After 29 December 1572 Catholic services in Delft only took place in the hospitals, D.P. Oosterbaan, *Zeven eeuwen: Geschiedenis van het Oude en Nieuwe Gasthuis te Delft* (Delft, 1954), pp. 130–31. For the religious situation in Delft see also R. Fruin 'De wederopluiking van het katholicisme in Noord-Nederland, omstreeks den aanvang der XVIIe eeuw', *Verspreide geschriften* (The Hague, 1901), III, p. 268. Evidently Orange was criticised by some for restoring the mass, J. Smit, 'De vestiging van het protestantisme in Den Haag en zijn eerste voorgangers', *NAK*, n.s., XIX (1919), pp. 216–17.

writing from Delft on 22 February to Orange's brother, Count John VI of Nassau-Dillenburg, the mass had already been suspended in Dordrecht, Gorcum, Zaltbommel, Rotterdam, Leiden, Haarlem, Gouda and in 'den gantzen Waszerlandt'.[39] Whether Catholic services in these towns continued in the religious houses is not known, but soon afterwards even this consolation was denied the numerous adherents of the old religion in Delft. On 17 March Orange had again insisted that Catholics should be free to worship there, but on 23 April the Beggars, following a military setback, invaded the Oude Kerk and the religious houses because, as they put it, 'the Prince could not be victorious as long as the aforesaid ecclesiastical persons persisted with their idolatry in the town'. Orange was prepared to allow the monastics to remain on condition they should cease to practise their religion but many found these terms unacceptable and left.[40] Soon afterwards Orange's secretary, also writing from Delft, told Louis of Nassau that since 'la belle messe a esté chassé de ceste ville, nous y sommes ung peu plus à repos et en meilleur seureté'.[41] Whether Catholicism was generally proscribed at this time by the States of Holland is uncertain. Orange, in his Apology, refers to a decision of this sort, taken at a meeting of the States in Leiden. He may have had in mind an edict of around April 1573, which obliged the religious to take an oath of loyalty to his regime and the Reformed religion.[42] It made little difference whether Catholicism was outlawed by a general edict or piecemeal: either way the *religievrede* was at an end. Henceforth in those parts of Holland obedient to the Prince the mass was forbidden.

The *religievrede* collapsed because its supporters could not withstand the war hysteria, which was fed by rumours of Catholic plots. The war also seriously hampered the advance of Reformed Protestantism in many parts of Holland. Militarily the province can be roughly divided into three zones: the walled towns securely held by each side; the country districts dominated by the towns; and the frontier areas, where both armies preyed on the hapless rural population. Amsterdam and Utrecht buttressed the royalist position and during the next three years the central government recaptured Naarden (December 1572), Haarlem (July 1573), Leerdam, Asperen, Heukelom and Nieuwpoort (July 1574) and, finally, Oudewater and Schoonhoven (July-August 1575). The Hague and the villages of the Westland, occupied at the end of 1573, were only relinquished after Leiden had been relieved. The fall of Haarlem disrupted land communications between the rebels north of the IJ and those south of the Haarlemmermeer and the campaigns of

---

[39] *Archives ou correspondance*, p. 62.

[40] J.J. Van Vloten, 'De beeldenstorm te Delft in April 1573', *Studiën en bijdragen op 't gebeid der historische theologie*, III (1876), pp. 185–90.

[41] *Archives ou correspondance*, IV, pp. 92–93.

[42] *Dagboek*, I, p. 249, fn. 5; *Apologie ou defense de tresillustre Prince Guillaume*, ed. A. Lacroix (Brussels-Leipzig, 1858), p. 107.

1574 and 1575 threatened to drive a wedge between Holland and Zeeland. Aside from Voorne and Putten and West Friesland, the enemy harassed almost every town in rebel hands at some time: the sieges of Alkmaar, Leiden and Woerden are famous, but the Spanish also threatened Delft in the summer of 1574, while panic broke out in Dordrecht and Rotterdam in September 1575 at the approach of Hierges.[43] The central government controlled Amstelland, the Gooi and the villages on the *geest* lands of Kennemerland and a no-man's-land existed on the northern shore of the IJ. Rijnland too lay open to attack from the side of Utrecht. The threat represented by the presence of government troops can never have been far from the thoughts of the Reformed.

In the years immediately following 1572 the Reformed church was preoccupied with the introduction of the new discipline, but the grim military situation left its mark on the deliberations of the first provincial synod held at Dordrecht in June 1574.[44] Representatives from the churches in the Noorderkwartier did not appear: with the enemy in virtual control of the coastline from below Scheveningen to Egmond, and the heralds of Eric of Brunswick before the gates of Hoorn and Enkhuizen, this was no time for the ministers to be away.[45] Leiden's isolation was summed up in the laconic entry, 'From the *classis* of Leiden: no one'; when the synod divided South Holland into *classes*, these were carefully defined, with the significant exception of 'Leiden with all of Rijnland'.[46] Leerdam excused the absence of its minister from the synod because of 'lawful impediments', evidently an allusion to the impending siege, which within a month would end in the town's surrender and the hanging of the minister.[47] The church of Naaldwijk was also in disarray. When the synod opened the proximity of Spanish troops had already forced the minister there to leave and soon afterwards the consistory joined him at Delft. Reformed services did not resume at Naaldwijk until 9 February 1575.[48] A more serious blow to the Reformed was the Spanish occupation of The Hague, which lasted with only a short interruption from 30 October 1573 until the relief of Leiden. The war also impinged on church life outside central Holland. Enemy raids on Waterland forced Gerardus, the minister in De Rijp and Graft, to withdraw until October 1576 when the 'peryckel' was judged to be past.[49]

---

[43] For the situation in Dordrecht and Rotterdam in 1575, *Relations politiques*, VII, pp. 557, 567–69, 572–73, 581–82, 587–89; also 'Utrechtsche kroniek over 1566–1576', ed. H. Brugmans, *BMHG*, XXV (1904), pp. 241–42.

[44] In March 1573 the churches of North Holland had deferred a decision on Modet's proposal to hold a provincial synod because of the dangerous times, RV, I, p. 10.

[45] *WMV*, II, iii, pp. 132, 193–94.

[46] *WMV*, II, iii, pp. 132, 136.

[47] *WMV*, II, iii, pp. 183–84.

[48] *WMV*, II, iii, pp. 177–79; KA Naaldwijk, 8, 4 July 1574 and 9 February 1575.

[49] AC Alkmaar 19, 15 October 1576. Gerardus received assistance from the deacons of the Reformed church at Enkhuizen during that autumn, GA Enkhuizen, 489.

When the Beggars entered the towns in 1572 they could not impose their absolute will on the corporations. Even though the agreements made then were soon broken, they had nevertheless been negotiated, if under duress, rather than dictated. Often the unpurged corporations managed to postpone the day when the small Reformed congregations replaced the Catholics in the principal parish churches. At first the Reformed might have to content themselves with a chapel or monastic church, a solution tried at Gouda, Dordrecht, Haarlem and The Hague.[50] Where a town was divided into two or more parishes the Catholics continued to worship in the senior church, as happened at Leiden and Delft.[51] In the smaller towns like Hoorn, Schoonhoven and probably Alkmaar the parish church soon passed to the Reformed.[52] By the spring of 1573 the parish churches in the rebel towns were either closed to both confessions or already in use by the Reformed. The pace of change varied according to local circumstances. At Dordrecht the first Reformed services were not held in a church at all, but above the Kloveniersdoelen. Within a month of the town's *overgang*, however, these were taking place in the church of the Augustinians, though not until 23 November in the Grote or Oudekerk.[53] All the churches were closed in Leiden on 7 July 1572, though on 20 July the first Reformed service took place in Onze Lieve Vrouwe Kerk. After the arrival of Lumey and more Beggar troops on 31 July several religious houses suffered damage, which was repeated at the end of September. On 6 September all the other churches reopened for the Catholic services, but not for long: on 5 October the Reformed held their first sermon in the Pieterskerk.[54]

The formation of a consistory took place in town congregations within a year or so of the *overgang*. By the autumn of 1572 elders had been appointed in Enkhuizen and probably Schiedam, while in the unique case of Delft a consistory emerged into the open after a furtive existence 'under the cross'.[55] By 1573 the Reformed congregations established at

[50] At Gouda they took Onze Lieve Vrouwkapel, Kesper, 'Goudsche vroedschap', p. 396; they were given the Augustinian church at Dordrecht, Schotel, *Kerkelijk Dordrecht*, p. 69; at Haarlem the Bakernessekerk, Verwer, *Memoriaelbouck*, p. 8; and in The Hague the Dominican or Kloosterkerk, J. Smit, *Den Haag in den geuzentijd*, (The Hague, 1922) pp. 184, 364–65.

[51] The Reformed were given Onze Lieve Vrouwe in Leiden and the Nieuwe Kerk in Delft.

[52] Hoorn, Velius, *Chronyk*, p. 342; Schoonhoven, Van Berkum, *Beschryving*, p. 516; Alkmaar, H.E. van Gelder, 'Hervorming en hervormden te Alkmaar', *Alkmaarse opstellen* (Alkmaar, 1960), p. 62.

[53] Schotel, *Kerkelijk Dordrecht*, pp. 60, 69, 75; M. Balen, *Beschryvinge der stad Dordrecht*, p. 847.

[54] Jones, 'Nederduitse gereformeerde gemeente', p. 126; J.C. Boogman, 'De overgang van Gouda, Dordrecht, Leiden en Delft in de zomer van het jaar 1572', *TG*, LVII (1942), p. 102.

[55] J.H. Hessels, *Ecclesiae Londino-Batavae Archivum* (Cambridge, 1889), II, pp. 420–22; *ibid.*, III, i, pp. 178–79; Jaanus, *Hervormd Delft*, pp. 54–56.

Leiden, Gorcum, Alkmaar and Dordrecht had consistories;[56] The Hague, Gouda, Leerdam and Den Briel followed suit in the following year.[57] At Oudewater, Gouda and Dordrecht unconstitutional consistories preceded the election of properly appointed church officers.[58] The process is fully documented for Dordrecht. In September 1572 the two ministers there called those whom they considered fit to serve as temporary elders and deacons; but 'since most of these set little store by this office, the two aforesaid ministers of the Word had on many occasions to choose others provisionally until such time as lawful elders and deacons had been chosen'.[59] On 14 June 1573 the ministers and those magistrates 'who had made profession of their faith' presented a list of twelve names from which the congregation chose six elders. The first meeting of the new consistory took place a fortnight later when the chief business was the arrangements for communion. At the same time the consistory devised procedural rules for the conduct of business, the last of which stated that no meeting – and two meetings were proposed weekly, one of which was scheduled to begin at 2 p.m. – should continue beyond six o'clock![60] These first consistories naturally included the veterans of 1566–67 whose devotion to the Reformed cause had been tested: Protestants to the fore in 1566 appeared on the earliest consistories at Enkhuizen, Delft and Gorcum.[61] By 1600 elders often came from regent families, though this was certainly not common in the 1570s. The overlap between consistory and *vroedschap* in Holland, evident by the end of the century, shows the regents had come to accept the Reformed church as a permanent and

[56] Leiden, R.L. Jones, 'Nederduitse gereformeerde gemeente', p. 135; Gorcum, KA Kerkeraadsnotulen, 18 October 1573; Alkmaar, *Archives of the London-Dutch Church, Register of the Attestations or Certificates of Membership, Confessions of Guilt, Certificates of Marriages, Betrothals, Publications of Banns etc.*, ed. J.H. Hessels, (London, 1892), p. 1; for Dordrecht see fn. 59.

[57] The Hague, *WMV*, II, iii, p. 179; Gouda, *op. cit.*, pp. 182–83; Leerdam, *op. cit.*, pp. 183–84; Den Briel, KA Kerkeraadsnotulen, A 1, 4 & 11 December 1572, C. Veltenaar, *Het kerkelijk leven der gereformeerden in Den Briel tot 1816* (Amsterdam, 1915) p. 75. In *WMV*, II, iii, p. 188 a list of elders and deacons is given which could be the consistory at Den Briel in June 1574.

[58] Tukker, *Classis Dordrecht*, p. 8.

[59] *Uw rijk kome: Acta van de kerkeraad van de nederduitse gereformeerde gemeente te Dordrecht*, ed. Th. W. Jensma (Dordrecht, 1981), p. 1.

[60] *Acta van de kerkeraad ... Dordrecht*, pp. 2–8.

[61] KA Enkhuizen, 10a, Kerkeraadsnotulen. The membership roll, at the end of the *notulen*, opens with the names of the two ministers. There follows a list of persons known to have been active in 1566, although these are not described as elders or deacons, they probably made up the consistory in November 1572. Delft, Jaanus, *Hervormd Delft*, p. 56: those who had been members 'onder het kruis' continued to hold a special position in this church after 1572. For the consistory at Gorcum see KA Gorcum, Kerkeraadsnotulen, 18 October 1573: at least three of the twelve elders and deacons had been prominent in 1566. At Leiden, however, none of those described by Alva's commissioners as the 'hoofden, autheurs ende consistorialen van de nieuwe Religie' reappeared in the earliest consistory there, Jones, 'Nederduitse gereformeerde gemeente', pp. 134–35.

indispensable part of the political framework.[62]

Once provision had been made for the exercise of discipline, the next step was often the administration of the Lord's Supper 'uprightly in accordance with the institution of Jesus Christ'. At Dordrecht a bare week separated the two events. Dordrecht was not however the first congregation to hold such a communion: that honour probably belongs to Enkhuizen where, on 1 November 1572, 156 sat at the Lord's Table, after making profession of their faith.[63] This example was followed by Hoorn in January 1573, Naaldwijk on 24 May, Dordrecht on 5 July and Delft on 4 October.[64] Communicant rolls met an obvious administrative need, although the congregation at Enkhuizen was probably alone in Holland in possessing a register of all members from the beginning. In other churches membership lists were not at first kept separately: at Den Briel and in some villages the names of new communicants were recorded along with the business of the consistory. At both Dordrecht and Alkmaar the consistory decided in 1576 to compile an alphabetical register which included the names of all founder members then living.[65]

Numbers of communicants are available for only a few town congregations. At Dordrecht the consistory noted how many adults took communion on the first five occasions: 5 July 1573, 368; 13 December, 463; 21 March 1574, 536; 5 September, 536; 5 December, 520.[66] At Delft there were only 180 communicant members in 1572,[67] at Alkmaar only 156 in 1576.[68] Contemporaries agree that the earliest Calvinist congregations were small: the Reformed at Hoorn were described as 'few in number' in July 1572[69] and the prior Wouter Jacobsz. pours scorn on the *gosepredicant* in Gouda, who on Easter Sunday 1573 could only draw an audience of seven or eight.[70]

Coornhert was then justified when he declared that the Reformed were 'by far the smallest band'.[71] Nevertheless conclusions drawn from raw

[62] For the social background of the consistories *c.* 1600 see Van Deursen, *Bavianen en slijkgeuzen*, pp. 83–85. At Gorcum one burgomaster and two *raden* served on the first consistory there. In Scotland the kirk sessions enlisted prominent men but not usually the most powerful, W.R. Foster, *The Church before the Covenants: The Church of Scotland, 1596–1638*, (Edinburgh-London, 1975) pp. 69–71.

[63] KA Enkhuizen, 10a, Kerkeraadsnotulen.

[64] Hoorn, *Dagboek*, I, p. 158; Naaldwijk, KA Naaldwijk, 8, p. 5; Delft, KA Delft 1, fo. 1.

[65] *Acta van de kerkeraad ... Dordrecht*, p. 55; KA Alkmaar, 68, Lidmatenboek.

[66] Figures from *Acta van de kerkeraad ... Dordrecht*, pp. 2, 4, 16, 29.

[67] Jaanus, *Hervormd Delft*, p. 33.

[68] H.E. van Gelder, *Hervorming .... te Alkmaar*, pp. 63–64. The first Reformed communion at Haarlem in 1577 was attended by 129 of whom twenty-seven were burghers and the remainder, inhabitants and strangers, A.A. van Schelven, 'Briefwisseling van Thomas Tilius', *BMHG*, LV (1934), p. 131.

[69] Velius, *Chronyk*, p. 341.

[70] *Dagboek*, I, p. 217.

[71] Cited by P. Geyl, *Geschiedenis van de Nederlandse stam* (Amsterdam-Antwerpen, 1961), II, p. 336.

figures can be misleading. Membership of the Reformed church was neither easily gained nor very attractive. Those wishing to join were first examined on their faith, a daunting experience for some. At the provincial synod of 1574 the *classis* of Voorne and Putten asked about the procedures for the admission of new members. The *classis* wanted to know if such people should be examined before the congregation about their faith or whether a simple affirmative in the presence of the consistory would suffice. The *classis* explained that 'many who were otherwise well-disposed to the church did not enter the same out of fear of being too closely questioned'.[72] The same problem troubled the consistory of Dordrecht two years later, when it resolved that new members might choose to make their profession before a minister and two elders or the full consistory. This was done so that 'the elderly [who] are afraid to make their profession in public may not on that account be frightened away'.[73] In the turmoil of the Revolt the Reformed refused to relax the stringent discipline they had maintained in the face of persecution. Reformed fugitives, uprooted by the fortunes of war, had first to produce attestations from their former ministers before being allowed to take communion. If the receiving congregation had any doubts about these credentials corroborative evidence would be sought, if necessary from the refugee churches, rather than allow the unworthy to sit at the Lord's Table.

Calvin did not consider discipline to be one of the marks of the church, though it was essential to the well-being of the church. Discipline however received greater prominence in the Reformed confessions of faith. In the Scots Confession of 1560 'ecclesiastical discipline uprightly ministered' was declared one of the notes 'of the true Kirk of God', while 'les marques' of the true church, according to the Belgic Confession, included 'la discipline Ecclesiastique'.[74] In the Netherlands the opponents of Calvinist discipline dubbed the consistory 'de Geneefsche inquisitie' and spoke sarcastically about the 'nieu Pausdom' and the 'nieuwe monnikerye'.[75] In the United Provinces only professed members were subject

---

[72] *WMV*, II, iii, p. 200; the synod agreed 'in this youth of the church' to accept a simple affirmation, *ibid.*, p. 147, *cf.* RV, II, pp. 169–70.

[73] *Acta van de kerkeraad ... Dordrecht*, p. 50.

[74] J. Plomp, *De kerkelijke tucht bij Calvijn* (Kampen, 1969), pp. 122–28.

[75] This criticism touched a raw nerve. In 1575 the synod of South Holland felt obliged to set forth the character of the Calvinist church order to the States. 'And since the ministers and the governors [*i.e.* the elders] are on account of the practice of their orderly assemblies sometimes accused of seeking to introduce a new Spanish Inquisition and to usurp the office of the magistrates, we are bound to demonstrate, in order to vindicate and defend ourselves, that our ecclesiastical government neither entails that which has been aforesaid nor prejudices the political office.' RV, II, p. 160. In 1577 the Calvinists lamented: 'What is more obvious than that the chief men among the nobility and the States as well as countless from the common folk stay away from our [Reformed] assemblies simply because they fear a new domination and yoke of ecclesiastical jurisdiction', Brandt, I, pp. 589–90.

to this discipline: not only were papists, Lutherans and Mennonites exempt from consistorial scrutiny, but so also were all those who attended Reformed services without becoming members. Only when *members* inclined towards Catholicism or, as more often happened, Anabaptism did the consistory intervene.

Here we encounter the peculiar nature of the religious settlement in the rebel provinces. The Genevan *consistoire* and the Scottish kirk session exercised jurisdiction over all the inhabitants in the city or parish. In both states the Reformed church had been established by law: failure to attend church services was therefore an offence and membership of the church a requirement of office-holding. In the United Provinces, on the other hand, no Act of Uniformity imposed Reformed Protestantism on the inhabitants. Certainly the Reformed church was greatly privileged: since 1573 it was the sole public church permitted in Holland, its ministers were paid from the revenues of the Catholic church, the provincial States defended its claims at the peace conferences of Breda and Cologne and it provided chaplains to accompany the army or sail with the fleet. But it was not by law established. No one was compelled to become a member or even attend its services. In the absence of any sort of Test Act known Catholics retained their places on the town corporations so long as they loyally supported the new regime. Furthermore, the Reformed congregations in the Low Countries had perforce led a sectarian existence before 1572 and they could not immediately shrug off this experience.

They had also grown up alongside the Anabaptists, whose greatest appeal was their aspiration to realise as nearly as possible the church of Saints on earth. Often wayward members of the Reformed church would give as the reason for their association with the Anabaptists the 'widespread abuse of manners in the [Reformed] churches', the 'unruly conduct of some brethren and the slack discipline' or the 'offence caused by the baptism of children of godless persons ... and the evident shortcomings in the lives of some church members'.[76] In these early years the consistories were greatly concerned about members 'who ... begin to adhere to Anabaptism'. The Reformed church felt itself pulled in two different directions: it thought of itself as an established church and in some respects fulfilled the function of such a church, but the temptation of the gathered church with its rigorous discipline was hard to resist.[77]

It is not then surprising that only a small fraction of the population joined the Reformed church. As long as the armies of the central

[76] These remarks were made by different members of the Reformed congregation at Enkhuizen who had been rebuked for their ties with the Anabaptists, KA Enkhuizen, 10a, Kerkeraadsnotulen.

[77] For the similarities and differences between the ecclesiology of Calvin and the Anabaptists see W. Balke, *Calvijn en de doperse radikalen* (Amsterdam, 1973).

government were within striking distance of Holland – and during these years their troops could often be seen from the town walls – membership was hazardous. At least four ministers in towns recaptured by government forces in the 1570s were executed.[78] The persecution under Alva had taught men that discretion in the matter of religious affiliations was advisable. Besides membership meant acceptance of a restrictive discipline. In July 1578 the consistory at Delft investigated a report that Anabaptist literature had been printed on the press of Niesgen Bruynen, a member of the congregation. The consistory also enquired why her husband, the printer Aelbrecht Hendricxsz., had not joined the congregation, though that had been a condition of their marriage. His wife explained that he had not done so 'since he wanted to be free to print and to sell whatever books he pleased'.[79] Nor did consistorial discipline hold any attraction for the regents. The Reformed were not afraid to rebuke those magistrates who were professed members. In December 1574 the consistory at Dordrecht discussed whether the *schout* and a burgomaster, who had 'submitted themselves to the discipline', should be reprimanded privately or 'in front of the consistory', as was customary, and they adopted the latter course.[80] When the consistory at Enkhuizen severely censured a burgomaster for immorality, it decided that 'one shall have no more respect for him than for the least in the congregation'.[81] Moreover non-members could freely attend services without any of the drawbacks of membership. There is no way of estimating the number of such *liefhebbers*, as such persons were known, but many magistrates may have fallen into this category. According to Caspar Coolhaes all of the twenty-eight members of the Leiden *vroedschap* regularly attended divine service in 1579, though only five took communion.[82]

On the other hand Geyl and Rogier have argued plausibly that paupers

[78] Symoen Janssen, minister at Haarlem, beheaded July 1573; Joest de Jonge, minister at Leerdam, hanged July 1574; Quirin de Palme, minister, hanged at Leerdam July 1574; Jan Jansz., minister at Oudewater, hanged August 1575. A Lutheran military chaplain, Willem van Lubeeck, was probably executed at Haarlem in July 1573.

[79] Cited by J.G.C.A. Briels, *Zuidnederlandse boekdrukkers en boekverkopers in de Nederlanden, 1570–1630* (Nieuwkoop, 1974), p. 314; the synod of 1574 had called on church members who were printers not to publish or to sell heretical literature, RV, II, p. 132.

[80] *Acta van de kerkeraad ... Dordrecht*, p. 27. See also *ibid.*, p. 147 for the censure of a *schepen*.

[81] KA Enkhuizen, 10a, Kerkeraadsnotulen, 9 December 1578 and 1 January 1579.

[82] H.C. Rogge, *Caspar Janszoon Coolhaes, de voorloper van Arminius* (Amsterdam, 1858), I, pp. 91. The proportion of Calvinists among the town magistrates varied. At Alkmaar ten of the twenty-four members of the *vroedschap* belonged to the congregation in 1587, H.E. van Gelder, *Hervorming ...te Alkmaar*, p. 64. At Enkhuizen those joining the congregation in 1572 and January 1573 included one burgomaster in 1572; two *schepenen* in 1573, 1574, 1575; two burgomasters in 1574; three burgomasters in 1575. The new *schout*, appointed in 1573, was also a founder-member. At Dordrecht the *schout* and one of the burgomasters in 1574 are known to have been members. For the religious complexion of the States, see below p. 235–38.

joined the Reformed church in the hope of obtaining relief from the diaconate.[83] There may be some truth in this, although in the 1570s the Reformed church had few financial resources beyond the offerings of church-goers. In March 1579 the deacons at Enkhuizen protested that the burden of supporting fifty-five households, all members of the congregation, was beyond them. Yet they had no other remedy to propose except a house-to-house collection from members of the church.[84] The deacons were conscious that some might join 'for the wrong reasons' and the consistory warned that care be exercised 'before they admit unknown paupers and strangers to the congregation'.[85] In the absence of any analysis of the social composition of Reformed congregations, it is surely rash to conclude that the poor joined out of self-interest. In the period under discussion the uncertain material benefits of membership seem at least to have been counterbalanced by the political risks, yet congregations were definitely growing.

Wouter Jacobsz., once so scathing about the low attendance at Reformed services in Gouda, learned to his sorrow in June 1574 that more and more people there were now going to the sermons.[86] And in 1577 the prior noted that many at Weesp and Muiden had abandoned the mass for the sermons of the 'calvinisten ende mennisten'.[87] In only a few congregations can the pattern of growth be even broadly established, although at Enkhuizen the method of recording new communicants makes this possible.

Number of new members joining annually at Enkhuizen 1572–89,[88]

1572	156	1578	180	1584	28
1573	118	1579	123	1585	88
1574	67	1580	75	1586	122
1575	84	1581	53	1587	57
1576	54	1582	46	1588	95
1577	96	1583	77	1589	85

[83] Rogier, *Geschiedenis van het katholicisme*, II, p. 366; P. Geyl, *Geschiedenis van de nederlandse storm*, II, p. 380.

[84] KA Enkhuizen, 10a, Kerkeraadsnotulen, 14 March 1579.

[85] KA Enkhuizen, 10a, Kerkeraadsnotulen, November 1578. For a judicious discussion of the argument on poor relief see Van Deursen, *Bavianen en slijkgeuzen*, ch. VI.

[86] *Dagboek*, I, p. 415.

[87] *Dagboek*, II, p. 667.

[88] The number joining at each of the five communions held annually has been aggregated. In 1572 there was only one communion service. Drs. F. Wieringa kindly drew our attention to several serious errors in the original data. We are obliged to her for supplying us with revised figures which are used in the table above. See her unpublished thesis, 'Tucht en ontucht: Een onderzoek naar zonde en verzoening in de gereformeerde gemeente van Enkhuizen, 1572–93', (*doctoraalscriptie*, Amsterdam, 1980), p. 69.

These figures do not, of course, tell us the size of the congregation in a particular year nor, in the absence of demographic evidence for Enkhuizen, enable us to correlate the growth of the church and the expansion of the town. The rise in receipts from the collections taken at the communion services for 1574, 1577 and 1578 does however imply a substantial increase in the total membership.[89] More intriguing are the fluctuations in the pattern of admissions. The surge between 1577 and 1579 is remarkable. This reached a peak at the two communions held in November 1578 and January 1579 when a total of eighty-nine joined, more than at any other time in the seventeen-year period. It is tempting to see a connection between the fortunes of the congregation at Enkhuizen and the course of the Revolt in Holland and Friesland. With sizeable contingents from Amsterdam and Friesland Enkhuizen was naturally affected by events there. The number of new communicants at Den Briel between 1577 and 1586 also showed a sharp increase at the beginning of this period: on average twenty-five people joined each year, but in 1577 and 1578 thirty and seventy-five new members were recorded respectively.[90] Perhaps, too, the Pacification of Ghent had created a more favourable climate for the expansion of the Reformed church, for with the extension of the Revolt to the other provinces, the religious settlement in Holland took on a semblance of permanence. Master Wouter's journal certainly gives the impression that anticatholic feeling in Holland grew in intensity at this time, not only in the rebel-held towns but also in the strongholds of Catholicism.

In the countryside the arrival of the Beggars often meant the disruption of the local administration, so that the period of the *overgang* coincides with a gap in the records. Naaldwijk is probably the only village where the process of political and religious change can be closely followed.[91]

---

[89] GA Enkhuizen, 489. While the average collection in 1574 at each communion service was almost 38 carolus guilders, it had risen to almost 67 in 1577, only to fall back to 50 guilders in 1578, too much should not be made of these figures, though it is interesting to learn that the collection on Christmas Day 1601 at Enkhuizen amounted to 400 carolus guilders, Van Deursen, *Bavianen en slijkgeuzen*, p. 113.

[90] KA Den Briel A1, Kerkeraadsnotulen.

1577	30	1582	15
1578	75	1583	16
1579	27	1584	8
1580	17	1585	17
1581	15	1586	30

[91] These include the 'Recueil ende Corte Verclaringe van alle tgunt dat my Willem van hoof, als castelleyn van den huyse ende slot tot Honsholredyck ... overgekomen, wedervaeren ende gemoeyt is geweest'. This detailed defence of Van Hoof's stewardship for the benefit of his employer, the Countess of Aremberg has been published in full by Goetschalkx, 'Invoering van de hervorming te Naaldwijk', pp. 341–423. For additional information see J.J. van Vloten, 'Eerste aanstalten tot vestiging der hervormde kerk te Naaldwijk in 1572', *Kerkhistorisch archief*, II (1859), pp. 129–34. The Reformed church at Naaldwijk possesses one of the earliest extant minute books of any congregation in Holland.

Here the mass was celebrated for the last time in the collegiate church on 20 July 1572. Already the Beggars had ransacked churches in the villages of the Westland and soon afterwards most of the canons of Naaldwijk moved to the relative safety of Delft. A few days later a spokesman for the Reformed demanded the church for the new religion, but the Catholic *baljuw* refused. The Vrouwe van Naaldwijk, the Countess of Aremberg, had given him no such authority and he recalled Orange's promise 'that everyone might retain his property and his religion'.[92] The Reformed nonetheless took possession of the church on 9 August and purged it soon after 'of all idolatry'.[93] In October two clerics, a canon and a chaplain, abjured their faith and embraced Reformed Protestantism; both served in the first consistory chosen on 25 November 1572.[94] It proved however easier to seize the church-building than to tap the revenues of the Catholic church for the benefit of the new religious establishment. The *baljuw* turned a deaf ear to the petitions and deputations of the Reformed, even though these had the support of Orange. In April 1573 the *baljuw*, still loyal to the countess, was ejected from office and put under house arrest, charged with collusion with the enemy. Eventually he was forced to abandon Naaldwijk, leaving the Reformed in control.

Probably the Reformed party in Naaldwijk was more firmly entrenched than was usual in the countryside. As with Nieuwe Niedorp,[95] the Reformed in Naaldwijk could boast a pedigree which went back at least to 1566.[96] Even so they lacked the support of the village bigwigs. In January 1573 the minister tried in vain to prevail upon the *baljuw* to attend services with his family so as to set an example to the 'principal families [*ryckdommen*], magistrates and community' who would otherwise stay away. The minister confessed that without the *baljuw*'s presence his ministry would not prosper as it should.[97] At Nieuwe Niedorp only one of the twenty-six magistrates appeared on the roll of members in 1574.[98] Where Reformed congregations had been organised in rural areas, they received

[92] Goetschalkx, 'Invoering', p. 344. In rural areas the *religievrede* was especially difficult to realise because few villages had more than one church-building.

[93] KA Naaldwijk, 8 Kerkeraadsnotulen, p. 3. The *baljuw*'s opposition is corroborated by the church records. Confusion surrounds the date of the first Reformed service in the church. The minutes of the Reformed church give 9 August, but the *baljuw*'s account suggests 18 October or soon after.

[94] KA Naaldwijk, 8, Kerkeraadsnotulen, p. 3. The former chaplain Hartman Adriaenz. van Capenborch served as elder and deacon on several occasions. In March 1574 he became secretary of Naaldwijk.

[95] See A.C. Duke, 'Nieuwe Niedorp in hervormingstijd', *NAK*, n.s., XLVIII (1967), pp. 60–71.

[96] J. Marcus, *Sententiën en indagingen van den hertog van Alba* (Amsterdam, 1735), pp. 198–200. Rancour caused by earlier persecutions at Naaldwijk recoiled on the unfortunate *baljuw* after 1572, Goetschalkx, 'Invoering', pp. 357, 364–66.

[97] Goetschalkx, 'Invoering', p. 359.

[98] Duke, 'Nieuwe Niedorp', p. 69.

reinforcements from coreligionists in nearby villages without such facilities. This explains the presence at communion services at Naaldwijk of inhabitants from 's-Gravenzande, Monster and De Lier. For the same reasons visitors from Barsingerhorn, Langedijk and Winkel swelled the congregation at Nieuwe Niedorp.

The Reformed congregation at Ridderkerk was less fortunate but probably more typical of village churches.[99] The first minister began preaching in January 1574 and during his brief stay the images and altars were removed. But since he resided in Dordrecht his impact on the village was probably slight. His unsatisfactory successor was eventually replaced in 1579 after the congregation had repeatedly complained to the *classis*. Although elders were first chosen in 1579, the consistory did not apparently meet until June 1584. In this respect Ridderkerk was certainly not exceptional. Middelharnis still had no consistory in 1581,[100] and on the manors of the nobility its inception was often later: Warmond lacked a consistory in 1605, while Woubrugge and Waddinxveen still had none in 1620.[101] Although elders were present in many villages to the north and east of Alkmaar already by mid 1574, this does not prove that consistorial discipline had been introduced.[102] But because the Reformed synods insisted that the Lord's Supper should only be administered after provision for discipline had been made, we may infer, at least in the case of Holland, that where communion services were held consistories had already been set up.[103]

It was an uphill struggle to implant the Reformed church in the countryside. At Winkel in North Holland the congregation agreed in 1579 to release their minister Ulricus since 'very few profited from his

[99] KA Ridderkerk, 1, Kerkeraadsnotulen. The account of the Reformation at Ridderkerk was evidently written up some time later, though before 1587. Similar potted histories precede the minutes of the consistories in the case of Dordrecht and Naaldwijk.

[100] RV, II, p. 208; see also RV, III, p. 47; for the situation in the *classis* of Dordrecht see below, p. 247 and fn. 92.

[101] A.G. van der Steur, 'Johan van Duvenvoirde en Woude (1547–1610), heer van Warmond, admiraal van Holland', *Hollandse studiën*, VIII (1975), pp. 230–31. Gysbrecht van Duvenvoirde bade the inhabitants on his *heerlijkheid* of Opdam and Hensbroek bring their 'swaricheden in die gemeente' before him or his deputy and 'niet in die consistorio', RANH, Het Steeboeck van Opdam, 3 August 1576. For Woubrugge and Waddinxveen see Van Deursen, *Bavianen en slijkgeuzen*, p. 96.

[102] RV, I, p. 23. A petition from the 'ouderlingen, diakenen ende lidtmaten der gereformeerde Religie binnen Warmenhuysen' (RANH, Warmenhuizen, 105) is allegedly dated September 1572, although 1575 when the first minister came seems more probable. Though Nieuwe Niedorp had a consistory since 1574 the first disciplinary case recorded in the minutes was in January 1579.

[103] For this reason we may suppose that the Reformed Protestants on the island of Texel had a consistory by December 1576, when the first communion service took place, KA Nieuwe Niedorp, A1 Kerkeraadsnotulen, fo. 6v-7v. Because of the different character of the Reformation in the province of Utrecht there was no necessary connection there between discipline and the holding of the Lord's Supper, see below pp. 249–51.

teaching'. The village clerk indeed claimed that 'no one could under-stand what he said.'[104] When a preliminary meeting was proposed at Enkhuizen in 1581 to prepare for the forthcoming national synod, the secretary of one *classis* recommended that those attending it should meet their own expenses since 'church members are for the most part humble craftsmen'.[105] The letters of Winandus Beeck Gerhardi, the minister at Zoetermeer, show how difficult and dispiriting was the task of a village *predikant* in the early 1580s: the local inhabitants ignored national fast days, profaned the Sabbath with dancing, drinking and games, and the local magistrates did nothing to check Catholic insolence.[106]

The accounts of dilapidated churches, contempt for Reformed dis-cipline and the indifference of local authorities suggest that the odds were stacked heavily against rural ministers. Rogier has described them, in a telling phrase, as 'generals without an army'.[107] In the sense that they had few members this is true,[108] but they were not therefore idle. Since the Catholic clergy had been driven out, the ministers of the Reformed church supplied the villagers' religious needs, administering baptism and marriage to all and sundry. They could be expected to make representations to the higher powers on behalf of the entire community in time of need and occasionally to provide some elementary education. On that account the village magistrates sometimes pressed the *classis* for a minister, for a community deprived of spiritual and pastoral care was difficult to imagine.[109]

Yet even as late as 1578 the Reformed church was still quite unable to man the rural parishes in Holland. Its success was naturally greater in those parts controlled throughout the civil war by the Beggars. The following table shows significant regional discrepancies. To allow com-parison with the pre-1572 situation certain rural deaneries have been selected.

In the countryside the Reformed presence was yet more feeble than these figures might seem to suggest. The appearance of a Reformed minister cannot be taken as proof of a continuous ministry thenceforth: in Rijnland and Kennemerland the war interrupted the work of the new church in the villages. Nor were all the *predicanten* at this time recognised by the *classis*: unqualified clergy were not uncommon and these inter-

---

[104] AC Alkmaar, 19, 29 October 1579.

[105] AC Alkmaar 19, 13 March 1581. *cf* below p. 238.

[106] L. Knappert, 'Stukken uit den stichtingstijd der Nederlandsche Hervormde Kerk', *NAK*, n.s., VII (1910), pp. 246–61.

[107] Rogier, *Geschiedenis van het katholicisme*, II, p. 337.

[108] Numbers of new members for Naaldwijk: 24 May 1573, thirty-seven; 20 September 1573, nineteen; 10 April 1574, thirteen. During 1574 a total of eighty-eight people took communion in Nieuwe Niedorp.

[109] See correspondence with *classis* of Alkmaar, AC Alkmaar, 19 from civil authorities of Oosthuizen, Graft, Winkel and Valkoog.

Number of parishes served for the first time by Reformed ministers[110]

Deanery	Parishes	1572	1573	1574	1575	1576	1577	1578	Total
Voorne	c. 17	1 (Den Briel)	–	11	–	–	1	–	13
Putten	c. 14	1 (Beijerland)	–	7	–	1	–	2	11
Rijnlandia	c. 39	3 (Leiden)	–	2	1	2	4	4	16
Kennemaria	c. 50	1 (Haarlem) 1 (Alkmaar)	4	7	1/2	2/3	4/7	1	21/26
West Frisia	c. 59	1 (Hoorn) 2 (Enkhuizen)	16	20	4	1	–	1	45

lopers, who gadded from one parish to another, did not necessarily advance the Calvinist cause.[111] The acute shortage of ministers meant two or more parishes might be served by the same man: Reyer Jansz. worked in Hoogmade, Koudekerk and Leiderdorp as 'minister of the Holy Gospel', while Jan Michiels was commissioned in September 1577 to preach 'after the manner of the Reformed church' in the villages in

[110] The information summarised in this table has been taken from a wide range of sources. For the parishes on the eve of the Reformation see S. Muller, 'De kerkelijke indeeling omstreeks 1550', *Geschiedkundige Atlas van Nederland* (The Hague, 1921) and the *Register op de parochiën, altaren, vicarieën en de bedienaars*, 7 vols., ed. P.M. Grijpink, C.P.M. Holtkamp et al., (Amsterdam-Haarlem, 1914–37). For the situation in Voorne and Putten where several parishes had already been combined before 1572, *Verslagen en kerkvisitatiën in het bisdom Utrecht uit de zestiende eeuw* (Amsterdam, 1911), pp. 241–338. Information on the ministers has been taken from printed sources. These include RV; *WMV*; J. Smit, 'Eenige gegevens voor de oudste geschiedenis van enkele Zuidhollandsche Protestantsche gemeenten', *NAK*, n.s., XXV (1932), pp. 239–45; W.M.C. Regt, 'Aanvullingen en verbeteringen op de naamlijst van predikanten in Zuid-Holland', *NAK*, n.s., XXVIII (1936), pp. 46–55, 176–85, 242–52; XXIX (1937), pp. 111–20, 177–86; XXX (1938), pp. 105–12. In addition the archival sources cited in the footnotes have also been used. Though M.V.L. van Alphen, 'Naamlijsten van Hervormde predikanten sedert de Reformatie' *Nieuw kerkelijk handboek*, (1908, 1909) was consulted no reliance was placed on this list because sources are not given and the information for this early period is sometimes inaccurate. The aim has been to establish the minimum number of parishes served by the Reformed church. Fuller use of church records would certainly yield fresh information, though we do not think it would substantially alter the picture here presented. It was not possible to make proper use of the records of the *classes* of Dordrecht and The Hague, or the consistorial records of Delft. Nor could we consult the Borger Handschrift in the Universiteitsbibliotheek at Amsterdam. When assessing the information in this table we should remember that virtually no information is available for Voorne and Putten before 1574, though the Reformed church had evidently begun to organise congregations earlier. Secondly the deanery of Kennemaria includes eleven island parishes (Wieringen, Texel and Vlieland), for which it had been difficult, even before 1572, to find priests.

[111] See career of Michiel Andriesz., *NNBW*, IX, col. 25–26.

the Noorderkwartier lacking a minister of their own.[112] Texel too was covered at first by a rota of ministers from the mainland.[113] Even in Voorne and Putten and West Friesland, where the Reformed church was on the whole successful in providing a regular ministry in the villages, difficulties arose. In February 1576 the ministers of Enkhuizen told Emden they could find vacancies for as many as 'six or eight ministers',[114] while Den Briel wrote in April 1577 that 'in our *classis* we have some three or four excellent charges ... with a good livelihood' for suitable ministers.[115] In such circumstances the sudden loss of three ministers on Voorne in 1574, all plague victims, was a serious blow.[116]

Inadequate and unsatisfactory financial arrangements also hampered the Reformed church. During in 1575 the *Gecommitteerden Raden* in the Noorderkwartier discussed how to make more rational use of the available resources.[117] The problems were most acute in the rural parishes. In 1577 the *Geestelijk Kantoor* was set up at Delft to administer the payment of stipends to the ministers in the countryside of South Holland. In the Noorderkwartier opposition to a central ecclesiastical office was so strong that the responsibility reverted to the parochial *kerkmeesters*.[118] Even so stipends were often paid in arrears or only in part. As late as 1580 the *schout* of Texel had still not compiled an inventory of church property 'to the great contempt of the Holy Gospel'.[119] The larger towns made their own arrangements but these took time to organise; in the meanwhile the ministers were paid on an *ad hoc* basis.

The names of around 250 ministers serving in Holland at this time have been recorded.[120] Of these at least forty-two and possibly as many as fifty-seven had been secular clergy. Ex-religious, on the other hand, were comparatively rare: only twelve monks definitely served as Reformed

---

[112] *Resolutiën der Staten van Holland*, 10 April 1577, pp. 44–45; RANH, Archief van Gecommitteerde Raden van de Staten van Holland ... in West-Friesland en het Noorderk-wartier, 13ii fo. 69v.

[113] RV, I, pp. 18, 28.

[114] E. Meiners, *Oostvrieschlandts kerkelyke geschiedenisse*, 2 vols. (Groningen, 1738–39), II, p. 45.

[115] Emden, 320 A. 99. 6 April 1577. In February 1577 Emden refused a request from Gerobulus for 'etlicke predigeren', Emden, 329/4, fo. 69v.

[116] *WMV*, III, v, p. 308.

[117] GA Alkmaar, Resolutien van Gecommitteerden Raden van West-Friesland in het Noorderkwartier, 22 January 1575, 30 July 1575; RANH, Archief van Gecommitteerde Raden van de Staten van Holland ... in West-Friesland en het Noorderkwartier, 13ii, fo. 98.

[118] RANH, Archief van Gecommitteerde Raden van de Staten van Holland ... in West-Friesland en het Noorderkwartier, 13ii, fo. 97v-99.

[119] *Ibid.*, 13iii, fo. 17.

[120] See fn. 110 on sources. Information on 258 ministers was gathered, though these may include a few double-entries. Ministers with no parochial responsibility have been omitted: for that reason Lievin Callewaert, Petrus Dathenus and Jacques Taffin have not been counted, although they were in Holland at this time.

ministers in Holland, among whom the only prelate, Thomas van Tielt the former Cistercian abbot of St. Bernard near Antwerp.[121] Probably the proportion of former clergy was still larger, for half of twenty or so leading ministers, whose antecedents are better known, had been priests.[122] Yet only a tiny fraction of the contemporary secular and regular clergy were fit or willing to serve in the new church. Many Catholic clergy fled from the rebel towns and took refuge in Amsterdam, Utrecht or the southern Netherlands; others abandoned their priestly vocation and returned to lay society, in a few cases even becoming elders or deacons in the Reformed church.[123] Most withdrew into obscurity, somehow eking out a living until their pensions could be paid. A few tried unsuccessfully to adapt themselves to the new circumstances. For example the priests on Texel told a Reformed synod in July 1573 that they had laid aside 'all ceremonies' the previous summer and now concentrated on preaching the Word. It was not enough. Their failure to sing the psalms and refusal to submit to the *classis* caused the synod to declare them 'unprofitable for the service of the Word'.[124] Ex-priests did not readily become Reformed ministers and one can sympathise with Jan Jansz. of Broek-op-Langendijk: aged about sixty-five in 1572, by which time he had served there for almost thirty years, he found it hard to learn new tricks.[125]

A qualitative distinction is sometimes drawn between priests who were converted in 1566 and those who joined the Reformed church after 1572. Yet it would be wrong to conclude that all those who entered later were carpetbaggers or mercenaries. Though the Reformed church in the 1570s was led by the earlier wave of converts, the fifteen or so secular clergy recruited in 1572 included several who were to give distinguished service as ministers. Conversely some of the most troublesome ministers had left the Catholic church in 1566. Those priests who entered the

[121] The singular absence of converts among Catholic prelates may have eased the introduction of a presbyterian church order. In Scotland the acceptance of the Reformation by some Catholic bishops helped to ensure the retention of the episcopal office alongside a presbyterian polity.

[122] Andries Cornelisz. (Den Briel), Andries Dircksz. (Enkhuizen), Arent Cornelisz.(Delft), Bartholdus Wilhelmi (Dordrecht), Christianus Sinapius (Dordrecht), Caspar Jansz. Coolhaes (Leiden), Clement Martensz. (Hoorn), Egidius Joannes Frisius (Den Briel), Herman Herberts (Dordrecht), Jacobus Michaelis (Dordrecht-Gorcum), Jan Arentsz.(Alkmaar), Jan Lippens (Dordrecht), Jan Pietersz (The Hague), Jan van Venray (Zaltbommel), Pieter Cornelisz. (Alkmaar), Pieter Cornelisz. uyten Briel (Leiden), Pieter Dircksz. (Nieuwe Niedorp), Pieter Jansz. (Schoonhoven), Mr. Roelof van Welt (Gorcum), Ruardus Acronius (Alkmaar), Thomas van Tielt (Delft).

[123] See fn.94. In March 1578 the consistory of Dordrecht gave financial assistance to a former monk from Genk to learn a craft, *Acta van de kerkeraad ... Dordrecht*, p. 101.

[124] AC Alkmaar, 19, 3 July 1573; RV, I, pp. 15–17. The priests on Texel bluntly declared that they would not blindly join some 'private consistory' although they would submit to such 'general reformation' as the King, Orange and the States might establish.

[125] RV, I, pp. 32, 34; AC Alkmaar 19, 24 April 1575, 3 October 1575, 1 February 1577.

Reformed church in 1572 were not generally time-servers, for it was scarcely less dangerous for a Catholic cleric to become a minister then than it had been in 1566.

The ministers at work in Holland included a large number of strangers to the province. At least one-fifth and possibly one-quarter came from outside Holland. Friesland contributed the largest contingent: twenty or more ministers were natives of this province, among whom were eleven of the seventy-eight clergy banished by Alva for their conduct in 1566.[126] Another ten had Flemish origins, while the other Dutch-speaking provinces, Zeeland excepted, contributed two or three apiece. To this extent the Reformed church in Holland gained from the failure of the Revolt elsewhere in 1572. Conversely when the situation for the Reformed improved in the other provinces after 1578 the parishes of Holland were deprived of forty or so ministers in a very short space. Rhinelanders too were prominent in these years: indeed the congregation at Gorcum showed a marked preference for ministers from that region.[127] The restoration of Lutheranism in the Palatinate in 1576 worked to the advantage of the Reformed church in Holland, for numerous Netherlanders returned, bringing with them experienced German ministers.[128] In addition many Netherlanders had themselves been in exile. At least twenty-six of the ministers active in Holland after 1572 had spent some time in Emden; another six had matriculated at Heidelberg and many more had been refugees in Wesel, Emmerich, Goch, Aachen and Cologne. A smaller number had been in England and fewer still in Geneva. In these ways the churches in Holland acquired the cosmopolitan outlook, which was so remarkable a feature of Reformed Protestantism.

These diverse and divergent influences took time to assimilate. At first the ministers in Holland lacked the coherence which acceptance of a single rule of faith or a common schooling would have given. They had come to the Reformed church by many different routes. Some had been to Heidelberg, others had received their higher education many years earlier at Leuven or Cologne and the great majority had never been to university at all. Very few had been born into Protestant families: of those brought up in the Catholic faith, some had broken suddenly and

[126] A.J. Andreae, 'Het verzet der Friesen tegen de Spaansche dwingelandij', *Vrije Fries*, XVII (1887), pp. 7–18.

[127] Henricus Rolandus Vellemius had been a minister in Cologne, Roelof van Welt had links with Wesel and Soest, Jacobus Michaelis had worked in the Lower Rhine and Henricus Middesdorf probably also came from these parts.

[128] The late Dr. J.P. van Dooren generously made available his copy of a list of Palatinate ministers in the Netherlands. It was drawn up late in 1578 or shortly thereafter. This gives the names of eighty Palatinate ministers then either employed as preachers or schoolmasters or at least resident in towns and villages in the Low Countries and the Lower Rhineland. The original may be found in KA Delft, Collectie Arent Cornelisz.

definitively, but for many the transition had been so gradual that their apostasy cannot be dated. A few ministers entered the Reformed church after service in German evangelical circles. With such a diversity of religious experience and so little formal grounding in Reformed theology or ecclesiastical discipline, it is hardly surprising that bitter disputes occurred. At this time the harmony of several town congregations was marred by antagonisms between their ministers: Coolhaes and Pieter Cornelisz. at Leiden, Jan Pietersz. and Hieronimus Hortensius in The Hague, Willem Gerritsz. and Cornelis van Braeckel at Gouda and Christianus Sinapius and the other ministers at Dordrecht.[129] Whereas the Calvinists of France naturally took their cue from Geneva, the Reformed church in Holland, so long exposed to a variety of religious influences, only slowly acquired a greater uniformity.

In this sifting process the *classis* played a most important part. The synod of North Holland decided in 1573 that the ministers of the churches in the Noorderkwartier should meet each Monday in five separate *coetus* in order to discuss doctrine.[130] We do not know for how long they maintained such assiduity, but in the *classis* of Voorne and Putten the ministers used to come together about once a month, with a break in the winter on account of the inclement weather. Attendance was obligatory and defaulters were reprimanded and liable to a fine. Such regular meetings helped to cultivate an *esprit de corps* as well as furnishing an opportunity for the supervision and counselling of the inexperienced and the correction of the headstrong and self-conceited. Even after a faculty of theology existed at Leiden the *classis* of Dordrecht continued to nurture candidates for the ministry and to retrain ex-priests.[131] The *classis*, too, had the weight to press the claims of the church when the civil authorities were obstructive. In short the *classis* might fairly be described as the lynch-pin of the Reformed polity: where it was prevented by war or where, as in the case of Rijnland,[132] it was slow to develop, the impact of the Calvinist Reformation was seriously weakened.

The Pacification of Ghent gave implicit recognition to Reformed Protestantism in Holland, although by referring the religious issue to the States General it gave a glimmer of hope to Catholics there. The treaty placed those towns in Holland which had not acknowledged Orange's authority

---

[129] For the quarrel between the ministers at Gouda, see C.C. Hibben, *Gouda in Revolt: Particularism and Pacificism in the Revolt of the Netherlands, 1572–88* (Utrecht, 1983), pp. 112–13.

[130] RV, I, pp. 13–14, 28, 39–40.

[131] For the role of the *classis* in the training of ministers see C.A. Tukker, 'The Recruitment and Training of Protestant Ministers in the Netherlands in the Sixteenth Century', *Miscellanea Historiae Ecclesiasticiae*, ed. D. Baker (Leuven, 1970), III, pp. 198–215.

[132] Jones, 'Nederduitse gereformeerde gemeente', p. 40. For the situation in Utrecht see below ch. X.

in a state of political limbo: excluded from the Pacification until they came to terms with the Prince, they therefore remained at war with the Beggars. Catholicism remained the only officially permitted religion in Schoonhoven, Oudewater, Haarlem, Amsterdam and the towns in the Gooi. During 1577 all save Amsterdam recognised the Prince, but the religious settlement varied. At Haarlem the *religievrede* was restored, but at Schoonhoven no concessions at all were made to the Reformed. In practice it made little difference whether or not they had been granted freedom of worship: at Schoonhoven they held their services in defiance of the agreement,[133] and at Haarlem, where they had been given a church, they still pressed for the abolition of the mass.

Meanwhile Amsterdam was virtually blockaded: in November 1577 the Beggars tried to take the town by surprise, but were bloodily repulsed.[134] A treaty with Orange was eventually concluded on 8 February 1578. No provision was made for Reformed worship within the municipal jurisdiction, for the corporation foresaw that a *religievrede* would only invite disorder. It is a measure of the dilemma facing town governments at this time that the policy adopted by the corporation held out no better prospect of peace: the exiles were allowed to return and the heresy edicts were suspended, yet the Reformed were denied freedom of worship. The frustrated Protestants could therefore press their demands with impunity. The journal of Wouter Jacobsz. shows how in the weeks preceding the *Alteratie*, the authority of the magistrates in Amsterdam was undermined by the insolence of the Protestants, who flouted Catholic festivals and held their own services provocatively close to the town. On 26 May 1578 the Beggars took control and within days Reformed started to preach in the Heilige Stede, for generations past the focus of Catholic devotion in Amsterdam. A few days later, on Corpus Christi, the experiment in confessional pluralism at Haarlem ended abruptly and violently, when the churches were pillaged and the Catholic clergy manhandled.

Just as these endeavours to obtain a *modus vivendi* in religion were breaking down in Holland Orange launched his 'amable accord et religion frid' in the south. Yet the article which permitted the restoration of the Roman religion in Holland where this was the wish of a hundred households remained a dead letter,[135] and the Union of Utrecht explicitly released Holland and Zeeland from the conditions of the *religievrede*.

The breakdown of religious peace followed by the abolition of Catholic worship was a familiar pattern in the Netherlands during the early years of the Revolt. This sequence of events had its own logic. For theological

---

[133] *Dagboek*, II, p. 674. For the terms of the *satisfactie* see Bor, I, pp. 778–79 [bk. 10, fo. 216–17].

[134] *Dagboek*, II, pp. 685–88.

[135] E. Hubert, *De Charles-Quint à Joseph II: Étude sur la condition des protestants en Belgique* (Brussels, 1882), p. 169.

reasons the Reformed ministers could no more tolerate the public exercise of Catholicism than Elijah and Jehu could suffer the worship of Baal. Though few in number the Reformed could exert their political influence within the Revolt to upset the delicate equilibrium. To Rogier the fact that so few were prepared to join the Reformed church, despite the obstacles placed in the way of Catholicism, is evident proof that Reformed Protestantism only triumphed as a result of political pressure. Such a view badly underestimates the deep-seated sense of insecurity felt by the Reformed church as a result of the haphazard and uncertain religious settlement in Holland. The support of the political establishment, as yet largely unpurged, remained lukewarm, the outcome of the Revolt still in doubt and the membership of the churches exiguous. The circumstances for building up a Reformed polity were far from propitious and the Reformed naturally feared Catholic competition. The unknown minister who told his congregation in Haarlem, in July 1577, 'that he could not be expected to make much headway unless they only permitted one religion' frankly admitted as much.[136]

---

[136] *Dagboek*, II, pp. 673–74.

10

The Reformation of the Backwoods: The Struggle for a Calvinist and Presbyterian Church Order in the Countryside of South Holland and Utrecht before 1620[1]

In June 1586 the National Synod, then meeting in The Hague, resolved to press the civil authorities 'to abolish sundry superstitions, pilgrimages, surviving altars and such like'.[2] The synod also deplored 'the manifold and abominable profanations of Sunday and of other days when there are religious assemblies'.[3] Winandus Beeck Gerardi, a minister with a rural charge, heartily endorsed this decision, and to lend weight to the synod's remonstrance he hastened to address the following letter to Arent Cornelisz., the synodal assessor. Here he recounted his recent experiences at Zoetermeer whose inhabitants made their living by cutting peat for sale in the neighbouring towns of Delft, Leiden and The Hague:[4]

I cannot in conscience conceal from you that on the fast-day appointed for 18 June last,[5] an officer of my lord, the *baljuw* of Rijnland, was here and the same entered the house of a smith, by name Master Jacob from Brabant, who was then advising a large number of peasants how to sell and how to sharpen their farming implements (as he also does every Sunday). To the best of my knowledge nothing much was done because the aforesaid sergeant is a very papist (the aforesaid smith is likewise also very papistical and an enemy of the truth), who on 4 July last read out an offensive ditty against our superior

---

[1] Earlier and shorter versions of this paper were read to the Seminar for the Reformation and Early Modern History at the University of St. Andrews, to the Low Countries Seminar at the Institute of Historical Research, to the Sir Thomas Browne Institute at Leiden and to the Stubbs Society at Oxford. I wish to record my thanks for their comments and criticisms. I am particularly indebted to Dr. Andrew Pettegree for his advice and encouragement. This essay builds upon the researches of Dr. J.P. van Dooren, the former archivist of the Nederlandse Hervormde Kerk, who died in 1984. It is dedicated to his memory.

[2] *WMV*, ser. II, deel iii, p. 544.

[3] *Ibid.*, p. 549.

[4] L. Knappert, 'Stukken uit den stichtingstijd der nederlandsche hervormde kerk, ii, Eene plattelandsgemeente anno 1582', *NAK*, n.s., VII (1910), pp. 259–61; *Informacie up den staet faculteyt ende gelegentheyt van de steden ende dorpen van Holland ende Vrieslant ... gedaen in den jaere MDXIV*, ed. R. Fruin (Leiden, 1866), p. 301.

[5] Leicester had convoked the synod for 20 June 1586.

magistrates while sitting on board a barge. Besides the aforesaid officer freely takes, so it is said here, bribes. The minister at Hazerswoude has also complained to me that on the said most recent fast-day the secretary, on his way to oversee the partition of some estate, rode through the village of Hazerswoude in a wagon with some others, in the presence of many peasants, at the same time as the bell to announce the sermon was rung for the third time. Nor can I conceal from you that during the administration of the Lord's Supper on 22 June last somebody fired a gun or hackbut in the yard of an innkeeper or tapster, which lies two houses away from the churchyard and the same thing has happened on two or three previous occasions. I do not know what they intend by this, but drunkards and other frivolous persons, along with all the tavern keepers or tapsters, congregate in large numbers during the Sunday sermon.

And I can scarcely find words to describe the superstitious practices used by the papists when they bury their dead. They have so many strange fancies about making the shroud, they place the body in this way or that in the charnel house, go to the graveside or to the church to pray, assist or kiss the bier and make many unprofitable pilgrimages for the benefit of the deceased and, after the funeral, they lay on a veritable feast ... Nor can I refrain from telling you that for several days past here, and especially yesterday, the papists on the barges which carry goods to the market ... have behaved very menacingly and insolently. They say that the ministers and others will certainly pay because the pilgrims to Wilsveen had been arrested.[6] They also spoke scornfully, to the effect that the *procureur-generaal* dare not release these now and that they had taken measures to make sure that it would be some while before pilgrims were again arrested. In short, unless the papists are curbed, they will eventually do as they please, if nothing is done to improve matters.

The lot of a Reformed minister in the villages was not easy. The official proceedings of the church bear witness to the villagers' scant regard for the Lord's Day, their stubborn attachment to 'superstition' and the assertive spirit of Dutch Catholics in the late sixteenth century. Even in the comparatively well-run *classis* of Dordrecht, established less than a year after the outbreak of the Revolt in Holland, the ministers of some villages had almost ten years later still not succeeded in gathering even a rudimentary Reformed congregation.[7] In 1589 the classical *gedeputeerden* carried out an inspection of ten of the thirty or so villages in the *classis*. In three villages the churches still lacked that indispensable instrument of Calvinist discipline – the consistory.[8] In at least four villages poor relief still remained the responsibility of parochial overseers rather than of deacons appointed by the Reformed congregation.[9] Minis-

[6] A miraculous statue at Wilsveen, near Zoetermeer. It continued to draw many pilgrims in the late sixteenth and early seventeenth century.

[7] *CAD*, p. 113.

[8] In Scotland parishes without a kirk session in the early seventeenth century were known as 'desolate', W.R. Foster, *The Church before the Covenants: The Church of Scotland, 1596–1638* (Edinburgh, 1975), p. 71.

[9] *CAD*, pp. 265–69.

ters in such villages had to learn with St. Paul that though they planted and watered, the Lord granted the increase. Some grew fainthearted. The ministry of Johannes Simonsz. at Puttershoek began in 1575 but, after five years, he asked leave of the *classis* to seek another charge because 'he could not bring forth any fruit there'.[10] The *classis*, however, made him wait until 1586 before allowing him to accept another call 'in order to discover whether he would be more fruitful there than in his previous place'.[11] His successor at Puttershoek fared scarcely any better for the visitors heard in 1589 that the small number of church members still made it impracticable to introduce a consistory there.[12]

In Utrecht one searches almost in vain for evidence of organised Reformed congregations in the villages, very few of which, if any, had proper consistories by 1600.[13] In 1606, twenty-six years after the provincial States there had forbidden the 'public exercise of the Roman religion',[14] the civil authorities finally consented to summon a synod of the (Reformed) ministers to propose remedies for 'the irregularities which may have crept into the churches of this province'.[15] The ministers from the five towns and thirty-three villages present on that occasion reported briefly to the synod on the state of affairs in their local churches. In turn they gave information about the attendance at the services, the number of communicants and the religious leanings of the sexton, schoolmaster and other parish officials. Although ministers had administered communion in about two-thirds of these villages, only six congregations apparently had elders. In many villages the presence of *papen* hampered the work of the ministers, especially where the former priests continued to live amongst their one-time parishioners and to baptise their children. The minister at Houten had to compete with a former priest who, on his visits from the nearby town of Utrecht, used to warn the inhabitants not to attend the Reformed services on pain of eternal damnation. The peasants here still clung to the old practices. On Whitsun and other festivals they brought their talismans, waxen representations of parts of the body and of domestic animals, to the church. The *kerkmeesters* received these, along with gifts of money, in a chapel within the church even while the minister was in the pulpit.[16] His colleagues at Leusden, close to

[10] *CAD*, p. 83.
[11] *CAD*, p. 212.
[12] *CAD*, p. 267. The classical 'deputies' exhorted the members to order their affairs against the time 'when God shall grant a greater increase'; by 1595 the congregation had a consistory and five years later a classical visitation found the church there 'in a reasonably good state'.
[13] OSA, 73, fo. 5. For the 'consistories' in 1606 see below, note 104.
[14] D.G. Rengers Hora Siccama, *De geestelijke en kerkelijke goederen onder het canonieke, het gereformeerde en het neutrale recht*, I, *De canonieke en gereformeerde bedeeling* (Utrecht, 1905), pp. 251–52, 262–63.
[15] RV, VI, p. 302.
[16] OSA, 73, fo. 17, 76.

Amersfoort, told the synod that though he drew a fair congregation to the services, he had had to abandon his attempts to introduce the metrical psalms because he could not sing in tune and the sexton refused to give a lead. He complained that when he preached he had to contend with a buzz of conversation among the churchgoers and periodic interruptions of the bell, tolled by the sexton as the dead were being buried outside in the churchyard. To make matters worse, the local worthies set a wretched example: the *schout* advised the inhabitants to stay away from the minister's services and the sexton, who ran a tavern on the side, used to leave the church in order to serve his customers.[17] Though the Reformed church enjoyed wider support in a few villages, the synod did not exaggerate when it told the States that idolatry and superstition still prevailed throughout the province so that 'the people were turned against the hearing of God's Word [and] were indeed so bitterly opposed to it that in some places very few children, in others none at all, were brought for baptism' to the ministers.[18]

From consistorial minute books to the acts of the national synods, the records of the Reformed churches testify that the rural inhabitants acquiesced in rather than welcomed the 'reformation' of the parish church in the late sixteenth century, where they did not oppose it. The ministers did not gloss over their difficulties and disappointments as they laboured 'to establish Religion' in the villages. In this straightforward sense, the reformation of the countryside failed. Yet the Reformed ministers, unlike the Lutheran pastors in Germany, did not generally admit to failure,[19] possibly because the Calvinist teaching on election afforded a theological explanation for their small success. Those who rejected 'the shining light of the gospel', after hearing the Word of God preached, thereby declared their own perversity.[20] Terms like 'success' and 'failure' are not absolute: they are bound in time to a particular culture and set of values. A democratic and secular society makes popularity at the polls the determinant of political success and accords particular weight to arguments based on quantitative data. The Dutch Calvinists of the late sixteenth century employed a different frame of reference. Though not indifferent to the numerical argument, they were disinclined to equate popular support with 'success'. Their familiarity with the history of God's chosen people and with the meditations of the Psalmist convinced them that the Lord prized faithfulness to His commandments above worldly prosperity or political advantage. 'Success' also

[17] RV, VI, pp. 309–10.

[18] RV, VI, p. 320.

[19] G. Strauss, 'Success and Failure in the German Reformation', *Past and Present*, LXVII (1975), pp. 30–63.

[20] There is a need for a study of the effect of the Calvinists' doctrine of election on their *Weltanschauung*.

[21] RV, I, p. 1.

depends on the goals of attainment. Winandus Beeck's letter cited above betrays expectations of social harmony and religious conformity which, given the recent upheavals, were probably unrealistic. On the other hand students of the Dutch Reformation have overlooked certain 'achievements' which deserve greater recognition, notably the introduction of a Presbyterian church order in Utrecht against the wishes of the civil powers.

In order to understand both the failures and the successes of the Reformed churches in the countryside, we shall need to take account of the rural population's lack of interest in the new doctrines before the onset of the Revolt. Secondly, due weight should be given to the political and institutional impediments, which subsequently hindered the Calvinists as they nurtured small congregations in the villages and sought to implement their vision of the church set forth in the synod of Emden in 1571. Lastly, we shall explore what the Calvinists understood by the 'true Reformation of the church' in order to underscore its radical character. At the very first Reformed synod in North Holland, which met in August 1572, those present discussed 'how those priests who wished to enter into the service of the holy gospel should be reformed'. This is what contemporaries understood by the *reformatie der papen*.[21] Then there were the 'reformations' of the church-building and furnishing, the liturgy, the institutions of the parish, and the church order, to say nothing of the 'reformation of manners' or as the National Synod of Dordrecht expressed it in 1619 'the stricter discipline of the people'.[22] There was, of course, even within the ranks of the Reformed ministers disagreement about the precise nature of these several 'reformations'. Partly for this reason, but partly also because the political elites reacted in different ways to the demands of the synods, the fortunes of the Reformed churches in the countryside varied greatly.

Though the countryside in the Low Countries remained broadly untouched by the 'new teaching' during the fifty years which followed the execution of Luther's two Augustinian disciples at Brussels in 1523, there were, of course, significant exceptions. Calvinism, for example, penetrated the Flemish Westkwartier in the late 1550s, where craftsmen, unskilled labourers and textile workers rallied to the new religion.[23] In Holland the small towns and fishing villages of the Zaanstreek and Waterland had gained a reputation for religious radicalism even before the apocalyptic gospel of the Melchiorite Anabaptism caught the ear of

[22] H.H. Kuyper, *De post-acta of nahandelingen van de nationale synode van Dordrecht in 1618 en 1619 gehouden* (Amsterdam, 1899), p. 124.

[23] J. Decavele, 'De correlatie tussen de sociale en professionele struktuur en de godsdienstkeuze op het Vlaamse platteland (1560–1567)', *Bronnen voor de religieuze geschiedenis van België* (Bibliothèque de la revue d'histoire ecclésiastique XLVII) (Leuven, 1968), pp. 280–85.

the seafaring classes here. The dissenting tradition persisted here.[24] By the early seventeenth century a devout Catholic described Waterland as 'an heretical wilderness, where scarce any good, that is Catholic people, can be found'.[25] Sometimes the jurisdictional privileges belonging to certain lordships and manors encouraged heretics to congregate there. This explains the concentration of Anabaptists in the mid-1530s in the otherwise unlikely setting of Hazerswoude.[26] Where 'protestantising' nobles enjoyed a greater measure of legal and administrative autonomy, they could present priests of dubious orthodoxy and appoint indulgent officers. In the 1560s the lords of Asperen, Brederode and Culemborg promoted a seigneurial Protestantism in their lands along the Lek and Linge which however attracted little indigenous support. Ironically the nobility in this same region later connived at the activities of Catholic priests in their lordships and held the authority claimed by the *classes* and synods of the Reformed church in contempt.[27] Occasionally a priest startled his parishioners by renouncing his Catholic faith and then using his pulpit to expound the new doctrines. But such spectacular apostasies usually turned out to be nine-day wonders, insufficient in themselves to bring about a lasting change in local religious practices.[28] These apparent exceptions to the rule that the early Reformation in the Low Countries, no less than in Germany, was 'an urban event' are in fact exceptions that prove the rule. Only where the countryside shed its agricultural character did Protestantism leave its mark before the Revolt. Elsewhere the rural Reformation resembles an exotic plant, only able to flourish in an exceptional microclimate.

This failure is at once significant and puzzling. It is significant because even in urbanised Holland the rural population still accounted for

[24] The 'lutersche ketterie' penetrated the villages to the north of Alkmaar by 1533, ARAG, Grafelijkheidsrekenkamer, 4240, fo. 5v-6v; 7v-8. For rural Anabaptism see A.F. Mellink, *De wederdopers in de noordelijke Nederlanden, 1531–1544*, (Groningen-Djakarta, 1953) pp. 156–231; K. Vos, 'De dooplijst van Leenaert Bouwens', *BMHG*, XXXVI (1915), pp. 39–70; W. Troost and J.J. Woltjer, 'Brielle in hervormingstijd', *BMGN*, LXXXVII (1972), pp. 341, 344–47.

[25] A. Driessen, 'Waterland V; Monnickendam vóór de hervorming', *BBH*, XXXI (1908), p. 29.

[26] J.D. Bangs, 'Waarom zou je het Nieuwe Jeruzalem zoeken in Hazerswoude, 1535–1536', *Doopsgezinde bijdragen*, n.r. VII (1981), pp. 82–91.

[27] See A.C. Duke, 'An Enquiry into the Troubles in Asperen, 1566–1567', *BMHG*, LXXXII (1968), pp. 207–27; O.J. de Jong, *De reformatie in Culemborg* (Assen, n.d. = 1957), ch. III; H. de la Fontaine Verwey, 'Hendrik van Brederode en de drukkerijen van Vianen', *Het Boek*, XXX (1949–51), pp. 3–41; Floris van Egmond may have connived at the evangelicals who found refuge in his lordship at IJsselstein in the 1520s and 1530s.

[28] Such sensational conversions occurred, for example, at IJsselmonde, De Lier and Brandwijk in 1566. At Brandwijk the support briefly enjoyed by the apostate priest quickly evaporated for no Reformed ministry was established here until 1584. At Nichtevecht, however, the memory of the priest who dramatically denounced the mass as idolatrous midway through the service in 1567 still burned bright in 1604, when the church there boasted that it was 'the oldest and first congregation' to have adopted the Word of God in 'all these United Netherlands provinces', Rengers Hora Siccama, *Geestelijke en kerkelijke goederen*, pp. 259–60.

around two-fifths of all the province's inhabitants in 1622; in the case of Utrecht a similar proportion lived in the countryside in 1632.[29] It is puzzling because the villages in Holland and Utrecht were not remote communities. Thanks to a well-developed network of waterways most villages had close links with the towns, while the indented coastline and deltas gave many rural inhabitants access to the North Sea. As the process of occupational specialisation gathered momentum in the country-side the surplus of landless workers migrated to the towns. The rural economy meshed tightly with, and sometimes competed with, that of the cities. An enquiry in 1514, which investigated most villages in Holland revealed that in addition to the herring fisheries and traditional agri-cultural pursuits, a substantial minority of country people already gained, or at least supplemented, their livelihood by digging peat for sale in the towns, spinning wool for urban cloth manufacturers or carrying goods as carters and bargees. Each of the large towns in Holland had its own *contado*, where a substantial proportion of the land in the rural parishes, sometimes more than one-half, belonged to the burghers, and where villagers had an obligation to bring their produce to the town market.[30] As Amsterdam expanded rapidly at the close of the sixteenth century, the villages drawn into its gravitational field concentrated on dairy produce and market gardening in order to supply the needs of the metropolis. As the supply of grain from the Baltic became more assured, local farmers began to turn away from cereals to the cultivation of industrial crops such as hemp, madder and coleseed.

The intellectual preoccupations of this rural society cannot be so readily discovered. Village schools were certainly not uncommon in the sixteenth century. In many the sexton gave a rudimentary education, though often only during the winter months. Perhaps we may surmise that the pupils of the 'clownish ignorant parish dominie' learned to read,[31] though not for pleasure, and less certainly to write.[32] Ludovico Guicciardini tells us indeed that 'the common people have for the most

[29] J. de Vries, *The Dutch Rural Economy in the Golden Age, 1500–1700* (New Haven, 1974), pp. 87, 97.

[30] Based on the returns in the *Informacie*, E.C.G. Brünner, *De order op de buitennering van 1531: Bijdrage tot de kennis van economische geschiedenis van het graafschap Holland in den tijd van Karel V* (Utrecht, 1918) and H.A. Enno van Gelder, *Nederlandse dorpen in de zestiende eeuw* (Verhandelingen der koninklijke nederlandse akademie van wetenschappen, afdeling Letterkunde, n.r. LXIX, no.2) (Amsterdam, 1953).

[31] E.P. de Booy, 'Volksonderwijs in de noordelijke Nederlanden', (Nieuwe) *AGN*, VII, p. 264.

[32] Books only occasionally feature in the inventories of farmers, for which consult *Gegevens betreffende roerend en onroerend bezit in de Nederlanden in de 16e eeuw*, I, *Adel, boeren, handel en verkeer*, RGP Grote serie 140, ed. H.A. Enno van Gelder, pp. 307–64. Heretical literature did, however, reach the villages. A pedlar, put to death at Gouda in 1547, confessed to having forbidden books among the wares he had sold in Winkel and Abbekerk. GA Gouda ORA 176, pp. 208–9.

part the rudiments of grammar and almost everyone, even the farmers and rustics can at least read and write'.[33] Perhaps the Florentine allowed his admiration for the Low Countries to colour his judgment, for certainly not all of the petty officials and dignitaries in the villages of Holland had mastered the skill of writing their own names.[34] Apparently the deacons chosen by the Reformed congregation of Sliedrecht were often unable to write and could not, therefore, keep proper accounts.[35] Given the economic interaction between the town and country in Holland and, to a lesser degree, Utrecht, the indifference of the the rural population to the Reformation begs questions which cannot yet be satisfactorily explained. For whatever the reason, the Reformed ministers who began to preach in the villages after the Revolt rarely found fields 'white already to harvest'.

Dutch Calvinism rode on the back of the Revolt and for as long as its future outcome remained in doubt, Reformed Protestants were haunted by a deep sense of their own insecurity. Rumours of Catholic conspiracies in the towns of Holland or defeat at the hands of the royalist army easily provoked a Calvinist backlash, expressed in spasms of iconoclastic activity and strident demands for the suppression of the mass. Of course thoroughgoing Calvinists could place their trust in divine providence. Hendrik van den Corput, a minister in Dordrecht, writing from Antwerp only a few days before that city surrendered to Parma in August 1585, articulated that confidence when he said that the Lord 'has set limits to our enemies which they shall not transgress' and therefore they should obediently await this help, 'praying and building in hope'.[36] Many found it impossible to sustain this faith when the fortunes of war threatened to undo the Calvinist achievement. Mutual religious mistrust undermined the precarious *religievrede* Orange supported in Holland after 1572. In a letter to Louis of Nassau, written in May 1573, William's own secretary confided his feelings of relief now that 'la belle masse' had been driven from Delft: 'nous y sommes ung peu plus à repos et en meilleur seureté'.[37] By 1585 the future looked especially bleak: the 'bon et sage pilotte', as Marnix called Orange, who had steered the Revolt through so many difficulties, had been assassinated one year ago and internal divisions

---

[33] L. Guicciardini, *Beschryvinghe van alle Neder-landen anderssins ghenoemt Neder-Duytslandt* (Amsterdam 1612, repr. 1979), p. 27. The original Italian edition appeared in 1567.

[34] For a brief discussion of literacy in the Low Countries see A.M. van der Woude, 'De alfabetisering', (Nieuwe) *AGN*, VII, pp. 257–64; an analysis of the depositions made by officers and petty magistrates from the villages in the Noorderkwartier before the Council of Troubles in 1567–68 shows that while all the *baljuws* and eleven of the fourteen *schouten* could sign their names, more than half of the twenty-one *schepenen* made a mark to authenticate their statements. See also *Gegevens betreffende roerend en onroerend bezit*, I, pp. 622–23, fn.1.

[35] *CAD*, p. 257.

[36] *WMV*, ser. III deel ii (2e stuk), p. 257.

[37] *Archives ou correspondance*, IV, pp. 92–93.

threatened to paralyse the rebels. Parma's victories had restored Catholicism in Flanders and Brabant, where so recently the Calvinist cause had seemed triumphant. Even after Groningen fell in 1594 to Maurice and Willem Lodewijk, the borders of Holland and Utrecht remained under threat. From the Betuwe Spinola planned to invade Utrecht in 1606 and in 1629 a Habsburg army captured Amersfoort and reinstated the mass in the churches there. Such alarms and reverses underscored the precarious position of the Union of Utrecht and the vulnerability of Reformed Protestantism.

The many Catholics in Holland and Utrecht looked forward keenly to the day when they would repossess the parish churches. When the 'papists' of a village in West Friesland heard in 1582 that Anjou openly went to mass in Antwerp, they gained entry to the local church one night, with the connivance of the village regents and *kerkmeesters*, most of whom were also Catholics, and celebrated sung masses.[38] Military defeats suffered by the Republic sometimes gave Catholics reason to crow. According to the minister at Uitgeest the local 'papists' had displayed great 'bitterness towards our province and church' when Montecuccoli invaded in 1629.[39] At Montfoort, where the Catholic clergy could reckon on the support of the governor and magistrates long after the provincial States had proscribed the mass, the priests incited the people in 1600 against the authorities and predicted an improvement in the position of Catholics: 'then Montfoort shall rule the roost and then shall come the time to root out the Beggars completely'.[40] Others gazed more frivolously into their crystal ball. Two men from a village near Amsterdam wagered a windmill in 1599 that within so many years the mass would once more be celebrated in the parish churches of the town 'with the surplice worn over the cassock', as it had been before 1578.[41] Calvinists in 1600, least of all those in the villages, could not yet look to the future with confidence.

No doubt they would have felt more assured if they had been certain that the 'superior magistrates' were, as these asseverated, indeed committed to the maintenance of the 'true Christian Reformed religion'. The Reformed church honoured the magistracy whose office was, according to the Belgic Confession, 'not only to watch over and maintain civil order, but also to uphold the true worship of God, to prevent and root out idolatry and false religion and to overthrow the kingdom of the

---

[38] RANH, Handschrift 1134. Claes Baerntsz., 'Kort verhael der Gedenckwaerdijgeste gheschiedenissen van Westvrieslant vervaet in vii deelen' (Hauwert, 1636), fo. 117–18.

[39] F.S. Knipscheer, 'Abdias Widmarius, predikant te Uitgeest en het kerkelijke leven eener gereformeerde gemeente in de XVIIe eeuw', *NAK*, n.s. III (1905), pp. 315, 316. The Calvinist youth replied by burning 'small old wooden crosses' during the festivities to mark the capture of 's-Hertogenbosch.

[40] OSA, 73, fo. 70.

[41] J.W. Groesbeek, *Amstelveen: acht eeuwen geschiedenis* (Amsterdam, 1966), p. 91.

Antichrist'.[42] Taking their cue from Calvin whose idealised rulers served as 'patrones religionis et nutricios ecclesiae' (protectors of religion and tutors of the church),[43] the church in its solemn declarations optimistically addressed the provincial states as 'voesterheeren der kercken' or, in Scots presbyterian parlance, 'nourishers of the kirk'.[44] Officially the Reformed synods esteemed the *Heeren Staten* as 'Christian Magistrates'.

Off the record, in their private letters and in the relative seclusion of the *classis*, the ministers voiced their misgivings. When Hendrik van den Corput reflected sadly in 1579 on the discord and disorder among the ministers, he also deplored the 'feeble assistance received by the church from the magistracy which is called Christian'.[45] Such ministers wanted the civil government to manifest its 'Christian' character by uprooting idolatry and endorsing a specifically Presbyterian polity – anything less smacked of libertinism. For their part, the town corporations and States of Holland considered they had amply proved their 'Christian' credentials. They had proscribed the mass and given official recognition and financial support to the Reformed church, when only a small fraction of the population professed membership of the 'Religion' – anything more jeopardised the principle of individual freedom of conscience entrenched in the Union of Utrecht. The discrepancy between these two positions explains why the States of Holland and the Reformed synods failed to devise a mutually acceptable church order. Outside Holland the status of the Reformed church seemed less secure. An attempt in 1583 to amend Article XIII of the Union of Utrecht so as to exclude any form of Protestantism other than the Reformed religion foundered because it was held to infringe the principle of provincial sovereignty. The States of Utrecht, in particular, insisted that they should determine religious policy within their province.[46]

[42] Confessio Belgica, art. XXXVI. See *De nederlandse belijdenisgeschriften in authentieke teksten met inleiding en tekstvergelijkingen*, 2de druk, ed. J.N. Bakhuizen van den Brink (Amsterdam, 1976), p. 141.

[43] Cited by H.A. Enno van Gelder, *Getemperde vrijheid: Een verhandeling over de verhouding van Kerk en Staat in de Republiek der Verenigde Nederlanden ... gedurende de 17e eeuw* (Groningen, 1972), p. 6, fn. 14a.

[44] For the description 'voedsterheren' see RV, VI, p. 323 and D.J. Roorda, 'Contrasting and Converging Patterns: Relations between the Church and State in Western Europe, 1660–1715' *BN*, VII, *Church and State since the Reformation*, ed. A.C.Duke and C.A.Tamse (The Hague, 1981), p. 144.

[45] *WMV*, ser. III, deel ii (2e stuk), p. 119.

[46] For the interpretation of Article XIII of the Union of Utrecht and of the debate in 1583 see J. den Tex, *Oldenbarnevelt*, IV, *Documentatie* (Haarlem, 1970), excursus lvi, pp. 242–57; O.J. de Jong, 'Unie en religie' *De Unie van Utrecht: Wording en werking van een verbond en een verbondsakte*, ed. S.Groenveld and H.L.Ph.Leeuwenberg (The Hague, 1979), pp. 176–77. When Maurice was offered the *stadhouderschap* of Utrecht in March 1590, it was stipulated that he should uphold 'the true Christian evangelical religion in accordance with the ordinance already made and yet to be made by the States of the province of Utrecht, as the aforesaid States understand regulation in the matter of religion belongs to them by virtue of Article XIII of the Union of Utrecht', Bor, III, p. 512 [bk. 27, fo. 16].

Since as Abel Eppens, a Calvinist farmer from the Frisian Ommelanden remarked in his chronicle, 'most of the chief men in the councils and towns had no understanding of the [ecclesiastical] reformation',[47] the Reformed found themselves in a cleft stick. They sensed that the *hoge overheid*, or the 'superior magistrates' were for the most part either Catholics at heart, religious trimmers or advocates of a comprehensive and Erastian church settlement. At any rate few of them were committed Calvinists.[48] During discussions with the States of Holland in 1587, a delegation of ministers felt moved to protest:

> that the common people ... do not know what to think. Although the Reformed religion is upheld and the *Heeren Staten* make protestations on every side to that effect, yet many of the same rarely come to hear the Word of God and most of them do not themselves profess the same ... and consequently the common people think they have reason to suppose that some of the members of the States are not seriously concerned to advance the same Religion. And since the common people set great store by the example and pattern of their magistrates, as is always the way in this world, you should consider carefully that the Reformed Religion is for that reason less esteemed by the common people.[49]

Yet the synods did not dare to withhold from the magistrates their 'Christian' title simply because these had not entered into membership of the Reformed church.[50] But in this marriage of convenience between

[47] W. Bergsma, 'Zestiende-eeuwse godsdienstige pluriformiteit: Overwegingen naar aanleiding van Abel Eppens', *Historisch bewogen: Opstellen over de radicale reformatie ... aangeboden aan Prof. dr. A.F. Mellink* (Groningen, 1984), p. 10.

[48] See above, p. 214 fn.82. In 1582 Hendrik van den Corput considered a general synod necessary, but he anticipated opposition from the States General because 'few members of the church attended that assembly', *WMV*, ser. III, deel ii (2e stuk), p. 199. According to L.J.Rogier only fourteen of the fifty-five members who composed the nobility of Holland between 1581 and 1619 were Protestant; *Geschiedenis van het katholicisme in Noord Nederland in de zestiende en de zeventiende eeuw* I (Amsterdam, 1947), p. 482. Four of the thirteen nobles who regularly attended the meetings of the States of Holland were Catholics, H.F. van Nierop, *Van ridders tot regenten: De Hollandse adel in de zestiende en de eerste helft van de zeventiende eeuw* (Dieren, 1984), p. 208. In the province of Utrecht Catholics dominated the political establishment. Helmichius, a minister at Utrecht, claimed in 1587 that 'not one out of all the nobility properly professed the Religion and [that] the greater part are enemies of the same', *WMV*, ser. III, deel iv, p. 62. In 1601 another local minister ascribed the provincial States' hostility to Reformed *classes* to the 'many papists in the government of the States', OSA, 73, fo. 68. When in 1610 the *burgerij* of Utrecht demanded that the *geëligeerden* should be Reformed Protestants, it was told that this was not feasible since there 'are scarcely any more [qualified representatives] of the [Reformed] Religion than already attend', D.A. Felix, 'Het oproer te Utrecht in 1610', *Utrechtse bijdragen voor letterkunde en geschiedenis*, XVI (Utrecht, 1923), p. xxx.

[49] Bor, II, p. 977 [bk. 22, fo. 90].

[50] Caspar Coolhaes truly called the Calvinists' bluff in 1582. He pointed out that they had refused to recognise a leading magistrate of Leiden as 'Christian' because he did not profess the Reformed faith. For the same reason they should deny the title of 'Christian' to the provincial magistracy, H.C. Rogge, *Caspar Janszoon Coolhaes de voorloper van Arminius*, I (Amsterdam, 1858), p. 126, fn. 45.

the Reformed church and the civil authorities, the former was concerned to retain its autonomy lest the magistrates should, in the future, prove themselves quite unworthy of their Christian calling. The synods therefore resisted those Erastians, including some ministers, who argued that consistories had no place in a polity ruled by godly magistrates.[51]

The *predikanten* in the villages moved in the less exalted company of the so-called 'lesser authorities' (*minder overheit*), but the arguments and concerns were similar. Here the conduct of the gentry and village notables could determine the standing of the Calvinist cause. The minister at Naaldwijk candidly acknowledged that if the leading families did not appear when he preached on Sunday, 'he could not foster God's Word to such effect as he would otherwise have expected'. Early in 1573 – less than six months after the Reformed had usurped the church – he told the *baljuw*, whom the absentee Catholic lady of the manor had appointed, that as long as that officer and his household stayed away from the services, the well-to-do and magistrates would also absent themselves from the sermon.[52] Whether in fact the village regents and more substantial farmers were under represented in the early Calvinist congregations is unknown. There are stray remarks which suggest that 'the simplest and poorest' inhabitants proved more amenable to the new religion than those higher up the social hierarchy.[53] Certainly the humble origins of the tiny Reformed congregation at Barendrecht induced the minister there to postpone the Lord's Supper lest the inhabitants would ridicule a service attended by a handful of poor villagers.[54] Sometimes the ministers in the *classis* seemed almost to take the hostility of the magistrates to the Reformed church for granted. The *classis* of Dordrecht once admonished a minister for having obtained a character reference from the *gerechts-persoonen*, or aldermen, 'who are ... enemies of the truth and seldom or

---

[51] Rogge, *op. cit.*, I, p. 80. Gerardus Blockhoven, a minister at Utrecht, was accused of subscribing to the opinion 'that where the magistracy makes profession of the Religion, elders are redundant', Bor, III, p. 736, [bk. 30, fo. 48]. C.P.Hooft also argued that where the church enjoyed the protection of a Christian magistracy, it should not exercise any authority independent of the civil government, *Memoriën en adviezen van C.P.Hooft* (Utrecht, 1871), p. 222.

[52] P.J. Goetschalkx, 'Invoering van de hervorming te Naaldwijk, Honsholredijk en andere plaatsen rond de stad Delft', *BBH*, XXVII (1903), p. 359.

[53] In 1579 two ministers from the *classis* of Brabant reported that 'in these first beginnings mostly poor people attend the [Reformed] churches and the rich generally follow later when everything is in a good and tranquil state', cit. J.J. Woltjer, 'De vredemakers', *TG* LXXXIX (1976), p. 318 fn. 75. A.C. Duke, 'Nieuwe Niedorp in hervormingstijd', *NAK*, XLVIII (1967), p. 69; KA Ridderkerk, I, p. 14.

[54] *CAD*, p. 231. The *gedeputeerden* from the *classis* upbraided the minister at Barendrecht for his timidity. To swell the congregation there the minister at Ridderkerk promised to send some of his members. The *schout*, who had shown some sympathy for the religion, was also to be asked to become a member.

never come to hear the Word of God'.[55] Helmichius described the civil powers of Utrecht as 'verae Reformationis adversarii' because they had supported a minister, who had been in his opinion properly suspended by the church for pelagianism.[56]

The Reformed synods denounced the subaltern officers, the *baljuws*, *schouten*, *maarschalken* and their minions the *gerechtsdienaeren*, who played the part of Dutch dogberries. According to the synods, these failed to bring charges against sabbath-breakers, took bribes from known 'papists' in return for ignoring their assemblies and stood idly by while the irreverent transmuted solemn fast-days into bacchanalia.[57] In 1619, the churches of South Holland decided to petition the States of Holland for the appointment of officers, 'who favoured the Reformed religion or [who] were, at least, not hostile to the same',[58] but even this modest objective proved unattainable. When in the 1650s the States conducted an enquiry into 'papist' magistrates and officers in the countryside, they uncovered numerous Catholic burgomasters, *schepenen*, *kerkmeesters*, overseers of the poor, *heemraden* and masters of orphanages. In some villages there were too few Calvinists of sufficient substance to replace the Catholic office-holders.[59] The presence of so many Catholics in strategic positions in the villages until late into the seventeenth century must surely have hindered, where it did not prevent, the 'calvinisation' of the countryside.

The creation of indigenous Protestant churches did not properly begin until informal groups of evangelically-minded dissidents broke with the Roman church. Leaving aside the earlier precedent of Anabaptist conventicles, this schismatic process first became apparent in the southern Low Countries in the later 1540s and early 1550s. At this time small numbers of evangelicals, persuaded by Calvin's denunciation of 'nico-demism', decided to withdraw from the *services papistiques* and to call

---

[55] *CAD*, p. 261; cf. p. 284.

[56] *WMV*, ser. III, deel iv, p. 43.

[57] See, for example, RV, II, pp. 322–23; III, p. 247. For the 'bacchusdagen' see OSA, 73, fo. 13, 73. The minister at Wilnis alleged in 1600 that the 'papists' around Vinkeveen had presented the local law officer with a foal to keep him sweet, *ibid.*, fo. 81.

[58] RV, III, pp. 396–97.

[59] W.P.C. Knuttel, *De toestand der nederlandsche katholieken ten tijde der Republiek*, I (The Hague, 1892), pp. 347–54. In 1655 the Reformed minister of Baardwijk (Waalwijk) declared in 1655 that the Calvinist congregation there was too small to furnish sufficient men of the right calibre (*stoffe*) to fill all the available posts. Indeed he argued that the burdens of office would deter people from joining the Reformed congregation. Rumours about the 'reformation of the regents' had already caused some to withdraw from the Reformed church. I hope shortly to publish an article about the enquiry into the 'papist' magistrates and officers. I know of no comparable evidence on the confessional loyalties of the petty magistrates and officers in Utrecht. At Wijk bij Duurstede the relatively well-to-do Calvinists dominated the town corporation by 1620, though several non-Calvinists and even some Catholics still found a place, J.W. van Brakel, 'Wijk bij Duurstede in de periode van de hervorming', *Oud Utrecht* (1984), pp. 30–31.

their own minister to preach the Word and to administer the sacraments. By 1566 small Calvinist congregations existed in the chief towns of Wallonia, Flanders, Brabant, Zeeland (Walcheren) and, possibly, at Amsterdam.[60] Gradually an informal supra-congregational organisation developed. In the Reformed churches of East Friesland and the stranger-churches of London ministers would meet regularly in the *coetus*, which bears comparison with the *Compagnie des pasteurs* in Geneva. In the southern Netherlands ministers came together from 1563 in gatherings dignified as 'provincial synods', to discuss the practical problems experienced by a persecuted minority. Here the crucial Presbyterian principle of parity between churches was enunciated in terms which betray how heavily the Calvinists in the Low Countries drew on the French Reformed churches, and, in particular, the *Discipline ecclésiastique*.[61] It was necessary, Marnix observed in 1570, 'to incorporate all the congregations of the Low Countries into a single body so that they strive to build up the church of God, while keeping in step with one another'.[62] The first national synod, held at Emden in 1571, proceeded to adopt an explicitly Presbyterian church order for the Netherlands congregations, 'which are under the cross and which are scattered through Germany and East Friesland'. The churches, both at home and abroad, were divided up into *classes* and provision made for regular provincial and national synods. It was an ambitious blueprint, whose realisation depended of course on favourable political circumstances.

After Emden Presbyterianism gradually came to be seen in Reformed circles as the only acceptable form of church government. Yet if the Calvinist leadership had a clear notion of how the churches in the Low Countries should be reformed, their vision did not command universal support, even among the Protestants. Apart from the Anabaptists, who outnumbered the Reformed at this stage in some parts of the northern provinces, and a select company of uncompromising Lutherans, there remained an untold number of evangelicals, who still clung to the hope that all Christians might be accommodated within a purified Catholic church. Nor should we forget that the excitable crowds who flocked to the field services in the summer of 1566 had only the haziest idea about Reformed theology and almost certainly no experience of consistorial

[60] Even before the organisation of the hedge services in Holland a minister used to give instruction on the Heidelberg Catechism in Amsterdam 'and those who belonged to the congregation came to hear him, a few at a time' Brandt, I, p. 315.

[61] F.R.J. Knetsch, 'Kerkordelijke bepalingen van de nederlandse synoden "onder het kruis" (1563–1566) vergeleken met die van de franse (1559–1564)', *Feestbundel uitgegeven ter gelegenheid van 80-jarig bestaan van het kerkhistorisch gezelschap S.S.S.*, ed. J. Fabius *et al.* (Leiden, 1982), pp. 29–44. At the synod of Emden the ministers testified to their 'common faith' with the French church by urging subscription to the *Confessio Gallicana*.

[62] Ph. van Marnix van St. Aldegonde, *Godsdienstige en kerkelijke geschriften: Aanhangsel*, ed. J.J. van Toorenenbergen (The Hague, 1878), p. 16.

discipline. Once the initial mood of exhilaration had faded popular support for the hedge preachers tended to fall away to reveal only a small and relatively isolated core of zealous Calvinists. The ruling elites too knew little or nothing about a church order drawn up outside the Netherlands in which they had had no part.[63] When the Revolt began in Holland and Zeeland, the civil authorities there naturally looked with incomprehension, if not suspicion, upon an ecclesiastical system devised without their knowledge or consent.

The plans optimistically laid at Emden in 1571 matured unexpectedly when the Sea Beggars gained admission to most towns in Holland and Zeeland in the following year. Small Reformed congregations now appeared in the rebel-held towns, sometimes for the first time. Ministers were called, makeshift consistories chosen, discipline established and the Lord's Supper administered according to the Reformed rite. Within the next few years the over-arching hierarchy of *classes* and *particuliere* and provincial synods began to function.[64] In the same period the Catholic establishment disintegrated. This did not happen at once: no acts of supremacy and dissolution severed the ties with Rome and abolished the religious houses. The authority of the Catholic church was eroded piecemeal. The agreements negotiated in 1572 between the town corporations and the Sea Beggars had guaranteed the continuation of the mass and gave protection to the priests, the religious and church-buildings. But these terms proved unenforceable and the Orangist policy of religious peace soon fell into disarray. The virulent anti-popery of the ill-disciplined Beggar army found expression in the looting of religious houses, the destruction of Catholic shrines and the persecution of priests and religious. To prevent still worse disorder the magistrates closed the parish churches for a month or so; when these were reopened, the priest at the altar had often made way for the minister of the Word. The mass, dislodged from the parish churches, lingered for a while in the religious houses and hospitals until sometime in February or April 1573 the States of Holland officially forbade its celebration in public.

In the countryside of Holland the confusion was greater and, in the absence of parochial and ecclesiastical records, the 'reformation' of the local churches usually went undocumented. The process may, however, be followed more closely at Ridderkerk. In this village situated in the Riederwaard to the north-east of Dordrecht 'the reformation in the congregation (*gemeynte*)' only started in January 1574 when Caspar van Gent preached there. During his ministry the interior of the church was

---

[63] Orange had, of course, encouraged the synod of Emden in a bid to improve links between the groups of exiles, J.J. Woltjer, 'De politieke betekenis van de Emdense synode', *De synode van Emden, 1571–1971* (Kampen, 1971), pp. 39–49.

[64] The county of Holland was divided for ecclesiastical purposes, into the synods of North and South Holland, known as *particuliere* synods; all other provinces had a single synod, therefore known as a *provinciale* synod.

cleared of statues, altars and 'other idols', but the minister, who did not live in the village, failed to introduce discipline before he left in April 1575. In the time of his unsatisfactory successor we hear of 'elders',[65] but the first Lord's Supper was probably not held until early in 1579. Poor relief remained in its old, unreformed state for several more years because the Reformed congregation lacked men of sufficient substance to serve as overseers of the poor. In 1585 the magistrates did appoint a former elder to serve in this capacity, but the *schout* and the authorities only agreed in 1588 that the responsibility for choosing 'deacons' belonged to the consistory. Even then the consistory took care to invite members of the polder board to attend the audit in the church in order to avoid malicious gossip.[66] Some ministers did succeed in arranging communion services within a year or so of the start of the Revolt in Holland,[67] but the protracted transition at Ridderkerk seems to have been more typical. Indeed the 'reformation' went forward more smoothly here than in some other parts of the Dordrecht *classis*, notably in the villages in the Alblasserwaard.

The Reformation of the Dutch countryside depended preeminently on the dedication, tact and resourcefulness of the first *predikanten*. In many villages the minister would at first be the sole representative of the Reformed church. When the question was raised at the synod of Dordrecht in 1574 whether non-graduates, who wished to serve in the ministry, might be licensed to preach, the synod decided only to admit those with all the following qualities: 'first godliness and humility; secondly, the gift of eloquence and, thirdly, good understanding and discernment'.[68] As the demand for ministers outstripped the supply of such paragons, the synods had to choose between admitting a significant proportion of former priests and renegade monks to the Reformed ministry or leaving many villages bereft of doctrinal instruction and pastoral care.[69] The Reformation in the countryside therefore began with the *reformatie der papen*. Indeed the first Reformed synod to be held on the soil of Holland opened with a discussion about 'how to reform the priests who wish to enter the service of the holy gospel'.[70] Between 1572 and 1578 apostate priests and ex-religious accounted for one in four of the ministers then at work in Holland.[71]

---

[65] *Uw rijk kome: Acta van de kerkeraad van de nederduitse gereformeerde gemeente te Dordrecht, 1573–1579*, ed. Th.W. Jensma (Dordrecht, 1981), p. 96.

[66] KA Ridderkerk, 1, pp. 3, 7, 8, 12–13, 15, 23–24.

[67] Above, p. 211.

[68] *WMV*, ser. II, deel iii, p. 140.

[69] Helmichius estimated that there were barely fifty ministers throughout Holland in 1582, *WMV*, ser. III, deel iv, p. 32.

[70] RV, I, pp. 1–2.

[71] Above, p. 221. Twenty-four of the sixty-seven ministers active in the *classis* of Sneek (Friesland) before 1600 had been priests or monks, *Een kerk in ophouw: Classisboek Sneek, 1583–1624*, ed. J.J. Kalma (Leeuwarden, n.d.), p. xiv.

The first generation of ministers has received a bad press. Caspar Coolhaes, who had himself left the Carthusian order in 1560, had no very high opinion of his clerical colleagues: they were 'for the most part mass priests and monastics, who had not so much deserted, as been deserted by, the papacy'.[72] The Amsterdam burgomaster, Cornelis Pietersz. Hooft, likewise held the Reformed ministers in contempt as foreigners from Flanders and persons of 'mean estate and modest ability'. Self-interest rather than religious convictions prompted the turncoat priests to become ministers according to Hooft.[73] The synods knew of course only too well how risky it was to admit such men to the Reformed ministry; they therefore required such as wanted to take this step to make public profession of their new faith and to marry their common law wives before the congregation. When the *classis* of the Neder-Veluwe met in 1592 for the first time, the village priests present had to state their opinions on several contentious matters of doctrine, including free will, justification and good works, and the manner of Christ's presence in the communion. In this way the *classis* hoped to identify those priests who might make passable ministers and to weed out the principled 'papists'.[74] It was the task too of the *classis* to monitor such one-time priests carefully until these had proved their suitability for the ministry and their doctrinal soundness. Despite such vigilance, the church still had to contend with 'catholicising' ministers, schismatics, interlopers and other freelance preachers, who neither owned the Calvinist confessions of faith nor respected the authority of the *classis*.[75] In Holland, where the regular classical assemblies enabled the church to maintain the pressure, the influence of these non-Calvinist ministers and vagabond preachers was gradually confined to the *heerlijkheden* of certain gentry, who refused to acknowledge the competence of the *classes* and the synods. But in Utrecht, where the *classes* did not function until after the national synod of Dordrecht in 1619, the Reformed church was usually powerless to remove unsatisfactory ministers.

In March 1593 the Reformed consistory at Utrecht petitioned the provincial states, not for the first time, to discharge their responsibility as Christian magistrates by establishing a fit and regular ministry in the

[72] Rogge, *Coolhaes*, I, p. 37.

[73] C.P. Hooft, *Memoriën en adviezen*, II, ed. H.A. Enno van Gelder (Utrecht, 1925), p. 131.

[74] *Acta van de classis Neder-Veluwe (Harderwijk) van 1592–1620*, ed. G. van der Zee (Goes, n.d.), pp. 5–16.

[75] Adrianus Cornelisz. and Michiel Egidii, both apostate priests and interlopers, were forced out by the *classis* of Dordrecht, C.A. Tukker, *De classis Dordrecht van 1573 tot 1609* (Leiden, 1965), pp. 141–51.

countryside.[76] On this occasion the States agreed to conduct a visitation to consider, among other matters, the condition of the parish clergy and they appointed a four-man commission.[77] At the end of October the commissioners tabled their report and made their recommendations. These included proposals for the combination of some charges to ensure more effective use of the restricted number of Reformed ministers then available. They submitted reports on the religious situation in fifty-six villages, excluding the hearsay information about Montfoort, several of which had chapels of ease rather than parish churches. According to the fairly undemanding criteria used by the commissioners some twenty of the forty-eight clerics visited were reckoned to qualify as 'Reformed ministers' and another eight were considered to be 'inclined to reformation'. They divided the other twenty priests into two categories: six were regarded as 'tolerable' in the short term, but the other fourteen were classified as 'intolerable and unedifying'.[78] By 1602 at least five of the last group had been removed and no trace can be found of six others. Of the remaining three, the incumbent at Bunschoten, damned in the report of 1593 for his 'dissolute and shameless conduct' evidently made sufficient amends to become the minister there until at least 1612,[79] but the priests at Ankeveen and Vinkeveen continued to defy the Reformation until they died in or shortly before 1602. The wily priest at Ankeveen had, it is true, tried to play the part of the pious minister, receiving the visitors psalter in hand, but they were unimpressed. When this priest joined his parishioners on the alehouse bench, he used to jest, 'Now it's off with the minister. I draw it [i.e. my religion] from another barrel. I'm no consistorial'. He continued to hear confessions, consecrate water and to distribute hosts.[80] His colleague at Vinkeveen was no exemplar of Catholic piety. Commonly known as 'the great god of Vinkeveen', this toper taught his parishioners that though drunkards might enter heaven, certain damnation awaited the Beggars. The Calvinists may have seen the

---

[76] B.M. de Jonge van Ellemeet, 'De organisatie der Utrechtse gereformeerde kerken vóór de invoering der Dordtse kerkenorde', *NAK*, n.s. XXXVI (1948–49), pp. 56–57; 'Visitatie der kerken ten platten lande in het sticht van Utrecht ten jare 1593', *BMHG*, VII (1884), pp. 186–89. See also G. van der Zee, 'Schets van de crisis der kerkelijke reformatie in de dorpen van provincie Utrecht ± 1580–1620', *Jaarboekje van het oudheidkundige genootschap "Niftarlake"* (1956) pp. 1–99. The author conveniently summarises the religious situation in each village in turn using the visitation of 1593 and the reports given by the ministers in 1606 but he offers no interpretation of the evidence.

[77] 'Visitatie', p. 190; the commission consisted of two ministers of Utrecht, Frederick van Zuylen van Nyvelt, one of the rare Protestant nobles in the province and Hendrik Buth, an elder in the Utrecht consistory and a *geëligeerde*.

[78] 'Visitatie', pp. 253–58.

[79] 'Visitatie', pp. 213–14; OSA, 73, fo. 17; RV, VI, pp. 296, 330.

[80] 'Visitatie', p. 230; OSA, 73, fo. 17. In Utrecht the label *consistoriant* was applied to the Calvinist party; the followers of Duifhuis were known as 'van de gesintheyt van Sint Jacob', Bor, II, p. 839, [bk. 21, fo. 112], or 'van 't Oude en Nieuwe Testament', 'Visitatie', p. 223; Brandt, I, p. 672.

hand of providence in the manner of this priest's death for he fell into the cauldron before the fire and drowned while in his cups.[81] Only one of the eight priests considered in 1593 as potential Reformed ministers in fact came up to the mark. Three relapsed into Catholicism, a fourth was removed after having failed his examination before the consistory at Utrecht, while another remained an inadequate 'reader'.[82]

In this time of doctrinal uncertainty and liturgical compromise several incumbents were prepared to do 'as the people wished', marrying and baptising in Latin or Dutch, according to the circumstances.[83] But few could match the versatility of Pibo Ovitius Abbema, the minister at Hagestein in 1602. He displayed a remarkable ability for survival by being all things to all men: this clerical chameleon served as minister or priest, as seemed appropriate, in no fewer than fifteen places, mainly in Gelderland and Utrecht, between 1586 and 1606.[84] Though he fell foul of both the bishop of Roermond and of several Reformed synods, the acute shortage of priests and ministers, the breakdown of ecclesiastical jurisdiction and the blurring of confessional lines, especially in the eastern Netherlands, enabled Pibo to find patrons and churches despite his chequered past and his sinister reputation as a werewolf!

When the so-called 'aristocratic' and anti-Leicesterian faction reasserted its control in the city and States of Utrecht in 1588, the beleaguered minority of Calvinists in the province discovered they could no longer directly influence ecclesiastical policy. In their need they turned to the synod of South Holland to whom they fed information about the state of the church in Utrecht. In 1601 the Holland synods decided to prepare a remonstrance on this subject for Maurice of Nassau, who was both *stadhouder* of Holland and Utrecht. In preparation the commission, appointed by the synod, received critical reports on some thirty-one ministers then at work in the villages of Utrecht. According to their findings only six ministers deserved the qualification 'Reformed'. No doubt they represented the position of the Reformed church in the Sticht in the worst light in order to reinforce the need for intervention by Maurice. By applying less rigorous standards, one might describe eighteen as Protestants of a sort, though these were by no means all convinced Calvinists or patterns of moral virtue and spiritual edification.[85] Thanks in part to the discreet pressure exerted by the synods of

[81] 'Visitatie' p. 235; OSA, 73, fo. 12, 40, 75.

[82] Only the former priest at Doorn went on to become a recognised minister; the priest at Kokkengen continued in his post until 1602, but his doctrinal inconsistency inspired no confidence.

[83] *E.g.* the priests at Kortenhoef and Kokkengen.

[84] See entry *s.v.* Abbema, Pibo Ovitius in *BLGNP*, III, pp. 13–15.

[85] Five of remaining thirteen clergy steered a course midway between the confesions and the other eight showed themselves to be Catholics of one sort or another of conviction. For the six 'Reformed Protestant' ministers see J.P. van Dooren, 'Kerkelijke toestanden in de provincie Utrecht omstreeks 1600', *NAK*, n.s. XLIX (1969), p. 193.

Holland the *reformatie der papen* in Utrecht went forward slowly, but incontrovertibly. By 1606, when the first synod of the Reformed churches in the province met, some thirty-five villages had Protestant ministers.[86]

When we compare the time taken to produce a 'Reformed' ministry in the villages of Holland and of Utrecht, we discover that the pace of change was markedly slower in the case of the Sticht. Because the States of Utrecht refused to sanction classical assemblies,[87] the church there was deprived of the means, which, on the analogy of Holland, would have enabled it to sift the priests and to provide practical training for the ministers. It was harder in Utrecht to remove obstinate 'papists' and dubious Protestants from office. In November 1596 a Calvinist minister in Utrecht complained to a colleague in Holland about the refusal, as he saw it, of the States to proceed to a thorough Reformation of the countryside: consequently, he wrote, 'outside [the city of Utrecht] almost everything runs wild as is only to be expected from those who are subject to neither regulation, order nor discipline'.[88]

Probably the most distinctive feature of Dutch Calvinism was the creation, within the parish community, of the Reformed congregation, the *broeders der gemeinte*, who alone were admitted to the Lord's Table. Membership was open to all adults provided they first submitted themselves to the instruction and discipline of the church, 'bowing', as the Belgic Confession said, 'their necks under the yoke of Jesus Christ'.[89] Before the Reformation every parishioner had been required by canon law to make his communion in his parish church at Easter; in Holland after 1572, according to the Reformed synods, only the Calvinist membership might attend. Consequently the new religious order in Holland gave rise to a novel distinction between those 'outside' and those 'inside' that congregation. Discipline within the Calvinist congregation was maintained by the consistory, which had, however, no authority over the wider parish community.[90] While Calvin had declared 'discipline' to be essential for

[86] RV, VI, pp. 296–97. Thirty-two village ministers appeared at the outset; the minister from Ter Aa arrived late and two others sent their apologies. According to van der Zee, 'Schets van de crisis', pp. 96–97 there were forty Reformed congregations in the province in 1612 and fifty in 1650.

[87] *Cf.* Jonge van Ellemeet, 'Organisatie', p. 257, fn.2.

[88] OSA, 73, fo. 51. *cf.* J. Hania, *Wernerus Helmichius* (Utrecht, 1895), pp. 115–16.

[89] *Nederlandse belijdenisgeschriften*, p. 123 (Article XXVIII).

[90] When it was suggested in 1578 that the ministers might exercise discipline more generally, Hendrik van den Corput replied that the consistorial discipline only applies to 'those who obey the Word, who are the least part, and that the discipline does not go beyond the correction of consciences', WMV, ser. III, deel ii (2e stuk), p. 95. When a church in the *classis* of East Flanders once asked whether a drunken overseer of the poor, who came to the Reformed services, but was not a church member might be admonished, it was told 'that the discipline does not come into effect unless he is a member', Janssen, *De kerkhervorming in Vlaanderen* (Arnhem, 1868), II, p. 188. Exceptionally the consistory at Dordrecht reprimanded a woman 'although she does not belong to the congregation', *Acta van de kerkeraad … Dordrecht*, p. 121.

the well-being (*bene esse*) of the church, the authors of the Belgic Confession went a step further and made discipline one of the three dispensable 'notes' of the true church.[91] Consistories had kept discipline in the Calvinist churches 'under the cross', in the stranger churches in England and the Rhineland, and in Emden that 'haven of God's church', as the religious refugees from the Low Countries called it. The principle and practice of consistorial discipline was therefore ingrained in Dutch Calvinism before 1572. In the wake of the Revolt the synods and *classes* gave a high priority to the formation of consistories, first of all in the towns, but subsequently in the villages. The official proceedings of the *classis* of Dordrecht enable us to follow that process. Of the thirty or so villages within the *classis*, five certainly had consistories by 1580 and their number increased to fifteen by 1590.[92] On the admittedly slender basis of the consistorial act book for Ridderkerk, it would seem the infant Calvinist congregations in the villages were subject to close, but patient, scrutiny. Apparently the concern to protect the good name of the congregation within the parish at large by strict discipline was offset by the desire not to lose errant members by hasty expulsion. Excommunications were therefore rare and only implemented after repeated attempts, made over many months, even years, to bring the backslider to repentance. Even then the consistory had to obtain the advice of the *classis* before applying the ultimate spiritual sanction.[93]

By no means all Dutch Protestants attached the same importance to discipline. In 1595 the synod of South Holland sternly rebuked certain ministers who had questioned the necessity for consistories: discipline, the synod stated, was 'not a matter of indifference, but God's ordinance and express commandment'.[94] The regent-magistrates displayed, as we have already noticed, no great enthusiasm for the Calvinist church order. In the first place they distrusted any form of jurisdiction not under their direct control. Secondly, some of them disliked the visitation

[91] See pp. 212; 284–85.

[92] The records of the *classis* of Dordrecht enable us to follow the expansion of consistories in the villages, as follows: by 1575 Oud-Beierland, Cillarshoek, Klaaswaal and (?) Klundert; by 1578 Ridderkerk, Zwijndrecht; by 1581 Maasdam, Strijen, Westmaas; *c.* 1582 Mijnsheerenland; by 1583 Barendrecht, Groote Lindt, Hendrik-Ido-Ambacht (deacons); by 1588 Streefkerk; by 1589 Alblasserdam, Fijnaart, Sliedrecht; by 1595 Puttershoek; *c.* 1598 's-Gravendeel (new settlement). No consistories existed at Bleskensgraaf, Brandwijk and Molenaarsgraaf in 1582; St. Anthonypolder in 1588. Nothing is known about Giessen Nieuwkerk, Giessen-Oudkerk, Goudriaan-Ottoland, Oud-Alblas, Papendrecht, Heerjansdam, though silence probably indicates the absence of any organised congregation.

[93] For example, the conduct of one wayward member of the congregation at Ridderkerk first caused concern *c.* 1580 and his name regularly appeared on the agenda of the consistory for the next twelve or so years. The consistory consulted the *classis* about excommunication but it did not take the ultimate step. In 1600 the consistory met to discuss the case of another offender on six occasions in less than a month after which the backslider repented of his unknown misdeed.

[94] RV, III, p. 47.

of members carried out by the consistory before the Lord's Supper and they discerned here a new form of spiritual tyranny which they compared unflatteringly with the papist inquisition or the Roman confession. Thirdly, they regarded the sectarian tendency lurking within Dutch Calvinism as being at odds with their vision of a comprehensive church settlement after the Erastian reformation of Zürich. Such anxieties surfaced in the States of Holland as early as 1575, when the parties discussed the conditions on which Orange would be granted greater authority. Rumours reached the synod of South Holland to the effect that the States intended to abolish 'all ecclesiastical assemblies together with the spiritual jurisdiction of the same' and the members responded with an elaborate defence of the Calvinist understanding of the relations between the civil and ecclesiastical orders.[95] Even so the States insisted that 'no other colleges, or consistory [be permitted] except on the advice, nomination and institution of the magistrates or the provincial states'.[96] The arguments about consistorial discipline rumbled on in Holland for years to come, but gradually the magistrates and the synods reached an understanding. The civil powers recognised that, as the Calvinist party had the upper hand in the church, consistories and Presbyterian synods could not be wished away, while the Reformed accepted that the magistrates had a legitimate interest in the business transacted in such ecclesiastical assemblies.

The auguries for the Calvinists in Utrecht were, as we have seen, far less propitious. Though the States of Utrecht had proscribed the mass in June 1580, the chapters, nobility and town magistrates in the province had done so primarily for political reasons. Nor could the Protestants in the city of Utrecht give a strong lead. The feuding between the evangelical, but non-Calvinist Jacobikerk, favoured by the magistrates, and the 'consistorials' continued from 1578 until 1586. The brief Calvinist triumph under Leicester did nothing to reconcile the leading families with the Calvinist cause: on the contrary, the Calvinists of Utrecht probably suffered from their association with the Brabanters who then held high office in the government of the province and city. After the overthrow of the Leicesterians in 1588, the Calvinist town ministers were replaced by men more attuned to the Erastian views of the magistrates. As a result the ministers at Utrecht found themselves at odds with the Reformed synods of Holland, while some local Calvinists in Utrecht felt sufficiently strongly about the changes that they seceded from the 'official' Protestant church and formed 'the protesting (*dolerende*) church

---

[95] RV, II, pp. 159–67; Orange informed the magistrates of Rotterdam that he considered synods, *classes* and consistories as necessary for the preservation of the church, H. ten Boom, *De reformatie in Rotterdam, 1530–1585* (Dieren, 1987), p. 163.

[96] Bor, I, p. 643 [bk. 8, fo. 119].

of Utrecht'.[97] The church order approved by the States of Utrecht in 1590 placed the 'true Christian religion' (*oprechte Christelijke religie*) in the province firmly under the tutelage of the patrons, the town magistracies and the States, who appointed the ministers and officebearers. The ministers were forbidden to hold any *classes* or synods without the express permission of the States, who would have to approve the agenda and who would be represented in any ecclesiastical assembly by deputies.[98] In line with the States' bid to foster a more comprehensive church, the place of discipline, and therefore the importance of the consistory, was reduced.[99] Whereas in the Calvinist congregations in Holland the consistory examined the members in advance of the Lord's Supper, the Utrecht church order explicitly forbade any searching of consciences: intending communicants were simply called on to 'try' themselves.[100] It is tempting to attribute such Erastian views to Hubert Duifhuis, who until his death in 1581 had ministered to the evangelical congregation at the Jacobikerk. Duifhuis had administered communion to anyone who wished to receive and had regarded elders and deacons as unnecessary in view of the existence of the *kerkmeesters* and parochial overseers of the poor.[101] In truth such ideas did not originate with Duifhuis, who should rather be considered as the local exponent of an Erastian and comprehensive evangelical church, which found varying expression, in the Lutheran territorial churches, in Bullinger's Zurich and in the Elizabethan church settlement. Nor was Duifhuis the only minister to advocate such 'libertine'

[97] For the secessionist Calvinist congregation in Utrecht see van Dooren, 'Kerkelijke toestanden', pp. 187–88; for the resumption of field services and conventicles at Utrecht after 1589 see Bor, II, pp. 842–48 [bk. 21, fo. 114–118]; for the reference to the 'dolerende kerke van Utrecht' see Bor, III, p. 731 [bk. 30, fo. 44].

[98] *Oude kerkordeningen*, pp. 293–98.

[99] We may gauge the subordinate place discipline held in the thinking of certain ministers at Utrecht from a letter by a local Calvinist to the ministers at Dordrecht in 1600. He wrote to ask whether he and his fellow-believers should sit at the Lord's Table with Johannes Bergarius, whom the town magistrates had appointed as a minister despite his controversial past. The ministers at Utrecht had tried to reassure our correspondent about the purity of the church at Utrecht. He was advised that 'the church was defined by these two marks, namely the proclamation of God's Word and the administration of the sacraments and both of these were pure [at Utrecht]; as for discipline, it was a bonus if one could obtain this, but the church or congregation could exist without it', OSA, 73, fo. 37. In support of their definition of the church the Utrecht ministers had cited both Bullinger and Calvin. *ibid.*, fo. 119. Such a definition of the church did not of course accord with that laid down in the Belgic Confession. The 'protesting' congregation at Utrecht also informed the synod of South Holland that the ministers, whom the town magistrates had appointed were guilty of profaning the sacraments because they made 'the Lord's Supper freely available to one and all without distinction'. Bor, III, p. 730 [bk. 30, fo. 44].

[100] *Oude kerkordeningen*, p. 297, but *cf.* the draft church order for Holland of 1576 (art. 28) and 1583 (art. 19). Reportedly the church order in preparation by Gerobulus *c.* 1602 had no place for excommunication, OSA, 73, fo. 153

[101] Bor, II, p. 832 [bk. 21, fo. 107–8].

ecclesiastical policies in Utrecht.[102]

The moderate Calvinist, Helmichius, writing from Utrecht in 1584, alleged that States sought to disseminate *Libertinismum Jacobaeanum* in the villages, by which he presumably meant a reformation of the sort Duifhuis had introduced in the congregation of the Jacobikerk.[103] Such a claim might seem far-fetched, the figment of an agitated Calvinist. The doctrinal, liturgical and ecclesiastical confusion in the rural churches in the first twenty or so years after the abolition of the mass in Utrecht seems so total as to belie any sort of considered policy of reformation. Yet, without wishing to gainsay the disorder in the parishes, there are certain features which suggest that the States did indeed seek to introduce a non-Calvinist church order in Utrecht. Consider the situation in 1606. At the synod held that year around two-thirds of the thirty-three ministers reported that they had held communion services, which were indifferently attended. Were such evidence available for any part of Holland, one might reasonably infer the presence of consistories in such churches: it was a Calvinist axiom that the congregation must be governed by a consistory before the Lord's Supper could be administered. Yet in Utrecht only six of these churches appear to have had consistories of any sort. In the case of Jutfaas and Maartensdijk the officers responsible to the parish for the church, the *kerkmeesters*, doubled as elders.[104] This may indeed reflect some official policy for a Calvinist minister alleged in 1602 that 'the States of Utrecht did not want the ministers in the countryside to have elders or deacons, but only *kerkmeesters*'.[105] Further doubt is cast on the Reformed character of such communion services by information about the practices of the minister at Harmelen. According to the visitation of 1593, when he was described as 'Reformed', this minister had already administered several communion services, once to as many as a hundred inhabitants.[106] Only later did the secret of his apparent success come to light, for we learn that this minister led the services in such a way that 'the papists took him for a papist, [and] the Lutherans

---

[102] Apart from Gerardus Blockhoven, whose views on the elders have already been quoted (see fn. 51), the seasoned anti-Calvinist minister, Andries Michielsz., freely acknowledged at Amersfoort that he was opposed to the discipline, *WMV*, ser. III, deel iv, p. 11. Erasmus Backer, a former colleague of Duifhuis and by 1593 the minister of Breukelen, refused to subscribe to the Belgic Confession. OSA, 73, fo. 15. Moreover several ministers, 'zijnde van de gesintheyt van Sint Jacobs', were ejected in 1586 because of their refusal to subscribe to the acts of the national synod held that year in The Hague, Bor, II, p. 839 [bk. 21, fo. 112].

[103] *WMV*, ser. III, deel iv, p. 43.

[104] RV, VI, pp. 300–12. Consistories are mentioned at Jutfaas, Maartensdijk, Nichtevecht, Westbroek and Zegveld. To these we may add Mijdrecht, 'Visitatie', p. 237. The deputies of the synod of South Holland took the view that only the church at Utrecht had a consistory, OSA, 73, fo. 5.

[105] OSA, 73, fo. 20.

[106] 'Visitatie', p. 244.

for a Lutheran'. Evidently anyone who cared to might participate at these communion services at which hosts and sometimes *krakelingen* were distributed.[107] This evidence coincides with the testimony of the troubled minister of Bunnik, who told the *gedeputeerden* of the synod of South Holland in 1602 that in the Sticht anyone who wished might take communion.[108]

In the four-tier Presbyterian polity with its hierarchy of consistories, *classes* and provincial and national synods, the *classis* provided the link between the consistory, which was chiefly concerned with the government of the *gemeente*, and both the 'lesser authorities' and the senior courts of the church. The *classis*, as we have already observed, watched over the training and orthodoxy of the ministers, initiated these into the Presbyterian system, regulated their calling and protected congregations against interlopers. The collective wisdom of the brethren in the *classis* provided a fund of expertise on which the newly-established and inexperienced village consistories could draw. Meeting in the case of the *classis* of Dordrecht four or five times a year, the *classis* could maintain a steady pressure on recalcitrant or indifferent village officials and magistrates, demanding the refurbishment of dilapidated church-buildings and manses, the 'reformation' of poor relief and of the schools, the proper observation of fast-days and the laws governing marriage. The *classis* also took up cudgels with the States of Holland to whom it addressed petitions concerning the payment of ministers' salaries and the support of their widows. Its business may seem humdrum and its successes fairly minor, but its sheer persistence made it, in the words of Professor van Deursen, 'pre-eminently the instrument of Calvinisation'.[109]

At first the States of Holland did not consider the *classis* as an indispensable part of the new ecclesiastical structure. The church order drafted in 1576 at the behest of the provincial States explicitly denied the *classis* any part in the appointment of ministers, reserving this to the magistrates. The same order also proposed that elders and ministers should go out from the towns once a year to visit the rural 'parishes' and report their findings to the town magistrates.[110] In fact this order was never approved and the role of the *classis* in the examination and appointment of ministers gradually came to be recognised with the exception of churches 'standing under free [*particuliere*] lords'. In April 1581 the synod of South Holland felt compelled to remonstrate with the marquis of Bergen-op-Zoom about a renegade friar who had not been examined

---

[107] OSA, 73, fo. 73. *Krakeling* was a type of bitter-sweet biscuit distributed in the church on Ash Wednesday and Maundy Thursday, J. Toussaert, *Le sentiment religieux en Flandre à la fin du Moyen-Age* (Paris, 1963), p. 184.

[108] OSA, 73, fo. 20.

[109] Van Deursen, *Bavianen en slijkgeuzen*, p. 9. For a succinct statement of the tasks discharged by the *classis*, ibid., pp. 5–11.

[110] *Oude kerkordeningen*, pp. 123, 127.

by the *classis*. Since the marquis was none other than William of Orange, to whom the Reformed church often looked for support, the synod adopted a deferential tone and assured him that the exercise of classical authority was 'without prejudice to his seigneurial rights'.[111] Orange's concern was not apparently allayed, for a short while afterwards he complained to the burgomasters of Dordrecht that the local *classis* 'was seeking some superiority in [that part of] Brabant under his jurisdiction'.[112] In 1597 the Protestant count of Hohenlohe, who had married the countess of Buren, ordered the ministers of that county not to attend the *classis* of Gorcum. The county of Buren acknowledged no superior apart from the count and Hohenlohe evidently feared the count's claim to 'absolute authority' would be impaired if the local ministers submitted to the jurisdiction of a *classis* in Holland.[113] After protracted discussions the parties eventually found a face-saving solution: the Reformed church created the separate *classis* of Buren in 1607, which however sent deputies to the synod of South Holland.[114]

In 1578 the national synod of Dordrecht proposed the division of the church in Utrecht into five *classes*,[115] but nothing came of this scheme. Though some ministers in Utrecht may have met together before 1589,[116] the States of Utrecht resolutely opposed the introduction of *classes* such as existed in Holland. Though the States pretended that *classes* were unnecessary on account of the province's small size, they feared that the classical system threatened their control of the provincial church and, by implication, their conservative approach to the ecclesiastical reformation. In Utrecht the supervision of the church belonged to a provincial synod of ministers, who all owed their appointment to lay patrons, magistrates or the States and who only came together at the invitation of

---

[111] RV, II, p. 208.

[112] *CAD*, p. 103.

[113] RV, III, pp. 94, 110–11, 242.

[114] In 1620 the easygoing count of Culemborg clashed with his local consistory and the *classis* of Gorcum concerning the appointment of a controversial minister. On that occasion the Count declared that 'we claim for ourselves the same rights within our territory in ecclesiastical affairs as German princes and counts exercise in their jurisdictions', de Jong, *Reformatie in Culemborg*, p. 224. From 1624 the ministers from Culemborg attended the newly-created *classis* of Buren.

[115] *WMV*, ser. II, deel iv, p. 280.

[116] The Utrecht church order of 1612 stated that *classes* 'have never been introduced on account of the small size of the province and other reasons', *Oude kerkordeningen*, p. 409. Informal meetings of ministers may have taken place. It is otherwise difficult to understand why the States in 1590 specifically forbade 'any *classes* or other assemblies', which might have taken place earlier. Around 1600 the ministers at Amersfoort were said to be working 'in order to have *classes* again' OSA, 73, fo. 5. Gerobulus' draft order of 1602 envisaged two *classes*, though these would have been controlled by the States *WMV*, ser. III, deel iv, p. 112. The minister at Houten crossed the border to attend a meeting of the *classis* of Overrijnland held at Waarder in July 1601, OSA, 73, fo. 77. Perhaps other Calvinist ministers from Utrecht unofficially attended *classes* in Holland.

civil powers. The synod in turn chose deputies who met regularly with colleagues appointed by the States and together these advised on ecclesiastical affairs and supervised the ministers.[117] Not surprisingly this body, whose constitution recalls the state-controlled *Konsistorium* or *Kirchenrat* typical of Lutheran territorial churches, failed to satisfy the Calvinists. It appeared to some inadequate to the task. One former minister at Utrecht, speaking admittedly with experience of the procedures in force before the church order of 1612, alleged that the ministers cited before this body simply claimed that the parishioners would attest their good conduct and then continued in their unruly ways. For that reason Blockhoven referred contemptuously to this form of supervision as the 'spurious [*blauwe*] visitation' and insisted that a proper reformation of the church in Utrecht depended on the introduction of *classes*.[118]

Both the States and the Calvinist party in Utrecht identified the *classis* as the critical institution: the eventual character of the Reformation in the province depended on whether or not the *classis* found a place in the ecclesiastical polity. While the church in Utrecht lacked *classes*, the States could control the direction and pace of the Reformation. In the Church order of 1612 the States tried to promote an Erastian church settlement whose broadbased evangelical character did not needlessly offend the powerful Catholic families still strongly entrenched in the first and second estates. During the 1590s the Calvinists in Utrecht called upon their colleagues in the Reformed synods of Holland in order to bring about with their help the Reformation they could not achieve by themselves. The Holland synods could not, of course, directly interfere in the ecclesiastical affairs of Utrecht. Instead they exerted indirect pressure on the political establishment of that province by refusing to recognise ministers from Utrecht as truly Reformed; by raising with the States of Holland the problem of Catholic activity in the lands of the provostry of St. Jan 'on the borders of Holland'; by petitioning Maurice, who was also the *stadhouder* of Utrecht, about 'the unruly ministers in the Sticht'; and by agitating for a national synod.[119] The replacement of the Utrecht church order of 1612 by that drawn up at Dordrecht in 1619 led directly to the establishment of *classes* in Utrecht.[120] No doubt the Calvinist triumph owed most to the political muscle of the Contra-Remonstrants

[117] *Oude kerkordeningen*, p. 409. See also W.F. Dankbaar, 'De kerkvisitatie in de nederlandse gereformeerde kerken in de 16de en 17de eeuw', *NAK*, n.s. XXXVIII (1951), p. 42.

[118] OSA, 73, fo. 79.

[119] For the remonstrances to Maurice see RV, II, pp. 377–78; 412–13; OSA, 73, *passim*. After 1601 the synods of Holland adopted special procedures for the examination of ministers 'from the Sticht or from other not properly Reformed parts', RV, I, p. 293; III, p. 171. The synod of South Holland already considered in 1604 that the strongest opposition to a national synod came from the States of Utrecht, RV, III, p. 212.

[120] The division of the church in Utrecht into three *classes* was approved in the synod held in August 1619 in the wake of the Contra-Remonstrant triumph at Dordrecht, RV, VI, pp. 424–25.

in Holland, but this may be only another way of saying that the over-whelmingly Catholic establishment in Utrecht lacked the political will to defend its own version of the Reformation.

In the Utrecht countryside the absence of *classes* left the ministers in the villages more isolated than their colleagues at work in, for example, the South Holland islands, whose inhabitants had demonstrated no strong attachment to the new religion before 1572. The loneliness felt by the conscientious Calvinist *predikant* in Utrecht at this time appears in the extant letters of Hendrik ten Brink, who served as minister at Wilnis at the turn of the century. With only four communicants by 1606, ten Brink looked on enviously as Catholics trekked in their hundreds to visit the shrine of Our Lady at Kokkengen or went in droves to attend mass at Vinkeveen, an hour from Wilnis. Stung by the taunts of the 'papists' and frustrated by the dereliction of the law officers, ten Brink felt compelled to take matters into his own hands and decided to beard the Catholics in their assemblies at some risk to his person.[121] His only comfort, as he confided to Johannes Uytenbogaert, who then still retained the trust of the Calvinists in Utrecht, was the knowledge that he discharged an office laid on him by the Lord, for 'you know in what sort of place I am and how uncouth the people are here'.[122] In these hostile surroundings the fellowship of the *classis* was sorely missed. When a former minister from Kudelstaart sought a charge in the *classis* of Dordrecht in 1591, he pleaded destitution – his stipend was badly in arrears – but he added that since the States of Utrecht had forbidden classical assemblies, 'he found himself so alone in those parts'.[123] This fugitive from the backwoods of Utrecht was soon after called to Barendrecht, whose own small Calvinist congregation may not have inspired great hope. But at least when the minister later complained about the ruinous condition of his manse and about his poverty, faced difficult decisions about baptism, matrimonial affairs or recalcitrant members, or protested about the administration of poor relief in the village, he could reckon on the support of the brethren of the *classis*.[124] When the *schout* and magistrates of Barendrecht tried to exclude the minister from the auditing of the poor relief accounts, the *classis* resolved to summon the *schout*, the *kerkmeesters* and the parochial overseers of the poor and this was duly carried out by the *gedeputeerden* of the *classis*.[125] A minister confronted by similar problems in the Sticht could only turn to the States or, perhaps, the consistory at Utrecht, with little prospect of sympathy from the former or practical assistance from

---

[121] OSA, 73 contains three letters from ten Brink to Johannes Uytenbogaert as well as the first hand account by the minister of Waverveen of a Catholic sermon which he had attended at Abcoude at Candlemas 1601.

[122] OSA, 73, fo. 39.

[123] *CAD*, p. 343; RV, II, pp. 393–94.

[124] *CAD*, pp. 368, 373, 381, 442, 469, 474, 511.

[125] *CAD*, pp. 405, 408, 411.

the latter. In this difference lies one of the chief reasons for the relatively greater success of the Reformed churches in the villages of the *classis* of Dordrecht.

By any standards the decisions of the provincial States of Holland and Utrecht to proscribe the mass were momentous. In Holland the endowments originally intended for the upkeep of the Catholic clergy – the glebe lands (*pastoriegoederen*) – were inventoried and their revenues diverted to support the Reformed ministers and schoolmasters.[126] Amid the confusion of the war the administrative apparatus of the medieval church gradually fell apart: monastic communities broke up, ruridecanal chapters (*seendgerechten*) and visitations ceased and the ecclesiastical courts, whose competence extended to the laity in testamentary and matrimonial cases, no longer sat. In the province of Utrecht similarly radical changes occurred after 1580. The disintegration of the institutional and legal structures, which had sustained the jurisdiction of the medieval church and maintained its army of clergy, prelates, monastics and administrators, left an enormous gap.

Yet the Reformed church did not begin with a clean slate. In particular it had to accommodate itself to the survival of the *jus patronatus* and of the parish, both of which cramped its freedom of action. After the recognition of the Reformed church as the 'true Reformed religion', it followed – at least in principle – that only ministers of this church might be presented by patrons. Even so the synods only accepted the *jus patronatus* with bad grace. In 1619 the synod of South Holland reminded the States that patronage had no foundation in scripture: it was 'a leaven from the Roman church and detrimental to the calling of ministers'.[127] For all its misgivings, the synod had, however, to acquiesce in the continuation of patronage.[128]

Catholic patrons could not brazenly flout the new religious order. On the other hand they did not think themselves duty bound to advance the Calvinist interpretation of what Fynes Moryson, an English traveller in the northern Netherlands, called 'the Reformation of the Christian Religion'.[129] Without doubt some Catholic patrons used their rights to impede the smooth running of the Reformed church. Johan van Duvenvoirde, the lord of Warmond, was typical of those Catholic nobles in Holland who took the side of the Revolt. He treated the churches in his

---

[126] J.F. van Beeck Calkoen, *Onderzoek naar den rechtstoestand der geestelijke en kerkelijke goederen in Holland na de reformatie* (Amsterdam, 1910), pp. 43–44.

[127] RV, III, p. 330.

[128] RV, III, p. 414. Though the synod of South Holland argued strongly at Dordrecht that the *jus patronatus* was contrary to God's Word, the National Synod hesitated to adopt a proposal which might cause the provincial States to withhold their approval of the church order, Kuyper, *Post-acta of nahandelingen*, pp. 112–19.

[129] (J.N. Jacobsen Jensen), 'Moryson's reis door en zijn karakteristiek van de Nederlanden', *BMHG*, XXXIX (1918), p. 281.

gift around Leiden as if these were still *Eigenkirchen*. When the receiver of the *Geestelijk Kantoor* of Delft tried in 1579 to recover the income arising from the glebe at Warmond and Jacobswoude in order to pay the stipends of ministers there, his lordship was alleged to have retorted 'that he would maintain a minister [from the glebe] there, if he so pleased'.[130] To the chagrin of the synods, the ministers who found favour with such patrons were not invariably drawn from the ranks of the Calvinists. In 1583 the synod of South Holland grew impatient with those nobles who appointed ministers to churches 'of which they claim to be patrons and collators', without regard for the procedures laid down by the church for the calling and examination of *predikanten*.[131] Van Duvenvoirde had just infuriated the synod by giving his protection to a certain Andries Michielsz., a known 'enemy of the [Calvinist] discipline'. He had lived at odds with the synods ever since 1573, flitting from pulpit to pulpit until his suspension from the Reformed ministry in 1581.[132] Nor was Michiel's successor at Jacobswoude any more to the liking of the synod. Before his appointment by van Duvenvoirde, Petrus Wassius had been declared unfit for the Reformed ministry in Flanders. In 1591 the synod admonished Wassius roundly: he stood accused of non-attendance at the *classis* of Leiden, failure to administer the Lord's Supper for many years and neglect of the matrimonial ordinances. Some members of the synod predicted that Wassius '[not even being well-versed in doctrine] would not build a church at Woubrugge'.[133] Wassius however survived this censure for he remained there until his death in 1604. The upbuilding of the Reformed congregation at Woubrugge proceeded at a snail's pace: in 1620 the church there still lacked a consistory and a few years later the synod suspected that the then lord of Warmond was still hindering the formation of a Reformed diaconate.[134]

In Utrecht, too, the rights of the patrons remained virtually intact after the Reformation. When a vacancy occurred, the patron presented his *predicant* to the States; the ministers at Utrecht then examined him in the presence of deputies from the States, after which the candidate was inducted by the patron and the States.[135] As a result of the Reformation the States assumed the part of the bishop, in much the same way as the Lutheran princes of Germany took upon themselves certain episcopal duties. Given the conservative religious disposition of the political establish-

---

[130] A.G. van der Steur, 'Johan van Duvenvoirde en Woude (1547–1610), heer van Warmond, admiraal van Holland', *Warmondse bijdragen*, VIII (1975), pp. 47–48.

[131] RV, II, p. 227.

[132] *NNBW*, IX, col.25–26 *s.v.*, Andrieszoon (Michiel).

[133] RV, II, pp. 380–81, 389–90. In the sources Woubrugge was also called Jacobswoude.

[134] RV, III, p. 429; *Acta der particuliere synoden van Zuid-Holland, 1621–1700*, I, *1621–1633*, RGP, Kleine serie 3, ed. W.P.C. Knuttel (The Hague, 1908), pp. 251, 294.

[135] Rengers Hora Siccama, *Geestelijke en kerkelijke goederen*, p. 500.

ment in Utrecht, we might expect that here too the *jus patronatus* worked to the disadvantage of the Calvinists. The careers of the first five Protestant ministers called to Montfoort show how the exercise of patronage could frustrate the Calvinist cause. The ministers who served in this small viscounty on the IJssel between 1583 and 1600 were, without exception, ill-qualified to advance the Calvinist cause in that Catholic bastion. The first had proved a thoroughly unsatisfactory minister at Ridderkerk and Westmaas in the *classis* of Dordrecht before his appointment to a church on Voorne in the gift of the lord of Montfoort, who hastily imported him as a stop gap to forestall the imposition of someone less compliant.[136] The second minister had fallen foul of the Reformed church on account of his pelagian and perfectionist opinions; the third had previously been excommunicated by the Utrecht consistory 'for his evil life'; the fourth teetered on the brink of Catholicism and suffered banishment from Holland and Utrecht on that account in 1596 when he was declared 'unfit for any ministry'.[137] The last of this quintet, Gerardus Blockhoven, had been charged by his colleagues in Utrecht with the dissemination of spiritualist and perfectionist doctrines in his sermons, though in later life he became reconciled with the Reformed synods.[138] Between such dissident and discredited Protestant ministers and their crypto-Catholic patrons a sort of symbiotic relationship evolved. At odds with the Calvinist leadership of the Reformed church and therefore treated as pariahs by the *classes* and synods, such ministers found a welcome from conservative patrons who by appointing them cocked a snook at the ecclesiastical authorities and kept more zealous Calvinists out of the pulpits in their churches. In 1580 the largely Catholic ruling classes in Utrecht found themselves obliged, for political reasons, to consent to the maintenance of the Reformed Christian religion. They were, however, concerned to resist for a variety of reasons the specifically Calvinist interpretation of that 'Reformation' and they deployed the *jus patronatus* to that end.

The parish also survived the politico-religious upheavals as a distinctive legal entity.[139] The parish was an independent corporate body, which existed alongside and overlapped with other corporations such as the

---

[136] On Matthias Pietersz. Dickinus at Ridderkerk see KA Ridderkerk, I, pp. 1–2; at Westmaas *CAD*, pp. 95, 103, 106, 114–15.

[137] On the first ministers at Montfoort see C. Dekker, 'De hervorming in Montfoort', *Heemtijdingen*, XV (1979), pp. 27–28; on Billichius see also *NNBW*, I, col. 352–53.

[138] On Blockhoven see Bor, III, pp. 735–38 [bk. 30, fo. 47–50]. Blockhoven subsequently became a strong defender of the Presbyterian system and he placed his first-hand experience of the ecclesiastical situation in Utrecht at the disposal of the deputies of South Holland.

[139] This paragraph draws heavily on L.J.A. van Apeldoorn, 'Het voortbestaan der parochies na de reformatie', *Rechtsgeleerde magazijn*, XLVIII (1929), pp. 1–55; Rengers Hora Siccama, *Geestelijke en kerkelijke goederen*, pp. 206–63; A.Th. van Deursen, 'Kerk of parochie? De kerkmeesters en de dood ten tijde van de Republiek', *TG*, LXXXIX (1976), pp. 531–37.

'village' and the 'manor'. The responsibility for the upkeep of the fabric of the parish church, and therefore the administration of the endowments for that purpose, belonged to the parish, which appointed *kerkmeesters* to that end. In the same way, and for similar reasons, the parish appointed overseers of the poor. Before the Reformation the independent juridical character of the parish had been partially obscured because the parochial and religious communities coincided; the medieval priest had dispensed the eucharist to all his parishioners, with the exception of very young children. When the Roman church yielded to the Reformed church a new situation arose. The Calvinist *predikant* discharged most of the religious functions formerly undertaken by the priest in respect of the parochial community: he preached the Word to all who would listen and he stood ready to baptise and to marry without charge any parishioner who called upon his services. But wherever a Calvinist congregation had been set up, access to the Lord's Table was restricted to those parishioners, who had made their profession of faith and submitted to the discipline of the consistory.[140] Conversely the consistory had, as we have already noted, no authority over other parishioners, even though these might regularly attend the church services. The Calvinist reformation led therefore to the creation of the *gemeente* within the parish, which had no medieval precedent and was indeed without parallel in all those states whose inhabitants were bound to worship in the church by law established. Since these Calvinist congregations often comprised only a small fraction of all the parishioners, the distinct and separate character of the parish now became glaringly obvious, even if it were not well understood by non-Calvinists. At Aarlanderveen, a village in Rijnland, the Reformed congregation in 1602 consisted of only six men and seven women. Yet many of those who did not belong to the congregation had nevertheless expressed a desire to be admitted when the minister, Johannes Lydius, next administered Lord's Supper at Whitsun. Though poorly informed about the fundamentals of the Reformed religion, these parishioners told him that they believed in Christ crucified, renounced works and placed their trust in Christ alone. The minister found himself in a dilemma. If he accepted so simple a profession of faith, there was a risk of admitting to the Lord's Table persons with an insufficient grounding in the faith. Yet if he debarred such persons, he feared none of his parishioners, who could 'scarcely tell A from B' would ever wish to join the church. In that case his tiny congregation would remain the butt of the local Lutherans, of whom there were evidently a large number in the village.[141] In Friesland the brethren of the classis spoke of the *breede*

[140] This as we have seen did not apply in Utrecht, for which reason the Calvinists in Holland regarded the churches there as not properly reformed.
[141] Fr.W. Cuno, *Franciscus Junius der Ältere: Professor der Theologie und Pastor, 1545–1602* (Amsterdam, 1891), pp. 391–92. I owe this reference to the kindness of Professor Posthumus Meyjes.

gemeente, by which they understood the parish community, to distinguish it from the *gemeente Christi*, as they called the professed membership of the Reformed church.[142]

Since the parish community, the parish priest or the patron chose the *kerkmeesters* and the overseers of the poor, these in turn presented their accounts to representatives of the parish – exceptionally some sort of *parochieraet*, as at De Lier, or more usually the *schout* and the *gerechte*, as at Barendrecht. In neither case did the consistory exercise any authority. When some ministers in the *classis* of Dordrecht proposed in 1582 that the church should supervise the *kerkmeesters* in the villages, they were reminded that this office fell under the lay magistrate. Complaints about the conduct of *kerkmeesters* should therefore be addressed to the appropriate *baljuw*.[143] As no religious test was imposed on officeholders after the mass was proscribed, Catholics remained eligible for parochial offices in Holland. Indeed *kerkmeesters* were not required by law to be members of the Reformed church until 1654.[144] The ownership of church-buildings, manses and churchyards continued to be vested in the parish. The abolition of the mass made not a whit of difference to their juridical status. The legal historian Rengers Hora Siccama explained the matter succinctly when he stated that at the Reformation 'only the use of the churches was changed ... whoever had been the owner remained so'.[145]

The Calvinists in the villages therefore could not simply banish from the churches the painted statues and altars they so abominated. In theory, they needed the consent of the guardians of the church-buildings. Of course much destruction did occur in Holland in the early 1570s and again in Utrecht in the early 1580s, but such acts lacked any legitimacy. When some Calvinist youths broke some 'rotten wooden crosses' in a churchyard in North Holland in 1631, the law officer promptly charged them with 'sacrilege and affray'.[146]

This explains why even in some villages on the South Holland islands, where the *classis* had assiduously driven forward the rural reformation, a few churches still retained their altars in the 1590s. In an effort to have the offending altar panel removed from the church at Giessen-Nieuwkerk, whose lord was a strong Catholic, the *classis* appealed first to the *baljuw* and then to the States. Even then the altar was restored so that the *classis* had again to invoke the assistance of the States.[147] In Utrecht, of course, many more churches retained their 'papist trappings'. At least twenty-six of the fifty-six churches and chapels had not yet been purged when the commissioners visited in 1593. Nor did the Catholics cease to

---

[142] *Een kerk in opbouw*, ed. J.J. Kalma, pp. 198, 254.

[143] *CAD*, p. 112.

[144] Van Deursen, 'Kerk of parochie?', p. 532.

[145] Rengers Hora Siccama, *Geestelijke en kerkelijke goederen*, p. 371.

[146] Knipscheer, 'Abdias Widmarius', pp. 318–19.

[147] *CAD*, pp. 428, 462, 466, 469, 478, 530.

use the parish churches for devotional purposes. At Stolwijk near Gouda devout Catholic women used to kneel in prayer by the graves of their forebears and they persisted even after the minister rebuked them for their 'superstitious insolence' from the pulpit.[148] In the churchyards, where the *kerkmeesters* held undisputed sway, the signs and sounds of popular Catholicism were even more evident: 'the superstitious and impotent crosses', the pilgrimages to Kokkengen, the Corpus Christi procession around the church at Wilnis, the thrice-daily angelus and the tolling of the bell as the dead were buried. The general effect only underlined the precarious character of the Reformation and contributed to the new church's sense of insecurity.

Of course the Calvinists used their influence in order to ensure the selection of *kerkmeesters*, schoolmasters and overseers of the poor who, if not members of the local Reformed congregation, were not downright hostile. In some villages, for example at Ridderkerk, the Calvinists did bring about the 'reformation' of parochial poor relief. Eventually deacons approved by the Calvinist *gemeente*, replaced the overseers of the poor, in which capacity, however, they distributed relief to all those in need, irrespective of their religious allegiance, and accounted to representatives of the parish, who might include the minister.[149] Naturally the *classes* and synods showed a keen interest in the religious outlook of the schoolmasters for the church regarded the school as 'the first nursery and seminary of Christian godliness'.[150] In the view of the Calvinists 'a good Reformed schoolmaster' should instruct the youth in the Heidelberg catechism and accompany the children to the Sunday sermon. But as the church neither appointed nor paid the schoolmasters, the synods could do little more than express pious hopes and urge local congregations to exert what influence they could. When the schoolmaster at Giessen-Nieuwkerk was admonished by the *classis* of Dordrecht for refusing to bring the children to the church services, he retorted that he was only answerable to the *schout* and local magistrates, who had taken him into service.[151] There was little the *classis* could do except petition the States, upbraid unsatisfactory schoolmasters and seek to make good its claim to examine those appointed.[152]

The 'reformation of the parish', that is the substitution of Calvinists for Catholics in the administration of the parish, was a *travail de longue haleine*. As we have noticed the process in Holland was still far from complete by the mid-seventeenth century. Progress there was, but it was slow and unspectacular. It owed most to the persistent lobbying of the

[148] Van Deursen, *Bavianen en slijkgeuzen*, pp. 394–95.
[149] KA Ridderkerk, I, pp. 14, 15.
[150] RV, VI, p. 322. For the Reformed church's concern about schools see Tukker, *Classis Dordrecht*, pp. 87–99.
[151] *CAD*, p. 469.
[152] *CAD*, p. 526.

classis and its deputies and the outcome was not assured for a determined *ambachtsheer* could frustrate the efforts of the Reformed church.

The drastic nature of the changes demanded by the Calvinists may well have deterred the villagers from embracing the Reformation. To those familiar with the medieval mass the Reformed liturgy probably appeared strange and forbiddingly austere. Whereas Luther and Cranmer had deliberately retained the framework of the mass when they revised the liturgy, the Reformed broke ruthlessly with a form of worship they considered superstitious and idolatrous. Before the Reformation the liturgical year had led the faithful, almost without them being aware, through the cycle of Christ's life and introduced them to the chief doctrines of the Christian religion. The Reformed, however, abandoned the church year almost entirely, making concessions to tradition only for Christmas and the major festivals which fell on a Sunday.[153] In place of the homily based on the epistle or gospel of the day, the Reformed synods insisted on systematic preaching, as Christian humanists had recommended, preferably from the New Testament.[154] At Ridderkerk the minister did the bidding of the synods. In June 1584 the consistory decided that the minister should take Luke for the Sunday morning service and Haggai for the weekday service. Haggai, with its twenty-three verses, provided matter for about five months and the gospel, sermon material for almost five years.[154a] Though a Calvin might have held the rapt attention of his hearers with such expository sermons, we may wonder whether the sermons of the ubiquitous *duytsche klerken*,[155] who occupied most pulpits in the villages, held their restless congregations enthralled. Of course demands varied. At Mijnsheerenland the consistory complained that their minister's sermons were 'feeble and uninstructive': they felt that they left the church without having had any teaching, nourishment or comfort. Others, however, spoke more approvingly, although when questioned on the previous day's sermon, they could not recall anything 'to prove the edifying character of his preaching'. The village magistrates thought he taught well enough, but then they were not members of the Reformed congregation.[156]

Our doubts about the suitability of much preaching in the villages find support from a proposal to the national synod of Middelburg in 1581 from representatives of the synods of Overijssel and Friesland, where the spiritual needs of the rural population perhaps received greater recognition. They requested that the church permit sermons based on the 'Sunday gospels', in other words an exposition of the gospel appointed

---

[153] *WMV*, ser. II, deel iii, pp. 142, 252–53, 394, 501.

[154] *Ibid.*, p. 143.

[154a] KA Ridderkerk, I, pp. 5, 7, 19.

[155] On these 'Dutch clerks', so called because they had no formal education in Latin, see van Deursen, *Bavianen en slijkgeuzen*, pp. 34–36.

[156] *CAD*, pp. 263–65.

for the day.[157] Though the national synod then demurred, a few years later churches, especially in the countryside, were given the latitude to preach in this way, if it seemed appropriate.[158] In Utrecht, where there was a greater concern 'for those of tender conscience', ministers were required by the church order of 1590 to preach their Sunday sermons on the epistles and gospels and this concession to the 'simple country folk' reappeared in the revised order of 1612.[159]

Calvinism is commonly associated with the congregational singing of psalms. Yet, whatever the popularity of metrical psalms elsewhere, they did not at once win a place in the affections of rural congregations in the northern Netherlands. Part of the explanation may lie in the extreme difficulty untutored congregations found in singing the psalms. In 1587 the consistory at Ridderkerk decided to abandon the attempt 'because most of those who come to church are simple people, who cannot manage the psalms'.[160] Fifty or so years later Constantine Huygens, who campaigned vigorously for the use of organs to accompany congregations as they sang the psalms, left a vivid description of the cacophony produced when they sang without the benefit of musical accompaniment: 'the tones grate together like birds with different beaks, the measures contending with each other like well pails, the one falling as the other is rising'.[161] In the eastern Netherlands the Flemish character of Dathenus' translation may have alienated those who spoke the Low Saxon dialects. The national synod of 1581 therefore reluctantly allowed the church at Deventer to choose a dozen or so of the 'simplest' psalms and to have these printed with a few hymns in the 'Oostersche' dialect.[162] In Utrecht too there was some resistance to the metrical psalms, which had not been introduced everywhere by 1606. Indeed the village schoolmasters at Soest and Baarn had been threatened with dismissal if ever they acted as precentors.[163]

As part of their campaign to implant in the villages the *puriorem ecclesiam*, the Reformed synods waged incessant war against what they called 'papist superstition'. This conveniently elastic term of opprobrium applied to all aspects of Catholic worship, to the churchyard crosses, altars, statues and shrines, to the ceremonies which accompanied the traditional *rites de passage* and, especially, to 'the abominable mass'. Catholics who sprinkled holy water, knelt before the family grave, placed lighted candles in the churches, took part in Corpus Christi processions

[157] *WMV*, ser. II, deel iii, pp. 421, 407.
[158] *Ibid.*, pp. 551, 508.
[159] *Oude kerkordeningen*, pp. 298, 401.
[160] KA Ridderkerk, I, p. 14.
[161] Van Deursen, *Bavianen en slijkgeuzen*, p. 174.
[162] *WMV*, ser. II, deel iii, pp. 421, 372, 444.
[163] RV, VI, pp. 310, 311.
[164] K.V. Thomas, *Religion and the Decline of Magic* (London, 1971), ch. 2.

or went on pilgrimages were all condemned for participation in superstitious practices. The Calvinist offensive extended to the entire range of
what Keith Thomas has described as 'the magic of the medieval church',[164]
the protective amulets worn against epilepsy,[165] the wax charms or talismans, weapon salves and the paraliturgical ceremonies devised to reassure
women facing child-birth.[166] More generally the Reformed church dis-
approved of exorcism and denounced divination. Though the theologians distinguished between 'heathen fortune-telling' and 'papist
abuses', the Calvinists tended to confound superstition, idolatry, necro-
mancy, magic and witchcraft and associate these with 'popery'. The
reason is not far to seek. If the religious dissidents had sought to prove
that the clergy had deceived the laity with their wonder-working relics
and images, they also sometimes invested these artefacts with a demonic
power. They regarded the miracle of transubstantiation ambivalently: on
the one hand, as a piece of hocus-pocus, on the other as a form of
witchcraft. 'Superstition' and 'magic' were not, of course, the preserve of
the countryside, but whereas in the relative anonymity of the towns the
clash between the transcendent God of the Calvinists and the immanent
theology articulated in the Catholic church could to some extent be
avoided, the confrontation was more obvious in the villages. This may
explain why the problem of 'superstition' and 'magic' looms larger in
the records of the Reformed church concerned with the countryside.

As a rule the Reformed synods were reluctant to make concessions to
accommodate tender consciences. Infant baptism is a case in point. The
new ministers were certainly prepared to baptise any children brought to
them, but they insisted that baptism should only be administered during
the ordinary church services. Many of their parishioners, however, still
clung to the view that children who died without the benefit of the
sacrament would be consigned to limbo. The refusal of the Reformed
church to countenance private baptisms seemed incomprehensible and
insensitive. In the dozen or so villages in the vicinity of Oudewater,
there were no week-day services during the winter months: the inhabitants
had either to attend the one midweek service held in the town in the
evening or go without. The rural inhabitants therefore demanded that
the ministers administer baptisms outside the services, but this was
rejected. The parents reacted by calling down God's judgment on the
new ministers 'if their children should come to die without baptism' and
threatened to have their children baptised by the priest in nearby Montfoort. When the church at Oudewater consulted the synod, it was told
that though the ministers might preach more frequently – and therefore
provide proper opportunities for baptisms – they might on no account
administer baptisms privately.[167]

[165] RV, III, p. 173.
[166] RV, II, p. 93; VI, p. 306.
[167] RV, III, p. 271.

The medieval church had provided a host of rites and paraliturgical ceremonies which brought comfort and assurance to those in mortal danger or to those who had suffered some calamity. The Reformed church opposed such 'superstitious' practices and exhorted the ministers to teach their congregations to forsake such 'forbidden remedies' as exorcism and divination. Instead the people should seek their help from the Lord.[168] In 1601 the synod of South Holland commissioned the theologian Hendrik Boxhorn to compose a small treatise to warn 'the simple people' to avoid 'magical and superstitious cures' such as wearing amulets against fever or exorcism in the case of epilepsy.[169] The efficacy of such endeavours was probably limited: even members of the Reformed congregations were wont to consult exorcists, when their animals suffered from the staggers.[170] Although in the case of weapon salves the synod stated that the practice was contrary to 'natural medicine', it was the scriptural condemnation of magical remedies, which carried most weight. The Reformed believed no less strongly than the Catholics in the power of the Devil. Indeed when Catholics pointed to the miraculous cures at shrines as proof of the truth of their faith, the heretics replied that the Devil too could work marvels. As the Reformed were neither willing nor able to banish the Devil from the world, it was an act of great presumption on the part of the Reformed synods to ask parishioners, beset by all manner of ills, to abandon the 'superstitious' remedies and 'magical' antidotes which had brought comfort and consolation to previous generations. In advance of a scientific explanation for meteorological change and of effective remedies for disease, it required great faith to forsake such well-tried palliatives and protective measures. We should perhaps be not too surprised if only a few possessed that confidence.

In the wake of the Revolt against the political and religious policies of the Habsburg government some sort of reformation of the church was probably unavoidable. After the reconciliation of the Walloon provinces and Rennenberg's 'treason' in 1580, the pressure became irresistible. 'Reform' and 'reformation' were not however the exclusive property of the Calvinists. The political elites in the rebel provinces were no less concerned. The burning question was what sort of 'reformation'? Grotius, with his personal preference for an undogmatic and Erastian Protestantism, asserted that the civil magistrates understood by the term 'reformation' the introduction of a 'religion purged of all gross abuses, but not too narrowly defined in respect of opinions concerning controversial points'. For that reason, he claimed, they spoke of 'the Christian or evangelical Religion'.[171] To zealous Calvinists such reformation seemed

---

[168] RV, II, p. 346.
[169] RV, III, p. 173; see also pp. 206, 231.
[170] Janssen, *Kerkhervorming in Vlaanderen*, II, p. 170.
[171] Brandt, I, pp. 551–52.

insipid: it bore an 'unseemly and libertine appearance'.[172] To the Calvinists the *vera Reformatio* required 'the reformation of the priests', 'the reformation of the schools', 'the reformation of the officers' and the *reformatio veterum abusuum*, a catch-all which included everything from sabbath-breaking, papist superstitions, to ministers' stipends and sumptuary laws.[173] To accomplish such a 'root-and-branch' reformation the synods held consistorial discipline and a Presbyterian church order to be indispensable.

Yet the Presbyterian church order elaborated at Emden lacked any sort of standing with the States of Holland. Even among the ministers it did not command universal assent. Gradually, however, consistories and *classes* came to be accepted as part and parcel of the Reformed eccles-iastical organisation in Holland, although some lordships withstood the pressure for a time. In Utrecht the outcome was longer in doubt. The political establishment there prized its independence in ecclesiastical matters. The small band of indigenous Calvinists, bereft of the *classes*, could not exert the persistent pressure exerted by the *classes* and synods of Holland. The States of Utrecht did indeed introduce a church order of their own devising, which, if successful, would have created the framework for a comprehensive territorial Protestant church firmly under their control. The States succumbed, however, to the combined pressures applied by the synods of Holland, Maurice of Nassau and the States of Holland. Whatever the doctrine of provincial sovereignty, the exercise of that sovereignty by any province other than Holland was, in practice, limited. The threat to the political stability and unity of the United Provinces posed by a distinctively different church order in Utrecht was too grave to pass unchallenged. One may also doubt whether the political elites in Utrecht, still largely Catholic, had the strength of purpose to impose a Protestant religious settlement to which many did not, in their hearts, subscribe. Eventually the constellation of outside forces wore down the resistance of the States, who conceded a Presbyterian church polity after the national synod of Dordrecht.

Even if Presbyterianism had prevailed more easily in Holland, the Reformed synods could still not count on the unstinted support of the patrons, petty magistrates and officers on whose cooperation the successful introduction of the Reformation in the countryside depended. Where the Calvinists did enjoy such support much could be achieved in a remarkably short space of time. In this respect the comparison with the Calvinist Republic of Ghent is instructive. After 1578 the Reformed church there received the backing of the magistrates because it appeared to furnish an instrument whereby that city's political control could be extended to the rest of Flanders. The 'Calvinisation' of the local magis-tracies and officers, combined with the systematic destruction of the

<hr>

[172] *WMV*, ser. III, deel iv, p. 43.

[173] Kuyper, *Post-acta of nahandelingen*, p. 426.

institutions of the Catholic church in Flanders was impressively rapid. Within a few months of field services beginning around Ghent in the summer of 1578 some fifty ministers were at work in the county which had a network of *classes* by 1579.[174] No such political imperative persuaded the States of Holland to embark on a campaign of 'protestantisation' and the Reformed church received less wholehearted support from the civil powers than the synods felt entitled to expect.

The uncompromising character of the Calvinist Reformation polarised religious attitudes. The synods wanted to foster 'true godliness' and to that end they would have no truck with the old religious forms or with 'the vanity and dissoluteness of this world'.[175] Society, in the view of the respected Reformed minister, Hendrik van de Corput, could be divided between those under 'the yoke of Christ' and those under 'the yoke of the Devil'.[176] It was the stern duty of the church to expose, not to gloss over, this fundamental difference.

The Calvinist church was then relatively indifferent to worldly success. Yet we should remember that the influence of the ministers was not limited to the quite small membership of the *gemeente*. The returns of attendance at services in the villages of Utrecht in 1606 show that many more inhabitants came to the church on Sunday than took communion.[177] Nor were ministers simply imposed on the villages. In 1590 the *classis* of Dordrecht received a request from St. Anthonypolder for its own minister. Previously the village had been served in combination with another. But it happened that on occasion the sick could not be visited; besides they wanted a minister to act as a schoolmaster to teach the youth. This request came from 'the entire village' (*den gantschen dorpe*)[178] not just the Reformed *gemeente*. Perhaps the villagers wanted a schoolmaster on the cheap, but it seems as if the inhabitants had come to regard the minister as someone whom a self-respecting community could not do without. Nor was this the only such request. In 1599 the *schout* of Hendrik-Ido-Ambacht drew the attention of the *classis* to the dissatisfaction of the inhabitants 'because the minister did not reside with them'.[179] In Gelderland the *classis* of the Neder-Veluwe heard in 1601 how the parishioners complained that without the services of a resident

[174] J. Decavele, 'Genève van Vlaanderen', *Het eind van een rebelse droom*, ed. J. Decavele *et al.* (Ghent, 1984), pp. 32–62.

[175] Kuyper, *op. cit.*, p. 269.

[176] *WMV*, ser. III, deel ii, p. 267.

[177] RV, VI, pp. 299–312. For example 100–150 attended at Amerongen and about 200 attended at Eemnes, though communion was not administered at either; at Veenendaal eighty to a hundred came to the services, and forty-three to the communion; at Wilnis thirty to forty came to the services, but only four took communion. Caution is of course necessary, for the Reformation in late sixteenth-century Utrecht cannot be characterised as Calvinist.

[178] *CAD*, pp. 292–93; 303.

[179] *CAD*, p. 528.

minister, they would die 'like cattle'.[180] It is difficult to know whether such demands should be accounted a mark of the 'success' of the Reformed church: but it does suggest that in the villages the minister had, to an extent, taken the place of the priest.

Appendix I

Chronology of the Reformation of the Church
in the Province of Utrecht, 1577–1620

9 October	1577	*Satisfactie:* monopoly of Roman church upheld; anti-heresy legislation suspended.
June	1578	Duifhuis leaves post as parish priest of Jacobikerk in Utrecht.
12 July		*Religievrede* published by States General.
7 August		Duifhuis invited back to Utrecht as minister of Jacobikerk.
August		'Consistorial' party takes possession of Franciscan church in Utrecht.
16 January	1579	*Religievrede* proclaimed at Utrecht: Protestants allocated two churches.
23 January		Union of Utrecht.
March		'Consistorial' congregation holds Lord's Supper.
June		Sporadic iconoclasm at Utrecht and Amersfoort.
15 June		*Religievrede* revised in favour of Protestants.
7 March	1580	Rennenberg's 'treason' (3 March) known in Utrecht; provoked sporadic iconoclasm in the town.
18 March		Mass suspended at Amersfoort.
18 June		Mass suspended in the town of Utrecht.
28 June		Mass suspended throughout Province; ordinance concerning ecclesiastical property issued by States.
3 April	1581	Death of Duifhuis.
29 July		Instructions for commissioners appointed by States to supervise monastic property.
2 August	1582	Magistrates of Utrecht refuse to impose Calvinist discipline on Jacobikerk.
26 April	1586	Forced union of Jacobikerk with Calvinists.
June		Church of Utrecht represented at National Synod of The Hague.
September		Church Order of The Hague accepted by States of Utrecht but not enforced.

[180] *Acta van de Classis Neder-Veluwe*, p. 78.

14 September	1588	Aristocratic (anti-Calvinist) party recovers control in Utrecht.
21 November	1589	Utrecht magistrates decide to remove four Calvinist ministers.
17 December		Ministers ejected.
6 February	1590	States of Utrecht approve new church order.
6 March		Maurice accepts *stadhouderschap* of Utrecht.
4 May		Utrecht magistrates empowered to nominate Consistory.
August		States of Utrecht prohibit 'any *classis* or other '[ecclesiastical] assembly'; Synod of South Holland petition *stadhouder* (Maurice) and the States of Holland about ecclesiastical affairs in Utrecht.
October	1591	Church at Utrecht asks again for help from the synod of South Holland.
26 September	1592	Ministers at Utrecht petition States to reform rural churches.
13 March	1593	Ministers petition States again to reform rural churches.
3 July		States appoint commissioners to make a visitation of rural churches.
31 October		Commission submits its report to States.
16 January	1600	Ministers at Utrecht petition States for uniform church order.
August	1601	Synod of South Holland decides to 'try' ministers who came from parts 'not properly reformed', especially Utrecht.
September		Synod of South Holland prepares petition on ecclesiastical situation in Utrecht for *stadhouder*.
July	1606	First Synod of Utrecht churches called by States to propose remedies for 'irregularities'.
27 August	1612	Second Synod called by States about church order.
28 August		Church order published by States.
29 July	1618	States of Utrecht agree to National Synod.
October		Remonstrant and Contra-Remonstrant synods meet separately to prepare for this Synod.
November	1618	National Synod of Dordrecht; concluded May 1619.
6 August	1619	Committee of States recommend qualified acceptance of Dordrecht Church Order.
10 August		Fourth Synod of Utrecht churches; introduction of *classes*.

11

The Ambivalent Face of Calvinism in
the Netherlands, 1561–1618

'Seeing it has pleased the Lord God to set apart from the whole human race
and to gather together ... a people and a church through the preaching of
the Word of God ... He will grant to that church quite undeservedly (as the
beloved bride of His son Jesus Christ, not having spot or wrinkle) eternal
salvation and blessed everlasting life'. From the preamble to the 'Acta van
de classis Zuid-Beveland, 1579–1581', ed. J.P. van Dooren, *De nationale synode
te Middelburg in 1581: Calvinisme in opbouw in de noordelijke en zuidelijke
Nederlanden* (Middelburg, 1981), p. 218.

'But in my opinion ... the evangelical net should be cast as far and as widely
as possible in order that many people may be gathered to the Lord'. From a
speech delivered by Cornelis Pietersz. Hooft on 16 August 1617. *Memoriën en
adviezen van Cornelis Pietersz. Hooft* (Utrecht, 1871), p. 202.

When the States of Holland finally outlawed the mass in March 1581,
shortly before the States General declared that Philip II had forfeited his
sovereignty over the United Netherlands, only a small fraction of that
province professed the Reformed faith. In 1587 the provincial States,
incensed by the pulpit tirades directed against the magistrates, pointedly
reminded some leading ministers that fewer than one in ten Hollanders
belonged to the Reformed church.[1] Though support for the new religion
grew, the French ambassador to the United Provinces reported in 1600
that Roman Catholics still formed the majority of the population,[2] and
less than two years before the national synod of Dordrecht, Oldenbarnevelt, the Advocate of Holland, informed Dudley Carleton, the
English diplomat, that the Protestants made up only one-third of the
population: 'la plus saine et plus riche partie' had remained loyal to the
Catholic church.[3]

Recent local studies have confirmed the accuracy of these contemporary
estimates, although the religious complexion varied greatly between one
town and another. By comparing the sporadic information about the

---

[1] Bor, II, pp. 975–76 [bk.22, fo.88].

[2] J. Briels, *De nederlandse emigratie, 1572–1630* (Haarlem, 1978), p. 98, fn. 13.

[3] J. den Tex, *Oldenbarnevelt*, 2 vols. (Cambridge, 1973), II, p. 574.

adult membership of some Reformed congregations in the early seventeenth century with the census of 1622 we can discover the relative strength of the Calvinist community in a few towns. At Den Briel, a small fishing-port at the mouth of the Maas, about one-fifth of the entire population belonged to the Reformed church at this time, while at Enkhuizen, then at the peak of its prosperity with almost 21,000 inhabitants, the Reformed church had a membership of 3,000.[4] At Alkmaar, however, the Calvinists accounted for a meagre five per cent of the 12,000 townspeople.[5] Despite the continued expansion of the towns in the province of Holland, in 1622 almost half the population still lived in the countryside. Here the disparities between the Calvinist communities were even more striking. In a handful of villages the Reformed church drew considerable support, while in many others only three or four came to the Lord's Supper, the focal point of Reformed worship. For a dozen villages, with a total population of over 12,000 in 1622, the number of Reformed members is known from casual entries made between 1590 and 1620. Taking the figure closest to 1622, we find a total of 700 Calvinists, or almost six per cent of the entire population.[6]

Outside Holland and Zeeland support for the Reformed church grew even more slowly. Catholic services ceased, at least officially, in June 1580 in the adjoining province of Utrecht, yet returns from the rural parishes in 1606 show that the Reformed churches had made little headway. In that year forty-one ministers from the countryside reported to the provincial synod on the state of religion in their parishes. In only five villages had the new religion secured a measure of popular support, and in only half the parishes had the Lord's Supper been held, often attended by fewer than a dozen communicants.[7] Calvinist *predikanten* strove to convince their bemused parishioners of the superior virtues of metrical psalm-singing, the Heidelberg catechism, and public baptisms.

---

[4] A.Th. van Deursen, *Bavianen en slijkgeuzen: Kerk en kerkvolk ten tijde van Maurits en Oldenbarnevelt* (Assen, 1974), p. 133. As these figures only relate to adult members, we may assume that, if allowance were made for the children of Reformed parents, the proportion of Calvinists in the local population would be substantially higher.

[5] H.E. van Gelder, 'Hervorming en hervormden te Alkmaar', *Alkmaarse opstellen* (Alkmaar, 1960), p. 67. First published in *Oud-Holland*, XL (1922). This figure omits the Remonstrants who formed a separate congregation.

[6] Derived from data in van Deursen, *Bavianen*, p. 132.

[7] For the religious condition in the countryside of Utrecht see 'Visitatie der kerken ten platten lande in het sticht van Utrecht ten jare 1693', *BMHG*, VII (1884), pp. 186–267; J.P. van Dooren, 'Kerkelijke toestanden in de provincie Utrecht omstreeks 1600', *NAK*, n.s. XLIX (1969), pp. 183–93; RV, VI (Groningen, 1897), pp. 294–328. Even in East Friesland, whose count had not opposed Protestantism, the Reformed church reported in 1576 that in many villages the Lord's Supper was never or only rarely held, and then with as few as four or five communicants, *Die evangelischen Kirchenordnungen des XVI. Jahrhunderts*, VII, *Niedersachsen*, ed. E. Sehling (Tübingen, 1963), p. 437.

But these continued to display a wayward affection for pilgrimages, crucifixes, and votive offerings. To keep the Devil at bay during thunderstorms they still resorted to the 'superstitious' ringing of the church bells. If it was difficult to build Jerusalem in Amsterdam, it was still more difficult to win the inhabitants in the remoter parts of northern Brabant to 'the pure doctrine'. Here the ministers, often from Holland, appeared to the overwhelmingly Catholic villagers as carpetbaggers, their earliest congregations composed of deserters and opportunists.[8] Sometimes the task exhausted the patience of the most diligent minister. In 1588 Ds. Johannes Hartmanni left his charge at Heusden, a fortified town on the Maas, because he had become so discouraged by the godless conduct of its inhabitants and their 'great contempt for the Word of God'. Hartman moved to a village in south Holland, but though it is not known how he fared there, the correspondence of a *predikant* in the neighbourhood, with its litany of complaints about the disregard for the sabbath and fast-days and the insolence of the papists, suggests that he would find himself once more casting his pearls before swine.[9]

Scholars of the Reformation in Germany and England have recently discovered that even with the backing of the prince the inhabitants in these countries accepted Protestantism slowly, and then only partially. But as long ago as 1930 the late Pieter Geyl alerted Dutch historians to the 'slow reformation', when he drew attention to the tardy reception of Calvinism in rural Utrecht and the lack of enthusiasm for the Sea Beggars in the towns of Holland in 1572.[10] At one stroke Geyl disposed of the myth that the Dutch had embraced Calvinism spontaneously: insofar as they adopted the Reformed religion, they did so under duress; in other words, they had been 'Protestantised'. L.J. Rogier (1894–1974), the foremost historian of Dutch Catholicism, demonstrated the resilience of the old church by combining the evidence from the Reformed synods with the returns made by missionary priests.[11] The population in large parts of the Republic, especially in the eastern Netherlands and in the 'conquered' lands of the Generality in the south, and also in parts of Holland itself, remained loyal to the Catholic church throughout the period of the Calvinist ascendancy. The first ministers in most villages

[8] The exceptionally well-documented historical novel by A. Roothaert, *Die verkeerde weereldt* (Utrecht, n.d.) gives an evocative account of the religious tensions in the Peelland of north Brabant.

[9] G. Hamoen, *Het begin van de reformatie in de ring Heusden* (Heusden, 1980), p. 16; L. Knappert, 'Stukken uit den stichtingstijd der Nederlandsche Hervormde Kerk', *NAK*, n.s. VII (1910), pp. 246–61.

[10] P. Geyl, 'De protestantisering van Noord-Nederland', *Leiding*, I (1930), pp. 111–23; the substance of this article appears in his *History of the Low Countries: Episodes and Problems* (London, 1964), pp. 32–42.

[11] L.J. Rogier, *Geschiedenis van het katholicisme in Noord-Nederland in de zestiende en zeventiende eeuw*, 3 vols. (Amsterdam, 1947).

resembled, in Rogier's vivid phrase, 'generals without an army'.[12] By establishing the continuity of the Catholic tradition, Rogier subtly shifted the emphasis of the debate on the Reformation. The successes achieved by the Calvinists were attributed to the intervention of a particular set of circumstances. Only where the misconduct of the late medieval clergy had brought the church into local disrepute, where the civil authorities staunchly supported the new religion after 1572, or where the Catholic cure of souls had been interrupted as a result of the fighting for a prolonged period did the course of 'Protestantisation' run smoothly.[13]

Rogier's history of Dutch Catholicism in the early modern period first appeared almost forty years ago, but the discussion he provoked continues, though less stridently. In two respects our understanding of the Reformation in the Low Countries has changed significantly. Historians no longer write about the Reformation there as though it were a three-stage rocket, with distinct Lutheran, Anabaptist, and Calvinist phases. The pluriform character of both Catholicism and Reformed Protestantism is better understood, while the importance of the middle groups, the *politiques*, the *neutrales* as they were sometimes known, is generally recognised.[14] Secondly, the support given to the Reformed by the provincial States and the magistracies appears to have been rather less wholehearted than Rogier supposed. Insofar as these had a coherent religious policy, it stemmed from their fear of Spain (and therefore their concern not to drive Dutch Catholics into association with the enemy), their wish to maintain harmony in the local community, and their understanding of the demands of commerce. The Catholic religion was considered politically dangerous, whereas to the Reformed synods 'popery' was idolatrous, to be abolished lock, stock, and barrel. In practice the impact of the ostensibly repressive and numerous anticatholic edicts and ordinances was blunted by the connivance of those in authority. These were less concerned to further the Calvinisation of Dutch society, than to render Dutch Catholicism politically docile.[15] But neither of these revisions has invalidated Rogier's conclusion that in the northern Netherlands, at least, the Calvinist churches originally lacked popular support.

No student of the Dutch Reformation would dissent from this conclusion: the evidence for the small size and slow growth of the early Reformed congregations is unassailable. There is less agreement about the reasons for the sluggish response to Calvinism. For many historians the failures of the Reformed church stem from the continuing vitality of

[12] *Ibid.*, I, p. 442.

[13] *Ibid.*, I, p. 444.

[14] The importance of the middle groups is well-illustrated by J.J. Woltjer, 'De vrede-makers', *TG*, LXXXIX (1976), pp. 299–321.

[15] O.J. de Jong, 'Is Nederland geprotestantiseerd?' *Rondom het Woord*, IX (1967), pp. 65–7.

the traditional forms of piety. In this respect the evidence from the rural parts speaks eloquently. Then, too, we should not forget that the fluctuating fortunes of the rebel provinces in their war with Spain may well have deterred many from entering into membership of the Reformed church. As late as 1629 Habsburg forces under Ernest Montecuccoli invaded the heart of the Republic: Catholic worship was restored at Amersfoort and Holland itself threatened.

An important, and rather neglected, obstacle to the rapid growth of the Reformed churches in the northern Netherlands was self-imposed, for the Dutch Calvinists insisted that access to communion should be restricted to those who had placed themselves under the 'discipline of Christ'. In this way they drew a distinction between 'those of the church' and the 'children of the world'.[16] The patriotism of the diehard Calvinist was tempered by his conviction that the cause of the Gospel should take precedence over 'the restoration of the Netherlands'. As Gaspar van der Heyden, who had been the first Reformed minister at Antwerp, put it in a letter to a colleague in 1573, 'what profits us the possession of many towns and walled places, if Jerusalem be not built there, for that is more pleasing to the Lord than all Jacob's dwellings'.[17]

By then the Reformation in the Low Countries had been in ferment for fifty years. The protracted gestation of Dutch Protestantism affected the subsequent development of the Reformed churches in ways that were still apparent in the early seventeenth century. To begin with, the evangelicals in the Low Countries drew their inspiration from Germany. Without question the *auctor intellectualis* here, as elsewhere, was Luther.[18] In the 1520s evangelicals in the Netherlands had no quarrel with Luther, the Wittenberger, whose eucharistic theology was still evolving.[19] Support for the new doctrines came above all from the *mediocriter litterati* – the clerics, schoolmasters, printers, and skilled craftsmen. Such men flocked to Wittenberg to hear Luther, while at home they found spiritual comfort from reading his works, as well as others by lesser-known German Evangelicals, including Urbanus Rhegius, Otto Brunfels, and Caspar Huberinus. But Charles V's hostility to the new ideas led to the

[16] From the chronicle of the Groninger Calvinist Abel Eppens, cited by W. Bergsma, 'Zestiende-eeuwse godsdienstig pluriformiteit: Overwegingen naar aanleiding van Abel Eppens', *Historisch bewogen. Opstellen over de radicale reformatie ... aangeboden aan Prof. Dr. A.F. Mellink* (Groningen, 1984), p. 9.

[17] M.F. van Lennep, *Gaspar van der Heyden, 1530–1586* (Amsterdam, 1884), p. 208.

[18] C.Ch.G. Visser, *Luther's geschriften in de Nederlanden tot 1546* (Assen, 1969). Andrew Johnston has shown that this debt to Luther was even greater than has been supposed, see 'The Eclectic Reformation: Vernacular Evangelical Pamphlet Literature in the Dutch-speaking Low Countries, 1520–1565' (unpub. Ph. D. Southampton, 1987).

[19] Explicit denials of the Real Presence amoung evangelicals in the Low Countries do not occur before 1525, see J. Trapman, 'Le rôle des "sacramentaires" des origines de la réforme jusqu'en 1530 aux Pays-Bas', *NAK*, LXIII (1983), pp. 1–24.

savage repression of their proponents in the Netherlands. As a result the evangelical movements in Germany and the Low Countries began to draw apart in the 1530s and 1540s.

After the Peasants' War, which had gravely compromised the Reformation, the evangelical theologians and jurists in Germany drew up church orders, catechisms, and liturgies in order to ensure a measure of doctrinal stability and institutional permanence. In this way Luther's religious revolution was secured against the Romanists, but equally against the blandishments of the *Schwärmer* and the *Sakramentslästerer*, as the Anabaptists and the Zwinglians were known. Eucharistic theology among German evangelicals came to be defined by the standard of the *Confessio Augustana* and this, in turn, ensured adherence to Luther's emphasis on the real presence. In this process the Schmalkaldic League, which the evangelical estates set up in 1531 in self-defence against the Emperor, played some part. Subscription to the Augsburg Confession was not required by the members, but the League's domination by the Lutheran princes and the dependence of the south German cities, which had previously been influenced by Zwingli, on their protection made it difficult for them to maintain their distinctive theology. The religious peace of Augsburg (1555) sealed the Lutheran triumph in Germany by denying recognition to Reformed Protestantism. In the Habsburg Netherlands, where the religious agreements reached in Germany had no legal validity, Lutheranism had no such entrée. This may explain why, despite Luther's immense influence, his eucharistic theology seems to have aroused little or no interest amongst Dutch evangelicals.[20]

Moreover, as Lutheranism edged towards respectability in the Empire, orthodox Lutherans found it hard to minister to the 'good Christians' living 'under the cross' in the Low Countries. As early as 1531 Luther had apparently warned evangelicals at Antwerp not to meet in secret assemblies.[21] The estrangement between Protestants in Germany and the Low Countries only became obvious in the early 1550s, with the outbreak of the second sacramentarian controversy. The rift came to light when the Lutherans of north Germany pointedly refused hospitality during the winter of 1553–54 to a company of Reformed Protestants from the Netherlands, who had been in exile at London until the accession of Mary Tudor caused them to leave. Between the colloquy of Marburg in 1529 and the religious peace of Augsburg the Reformation in the Low Countries slipped out of the Lutheran orbit. When the sacramentarian controversy broke out again the Dutch evangelicals found themselves in opposition to leading Lutheran spokesmen such as Westphal. When in

---

[20] J.W. Pont, *Geschiedenis van het lutheranisme in de Nederlanden tot 1618* (Haarlem, 1911), p. 41.

[21] *Ibid*, pp. 38, 42–43, 330. For the letter from an Antwerp evangelical, dated 12 September 1531, to Luther on the legitimacy of conventicles see M. Luther, *Werke. Kritische Gesamtausgabe: Briefwechsel*, VI (Weimar, 1935), pp. 189–91.

1566 the Lutherans did organise a church at Antwerp, they brought in German theologians, who provided the congregation with a church order and liturgy based on German models. In the Low Countries confessional Lutheranism consequently appeared to be an exotic growth.

Evangelicals who abhorred the Roman church as the abode of Antichrist were bound, for salvation's sake, to withdraw from this 'congregation of evil-doers'. By 1531 the previously informal conventicles had begun among the Anabaptists at Amsterdam to acquire the features of a gathered church. As well as reading the Scripture, they commemorated the Lord's Supper, and deacons dispensed alms.[22] Those admitted to baptism first promised not to go to mass, or to indulge in drinking or gossiping. By baptism they bid farewell to the world, including the Roman church, and entered the covenant; they therefore called themselves 'covenanters'.[23]

The Dutch Anabaptists defined the church as a voluntary fellowship of holy beings, 'an assembly of the righteous', as Menno Simons said, at odds with the world.[24] This notion of the church as a remnant in conflict with the forces of Antichrist chimed with their own experience as a persecuted minority and gave meaning to their present tribulation. Their sufferings put their faith to the test: as a result the saints would be purified and the dross purged.[25] The Anabaptists did not rely only on the external instrument of persecution in order to keep holy the congregation of God; discipline was also necessary. 'As a city without walls and gates, or as a field without ditches or fences', wrote Menno, 'so also is a church which has not the apostolic exclusion or ban'.[26] Following in the wake of the Swiss Brethren, the Dutch Anabaptists insisted that 'without discipline there could be no church'.[27] At first they used excommunication to bring the sinner to repentance, but before long their concern shifted to the preservation of the congregation. Both Menno Simons and Dirk Philips yearned to bring about the church 'having no spot or wrinkle' and discipline was indispensable for this purpose.[28] The rigorists among them went so far as to demand that in order to keep the congregation unblemished the excommunicant should be shunned even by his spouse.[29]

---

[22] A. Mellink, *Amsterdam en de wederdopers in de zestiende eeuw* (Nijmegen, 1978), p. 21.

[23] G. Grosheide, *Bijdrage tot de geschiedenis der anabaptisten in Amsterdam* (Hilversum, 1938), p. 95. The religious dissidents distinguished themselves between 'convenanters' and 'evangelicals', Hoop Scheffer, p. 110.

[24] Menno Simons, *Complete Writings* (Scottdale, Pa., 1956), p. 234.

[25] W.E. Keeney, *Dutch Anabaptist Thought and Practice, 1539–1564* (Nieuwkoop, 1968), p. 182.

[26] Simons, *Complete Writings*, p. 962.

[27] K.R. Davis, 'No Discipline, No Church: an Anabaptist Contribution to the Reformed Tradition', *Sixteenth Century Journal*, XIII (1982), pp. 45–49.

[28] Keeney, *Dutch Anabaptist Thought*, p. 150.

[29] *Ibid*, pp. 163–65.

The Anabaptists chided the magisterial reformers for the lax discipline in their churches. Among the Reformed this reproach did not pass unheeded. The Polish Reformer John à Lasco responded, when he was superintendent of the evangelical church in East Friesland, to the Anabaptists' complaint about the absence of discipline in the territorial church by appointing laymen in 1544 to oversee the conduct of the people.[30] In the Low Countries the Anabaptists remained a thorn in the flesh of the Reformed throughout the sixteenth century and beyond. Disaffected Calvinists, offended by the 'disorderly conduct ... and the lax discipline' in their own ranks, might well be drawn to the gathered Anabaptist congregations.[31] Theologians and church historians have remarked on the affinities between the Calvinist and Anabaptist doctrine of the church.[32] But as the Anabaptists made almost no headway in the French-speaking world, the Calvinists there were not confronted in practice with this challenge; by contrast, in the Netherlands the Anabaptists' reputation for virtuous living put the Reformed on their mettle. In this respect the presence of the Anabaptists probably reinforced the sectarian tendencies latent in Dutch Calvinism.

The disintegration of Dutch Anabaptism after 1555 into a host of splinter congregations served however as a warning of what might happen if authority depended on the subjective judgment of strong-willed leaders. The first Dutch Anabaptist confession of faith was not drawn up until 1577. With this example before them the Dutch Reformed churches were perhaps more willing to be bound by the presbyterian system of church government than were the French churches. Certainly the violent quarrel between the presbyterian and congregationalist parties which troubled the French Reformed church in the decade before the massacre of St. Bartholomew seems not to have greatly affected the Calvinists in the Low Countries.[33] But the Reformed theologians working in the Low Countries were obliged to repudiate explicitly certain doctrines characteristic of the Dutch Anabaptists. The debate held at Wismar between Marten Micron and Menno Simons in 1554 on the

[30] A. van Ginkel, *De ouderling: Oorsprong en ontwikkeling van het ambt van ouderling en de functie daarvan in de gereformeerde kerk der Nederlanden in de 16e en 17e eeuw* (Amsterdam, 1975), p. 164.

[31] See above, p. 213; A.Th. van Deursen, *Het kopergeld van de Gouden Eeuw*, IV, *Hel en hemel* (Assen, 1980) p. 118; J.H. Wessel, *De leerstellige strijd tusschen nederlandsche gereformeerden en doopsgezinden in de zestiende eeuw* (Assen, 1945), pp. 22–29.

[32] See esp. W. Balke, *Calvijn en de doperse radikalen* (Amsterdam, 1973); English tr. *Calvin and the Anabaptist Radicals* (Grand Rapids, 1982).

[33] R.M. Kingdon, *Geneva and the Consolidation of the French Protestant Movement, 1564–1572* (Geneva, 1967), pp. 62–137; Kingdon's suggestion that synodal government had its critics among Netherlands Protestants at this time receives some support from W. van 't Spijker, 'Stromingen onder de reformatorische gezinden te Emden', *De synode van Emden, 1571–1971*, ed. D.Nauta *et al.* (Kampen, 1971), pp. 63–66. The main attack on synods came from the Erastians, not from the 'congregationalists'.

Incarnation inaugurated a polemic which was to be pursued in formal disputations and in doctrinal refutations for the rest of the century.[34] This preoccupation with the Anabaptists sets the Netherlands Confession of Faith apart from the French or Scots Confessions. The authors of the Netherlands Confession condemned the teaching of the Anabaptists on the Incarnation, baptism, and the civil powers.[35] In matters both of doctrine and discipline the radical Reformation provoked a sharp response from the Reformed churches in the Netherlands and so indirectly exerted an influence on the character of Dutch Calvinism.

Apart from the Anabaptists, the evangelicals in the Low Countries did not begin to form counter-churches until the mid-sixteenth century. Before then, they denounced certain doctrines of the church, and some engaged in blatantly anticatholic acts, but the sporadic attacks on the clergy and on the objects of Catholic ritual were carried out by isolated individuals. By contrast the iconoclastic riots of 1566 were concerted by the hedge-preachers and the consistories. Most evangelicals supplemented their attendance at mass by reading scriptures and edifying literature, usually of a Lutheran provenance, at home and in conventicles, where the religious issues of the day were discussed. Often evangelically-minded priests led these gatherings, while continuing to preach in the churches. Though eucharistic theology was discussed, the sacraments were almost certainly not administered, nor was there any sort of organisation beyond a rudimentary common chest to relieve those in need in their circle.[36]

The transition from dissent within the church to open schism accelerated in the 1540s. The colloquy at Regensburg (1541) seems to have precipitated a debate in evangelical circles about the status of the Roman church. Evidently the counsel of Capito, one of the Strassburg reformers, to the effect that evangelical Christians should not quit the Roman church for all its defects, circulated at this time in the northern Netherlands.[37] Calvin, on the other hand, regarded the mass as an abomination. He therefore advised evangelicals dwelling 'in the midst of papists' either to withdraw completely from idolatry (thereby risking persecution) or to leave for some place where the gospel was openly professed. In 1543 Calvin's *Petit traicté* brought consternation to evangelicals at Tournai and elsewhere in the Walloon provinces.[38] For the next generation this

---

[34] These polemics and disputations are treated in detail by Wessel, *Leerstellige strijd.*

[35] *De nederlandse belijdenisgeschriften in authentieke teksten*, ed. J.N. Bakhuizen van den Brink, 2nd. edn. (Amsterdam, 1976), Articles XVIII, XXXIV, XXXVI.

[36] The evangelicals at Tournai had such a 'boette' by 1531; G. Moreau, *Histoire du protestantisme à Tournai jusqu'à la veille de la Révolution des Pays-Bas* (Paris, 1962), p. 70, fn.1.

[37] P. Fraenkel, 'Bucer's Memorandum of 1541 and A "Lettera nicodemitica" of Capito's', *Bibliothèque d'humanisme*, XXXVI (1974), pp. 575–76.

[38] Moreau, *Histoire*, pp. 90–91. Significantly this was the first of Calvin's writings to be translated into English and Dutch and one of the earliest to be translated into Italian.

problem continued to exercise evangelicals in the Low Countries. Around 1550 à Lasco wrote in much the same vein: Christians might only go to mass if they were willing to bear witness there to their faith.[39] Anguished Protestants in Holland asked the church at Emden in 1558 whether they might attend 'papist sermons' while 'the brethren' from Middelburg sought guidance from the Dutch stranger-church in London a few years later.[40] Usually they were warned against making any compromise. To fortify their resolve the heroic conduct of the martyrs was set before them in Micron's account of the execution of Hoste van der Katelyne in 1555 and in the Reformed martyrologies of Crespin and van Haemstede, the first editions of which appeared in 1554 and 1559. For good measure Karel de Coninck, an erstwhile Carmelite from Ghent and himself to die a martyr's death at Bruges in 1557, translated the cautionary tale of Francesco Spiera, the Italian evangelical who had died in despair in 1548, having forsaken his faith two years earlier.[41] The moral could not have been plainer.

By no means all evangelicals looked on the Roman church as 'the church of Antichrist'. In 1557 a certain Jan Daelman, in a debate with the Reformed minister van Haemstede, maintained 'that the Roman church, for all its corrupt practices, is the church of Christ; that whoever leaves the Roman church, leaves the church of Christ; that a Christian may use all the Romanist superstitions and idolatry, without committing sin, provided he does not seek his salvation in such practices'.[42] Among the well-educated urban elites, whose piety had been coloured by the *Enchiridion*, such attitudes were not uncommon. Confessional boundaries also mattered rather less in the newly incorporated provinces of Friesland, Groningen, and Gelderland. Here a priest of an evangelical disposition might cease to celebrate mass, attend a Lutheran university, and still return to preach in the Catholic church.[43]

But those evangelicals who broke with the Roman church, while remaining in the Netherlands, were bound sooner or later to erect privy churches, where the Word might be preached purely and the sacraments rightly administered. For, as Calvin told the Walloon congregation of

[39] The Latin version had been written by August 1550. *De fugiendis papatus illicitus sacris* appeared in Dutch in 1557. The French text may be found in E. Droz, 'Musculus, Poullain et les temporiseurs', *Chemins de l'hérésie*, I (Geneva, 1970), pp. 234–47. Bertrand le Blas (1554) and Hans Tuscaens (1566) caused a sensation by desecrating the host at mass.

[40] Emden 329/1, 18 April 1558; *Kerkeraads-protocollen der nederduitsche vluchtelingen-kerk te Londen, 1560–1563*, ed. A.A. van Schelven (Amsterdam, 1921), p. 224.

[41] A.L.E. Verheyden, *Het brugsch martyrologium* (Brussels, n.d.), p. 40.

[42] J.Decavele, *De dageraad van de reformatie in Vlaanderen, 1520–1565*, 2 vols. (Brussels, 1975), I , p. 383.

[43] J.J. Woltjer, *Friesland in hervormingstijd* (Leiden, 1962), chs. VI, VIII, IX; E. van Dijk, 'Dr. Johannes Eelts, *c.* 1528–1588, persona te Groningen, en de tegenstelling katholicisme/ protestantisme in zijn tijd', *Groningse volksalmanak* (1970–1), pp. 15–48.

Antwerp in 1556, 'it is not enough to read and to hear [the Word]'.[44]
The informal Scripture-meetings became church services, the gadabout
hedgepreacher gradually gave way to a properly called minister, with a
pastoral responsibility for specific congregations, which were subject to
the discipline of the consistory. The first Reformed church of this sort
came into being at Antwerp in 1555, the same year as the Protestant
church at Paris was constituted.[45] Yet we should not jump to the
conclusion that by this time the Protestants in the Low Countries took
their theology and church order from Geneva. Luther's influence had
indeed receded, but other reformers besides Calvin were looked to for
guidance.

Joannes Uytenbogaert (1557–1644), whose Remonstrance in 1610 set
out the doctrinal position of the Arminian party, tells us that in his youth
at Utrecht he had studied a wide range of evangelical literature. These
included works by Luther, Melanchthon, and Bullinger, not to mention
the writings of several lesser-known Dutch evangelicals.[46] Given the unofficial nature of the Reformation in the Low Countries and the lack of
any central direction, such eclecticism was only natural. Netherlanders
had encountered Protestantism in many different guises as they travelled
to Wittenberg, Marburg, Strassburg,[47] and Zürich or across the North
German Plain, through East Friesland, Bremen, and eastwards to the
Baltic. In East Friesland they found a hybrid Reformation. Here à Lasco
had superimposed on the basically Lutheran church order of 1535 a
discipline and liturgy more in keeping with Strassburg than Wittenberg.
In the town of Norden Lutheran and Reformed liturgies were both in
use in the 1550s.[48] The church at Emden fulfilled certain of the roles
played by Geneva in the organisation of French Protestantism. Large
numbers of religious refugees from the Low Countries joined the town
church, whose consistory ministered as best it could to the needs of the
churches 'under the cross', giving advice and sometimes sending ministers. Emden, too, became the base for the Reformed printing industry in
north-western Europe after 1553. From the presses of the Netherlands,
emigré printers issued a stream of Bibles, metrical psalms, catechisms,
consolation-literature, and anticatholic polemic for Dutch Protestants
who found themselves in exile or still dwelling 'amidst the papists'. Nor
was Emden the only haven. The accession of Mary Tudor cut short the
first wave of stranger churches in England, but the church order devised

[44] Cited by F.L. Rutgers, *Calvijns invloed op de reformatie in de Nederlanden voor zooveel die door hemzelven is uitgeoefend*, 2nd edn. (Leiden, 1901), p. 223.

[45] A.J. Jelsma, *Adriaan van Haemstede en zijn martelaarsboek* (The Hague, 1970), p. 22.

[46] A.J. van 't Hooft, *De theologie van Heinrich Bullinger in betrekking tot de nederlandsche reformatie* (Amsterdam, 1888), p. 100.

[47] L.E. Halkin, 'Protestants des Pays-Bas et de la principauté de Liège réfugiés à Strasbourg', *Strasbourg au coeur religieux de XVIe siècle* (Strassburg, 1977), pp. 297–307.

[48] M. Smid, *Ostfriesische Kirchengeschichte* (Pewsum, 1974), pp. 179–82.

for the Dutch church in London under Edward VI left its mark on Reformed Protestantism in the Low Countries for a long time to come.[49] Dutch and French-speaking communities of exiles settled in the Lower Rhineland and at Frankfurt, each with its own ethos.

In the Walloon provinces the Reformation moved in step with the evolution of French Protestantism. When French evangelicals began to prefer Geneva to Strassburg as a place of refuge after 1550, their counterparts from Tournai, Valenciennes, and Arras followed suit. Likewise, the religious literature then coming off the Genevan presses found a market in the Francophone provinces.[50] By 1553 French-speaking artisans, who had probably drifted to Flanders proper in search of employment, were trying to win over their fellow workers to the teachings of Calvin.[51] Through the French-speaking minorities in the Flemish towns and the close connections between the French and Dutch stranger-churches in London and Emden, Calvinism *pur sang* surmounted the language barrier, which Anabaptism had failed to overcome in the other direction. By 1560 Calvin was well enough known in Flanders for a Protestant barber-surgeon to include him in his pantheon of great reformers along with Zwingli, à Lasco, and Micron.[52]

Reformed Protestants in the Low Countries, and especially in the Dutch-speaking parts, never depended on Geneva as closely as their co-religionists in France. Whereas the Genevan church formally despatched at least eighty-eight pastors to French congregations between 1555 and 1562, only a dozen of the eighty-four preachers active in the southern Netherlands before 1566 had ties with Geneva, of whom four had matriculated at the Academy.[53] Netherlanders certainly resided in Geneva: seventy indeed enrolled as *habitants* between 1549 and 1560, and therefore took an oath to live 'selon la Sainte Religion évangelique ici purement annoncée', but most of these hailed from the Walloon provinces.[54]

[49] The London stranger-churches have been the subject of two recent theses: P. Denis, 'Les églises étrangères à Londres jusqu'à la mort de Calvin: De l'église de Jean Lasco à l'établissement du calvinisme' (Liège, *Licence* 1973–74) and A. Pettegree, 'The Strangers and their Churches in London, 1550–1580', (Oxford Univ. D. Phil. thesis, 1983). I am indebted to Dr. Pettegree for allowing me to consult his thesis, which has since been published as *Foreign Protestant Communities in Sixteenth-Century London* (Oxford, 1986).

[50] G.Moreau, 'Un colporteur calviniste en 1563', *Bulletin de la Société de l'Histoire du Protestantisme Français*, CXVIII (1972), pp. 1–21. The Calvinist influence in the Walloon provinces is confirmed by *idem*. 'Catalogue des livres brûlés à Tournai par order du duc d'Albe (16 juin 1569)', *Horae Tornacenses* (1971), pp. 194–213.

[51] Decavele, *op. cit.* I p. 339.

[52] *Ibid.*, I, p. 630.

[53] P.M. Crew, *Calvinist Preaching and Iconoclasm in the Netherlands, 1544–1569* (Cambridge, 1978), pp. 84–7. Cf. R.M. Kingdon, *Geneva and the Coming of the Wars of Religion in France, 1555–1563* (Geneva, 1956) pp. 135–37.

[54] *Livre des habitants de Genève*, I, *1549–1560*, ed. P.F. Geisendorf (Geneva, 1957). Only five Flemings and two Hollanders enrolled. On the other hand, twelve inhabitants of Ghent obtained burgher status at Emden between 1553 and 1560.

Translations are not necessarily an accurate reflection of the popularity of their authors with the public, but translations may create a readership where none existed before. The Dutch evangelical without any Latin or French would have had limited opportunities to read Calvin for himself. When he died in 1564 only four of his writings had appeared in Dutch, far fewer than had been translated by this time into English, German, or even Italian.[55] Though the evidence is circumstantial, it suggests that the Genevan church had not as yet impinged deeply on the consciousness of Protestants in the Low Countries, above all those in the Dutch-speaking parts.

Yet the foremost Netherlands Protestants were well aware that Calvin's star was in the ascendant. By the later 1550s Cornelis Cooltuyn, Willem Gnapheus, and Anastasius Veluanus, were evidently familiar with the *Institutes*.[56] The leading ministers bracketed Calvin with Bullinger and Melanchthon and sought his opinion. Exiles from the Low Countries at Frankfurt turned to Calvin to resolve their internal conflicts and to guide them in their delicate negotiations with the Lutheran clergy.[57] The growing respect for the Genevan church among Dutch Protestants is brought out by the decision of the Reformed in Holland to enlist the aid of Calvin, and later Beza, in the early 1560s in order to refute the spiritualist views advanced by Dirk Volkertsz Coornhert.[58] One might otherwise have expected the Dutch Reformed still to seek guidance from the church at Emden, which had called the first ministers to serve in Holland only a few years earlier.

Familiarity with the *Institutes* and respect for the Genevan divines was no guarantee of Calvinist orthodoxy as we know from the later careers of those Remonstrant theologians Arminius, Uytenbogaert, and Vorstius, all of whom had enjoyed Beza's favour as students at Geneva. Several of the earlier Dutch evangelicals who thought well of Calvin, including Veluanus and Cooltuyn, disagreed with him on the doctrines of the real presence and election. The pluriformity of the Reformation in the Netherlands did not hinder Reformed Protestants with differing opinions about predestination from working together in order to build up a

[55] Based on A. Erichson, *Bibliographia Calviniana* (repr. Nieuwkoop, 1960) and *Index Aureliensis*, VI, *s.v.* Calvin, Jean. Books by Calvin began to appear in the northern Netherlands from 1557, when some were found at Culemborg, near Utrecht.

[56] Joannes Anastasius Veluanus cites Calvin in *Der leken wechwyser* (1554); Gnapheus borrowed material from *Institutes*, bk. iv for the dedicatory epistle in *Tobias ende Lazarus* (1557); Cooltuyn's denunciation of the mass as a sacrifice in *Dat evangeli der armen* (1559) leans heavily on Calvin's treatment of this matter in the *Institutes*. Andrew Johnston kindly drew my attention to the Cooltuyn parallel.

[57] Rutgers, *op. cit.* pp. 129–34, 137–40.

[58] H. de Vries Heekelingen, *Genève pépinière du calvinisme hollandais*, II (The Hague, 1924), pp. 263–86.

Reformed church in very trying circumstances.[59] These unresolved differences lay buried in Reformed Protestantism like a time bomb with a long fuse until it exploded in the last decade of the sixteenth century. Only with the decision to expel the Remonstrants at the synod of Dordrecht was the controversy within the Reformed church checked. In no time the publicists from both the Remonstrant and Contra-Remonstrant camps were laying claim to be the authentic heirs of the Dutch Reformation – and such was diversity of the Reformed inheritance that, by careful selection of the evidence, they could both advance plausible cases.

The Reformed Protestants in the Low Countries, like the French Calvinists, eventually adopted a presbyterian church order. This polity was intended to prevent any revival of 'proud prelacy'. The synod held at Emden in 1571 opened by affirming the central principle of presbyterianism, namely that 'no church shall exercise dominion over another church'.[60] This church came to be governed through a hierarchy of assemblies, beginning with the consistory or *kerkeraad*, and ascending through the *classis*, the provincial synods to the highest court, the national or general synod. This pattern accorded in many respects with the decentralised political tradition in the Habsburg Netherlands, where the prince's authority had been curtailed by the town corporations and provincial States. The consistory corresponded to the municipal corporations and the provincial synods to the states. On the other hand the biennial national synod envisaged at Emden remained a pious hope during the lifetime of the Republic. The provinces guarded their sovereign powers too jealously in the ecclesiastical, as well as in the political sphere, to allow this supra-provincial body to flourish.

When the first consistory came into being at Antwerp in 1555, this all-embracing synodal hierarchy still lay some years ahead. Our immediate concern is to examine the purpose and antecedents of this institution. Clearly the Reformed church order at this stage in the Low Countries did not stem directly from the Genevan *Ecclesiastical Ordinances*. Though these had been drawn up in 1541, they were not published for another twenty years. Besides, this order had been framed for a small city state, whose magistrates, citizens, and *habitants* had professed publicly their allegiance to the Reformation: in other words, for a Christian commonwealth. It was therefore quite unfitted for a church 'under the cross', where the magistrates remained papists. Orders which had been devised for stranger-churches, however, lent themselves more readily to such circumstances.

[59] W. Nijenhuis, 'Variants within Dutch Calvinsm in the Sixteenth Century', *The Low Countries History Yearbook*, XII (1979), pp. 48–64.

[60] *WMV*, ser. II, deel iii (Utrecht, 1889), p. 55. This gives the text in Latin and Dutch; for a modern German translation of the acts see D. Perlich, 'Die Akten der Synoden der niederlandischen Gemeinden ... gehalten in Emden, den 4 Oktober 1571', *Emder Synode, 1571–1971* (Neukirchen, 1973), pp. 49–66.

Calvin himself had developed piecemeal one such 'order' during his stay at Strassburg between 1538 and 1541. The magistrates of that city had given him *pleins pouvoirs* to weld the French-speaking evangelicals, who numbered some hundreds, into a church. As the minister to this congregation Calvin was not under the same restraints as the ministers of the parish churches. Here, for example, discipline could be closely linked to the Lord's Supper. Calvin denied unrepentant sinners admission to the Table lest these by their presence profane the solemn event. All those intending to communicate were expected to intimate their decision beforehand to Calvin.[61] In a revised form the order and liturgy of this *ecclesiola gallicana* was later published by Valérand Poullain, who had served the French exiles at Strassburg since 1544. Shortly after coming to England he published his *Liturgia sacra* in order to inform the revisers of the Prayer Book about the practice of the Strassburg church.[62] As one might expect discipline here was explicitly tied to the Lord's Supper.

Bucer too had advocated a stricter discipline in the Strassburg church, partly in order to answer his Anabaptist critics. Not until the crisis provoked by the Interim in 1548, and then only briefly, did he have an opportunity to realise at Strassburg the *christliche Gemeinschaft*. The members of this community voluntarily placed themselves under the supervision of *Seelsorgediener*, in effect elders. Those who refused to join these *corpora christianorum* were eventually to be asked to abstain from the Lord's Supper. These voluntary congregations did not long survive Bucer's departure from Strassburg in 1549.[63]

In Emden too the Anabaptists spurred on the magisterial reformers to strengthen discipline. In 1544 John à Lasco introduced the *Kirchenrat* for this purpose. Originally the four ministers sat with four lay assistants, the *cives* who doubled as church-wardens and as elders.[64] A Lasco seems to have derived the notion of the lay helper from the church order Bucer had drafted shortly before for Hermann von Wied, the evangelical prince-bishop of Cologne.[65] After the Interim, à Lasco left East Friesland to become the superintendent of the stranger-churches at London. It was he who devised the church order for them, though it was revised by Jan Utenhove and Micron, before the latter published it in Dutch for the first time in 1554. Cognate orders in Latin, French, and German appeared in the succeeding decade.[66] No doubt John à Lasco imported features characteristic of the church he had known at Emden, but he probably

---

[61] J. Plomp, *De kerkelijke tucht bij Calvijn* (Kampen, 1969), pp. 156–66.

[62] V. Pollanus, *Liturgia sacra (1551–1555)*, ed. A.C. Honders (Leiden, 1970).

[63] Van Ginkel, *op. cit.* pp. 99–101.

[64] Smid, *Ostfriesche Kirchengeschichte*, p. 166.

[65] Van Ginkel, *op. cit.* pp. 164–66.

[66] M. Micron, *De christlicke ordinanciën der nederlantscher ghemeinten te Londen* (1554), ed. W.F. Dankbaar (The Hague, 1956). A Lasco published the Latin version later as *Forma ac ratio tota ecclesiastici Ministerii* at Frankfurt in 1555.

also drew on Poullain's *Liturgia sacra*. Either way the antecedents of the London church may be traced, at least in part, to the *ecclesiola gallicana* at Strassburg and to Martin Bucer.[67]

By no means all the features of the London order derive from Strassburg. Micron and Jan Utenhove both knew the church at Zürich at first hand and would therefore have been familiar with the *Prophezei* there, which recur in the London order.[68] But in the specific matter of discipline à Lasco's order stood in a tradition which had originated in Strassburg. At Zurich the exercise of discipline fell to the Christian magistracy: they had the task of punishing recalcitrant sinners publicly. According to Bullinger excommunication had no place in the church. Not only did the practice lack adequate scriptural warrant, it defeated the purpose of the Lord's Supper, which had been instituted to give sinners an opportunity to render thanks to the Lord, not to remove the tares from the wheat.[69] At Geneva the consistory maintained discipline and barred unrepentant sinners from the Table. Since the Genevan elders were chosen annually from the municipal councils, their position differed from that held by their namesakes in the stranger-churches or the churches 'under the cross' in the Netherlands: in the latter the elders acted solely on behalf of the church.

This difference did not pass unremarked. In the early seventeenth century the anti-Calvinist regent of Amsterdam, Cornelis Pietersz. Hooft, sought to embarrass the Contra-Remonstrants when he pointed out that the elders in Holland were still chosen by the consistories, unlike the practice in Geneva.[70] To which his opponents might have retorted that Amsterdam scarcely resembled the Christian commonwealth of Geneva.

According to Luther the true church was to be found wherever the Word was preached faithfully and the sacraments properly administered, and the Lutherans never swerved from this definition.[71] Calvin came close to making discipline the third mark, but he stopped short.[72] Discipline, however, assured the safety of the church: 'for to hang together, the body of Christ must be bound together by discipline as

[67] Van Ginkel, *op. cit.*, p. 115.

[68] P. Denis, 'La prophétie dans les églises de la réforme au XVIe siècle', *Revue d'histoire ecclésiastique*, LXXII (1977), pp. 300–4; Pettegree, *Foreign Protestant Communities*, pp. 63–64.

[69] Plomp, *op. cit.*, pp. 28–9; J. Wayne Baker, 'In Defense of Magisterial Discipline: Bullinger's "Tractatus de excommunicatione" of 1568', *Heinrich Bullinger 1504–1578. Gesammelte Aufsätze zum 400. Todestag*, ed. U. Gäbler and F. Herkenrath (Zürich, 1975), pp. 147–49.

[70] Cornelius Pietersz. Hooft, *Memoriën en adviezen*, I (Utrecht, 1871), pp. 131, 157, 207, 296. In fact, of course, the corporations exercised a good deal of influence over consistorial appointments, but it suited Hooft's book to emphasise that the Dutch Calvinists had in this respect been unfaithful to the Genevan model.

[71] Plomp, *op. cit.*, p. 22.

[72] *Ibid.*, p. 124.

with sinews'.[73] In Calvin's teaching on the church a tension develops between his concern lest the Lord's Table be polluted by the attendance of shameless sinners and his abhorrence of schismatics, who broke the church's unity. When Reformed exiles at Wesel sought Calvin's advice in 1554 as to whether they should set up their own congregation on account of the objectionable Lutheran ceremonies used in the town church he warned them that separation on those grounds could not be justified.[74] For the same reason he considered the rigorism characteristic of the Anabaptists as a threat to the church's unity and to evangelical freedom.[75] Such concerns probably prevented him from including discipline as the third mark of the church.

Yet it was precisely the challenge presented by the Anabaptists which induced the Strassburg theologians to add discipline to the *notae ecclesiae*.[76] In 1538 Bucer succeeded in persuading a large number of Anabaptists in Hesse to return to the territorial church by conceding the principle that 'there cannot be a church without discipline'.[77] And this principle, which Bucer also maintained in his apologia for the church order of Cologne (c. 1543),[78] was to be put into practice by the influential stranger-churches at London. In 1551 Jan Utenhove boasted that 'our Netherlands nation never before had a congregation where the Word of God was so purely preached, the sacraments so uprightly administered and the Christian discipline so diligently and faithfully exercised'.[79] This threefold definition of the church recurs in the *Christlicke ordinancien*.[80] From London Dutch exiles like Jacob Dieussart carried it back to Flanders.[81] In 1561 the Netherlands Confession of faith duly included *la discipline ecclesiastique* among the signs of the church.[82]

Discipline became essential to the Reformed churches in the Low Countries. Without discipline the Lord's Supper could not be properly administered, as Calvin himself reminded a French congregation in

---

[73] *Ibid.*, pp. 125–27. Quotation from 'Calvin's Reply to Cardinal Sodolet', *Calvin: Theological Treatises*, ed. J.K.S. Reid (London, 1954), p. 245.

[74] G.R. Potter and M. Greengrass, *John Calvin* (London, 1983), p. 139.

[75] Balke, *Calvijn en de doperse radikalen*, pp. 225–40; Plomp, *op. cit.*, pp. 100–15.

[76] Davis, 'No Discipline', p. 50. Poullain reflected the Strassburg traditions when he included discipline as one of the three marks of the church in the confession he composed for the congregation at Glastonbury. Pollanus, *Liturgia sacra*, p. 207.

[77] Davis, 'No Discipline', p. 54

[78] B. Hall, 'Diakonia in Martin Butzer', *Service in Christ: Essays Presented to Karl Barth on his 80th Birthday*, ed. J.I. McCord and T.H.L. Parker (London, 1966), p. 96.

[79] Micron, *Christlicke ordinancien*, p. 1.

[80] *Ibid.*, p. 89.

[81] Dieussart had been a member of the London church before his arrest in Flanders in 1560; see Decavele, *op. cit.*, i, 411–12. For his martyr's testimony see (A. van Haemstede), *Geschiedenis der martelaren....tot het jaar* 1655 (Arnhem, 1868), p. 719.

[82] *Nederlandse belijdenisgeschriften*, Article XXIX. Significantly the French confession, drawn up in 1559, omits discipline as a true mark of the church.

1554.[83] But the process by which the clandestine Bible-reading assemblies became transformed into Reformed congregations with consistories was gradual and liable to be interrupted by the arrest of the principals. The metamorphosis took place in secrecy, and the historian has to piece together the evidence from the trial proceedings of those unfortunate enough to fall into the hands of the magistrates, and from stray remarks passed in the correspondence of the underground congregations and the consistory minutes of the stranger-churches. By 1566 churches in the chief Walloon towns [84] as well as at Ghent, Bruges, and Hondschoote in Flanders, had been *dressées*, as the French Calvinists described congregations with discipline. In Brabant, apart from Antwerp, which acted as the mother church for the duchy, only Breda certainly had a consistory by then,[85] though the 'brethren' at Brussels appear to have been quite precocious. In the records of the Dutch church at London there are passing references to the Calvinist communities on the island of Walcheren in Zeeland, which suggest that they, too, had a church order of sorts before 1566.[86] Holland lagged behind: there the embryonic congregations were served by a minister with a roving commission from the church at Emden.

Perforce the Calvinist churches in the Low Countries, as in France, come into existence as individual congregations: the presbyterian or synodal framework followed. Since 1562 meetings of the churches in the southern provinces had occurred at Antwerp.[87] In this development the French-speaking churches seem to have taken the lead, though these meetings were almost certainly also attended by the Dutch churches: the division of the French and Dutch Calvinist churches into separate synods did not take place until 1577. In the 1560s the Reformed churches in the Netherlands looked to the French Protestant church for the simple reason that the synodal system of government had been first introduced in France in 1559. In the matter of synods the church orders of the gathered churches could no more provide a model than those of the Reformed city states. This explains why the earliest synods held in the Low Countries set their course by the *Discipline ecclésiastique* of the French Calvinists.[88] In following the

---

[83] Potter and Greengrass, *John Calvin*, p. 152.

[84] Brully's ministry to the Walloon towns in 1544 ended after less than two months, giving him too little time to organise the churches. Though charged with preaching and teaching heretical doctrine about the real presence, he was not charged with administering communion, see C. Paillard, *Le procès de Pierre Brully* (Paris and The Hague, 1878), p. 80.

[85] A.J.M. Beenakker, *Breda in de eerste storm van de opstand: Van ketterij tot beeldenstorm, 1545–1569* (Tilburg, 1971), p. 41.

[86] From *Kerkeraads-protocollen ... 1560–1563*, pp. 121, 200, 224, 229–30, 236, 347, 349, 436.

[87] G. Moreau, 'Les synodes des églises wallonnes des Pays-Bas en 1563', *NAK*, n.s. XLVII (1965), p. 10.

[88] F.R.J. Knetsch, 'De nationale synode te Dordrecht 1578 en de positie der waalse kerken', *De nationale synode van Dordrecht 1578*, ed. D. Nauta *et al.* (Amsterdam, 1978), pp. 55–60; 'Kerkordelijke bepalingen van de nederlandse synoden "onder het kruis" (1563–1566) vergeleken met die van de franse (1559–1564)' *Kerkhistorische studiën*, J.Fabius *et al.* (Leiden, 1982), pp. 29–44.

French example, the Reformed churches in the Netherlands may thereby have fallen more directly under the influence of Calvin and Beza, who watched so vigilantly over the affairs of the French churches, than has been suspected. A Lasco deliberately included in his church order certain features which were intended to check the growth of clerical domination. These included congregational participation in the election of church officers and the institution of prophecy, by which the ministers could be called to account by the members for their preaching.[89] Yet by the synod of Emden in 1571 these practices had apparently fallen into a desuetude among the Reformed Protestants in the Low Countries. Beza, for one, would surely not have regretted their passing.

The arrival of Alva in the summer of 1567 forced many Protestants to flee the country. In the diaspora the need for closer liaison between the communities scattered through England and Germany and those in hiding in the Netherlands became more urgent. The campaigns orchestrated by William of Orange in 1568, 1570, and 1572 underlined the importance of concerted action. In the entourage of the prince the Calvinist consistories were regarded as a means of obtaining information about the enemy and raising money for the recruitment of troops. This, in turn, presupposed a greater coherence than had hitherto marked the Reformed churches. It was significantly the Calvinist scholar-statesman, Philippe Marnix de St. Aldegonde, at Orange's side by 1571, who championed the plan to 'incorporate all the congregations of the Netherlands into a single body'.[90] He had the example of the French church in mind, when he invited the Dutch church at London to attend the national synod at Emden in 1571.[91] The decision reached at Emden to subscribe to both the French and Netherlands confessions of faith was intended to seal the doctrinal unity of the two Reformed churches.[92] It also symbolised the triumph of the Calvinist church-order among the Reformed in the Low Countries, a triumph about which a minority of Protestants had some nagging doubts.

In 1572 the Lord, as it appeared to the Calvinists, opened 'the door

[89] In France Jean Morely's support for the practice had been brought into disrepute with the triumphant clericalist party in France; in the stranger-churches prophecy continued, albeit in an attenuated form, until the 1570s. At the so-called Convent of Wesel, which probably took place near Antwerp in 1567, the institution was discussed at length, but Emden made no mention of the practice. The memory, however, lingered on. The classis of the Neder-Veluwe discussed a proposal to revive prophecy in 1606, *Acta van de classis Neder-Veluwe (Harderwijk) van 1562–1620*, ed G. van der Zee (Goes, n.d.), p. 108. According to this the *exercitium prophetiae* still continued in East Friesland. Note the alarm of the Reformed church in the *classis* of Alkmaar in 1587 about 'the great assemblings of young people' who met to expound 'some passage in scripture by way of a sermon', Brandt, I, p. 728.

[90] Ph. Marnix de Sainte-Aldegonde, *Godsdienstige en kerkelijke geschriften: Aanhangsel* (The Hague, 1878), p. 16.

[91] W. van't Spijker, 'Stromingen', pp. 62–63.

[92] *WMV*, ser. II, deel iii, p. 56.

for the proclamation of his Word in the Netherlands'. Like the Israelites under Joshua, they were not to wrest control of the Promised Land without a struggle. When considering the slow advance of the Reformed church in Holland after 1572, we need to bear in mind how few of the inhabitants of Holland had any inkling of the Reformed church order. Because of this lack of experience the Reformed church at Dordrecht appealed in 1572 to the Dutch church at London for ministers' who were reasonably familiar with the regiment of the church'.[93] The existing political order did not immediately collapse when the Sea Beggars entered the towns. Some magistrates went into the wilderness in the first years of the revolt in Holland, but especially in the smaller towns, where the supply of men with the requisite political experience and wealth was limited, the families in control of the corporations under Alva retained their grip.[94] Even at Amsterdam, whose magistrates were drastically purged in 1578, ten Catholics sat on the revised town corporation.[95] The governing classes in Holland could not easily slough off traditional political habits or old religious loyalties.

On that account the convinced Calvinists in the Reformed church had difficulty in deciding whether they had indeed a truly 'Christian magistracy'. They knew that few wholeheartedly endorsed the political objectives of Orange or zealously backed the Calvinist cause. In 1572 the magistrates pointedly ignored the Beggars' demand that the Reformed should be allowed to worship in the principal church in the towns.[96] Instead the town corporations did all in their powers to secure the Catholic establishment by writing into their agreements with the Beggars clauses designed to safeguard the clergy and the churches from attack. Freedom of religion might be guaranteed, but no formal provision for Reformed worship was made. In a few towns the magistrates cast about in search of some sort of anodyne Catholicism, purged of those 'superstitious' ceremonies many humanist Catholics found objectionable. But these attempts to find a middle road between Rome and Geneva came to nothing with the exception of Huibert Duifhuis's congregation at Utrecht, which flourished with magisterial approval from 1578 until its demise in 1586.[97]

[93] Briels, *Zuidnederlandsche emigratie*, p. 26.

[94] C.C. Hibben, *Gouda in Revolt: Particularism and Pacifism in the Revolt of the Netherlands, 1572–1588* (Utrecht, 1983), pp. 67–76; S.A. Lamet, 'The Vroedschap of Leiden 1550–1600: The Impact of Tradition and Change on the Governing Elite of a Dutch City', *Sixteenth Century Journal*, XII (1981), pp. 19–20.

[95] H.A. Enno van Gelder, 'Nederland geprotestantiseerd?', *TG*, LXXXI (1968), p. 457.

[96] See above, pp. 205.

[97] *E.g.* at Gouda, Hibben, *Gouda*, p. 86; at Goes (Zeeland) in 1578, H.A. Enno van Gelder, *Revolutionnaire reformatie: De vestiging van de gereformeerde Kerk in de nederlandse gewesten ... 1575–1585* (Amsterdam, 1943) p. 45 and possibly also at Amersfoort in 1579, C.A. van Kalveen, ' "Een vast gelove, ende Christus vrede si met ons ende alle onse vianden mede": De definitieve vestiging van de reformatie te Amersfoort, 1579–1581', *NAK*, LXII (1982), p. 38; for Duifhuis at Utrecht, see Brandt, I, pp. 346–50, 370–71, 378–80.

Sooner or later Catholic worship ceased in the parish churches, and then in the religious houses, in most cases in the rebel-held towns in Holland, by the spring of 1573. The magistrates came to realise the need for them to work out a *modus vivendi* with the Reformed churches, of whose doctrine, catechisms, and church orders they had little knowledge. More or less willingly the civil authorities – the magistrates and the provincial States – lent their authority to the Reformed church. They paid the ministers' stipends from the endowments which previously had maintained the parish priests. The income from the famous Benedictine abbey at Egmond was diverted in order to pay the professors of the new university founded at Leiden in 1575 for the education of the rising generation of political and religious leaders. Calvinist ministers were engaged to serve as chaplains to the army and the fleet, pilgrimages were forbidden by placards and local ordinances, and schoolmasters were required to use the Heidelberg catechism. In these ways the civil authorities fulfilled, as they believed, the requirements of Christian magistrates.

To the Erastians among the civil authorities the Reformed church no longer had any need of consistories now that it lived under a Christian magistracy. Caspar Coolhaes, a minister at Leiden between 1574 and 1582, supported this opinion. In a treatise written in 1582 he argued 'wherever the Christian magistracy discharges the office of guardian towards the church ... there is no need for any consistory', and he pointed to the example of the church at Zürich.[98] In the early seventeenth century Cornelis Pietersz. Hooft complained that the contemporary Calvinist ministers had failed to distinguish between the circumstances 'of a church which is under the protection of a Christian magistracy and one which is under the cross'.[99] In other words, the consistory was only required by the church during persecution; otherwise, it served no purpose.

When Hooft wrote of a Christian magistracy he was, at least as far as his opponents were concerned, merely begging the question. In 1607 a minister in a synod at Delft declared that he would not acknowledge the civil powers as 'Christian' until they had expelled from the country everyone who refused to join the Reformed church.[100] An uncharacteristically extreme statement, no doubt, but it demonstrates the problem contemporaries had in reaching a consensus on the qualities expected of a Christian magistracy. The Calvinists had their own definitions. The authors of the Netherlands confession of faith laid on the magistrates

[98] H.C. Rogge, *Caspar Janszoon Coolhaes, de voorloper van Arminius en der Remonstranten*, I (Amsterdam, 1858), p. 230.

[99] Hooft, *Memoriën*, I, pp. 81, 222; Rogge, *Coolhaes*, I, pp. 126, fn. 45. See also R.H.Bremmer, *Reformatie en rebellie, Willem von Orange, de calvinisten en het recht van opstand: Tien onstuimige jaren: 1572–1581* (Franeker, 1984), pp. 133–34.

[100] Briels, *Zuidnederlandse emigratie*, p. 27.

the responsibility for the uprooting of all idolatry and false religion 'so that the kingdom of Antichrist may be overthrown and the kingdom of Christ Jesus advanced'.[101] The problems for the Reformed were twofold. Could magistrates, who themselves declined to submit to the Reformed discipline, fulfil such a charge? Secondly, should the Christian discipline be maintained, even where a Christian magistracy occurred?[102]

Even 'under the cross' there had been disagreements among the Reformed concerning the nature of the church. In 1557–58 a heated controversy broke out among the brethren at Antwerp. The consistory condemned as reckless and divisive the decision of one of their ministers to preach to the rich, who had not as yet entered the congregation and forsworn the Roman church. In their letter to Emden the elders and deacons explained their point of view:

> As we live in a place where the people, in their blindness, speak ill of the way of God, there must be a separation between the children of God and those of the world. This is most conveniently accomplished through the profession of faith and submission to the discipline of Christ.

The signatories did, however, preface these observations by saying that this problem would not exist if they dwelt 'in a free country'. Then all who wished might hear the Word.[103] After 1572 the Reformed found themselves 'in a free country' and they acknowledged that they had responsibilities to those outside the congregation. Petrus Dathenus, who was noted for his Calvinist fervour, confessed in a letter to Bullinger in 1570 that it would be unrealistic to expect the same strict discipline in a territorial church, such as was then being established in the Palatinate, or could be maintained in Geneva or in the Dutch stranger-church at London. As a minister who had to answer before the Lord for those committed to his care, he was satisfied if he could clearly distinguish his flock and if the sacraments could be protected against open profanation.[104] After 1572 the Reformed churches in Holland were prepared to make concessions to accommodate tender consciences 'in the youth of this church'. Wafers might be used at communion instead of bread, the custom of reading the Sunday gospel continued, and the elderly were permitted to make their profession of faith before the minister and two elders instead of in the face of the full consistory. Aware that the singing of the metrical psalms did not always catch on with village congregations, the national synod of Middelburg in 1581 permitted the church at Deventer to choose a dozen or so of the 'simplest' psalms and to publish

---

[101] *Nederlandse belidenisgeschriften*, p. 141; cf. also R.B. Evenhuis, *Ook dat was Amsterdam: De kerk der hervorming in de gouden eeuw*, I (Amsterdam, 1965), p. 182.

[102] *CAD*, p. 20.

[103] *WMV*, ser.III, deel ii (Ie stuk), pp. 71–72.

[104] Van't Spijker, 'Stromingen', p. 61.

these along with some carefully-chosen hymns in the local dialect. In this way the synod hoped to accustom Overijsselaars to Dathenus's psalms.[105] A much more significant response to the new circumstances came with the decision, reached with much heart-searching, to administer baptism to all children, including the offspring of 'papists'.[106] In this respect the Reformed dominee took the place vacated by the parish priest.

On one point the Dutch Calvinists remained inflexible. They would not surrender consistorial discipline. Admission to the Lord's Supper was to remain carefully supervised to ensure that those who sat at the Table ate 'worthily'. That was only possible with consistorial discipline: in the absence of discipline the Lord's Supper could not take place. In the early years in the countryside the minister might be the only member and arrangements had to be made so that he sat at the Lord's Table in a neighbouring church which had discipline.[107] The distinction which had existed 'under the cross' between the *prudents* and the *fidèles*, between those 'outside' and those 'within' the congregation, gave way after 1572 to one between the *liefhebbers*, who came to the sermons, and the *lidmaten*, or members, who had placed themselves 'under the sweet yoke of our chief shepherd Jesus Christ'. The fundamental distinction between 'the children of God' and 'the children of the world' did not change, for that was quintessential to Dutch Calvinism.

Ranged on the other side in this debate about the nature of the church were those for whom the Reformation had, above all else, put an end to the tyranny of penance, which had brought despair to sinners, and restored evangelical liberty. This was of course an outlook shared by all the reformers, including Calvin and the Reformed Protestants. Yet as soon as the reformers began to give permanent institutional expression to the new theology, they laid themselves open to the charge of reviving that very tyranny they had formerly denounced. Already by 1526 Erasmus compared the Lutheran yoke unfavourably with the burdens imposed by the papists.[108] Milton's familiar denunciation of the Presbyterians as the 'new forcers of conscience' has an ancestry which goes back to the earliest years of the Reformation.

In the Low Countries the Calvinists were accused by other evangelicals of forging a 'new monkery' and of setting up 'the Genevan inquisition', on account of the strict discipline which surrounded the Lord's Supper. To Duifhuis, for whom church orders belonged to the category of

[105] *WMV*, ser. II, deel iii, pp. 372, 444.

[106] Van Deursen, *Bavianen*, pp. 135–39.

[107] E.g. *Acta van de classis Neder-Veluwe*, p. 37. See also the Dordrecht church order of 1619: 'In those places where there is still no consistory, the *classis* shall discharge that which otherwise the consistory, in conformity with the church order, is required to discharge, *Oude kerkordeningen*, p. 453.

[108] P. Denis, 'Jean Laski et le retour au papisme', *Les Eglises et leurs institutions au XVIe siècle*, ed. M. Perronet (Montpellier, 1978), p. 14.

matters indifferent, any other sort of discipline than that exercised by
the magistrates represented a 'tyrannising over consciences, and a remnant
of the Popish yoke'.[109] Herman Herberts, another minister influenced by
the spiritualists, once shocked the Calvinists by describing the Heidelberg
catechism as 'a new monstrance in which they (*sc.* the Calvinists) want to
incarcerate Christ', because of the Reformed practice of expounding
some portion of the catechism each Sunday.[110] Others, like Coolhaes
and Hooft, likened the visitation conducted by the Calvinist elders on
the eve of the Lord's Supper to auricular confession in the Roman
church.[111]

   These critics of the Calvinists wanted a comprehensive church. In the
church orders drafted by the States of Holland in 1576 and 1591 the
Lord's Table would have been opened to all who wished to come.
Preparations were to have been limited to an exhortation by the minister
to remind the communicants to search their own consciences.[112] At
Utrecht Duifhuis allowed all who wished to sit at the Supper to come: no
profession of faith was required, no roll of members kept.[113] Oldenbarnevelt at his trial urged the public church to attract to its services
Lutherans, Mennonites, even papists,[114] while Hooft, who stood in this as
in other respects close to the Advocate, wanted the 'evangelical net' cast
widely to catch as many as possible. To this end the rigid insistence on
binding confessions, catechisms, consistorial discipline, in fact the whole
Calvinist paraphernalia, should be relaxed. With some, especially among
the magistrates, there was a natural desire to retain control of the new
church, but one may also detect an irritation at the refusal of the
Reformed churches to fulfil the part of a comprehensive church to
which all patriotic Dutchmen might belong. From the standpoint of the
civil powers the Calvinists' separation of society into two camps was
politically very inconvenient. No wonder some magistrates, notably at
Leiden, looked enviously on the Reformed church at Zürich, where
discipline remained unambiguously in the hands of the lay powers and
where consistories were unknown.[115]

   The Calvinists were not wholly convinced. They believed themselves to
belong to a people whom it had pleased God to call forth from the
nations. That they found themselves, at least for a time, in a small
minority caused them no surprise. After all, as their confession of faith
declared, the church might appear to the world to be 'very small', as in
the time of Ahab, yet even then the Lord had reserved to Himself seven

---

[109] Brandt, I, p. 349.
[110] Rogge, *Coolhaes*, II, pp. 180–81.
[111] Hooft, *Memoriën*, II, p. 126; Rogge, *op. cit.*, p. 52.
[112] *Oude kerkordeningen*, pp. 124, 344–45.
[113] Brandt, I, p. 349.
[114] J. den Tex, *Oldenbarnevelt*, III. *Bestand* (Haarlem, 1966), p. 31.
[115] Rogge, *Coolhaes*, I, pp. 62–86.

thousand, who had not bowed down to Baal.[116] In their trials the vicissitudes of God's people in the Old Testament remained a consistent source of comfort, as also did the doctrine of election. The state of their own society confirmed their reading of the scriptures. From this perspective success, as measured in terms of numerical support, was unimportant. Keeping faith with the Lord in prosperity, no less than in adversity, was what counted. Whatever the temptations the differences between 'the children of the church and the children of the world' should not be obscured. After all as Marnix remarked as early as 1568, the Lord might 'take the Word away from us and bestow His grace on other nations, who would put this to a better and more Christian use'.[117]

By the early seventeenth century the size and influence of the Reformed church had grown and gradually the magistrates, who had tended to stand aloof in the early years of the Revolt, began to enter the congregation and to take their places in the consistory. The national synod of Dordrecht in 1618 marked the triumph of Calvinist theology within Dutch Protestantism and the church became increasingly preoccupied with the creation of a Christian society. Perhaps for that reason the Calvinist divines became more inclined to draw parallels between the Dutch Republic and Israel in the seventeenth century.[118] Yet the Reformed church never became the church of all, or even a majority, of Dutchmen. Many reasons have been offered for this failure, as we has already been observed, but the search for the *purior ecclesia*, to which many Calvinists in the seventeenth century remained faithful, was surely a restraint on the popularity of the Reformed churches. The sense of being a chosen people, 'set apart from the whole human race', which had inspired the Calvinists in their tribulations under Philip II, could not be entirely blotted out by the worldly prosperity they came to enjoy. So the Dutch Calvinists in the seventeenth century remained in a debate with themselves, in which one party, probably by now the smaller, looked back with nostalgia to the heroic age of the Reformation.

---

[116] *Nederlandse belijdenisgeschriften*, Article XXVII.

[117] Marnix van St. Aldegonde, *Godsdienstige en kerkelijke geschriften*, I, ed. J.J. van Toorenenbergen (The Hague, 1871), p. 138.

[118] See G. Groenhuis, 'Calvinism and National Consciousness: the Dutch Republic and the New Israel' in *BN*, VII, *Church and State since the Reformation*, ed. A.C. Duke and C.A. Tamse (The Hague, 1981), pp. 118–33.

Glosssary

Accoord	Name given to agreement between Margaret of Parma and Compromise of 25 August 1566; Calvinists granted limited religious freedom; Compromise disbanded; great nobles sent to provinces to restore order.
Alteratie	Applied to overthrow of Catholic government of Amsterdam on 26 May 1578.
baljuw	Bailiff. Holland (excluding towns and lord-ships) divided into bailiwicks. Bailiff charged by prince with administration of justice and maintenance of order in his district; *s.v. schout.*
classis	Meeting of ministers and elders charged with oversight of Reformed churches in a district; *cf.* presbytery in Scottish Reformed church.
coetus	Used of weekly meetings of ministers at Emden; in Holland such meetings soon replaced by *classis.*
geest	Soil type (clay, peat and sand) found inland of sand dunes along coast of Holland.
Geestelijk Kantoor	Chamber of Ecclesiastical Receipts. Set up by States of Holland in 1577 to administer church property and to pay stipends of rural ministers in South Holland.
Gecommitteerde Raden	Standing committees of States of Holland formed after Revolt for North and South Quarters. William Temple described body as a 'Council of State of Holland'.
Gedeputeerden van de classis	Deputies who implemented decisions of *classis.*
gemeente	Commonalty. In Reformed Protestant circles, members of Calvinist church or congregation.
hoogheemraadschap	District waterboard charged with upkeep of

dykes and water control. Administered by *dijkgraaf* (dikereeve) with *heemraden*, elected representatives of landholders (*ingelanden*).

Heeren Staten   Sovereign Lords. Collective title for members of States of Holland.

heerlijkheid   Domain of manorial lord over which he exercised seigneurial rights.

Hof van Holland   Court of Holland. Advised *stadhouder* (*s.v.*); administered justice and registered edicts. Also called *Raad van Holland*. Comparable with *Parlement* in France.

hoogheid en heerlijkheid   Almost synonym for sovereignty. Authority claimed by medieval counts of Holland: out of respect for emperor's vestigial authority they avoided explicit claims to sovereignty.

kerkmeesters   Parish officers responsible for church fabric and parochial endowments. Appointed by patron or parishioners. *cf.* church wardens.

kleyne luyden   Persons of small means.

landsadvocaat   Legal adviser to States of Holland; known after Oldenbarnevelt as *raadpensionaris* (councillor or grand pensionary).

liefhebbers   'Favourers' or 'sympathisers'. Used of those who attended Reformed church without becoming communicant members; children of Calvinist parents also so described.

overgang   Term used by Dutch historians to describe 'defection' of towns to side of Sea Beggars and Orange in 1572.

papen   Priests; used pejoratively by Protestants.

poorter   Freeman.

predikant(en)   Reformed minister(s).

procureur-generaal   Procurator-General or public prosecutor. Demanded punishment of criminals by provincial court in name of prince.

Raad van Beroerten   Council of Troubles. Extraordinary court set up by Alva in 1567 chiefly to punish those involved in disturbances of 1566/67. Abolished 1576.

Raad van Brabant and *Raad van Vlaanderen*   *s.v. Hof van Holland*.

rederijkers-kamers   Chambers of rhetoric. Dramatic societies which performed morality plays in vernacular.

religievrede	Religious Peace. In 1578 Orange proposed a policy of religious freedom. From *Religionsfriede*.
rijkdom	See *vroedschap*.
satisfactie	Agreements made in 1577-78 between Orange and those towns in Holland, Zeeland and Utrecht which had remained loyal to King. Pacification of Ghent required Orange to give 'satisfaction' to these towns.
schepen(en)	Town magistrate(s) who judged civil and criminal causes. Appointed by *stadhouder*, acting before Revolt for prince, from shortlist submitted by *vroedschap* (*s.v.*).
schout	Local representative of lord of manor or prince. Demanded punishment of accused criminals. Supervised law and order in his district. *s.v. baljuw.*
schutter	Civic guard.
schutterij	Company of civic guards or train band.
stadhouder	Prince's lieutenant in province. Responsible for preservation of prince's prerogative and domain; law and order; defence and calling of provincial states. After the dismissal of the King's authority (1581) *stadhouders* chosen by provincial States, but the social standing of house of Orange and the military threat to the Dutch Republic gave them great political influence.
vroedschap	Town corporation. Formed closed college which drew up shortlist for appointment of burgomasters and schepenen. So-called because it represented collective wisdom (*vroetschap*) and wealth (*rijkdom*) of town. William Temple translated *vroedschap* as 'senate'.

Index

Aalst, 189

Aarlanderveen, 258

Aarschot, Philippe de Croy, duke of, 185

Aartsbergen, 133

Abbema, Pibo Ovitius, 245

Abbesz., Sixtus, 202 & fn.

Abcoude, Dirk van, 36

Adriaens, Johanna, 51

Aemsz., Pieter, 122

Agricola, Rudolf, 5

Aken, Gilles van, 114–15, 117

Alardus Aemstelredamus, 14, 61

Albada, Aggaeus de, 196

Alblasserwaard, 126, 242

Aleander, Girolamo (Hieronymus), 34

Alkmaar, Jorists at, 105; Reformed services at, 129, 139; Brederode at 131, 146–47; iconoclasm at, 132, 135, 137, 145; analysis of imagebreakers at, 136; consistory in 1566 at, 140; *schutters* at, 141; besieged, 208; Reformed church after 1572 at, 208, 209, 211, 270

Alva, Fernando Alvarez de Toledo, duke of, 176, 202

Ameide, 126, 149

Amelia von Neuenahr, 126, 127

Amersfoort, 101; Catholicism restored at, 235, 273

Ammonius, Livinus, 44, 155

Amsterdam, 14, 51, religious at, 81; anticlericalism at, 34, 35, 52, 75, 77; *rederijkers* at, 107; conventicles at, 38, 115; Anabaptism at, 85–88; 110–11, 112, 117–18; sacramentarianism at 45, 101, 121; hostility to persecutions at, 76, 157–58; and antiheresy measures, 160–61, 162, 166; Brederode at, 128, 149; Reformed organisation in 1566/67, 129, 138, 139, 140, 201; iconoclasm at, 132, 136, 137; *schutters* at, 74, 141–42; factions at, 96–97, 149–50; as Catholic and royalist

centre, 204, 207, 222; *Alteratie* at, 225; Catholic magistrates after 1578 at, 288; economic impact of, 233; Contra-Remonstrants at, 3

Anabaptism, 17fn, 57–59, 65, 71, 76, 85–89, 90, 121, 157, 159, 160–61, 163, 164, 165, 214, 231, 232, 240; failure of, in francophone region, 93, 280; organisation of, 114–18; social appeal of, 15, 86–88, 110–12; theology of, 106, 117–18, 213, 275–76, 285; and late medieval dissent, 27; and Reformed churches, 213, 276–77, 283, 285

Anjou, Francis Hercules, duke of, 182, 195

Ankeveen, 244

Anna, Andries, 45–46, 48, 50

anticlericalism, 1, 35, 61, 67, 80–81, 84–85, 105 & fn., 118–20, 137, 155–56, 200, 203–04, 277

antiheresy legislation, 32, 53–54, 73, 83–84, 153, 158–70, 176; and courts, 109–10; enforcement of, 73; dislike of, 85, 89, 109–10, 152–55, 157–59, 160–61, 163, 165–72, 176. *See* privileges

Antwerp, 9, 13, 15–16, 22, 26–27, 30–31, 33, 34, 36, 37, 41, 50, 62, 71, 77–78, 90, 114, 115, 117, 129, 131, 140, 149, 155, 189, 234, 274–75; printing at, 103, 156; Reformed congregation at, 92–93, 157, 279, 282, 290

apocalypticism, 86–87, 110–11

Aportanus, Georgius, 21

Aquinas, Thomas, on heresy, 162

Arendsz., Jan, 129, 130, 201

Armentières, 92

Arminius, Jacob, 281

Arras, 280

Artois, 178, 179fn.; States of, 182, 195

Asperen, 132–33, 138, 207

Augustinians and Reformation, 15,16 & fn., 17, 29, 30 & fn., 31, 46, 57, 77–78, 79

DATE	ISSUED TO

CONCORDIA COLLEGE LIBRARY
2811 NE Holman St.
Portland, OR 97211